FOOD SECURITY IN THE MIDDLE EAST

T0386558

ZAHRA BABAR and SUZI MIRGANI
Editors

Food Security
in the Middle East

GEORGETOWN UNIVERSITY

School *of* Foreign Service *in* Qatar
Center for International and Regional Studies

Published in Collaboration with
Georgetown University's Center for International and Regional Studies,
School of Foreign Service in Qatar

HURST & COMPANY, LONDON

First published in the United Kingdom in 2014 by
C. Hurst & Co. (Publishers) Ltd.,
41 Great Russell Street, London, WC1B 3PL
© Zahra Babar, Suzi Mirgani and the Contributors, 2014
All rights reserved.
Printed in India

The right of Zahra Babar, Suzi Mirgani and the Contributors to be identified
as the authors of this publication is asserted by them in accordance with the
Copyright, Designs and Patents Act, 1988.

A Cataloguing-in-Publication data record for this book
is available from the British Library.

ISBN: 978–1–84904–302–1

www.hurstpublishers.com

This book is printed on paper from registered sustainable
and managed sources.

CONTENTS

v

CONTENTS

LIST OF FIGURES

Figures

LIST OF FIGURES

LIST OF FIGURES

LIST OF FIGURES

APPENDICES

LIST OF FIGURES

ACKNOWLEDGEMENTS

The chapters in this volume grew out of two working group meetings held under the auspices of the Center for International and Regional Studies at the Georgetown University School of Foreign Service in Qatar. Grateful acknowledgement goes to all the participants of the working groups for their intellectual contribution to the project that eventually resulted in this book. We are particularly thankful to Mehran Kamrava, Fahad bin Mohammed Al Attiya, Abdulrahman Salih Al-Khalifa, Khalid Nahar Al-Rwis and Nahla Hwalla for their participation in our working group and their support for this project. Grateful acknowledgment goes to the Qatar Foundation for its support of research and other scholarly endeavors. Invaluable assistance also came from the dedicated and capable efforts of the staff of the Center for International and Regional Studies, namely, Flora Bayoud-Whitney, John Crist, Dwaa Osman, Nadia Talpur, Barbara Gillis, Nerida Child Dimasi, Elizabeth Wanucha, Salman Ahad Khan, Arwa Elsanosi and Maha Uraidi. We gratefully acknowledge their part in making this book possible.

ABOUT THE CONTRIBUTORS

Mounir Abi Said studied at the American University of Beirut (AUB) and at the University of Kent at Canterbury in the United Kingdom. He has been a part-time lecturer in several universities including the AUB and the Lebanese University. His research interests range from biodiversity conservation and resolving human wildlife conflict to sustainable development and use of natural resources. He is currently serving as the president of the Animal Encounter, a leading and educational centre for wildlife conservation. In addition, he is serving on different international boards related to biodiversity and sustainable development. His major challenges are to develop new approaches towards the sustainable use of natural resources and biodiversity conservation in the region.

Amin Al-Hakimi is Professor of Plant Breeding at the Faculty of Agriculture, Sanaʻa University, and Head of the Yemeni Association for Sustainable Agriculture Development-YASAD (www.yasadngo.org). He received his PhD in Agronomy and Plant Breeding from Ecole Pratique des Hautes Etudes (the Practical School of Higher Studies) and INRA-ENSA Montpellier France. Al-Hakimi served as Researcher in Agriculture Research and Extension Authority (AREA) and created and directed the Yemeni Genetic Resources Center (YGRC) from 1998 to 2007. He is a lecturer and researcher in the areas of crop improvement, sustainable rain-fed agriculture, traditional agriculture knowledge, plant biodiversity, food security, coffee production, medicinal plants, and participatory research. Al-Hakimi is also a national and international consultant and expert on urban agriculture, climate change in agriculture, biosafety, biotechnology, traditional food systems, eco-health, higher education, and utilization of biotechnology in agriculture adaptations, and production improvement.

Zahra Babar is Associate Director of Research at the Center for International and Regional Studies, Georgetown University School of Foreign Service in Qatar. Previously, she worked in the international aid, community development and poverty alleviation sectors. She has served with the International Labour Organisation and the United Nations Development Programme. Her current research interests lie in rural development, Gulf migration and labour policies, citizenship in the Persian Gulf states and GCC regional integration. Babar received her BA in Government from Smith College in Northampton, Massachusetts, and her MA from the School of International Studies at the Jawaharlal Nehru University, New Delhi.

Ray Bush is Professor of African Studies and Development Politics at the University of Leeds working on the political economy of Africa and the Near East. He has had visiting research appointments at the Norwegian Nobel Institute, Oslo, and the Social Science Research Centre at the American University in Cairo. Bush is a member of the editorial working group of *Review of African Political Economy*, and he recently completed a film with Habib Ayeb called *Fellahin*, which explores the forgotten voices of farmers in the uprisings of Tunisia and Egypt. Bush's research interests include the political economy of resources, political and economic reform, and rural transformation and resistance.

Elisa Cavatorta is a Lecturer in Political Economy at King's College London. Prior to joining King's, she was a Post-Doctoral Fellow at the School of Oriental and African Studies, University of London and an associate researcher at Birkbeck College, University of London, where she obtained her PhD. She has worked in the Middle East, holding research appointments at the FAO and regional research institutes. Cavatorta's research interests are in the fields of development economics and microeconomics; her current works focuses on the impact of shocks on individual decision-making in conflict zones and evaluations of health policy interventions.

Jad Chaaban joined the American University of Beirut (AUB) as an Assistant Professor of Economics in September 2006, where he currently teaches development and agricultural economics. Prior to working at AUB, he was an economist in the World Bank's regional office in Beirut, where he undertook research related to poverty reduction and economic management, covering Lebanon, Syria, Jordan and Egypt. Chaaban is the president and founding member of the Lebanese Economic Association. He also currently serves as an expert for the Middle East Youth Initiative at the Wolfensohn Center for Development at Brookings; and as an Associate Researcher with the Toulouse School of Economics in France. Chaaban holds an MBA from the European School of Management (2000), a Masters in Environmental and Natural Resources Economics from the Toulouse School of Economics (2001) and a PhD in Economics (2004) from the same university. His current research interests include poverty and inequality in polarised societies, youth development and the economics of agro-food industries. He has published several scientific articles in international academic journals.

Tahra ElObeid is Head of the Department of Health Sciences at the College of Arts and Sciences, Qatar University. ElObeid has taught at several institutions in Qatar, Sudan and Austria. She has also served as a consultant for a number of organisations, most notably the United Nations World Food Programme, the World Health Organization and the Qatar National Food Security Programme. She is a member of the Qatar Standardization Organization Committee for Food Standards. Her current areas of research interest are: food safety, novel and functional foods, analysis of indigenous foods, and micronutrient deficiency and fortification.

Hala Ghattas joined the American University of Beirut as Assistant Professor of Community Nutrition in 2009. Her research interests include nutrition-infection interactions, micronutrient interventions and the measurement and prevention of food insecurity and malnutrition. Ghattas holds an MSc in Public Health Nutrition from the London School of Hygiene and Tropical Medicine (2000) and a PhD from St George's, University of London (2004). She is a part-time lecturer at the London School of Hygiene and Tropical Medicine and Managing Editor of the BioMed Central journal *Emerging Themes in Epidemiology*. Ghattas's previous research focused on maternal and child nutrition and its interactions with immunity, morbidity and mortality in Gambia,

Zanzibar and the Ivory Coast. Ghattas is now based in Lebanon where she has been conducting research on the prevalence and determinants of food insecurity and malnutrition in marginalised populations and those vulnerable to emergencies in Lebanon, including Bedouin populations, Palestinian refugees and those living in conflict-prone areas.

Shadi Hamadeh studied at the American University of Beirut (AUB) and at New Mexico State University in the USA. He has been a professor of animal science at AUB since 1988. His research interests range from animal environment interactions to sustainable farming systems. He is currently leading the Environment and Sustainable Development Unit at AUB and serving on the executive board of the Resource Centers on Urban Agriculture and Food Security. His major challenge is to reconcile chaos theory with the bitter realities of rural development in the Arab world.

Jane Harrigan is Professor of Economics at the School of Oriental and African Studies, University of London. She has worked extensively on World Bank and IMF activities in sub-Saharan Africa and the MENA region and is co-author of three recent books on MENA: *Aid and Power in the Arab World: IMF and World Bank Policy-Based Lending in the Middle East and North Africa*; *Economic Liberalisation, Social Capital and Islamic Welfare Provision* and *Globalisation, Democratisation and Radicalisation in the Arab World*. Harrigan is author of the forthcoming book *The Political Economy of Arab Food Sovereignty* published with Palgrave Macmillan. She has also worked on the political economy of foreign aid to both Africa and MENA and on agricultural policy and food security issues in Africa. Harrigan has written eight books and is the author of numerous journal articles, including papers in *World Development, Food Policy, The Middle East Journal* and *Review of Middle East Economics and Finance*.

Abdelmonem Hassan is Associate Professor of Nutritional Sciences at Qatar University's College of Arts and Sciences. In 2012 he was elected Chair of Muslims in Dietetics & Nutrition, a member interest group of the Academy of Nutrition and Dietetics (formerly known as the American Dietetic Association). Hassan's research focuses on nutrition and obesity issues in Qatar and the GCC.

Mehran Kamrava is Professor and Director of the Center for International and Regional Studies at the Georgetown University School of Foreign Service in Qatar. He is the author of a number of journal articles and ten books, including, most recently, *Qatar: Small State, Big Politics, The Modern Middle East: A Political History since the First World War*, 3rd ed., and *Iran's Intellectual Revolution*. His recent edited books include *The International Politics of the Persian Gulf, Innovation in Islam: Traditions and Contributions, The Political Economy of the Persian Gulf, Migrant Labor in the Persian Gulf* (edited with Zahra Babar), and *The Nuclear Question in the Middle East*.

Suzi Mirgani is Manager and Editor for Publications at the Center for International and Regional Studies, Georgetown University School of Foreign Service in Qatar. She holds a PhD in Communication and Media Studies. Mirgani's research is based on critical discourse analyses of government and corporate-sponsored media messages and their influence on social attitudes towards issues of copyright and the circulation of cultural material. In addition, she writes creatively on the intersection of politics and popular culture. She has published in *Critical Studies in Media Communication; International Feminist Journal of Politics*; and *Anthology of Contemporary African Diasporic Experience*.

Toktam Mohtashami received her undergraduate degree from Ferdosi University with a specialisation in Agricultural Economics. She continued her MA and PhD in the Faculty of Economic and Agricultural Development, University of Tehran. Agricultural policy and Development is her major field of study. Mohtashami's research interests include time series modelling, quantitative agricultural sector analysis using positive mathematical programming, partial equilibrium modelling, analysis of trade-related issues in agriculture, credit scoring and agricultural policy analysis. She has published several articles in these fields and has participated in research projects supported by various Iranian organisations.

Martha Mundy is Professor Emerita of Anthropology at the London School of Economics and Research Associate at the American University of Beirut. Mundy's research has concerned anthropology of law, agrarian systems, and kinship and family. Before joining the LSE in 1996 she taught at Yarmouk University in Jordan (1982–92), University of California Los Angeles, Lyon 2 Lumière University, and the American University of Beirut. Her edited books include *Part time Farming: Agricultural development in the Zarqa River Basin* (1990); *The Transformation of Nomadic Society in the Arab East* (2000); *Law and Anthropology* (2002); and *Law, Anthropology and the Constitution of the Social: Making persons and things* (2004); and her authored books *Domestic Government: Kinship, community and politics in North Yemen* (1995) and *Governing Property, Making the Modern State: Law, administration and property in Ottoman Syria* (2007).

Mohamad Saeid Noori Naeini has served as the Ambassador of the Islamic Republic of Iran to the International Fund for Agricultural Development, Food and Agriculture Organization of the UN and the World Food Programme (WFP) as well as the President of the Executive Board of WFP. Naeini has also served as the Vice Chancellor of Shahid Beheshti University in Iran, as Deputy Dean of the Faculty of Economics and Political Science and as Professor of Agricultural Economics. He is the author of over thirty articles on various topics ranging from resource allocation in smallholder agriculture, food security and rural poverty alleviation projects to evaluation of agricultural projects and land tenure issues.

Frédéric Pelat is an agronomist who studied tropical agronomy in Toulouse (ENSAT) and Montpellier (CNEARC/IRC). He lived in Yemen from 1998 to 2011, working through the NGO that he created (Iddeales) on small development projects aiming at the enhancement of local resources and farmers' knowledge. He holds an MSc in social anthropology from the London School of Economics and is currently a PhD student in the anthropology and sociology of development at the Graduate Institute of Geneva. Pelat's recent publications include, 'Health issues in the mountains of Yemen: healing practices as part of farmers' traditional knowledge,' in *Herbal Medicine in Yemen: Traditional Knowledge and Practice and their Value for Today's World*, edited by I. Hehmeyer, H. Schonig and A. Regourd (Leiden: Brill Publishers, 2012), co-authored with Al-Hakimi and Ya'ni.

Habibollah Salami is Professor of Agricultural Economics and Director of the Centre of Excellence of Studies in Strategy of Agricultural Development at the University of Tehran. His expertise include econometrics and CGE modelling, production structure analysis and modelling, productivity measurement, measurement of technological change, trade and agricultural policy analysis, as well as income distribution, agricultural project and water pricing analysis. He is the author of over sixty journal articles on various topics ranging from productivity measurement in agriculture, food security and drought effects, measuring subsidy effects on income distribution, to forecasting effects of macro policies on investment and other macro variables.

Karin Seyfert is project manager of the AUB research project on 'Fresh Foods and Value Chains Project' a firm survey-based research project which compares Lebanon and Qatar. She also held an appointment as an economist in the Office of the Chief Economic Adviser with the Scottish Executive in Edinburgh. Seyfert is due to complete her PhD thesis with the School of Oriental and African Studies, University of London. Her research involves a critical assessment of NGOs' ability to foster sustainable rural development. She holds an MA in Arabic and Economics from the University of Edinburgh and an MSc from the Toulouse School of Economics.

Benjamin Shepherd is a PhD candidate in the Food Security programme at the Centre for International Security Studies, University of Sydney. Shepherd's research examines foreign investment in developing country farmlands. This project has included field research in the Philippines, Cambodia and Ethiopia. Shepherd was 2010 Research Fellow at the Centre for Non-Traditional Security Studies in Asia. Prior to embarking on the PhD, Shepherd had a corporate career which included selling and implementing data secrecy technologies with government agencies and financial institutions around the world.

Salwa Tohmé Tawk studied at the American University of Beirut (AUB) and at the Institut National de Recherche Agronomique Paris-Grignon France. She has been an associate researcher and lecturer at the American University of Beirut since 2005, and her research interests focus mainly on sustainable farming systems in the urban and rural context and in field surveys. She is currently leading the knowledge management activities at the Environment and Sustainable Development Unit at the

AUB, including training and facilitating various development projects covering countries in the Middle East and North Africa region (Lebanon, Jordan, Syria and Yemen). She is the editor of the Arabic version of an urban agriculture magazine; she is also serving on the board of MADA, a Lebanese non-governmental organisation.

Mary Ann Tétreault is Una Chapman Cox Distinguished Professor Emerita of International Affairs at Trinity University in Texas. She has also held positions at the American University of Kuwait, Iowa State University, Old Dominion University, Kuwait University, Kitakyushu University and Comenius University. She is a member of the Association of Genocide Scholars, International Studies Association, Middle East Studies Association and the Middle East Institute. She has published numerous journal articles and books. Among her recent books are: *Political Change in the Arab Gulf States: Stuck in Transition* (2011); *World Politics as if People Mattered* (2009); *Gods, Guns, and Globalization: Religious Resurgence and International Political Economy* (2004); *Feminist Approaches to Social Movements, Community, and Power* (2003); and *Stories of Democracy: Politics and Society in Contemporary Kuwait* (2000).

Deborah L. Wheeler is an Associate Professor of Political Science at the United States Naval Academy in Annapolis and a Visiting Professor of Political Science at the American University of Kuwait. Her interests in food security developed from a focus on questions of human security and political stability in the Middle East. Her research on food security in the Middle East adds another layer to considerations of ways in which non-traditional security questions affect political stability in the Middle East. Her publications include *The Internet and the Middle East: Global Expectations and Local Imaginations in Kuwait* (2006) and a wide range of articles and book chapters spanning a decade and a half of research on the Middle East. She has conducted fieldwork in Morocco, Tunisia, Egypt, Jordan, Israel/Palestine, United Arab Emirates, Syria, Turkey, Kuwait and Oman.

Sam Waples is an established geographical researcher with a strong track record in public policy and commercial applications of Geographical Information Systems (GIS) and other methods of data modelling and spatial analysis. He is a researcher at Birkbeck College, University of

London where he also teaches GIS. Waples is attached to the Governments Rural Evidence Research Centre hosted by Birkbeck, and previously contributed to both the National Sure Start Evaluation Project and the Home Offices National Evaluation of CCTV. Waples has a degree in geography from the University of Edinburgh and a MSc degree in GIS from the University of Nottingham.

Eckart Woertz is a senior research fellow at the Barcelona Centre for International Affairs (CIDOB). Formerly he was a visiting fellow at Princeton University, director of economic studies at the Gulf Research Center (GRC) in Dubai and worked for banks in Germany and the United Arab Emirates. He teaches at the Barcelona Institute of International Studies (IBEI) and has been visiting faculty at the Paris School of International Affairs (PSIA) at SciencesPo. He is author of *Oil for Food. The Global Food Crisis and the Middle East* (2013) and editor of *GCC Financial Markets: The World's New Money Centers* (2012). He holds a PhD in economics from Friedrich-Alexander University, Erlangen-Nuremberg.

1

FOOD SECURITY AND FOOD SOVEREIGNTY IN THE MIDDLE EAST

Zahra Babar and Mehran Kamrava

Soaring prices for agricultural commodities in 2007–8 and again in 2011 reinvigorated the global discussion on food security. According to the World Bank, by 2008 international food prices had increased by an alarming 83 per cent over the course of the previous three years.[1] For the Arab World, which imports over 50 per cent of its caloric needs every year, the impact of such an escalation in food costs cannot be overstated. The following year, the World Bank urged Arab states to try to contain the expected effects of a major food crisis in their countries.[2] Before long, however, in 2011, food prices once again spiked globally, pushing an estimated 44 million people into poverty.[3] This had particularly devastating consequences for the Middle East, as nearly one-quarter of the region's population is poor and about three-quarters of those people live in rural areas with, at best, uneven access to food resources.[4]

As part of their respective ruling bargains on which political rule was justified, almost all states of the Middle East heavily subsidise food prices, spurred especially by the so-called 'bread riots' of the late 1980s and the 1990s and the Arab Spring uprisings that have swept across the region since 2011.[5] Despite heavy state subsidies, however, international food price shocks tend to rapidly translate into price hikes in the domestic markets across the region. From 2006 to 2011, for example, food prices rose by an average of 10 per cent annually in Egypt, Iran and Yemen, and by nearly 5 per cent or more in Djibouti, Kuwait, Lebanon, Oman, Qatar, Saudi Arabia and the United Arab Emirates.[6] Ironically, although international food price increases are often quickly reflected in domestic markets across the Middle East, declines in world food prices are rarely similarly transmitted domestically.[7]

The reasons given for the spike in food prices are varied, with experts unable to agree on a single factor as the cause of the sudden jump. In reality, the soaring prices resulted from a coalescing of various structural, supply-side dynamics, including a slow down in global cereal productivity; insufficient cereal stockpiles worldwide; trade restrictions or export bans on key agricultural products; diversion of agricultural land for bio-fuel production; the high cost of petroleum and the resulting higher expenditures for fertiliser and energy; and speculative investment in commodities.[8] Demand-side pressures pushing up prices were also responsible for the rise in food prices, largely resulting from the increasing global population and changing patterns of consumption in the developing world. It was evident that such a dramatic rise in food costs presented a grave challenge to the whole international community, and in the spring of 2008 the United Nations Chief Executives Board established the multi-stakeholder High-Level Task Force on the Global Food Security Crisis.

While food prices have dropped since the 2008 highs, they remain significantly higher than pre-crisis levels. Expert opinion suggests that this will continue to be the case as the factors that led to elevated costs in the first place have not been adequately dealt with.[9] Bio-fuel production programmes continue to be encouraged in major grain-producing countries; global grain reserves have not been sufficiently enhanced in the intervening years; and food supplies have not kept pace with the increasing demands arising out of higher per capita incomes and changing consumption patterns in certain parts of the developing world.

We should state at the outset that 'food security' and 'food sovereignty' both remain contested notions that are often conceptualised differently depending on context, geography, and the political and policymaking priorities. There are multiple definitions of food security—many of them operationalised by the contributors of this volume—that are all equally valid. At the narrowest level, food security means that 'enough food is available, whether at the global, national, community, or household level'.[10] Along similar lines, in 1996, the United Nations Food and Agriculture Organisation adopted a definition that took into account food availability, access, utilisation and stability: 'Food security exists when all people, at all times, have physical and economic access to sufficient, safe and nutritious food that meets their dietary needs and food preferences for an active and healthy life'.[11]

Implicit in this definition are four critical dimensions of food security: the availability of sufficient quantities of food of appropriate quality; access to 'adequate resources for acquiring foods for a nutritious diet'; utilisation of food through adequate diet for a healthy and productive life; and the stability of food resources over time.[12]

Central to the notion of food security is vulnerability, or lack thereof, to shocks, both external and internal, over which one has little control.[13] Benjamin Shepherd, one of the contributors to this volume, has proposed a definition of food security that pays special attention to vulnerability: 'securing vulnerable populations from the structural violence of hunger'.[14] Shepherd calls for an expansion of traditional conceptions of security to include 'human beings experiencing or vulnerable to hunger'.[15] There is universal agreement that food insecurity, whether transitory or chronic, is caused mainly by poverty, and that the poor are the most vulnerable populations in any society.[16] Across the world today, more than one in seven people do not have access to sufficient protein and energy from their diet, 'and even more suffer from some form of micronutrient malnourishment'.[17]

'Food sovereignty' is a similarly debated term, and some scholars fear that applying it loosely and widely may dilute the original force of the concept.[18] The term first emerged in the West, out of community-based movements coalescing around people's rights to determine food access, food policy and food choices. It arose very much in opposition to state-operated policy and practice, and to challenge the notion that corporate or national interests regarding food resources, food production and food consumption should dominate the discussion.[19] The food sovereignty movement as such was an activist movement, and part of a broader confrontation against neo-liberal economic policies and state-derived notions of food security. At the behest of the international farm workers' organisation Via Campesina, the concept of food sovereignty was introduced into the global debate at the 1996 World Food Summit.[20]

Similar to food security, there is no universally agreed definition of 'food sovereignty'. In relation to the Middle East, the concept of food sovereignty has assumed a fluid dynamism that differs markedly from one country to another. In the smaller states of the Persian Gulf, most notably in the United Arab Emirates, food security is sought through land purchases abroad. An alternative route, pursued by Qatar, is sizeable investments in agricultural and livestock sectors at home and abroad through domestic public enterprises and stakes in international food companies. For others, the question of food availability bears on issues of sovereignty. 'National food sovereignty', therefore, is often viewed as 'the extent to which a country has the means to make available to its people the food needed or demanded, irrespective of whether the food is domestically produced or demanded'.[21] A country unable to produce or import the food its people need or demand does not have food sovereignty. Some policymakers, such as those in the Islamic Republic of Iran, define food security in terms of food self-sufficiency. As the contribution by Salami, Mohtashami, and Naeini in this volume makes clear, Iranian authorities have articulated domestic food self-sufficiency—food sovereignty—as food security. Harrigan similarly shows that after the food price shocks of 2007–8, both Lebanon and Jordan sought to enhance their food sovereignty by increasing food self-sufficiency. Increasing agricultural self-sufficiency, as in Iran, Jordan and Lebanon, may be a step in the right direction in enhancing food sovereignty but is not by itself necessarily sufficient in guaranteeing food security. According to a 2011 Food and Agriculture Organization (FAO) report, 'A food security strategy that relies on a combination of increased productivity and general openness to trade will be more effective than a strategy that relies primarily on the closure of borders.'[22]

In this volume we deliberately refrain from presenting a uniform definition for both terms precisely because of the different conceptualisations that have been employed by the principal actors involved, be they national governments, business and commercial conglomerates, or large and small farmers. This is further complicated by the various levels at which food security can be conceptualised, ranging from the global and national levels and descending down to the levels of the household and the individual. At the broadest level, somewhere between a state of absolute famine and food deprivation, and one of abundance and plenty, there exist zones of 'food security' and 'food insecurity'. Assessing what ensures one and mitigates the other is a complex process that needs to take into account different geographic, socioeconomic, agricultural and political resources and capacities within a community, a country or a region.[23] Within this broad description, we adopt the definition of food security at the household and individual levels offered by the World Food Programme: the daily ability of people to avail of nutritious and adequate amounts of foods that meet their dietary and caloric needs.[24]

At the national level, food security is often conceived of as the adequate availability of food to meet the needs of the populace. Food availability depends on domestic food production capacity combined with food imports. Assessing food availability determines food security. This assessment is particularly important for countries that are highly dependent on food imports, to which an overwhelming majority of Middle Eastern states belong. Nevertheless, a country that has low self-sufficiency and is highly dependent on food imports can still be food secure as long as it is able to finance its food imports.[25]

Several countries of the Middle East began experiencing an increasing 'food gap' in the 1970s as a result of population growth, rapid urbanisation and higher per capita incomes. Rising incomes resulted in changing local consumption patterns, leading to an increasing demand for grains, protein, and varied fruit and vegetable sources. Not surprisingly, over the last several decades, food self-sufficiency for many states in the region has dropped dramatically. Instead, an increasing dependency on food imports has become the norm. It is not possible to predict whether or not food prices will continue to remain high in the years to come, but observers uniformly agree that given its heavy reliance on external food supplies, the Middle East is particularly susceptible to fluctuations in both price and availability of global food stocks.[26]

Despite the significant gains made in terms of combating extreme poverty on a global scale, given the trend of heightened food prices, hunger-reduction in many regions of the developing world will continue to present a real challenge in the years and decades to come. The 2012 'Annual Report on the United Nations Millennium Development Goals' stresses a marked disconnect between poverty-reduction efforts and the persistence of hunger. While incomes have improved in many parts of the developing world and efforts to lower poverty levels have been effective, the number of hungry people around the planet continues to grow. These findings lead us to question the long-held assumption that combating poverty is in itself enough to mitigate hunger. It also underlines the need to more closely study the mechanisms that govern access to food.[27] The report adds that clearly food security needs to be addressed as a global problem, rather than as a national or regional one.[28]

The problematic globalisation of food

Within the growing body of literature on agricultural political economy, in the mid-1980s there emerged a new strand that saw agro-food systems, food production and food access as increasingly internationalised and a product of the historical progression of global capitalism. Existing state systems of agricultural production had become increasingly affected by the internationalisation and globalisation of the food economy.[29] As national, domestic agricultural systems became integrated into the globalised economy, national food security was delinked from local production and domestic agriculture became increasingly more aligned with the economic competitive advantages of international trade.[30] These internationalised forces shaping food production, food access and food consumption can be conceived of in terms of a 'food regime'.[31] What is often described as 'food regime theory', which over the past decades has been much elaborated upon—as well as contested—has its origins in theories of global political economy and world-systems theory. It draws attention to the politically calculated functioning of the world capitalist economy, and how this has incorporated agricultural production, impacted on farming practices and caused specific economic development trajectories.[32]

A 'food regime' refers to a set of factors that undergird the globalisation of food within the capitalist system, and comprises national and international policies, practices, institutions, regulations and interests that inform and structure the production and consumption of food.[33] Integration into the global economy has propelled states to promote export-oriented agricultural production, to institute policies that structure agricultural output in ways that maximise competitive economic advantages and thus rely on efficiently functioning world markets to secure domestic food needs. Some have argued that this process of permitting the logic of the global marketplace to dominate national agro-policy has had a direct and negative impact on local food supply and domestic food production, and, as a result, has increased the risk of food insecurity.[34] Food regime theory suggests that the global market does not exist purely along lines of economic rationality or 'free trade', but is rather politically supported and crafted by specific interests, be they national, international or corporate.[35] This is most obviously manifest in the North-South divide, where grain output in the North is frequently subsidised, protected and supported by the state, and heavily promoted on the international market at comparatively lower prices, thus rendering many domestic agricultural sectors in the South non-competitive.[36] The wheat sector in the United States is regularly held up as an example of this sort of manipulation of the international marketplace.[37]

Food regime theory maintains that while food might exist as a tradable commodity in the global marketplace, the provision of food is also considered to be a political and social right for which the state can be held accountable. As Philip McMichael argued back in 1991:

We are witness to growing political tensions as the contradiction between private (global) accumulation and the national-political legitimacy of states intensifies. One of the clearest currents in this development is the food security movement, which at its most elemental level expresses the decline of community and the subordination of the state to global economic forces.[38]

For nations to surrender their domestic food security to the needs of world markets may not be the wisest course. The global food marketplace does not always function optimally. The competing political or economic interests of other states may impinge upon domestic markets, particularly in terms of crises, such as during natural disasters. Exporting countries may choose to clamp down on certain key food exports that can cause disruption to the global marketplace, which may prove to be particularly difficult for high food-importing countries. The consequences of this were clearly felt in the Middle East in 2008, when several grain-exporting countries banned the sale of grains as a result of their own domestic pressures.[39]

Food security in the Middle East: from Yemen to Qatar

The Middle East is not one of the most severely food insecure regions of the world. It is in sub-Saharan Africa and South Asia that the highest percentages and largest aggregate numbers of the world's hungry reside.[40]

By contrast, the Middle East region has not in the recent past been plagued by severe famine and starvation. On the Global Hunger Index (GHI), which is a composite tool of measurement that goes beyond per capita caloric deficiency and takes into account several different indicators (including the proportion of the undernourished and the prevalence of underweight children), sub-Saharan Africa, South Asia, South-East Asia and Latin America all face far more severe food insecurity than the Middle East does.[41] In fact, by the GHI measurements, the Middle East as a whole is not a gravely food insecure region.

Across most of the Middle East, approximately 5 to 14 per cent of the total population suffers from undernourishment—a figure that is considered to reflect only a moderately low level of hunger.[42] In some countries, notably those of the Arabian Peninsula, that rate goes down to below 5 per cent of the total population, translating into a very low level of undernourishment. What becomes immediately apparent in relation to the Middle East is the discrepancy and disparity in conditions between some of the different countries that occupy the same geographical space. Generalising food security levels region-wide may mask critical levels of food insecurity that exist within pockets of the Middle East. Qatar and Yemen, for example, are both located in the Arabian Peninsula and are often lumped together for analytical purposes. One of them, however, boasts the highest per capita income in the world whereas the other teeters on the brink of socioeconomic collapse. Undernourishment in Qatar is of no measurable numerical significance; in fact, as Tahra ElObeid and Abdelmonem Hassan's contribution in this volume demonstrates, for Qatari nationals the most pressing food-related challenge has to do with the prevalence of unhealthy dietary habits and sedentary lifestyles leading to poor nutritional outcomes and ill-health. In Yemen, however, undernourishment affects between 25 to 35 per cent of the population and is unlikely to decrease any time soon.[43]

If food security is measured by household-level patterns of consumption and income, the range of values will show a huge divide between conditions in countries like Yemen, Djibouti and Sudan, where hunger and poverty are widespread, and the wealthier oil-rich countries of the Persian Gulf. Bahrain, Kuwait, Qatar, the UAE, Oman and Saudi Arabia are not considered to be food insecure because of their prosperity.[44] Certainly, the conceptions of, and approach towards, addressing food insecurity will differ between countries depending on their particular resources and vulnerabilities. Policymakers and governments across the Gulf Cooperation Council (GCC) all rate food security as being a grave concern and one which they are actively working to address, even if internationally their fears are dismissed as being baseless.

While malnutrition and mass starvation are by no means endemic features of the Middle East, food security is certainly an issue that affects all of the states across the region. Given that much of the geographic space the Middle East occupies is known for its arid and inhospitable climate, minimal arable acreage and critical lack of adequate water supply, it is hardly surprising that the region depends heavily on externally-supplied food. The scarcity of water is a geological limitation that is difficult to surmount, as is the limited amount of arable land available for expanding agricultural production. However, agricultural yields in the Middle East are well below the world average, and there is scope for improvement if adequate technological investments are made. Currently, among Middle Eastern countries only Lebanon, Syria, Iran and, to some extent, Egypt are considered to be adequately self-sufficient in agricultural production.[45]

The Arab states as a whole import close to 60 per cent of their food needs; are the largest grain-importers in the world;[46] and are, as a result, highly affected by spikes in food prices.[47] Six of the top ten wheat-importing countries in the world are located in the Middle East.[48] Increasingly, rising global food costs place severe pressures on both the states and the people of the Middle East, at both the national and the household levels.[49] Middle Eastern governments are also growing more alarmed at their deepening food dependency, and there is an increasing level of awareness concerning food security across the region. Not surprisingly, most Middle Eastern states have instituted explicit policies regarding the levels of strategic food storages required. Currently, storage capacity in the region averages about six months of consumption, with an estimated five months of ending stocks.[50]

The ensuing national and regional debates over how to best achieve food security have become somewhat polarised. A number of regional policymakers and scholars feel that individual countries must attempt to become self-sufficient in food supply. This would require increasing domestic food production and, if necessary, investment in overseas food production, not only by investing in overseas agro projects but also by purchasing stakes in international food companies. On the opposite side are those who argue that the limitations of natural resources across many parts of the Middle East make self-sufficiency prohibitively expensive, and, with increasing demands as populations grow, unsustainable.[51] These experts stress that food security translates into access to affordable food, not ownership or control over how it gets made. Given the high costs of water and land investment, they argue, greater domestic self-sufficiency for food production means that funds are taken away from other critically important development sectors, such as education and healthcare.

Most international organisations consider that economic growth, increasing incomes and targeted initiatives to combat poverty provide the key to ensuring food security. This arises out of a commonly-accepted assumption that if people can afford to buy food to feed themselves then they will be food secure. If macro-level security is measured by nutrition outcomes (as captured by GHI) then most of the Middle East is classified as not suffering grave food insecurity. On the other hand, the Middle East is certainly the part of the world that is most reliant on food imports, and it has extremely low self-sufficiency in food production. This dependency on external food supplies creates a fragility of sorts. The majority of countries in the region depend on purchasing their food on the international market in order to meet the needs of their populations. This food dependency is only expected to increase exponentially in the future as populations continue to grow and as consumption patterns keep changing.[52] The International Food Policy Research Institute (IFPRI) estimates that between 2000 and 2002, anywhere from 25 to 50 per cent of national consumption across the Middle East was met through food imports.[53] This varies broadly depending on the particular country. The six GCC states, for example, have much higher rates of food dependency than some of their regional neighbours, importing well over 60 per cent of their food needs every year.[54] Qatar and the UAE currently import roughly 90 per cent of their food needs.[55] This lack of ability to maintain self-sufficiency in terms of food production for their local populaces has led many of the GCC states to consider themselves to be in a precarious or 'food insecure' position. As a result, various policy initiatives have been launched to develop strategic mechanisms for curbing their heavy dependency on external food supplies.

Terminology can be confusing and has the potential to obscure the issues under discussion. In parts of the Middle East, the defining issue is not about the lack of access to adequate amounts of food, but that the food has to be brought in from far afield. Thus, the price of, availability of and access to global food supplies are viewed as being critical factors. According to a 2010 IFPRI report, in the Middle East, national or macro-level food security might exist but food self-sufficiency does not.[56] The region as a whole lacks adequate control over, and access to, its food sources and this dependency on external supply channels has been locally articulated as a lack of food sovereignty. Despite their wealth and affluence, high income countries such as Qatar, Kuwait, Saudi Arabia and the UAE lack control over their food sources and are highly dependent on imports—thus lack food sovereignty. Other countries, like Egypt, Syria, Iran, Morocco and Lebanon, actually have higher levels of agricultural production and are thus not lacking in food self-sufficiency, but they are actually still food insecure as nutritional outcomes for the population are poor. Yemen falls among that category of countries that are both food insecure and lack self-sufficiency in agricultural production.

Micro and macro impact of food price increases

Higher food prices have both micro- and macro-level effects across the Middle East. At the micro level, households have to spend more of their budget on food expenditure. There is little elasticity around food consumption, and consumers may find themselves suddenly spending a far larger share of their income for the same amount of food bought previously. Food price increases hurt the poorest the most, with lower income households in general spending the largest percentage of their budget on food items. In times of crisis or economic difficulty, the poor are often forced to divert funds from productive expenditure or to incur debt in order to meet their food needs.[57] Sudden sharp increases in food prices can quickly push more people below the poverty line. In those countries of the Middle East where incomes are lower and poverty is endemic, there is a far greater risk for this sort of slippage.

A 2012 World Food Programme report on Yemen, for example, indicated that household food security is critical, with the poorest households spending close to 35 per cent of their income on the purchase of bread alone.[58] According to a recent joint United Nations survey on Yemeni food security, close to 5 million people—more than a fifth of the population—are unable to meet their required food needs.[59] This is a dramatic increase and doubles the number of people assessed to be food insecure in Yemen in 2009.[60] As Yemen imports 96 per cent of its food needs it has been particularly hard hit by increases in global food prices. Escalating costs for food imports, combined with the lack of socio-economic stability and ongoing political conflict in the country, have directly impacted on peoples' capacity to feed themselves.

At a more macro level and in terms of governance, higher global food prices test the capacities of many Middle Eastern governments in particularly strenuous ways. Many of the regional governments have implemented food subsidy programmes for decades, which are costly and difficult to maintain. The International Monetary Fund has regularly pressed governments to pull back from food subsidy programmes that are considered inefficient and costly. Food price shocks, such as the ones in 2007–8 and 2011, force already-stretched government budgets in the region, as more subsidies were considered to be a necessity in mitigating against food inflation pressures on the populace. Wealthier resource-exporters such as the GCC states may be able to cope with these additional budgetary pressures. But for those states with less robust economies, the extra expenditure on food subsidies exposes them to greater economic and financial challenges.

The overall prognosis for food security—globally or in the Middle East—is not positive. As the chapters in this volume clearly illustrate, problems associated with food security, in the Middle East or elsewhere, are unlikely to be resolved anytime soon. By some estimates, the world at large will need 70 to 100 per cent more food by 2050 to be able to feed itself.[61] With the exception of Morocco, all countries of the Middle East and North Africa are currently food importers and are likely to remain so in the years and decades to come.[62] Food security is a product of a number of interlocking systems at both the national and international levels, not the least of which include water, land, energy, agriculture, national and international distributional networks, and—perhaps most significantly—public policy and national politics.[63] Ensuring equitable and sustainable food security requires a 'multifaceted and linked global strategy',[64] one that is unlikely to emerge or be forged in the foreseeable future. As the FAO concluded in 2011, in fact, 'high and volatile food prices are likely to continue' and to be exacerbated by additional shocks:

Demand from consumers in rapidly growing economies will increase, population continues to grow, and any further growth in biofuels will place additional demands on the food system… Food price volatility may increase because of stronger linkages between agricultural and energy markets, as well as an increased frequency of weather shocks.[65]

Not surprisingly, the institutional requirements for food security are not static and vary based on national, economic, and political contexts and circumstances.[66]

In specific relation to the Middle East, several structural factors particular to the region are likely to continue to aggravate issues of food insecurity and food sovereignty. Throughout the Middle East, arable farmlands tend to be highly fragmented due to successive land reform programmes by the region's many populist regimes. In Egypt, for example, some 90 per cent of landlords own less than 1 hectare. Landholdings elsewhere in the region—most notably in Algeria, Jordan, Saudi Arabia and Tunisia—tend to be also relatively small for largely similar reasons.[67] Aridity, periodic droughts and chronic water scarcity also tend to be endemic features of the Middle East, as are generally inefficient distribution networks of ports, roads, wholesale markets, supermarkets and other stores—one of the reasons wastage across the region tends to be extremely high. Finally, official rhetoric notwithstanding, most policymakers in the Middle East have an urban bias that results in the preferential treatment of modern industries located around urban centres, thus frequently neglecting rural areas and the agricultural sector.[68]

This volume

The contributions in this volume analyse both the historic trajectories of agricultural development in the Middle East, and how the globalisation of food production has impacted domestic food security. The volume draws on original research undertaken on the causes and consequences of macro-level Middle Eastern food security (at the national and regional levels), as well as the causes and consequences of food security at the micro-level (household and individual). As amply demonstrated in the chapters to come, there is historical memory of food shortages and scarcity in the region, and this has had an impact on the formulation of thinking on food security. If economic and political factors in the past have led to sudden disruptions in food availability, this provides a logical rationality for why Middle Eastern states might currently be considering means by which to make themselves food self-sufficient. Another consistent theme that runs through several chapters is the impact that rentier earnings have had on the development of agriculture in the Middle East or the lack of domestic investment in the agricultural sector. The ongoing sense of being food dependent, or forcibly having been made food dependent through food aid schemes and 'wheatification' of local diets, has informed much of regional thinking on food security.

The volume begins with an examination of the historic rise and fall of various food regimes by Eckart Woertz, who traces the dependence of the Middle East on long-distance food trade. The unhappy convergence of dynamics that have made the region a net importer of foodstuffs and agricultural goods, Woertz concludes, appear far too deeply entrenched to be easily reversed or remedied by states lacking the resources, or the political willpower, to implement policies needed to prevent another food price crisis. The volume then presents a series of in-depth case studies, examining the causes and consequences of dependence on food imports and the policy options available or taken by the states concerned with alleviating food insecurity. Jane Harrigan presents an economic analysis of food import dependence in Lebanon and Jordan, arguing that despite efforts by both states to increase domestic food production, which are not necessarily economically efficient, both are likely to remain dependent on imports and thus susceptible to price shocks in the foreseeable future. Ray Bush reaches similar conclusions in his analysis of Egypt, though his study focuses on the experience of Egyptian farmers and on rural relations of production and reproduction as shaped by political and economic power, patterns of land ownership and the integration of the Egyptian economy into the world economy. 'Urban peace' has been bought at the price of rural producers, Bush maintains, whereby large landholders and merchants, based overwhelmingly in the urban areas, have been able to exact increased profits from farmers with small plots of land. This has not increased rural competitiveness or productivity but has instead stymied rural growth and has facilitated the urban merchants' dominance over rural economies.

Iran and Yemen offer two contrasting examples of the role of the state and its efforts aimed at alleviating food insecurity. Salami, Mohtashami and Naeini examine the efforts of successive Iranian governments since the 1980s to enhance the domestic production of foodstuffs. For the most part these efforts have paid off, despite their apparent lack of economic soundness—Iran has achieved self-sufficiency in most food products except red meat and poultry. Nonetheless, such self-sufficiency appears tenuous at best and likely to be upset by any precipitous increases in domestic energy prices. This chapter provides an illuminating data-set on the efforts undertaken by the state to invest in food self-sufficiency. These self-sufficiency efforts—which for decades have been taken contrary to prevailing economic wisdom that encourages reliance on global food trade rather than domestic production—may have been initially motivated out of nationalist and revolutionary agendas. However, over time and as the Islamic Republic has grown increasingly politically and economically isolated from the international community, perhaps there is a logic to such efforts after all. Iran's current inability to trade freely provides a degree of justification for policymakers who caution against placing one's national food needs in the hands of global markets. It also raises normative questions of how just it is for the international community to punish a state by placing trade embargoes that impact food procurement and thus the food security of civilian populations. While the current sanctions regime on Iran does not target food procurement, it makes it close to impossible for food importers to conduct international transfers through banks.

In Yemen, meanwhile, a food crisis has been steadily brewing since the 1960s, aggravated by chronic national turmoil, political instability, and policy paralysis. As Mundy, Al-Hakimi and Pelat demonstrate, even after the unification of the Yemen Arab Republic and the People's Democratic Republic of Yemen in 1990, policy differences in land tenure, infrastructural investment, crop choice and marketing continued to characterise the nascent institutions of the new state. For the most part, however, the state relegated attention to agriculture to international aid agencies and instead focused on security issues, a task at which it also had little success. Not surprisingly, today Yemen has neither food security nor food sovereignty.

Small farms located on the margins of major urban centres often account for a sizeable portion of agricultural activity throughout the Middle East. Although often the sole source of food and income for their proprietors, the yield and efficiency of these peri-urban farms tend to be low and their productivity often marginal. Tawk, Abi Said and Hamadeh examine the agricultural sectors in two such peri-urban areas in Lebanon and Jordan—Bebnine and Wadi el Seer—respectively. Despite the prevalence of such urban agriculture, they argue, urban and peri-urban farmers and food producers tend to suffer from higher rates of poverty and food insecurity compared to non-producers. Nevertheless, they do find that targeted and supportive state policies, as those applied to the outskirts of Amman, can help alleviate peri-urban poverty and perhaps even lessen instances of food insecurity among peri-urban food producers.

Despite the continued prevalence of peri-urban food production across the Middle East, the region is undergoing both a 'nutrition transition'—with traditional diets being increasingly replaced with 'modern' diets that have larger portions of saturated fats, sugar and processed foods—and a 'supermarket transition'—whereby food production and processing in smaller units is being replaced, or at least complemented, by the activities of larger retail outlets that trade primarily with specialised wholesalers and large food producers. Seyfert, Chaaban and Ghattas examine nutrition and supermarket transitions in Lebanon and Qatar, finding that while both countries have undergone nutrition transitions, a supermarket transition has occurred in Qatar but not in Lebanon. Because of Qatar's high aridity and excessive temperatures, agricultural production is necessarily more industrial and requires much higher levels of state support, thus facilitating a comparatively higher level of supermarket transition in the country. This supermarket and nutrition transition, as we shall see presently, has not been without its adverse effects for public health. In Lebanon, by contrast, state policy towards the agricultural sector has been less interventionist, resulting in the perseverance of small-scale—and often inefficient—farms.

Seyfert, Chaaban and Ghattas demonstrate that among other factors, the small population size of Qatar has led increasingly to a dependency on globalised supermarket chains, a selective few of which dominate the Qatari food market. It is worth noting that out of the close to 2 million people residing in Qatar, a dominant percentage comprises lower income migrant workers. While the top tier of skilled, high-wage earning foreigners and the national population may find expensive supermarkets affordable, low-income migrant workers do not have the ability to afford high-quality supermarket produce. Further research will be needed to assess the food consumption and purchasing patterns of the Qatari migrant worker population.

Tétreault, Wheeler and Shepherd examine the growing phenomenon of overseas agricultural investments by the small Persian Gulf sheikhdoms in parts of Africa and Asia, focusing specifically on Cambodia and Ethiopia. These investments have drawn much public and policy discussion of late, discussion which has not been empirically backed up by hard facts on the ground regarding both the nature of these investments and their potential 'win-win' or problematic outcomes. Much of the discussion has aired the concern that these initiatives pose a threat and risk to the host countries. Tétreault, Wheeler and Shepherd argue however that, by and large, overseas agricultural investments are 'bad business' and are likely to result in 'lose-lose' scenarios that produce neither food sovereignty nor food security for both the host and the investor country. The chapter demonstrates that there is a high risk to potential GCC investors engaging in international land transactions. Poor governance structures, absence of rule of law, embedded corruption and the socio-economic fragility of farming communities provide little assurance that GCC investments would succeed.

The volume ends with two extreme, opposite cases, namely those of the Palestinian West Bank and Qatar. Most studies of food security, including many of the chapters in this volume, focus on national policies at the macro level. Using spatial mapping, Cavatorta and Waples examine instances of food security at the community level across the West Bank. They argue that apart from, and in addition to, macro-level, national policies aimed at ensuring food security, community-level variables such as employment rates, levels of economic development, agricultural potential and access to markets are important predictors of food security. In Qatar meanwhile, a country whose citizens enjoy one of the highest income levels in the world, under-nutrition and micronutrient deficiencies coexist with over-eating and extremely high rates of childhood obesity. The country's small size, the inordinate financial resources at the disposal of the state and its streamlined and focused leadership have enabled the state to proactively seek to stem what is steadily emerging as a public health crisis. Nevertheless, as ElObeid and Hassan's study shows, addressing entrenched dietary and consumption habits requires more than state efforts at sponsoring major sporting events and encouraging physical activity on the part of the citizenry.

As the various chapters here demonstrate, food sovereignty and food security, whether at the national or the household level, are rooted in several intertwined structural, economic, political and cultural dynamics. Across the Middle East, as in much of the rest of the world, there appears neither the necessary political will nor the resources needed to address issues related to food security and national food sovereignty. At the household level, food insecurity is intimately tied to poverty and insufficient or inadequate access to food sources, thus requiring states to devise and implement poverty-alleviation measures and policies at both the community and national levels. The reality on the ground, whether in Egypt, Lebanon, Iran, the West Bank or Yemen, is far too grave to promise wide-scale alleviation of poverty in the near future. At the national level, meanwhile, managing future food security must include strategic choices about securing access to food through a mix of domestic investments (agriculture and food stocks), international market arrangements (trade agreements and hedging) and, when possible, potential innovative mechanisms (such as virtual reserves). All are tall orders for any state, but they are especially arduous for states in a region as chaotic and politically unstable as the Middle East.

Through this volume, multidisciplinary by design, we hope to start academic and policy dialogues on a topic seldom discussed and even less often studied. The studies here offer preliminary glimpses into some of the fundamental research questions that future analyses of food security and food sovereignty, whether in the Middle East or elsewhere, ought to examine. Our hope is to have paved the way for future directions in research and inquiry on a topic that's critical importance transcends purely academic endeavours and touches on the most basic needs of individuals, communities and entire countries. Much research is still needed, especially in those parts of the Middle East—such as Libya, Syria and Iraq—where at the time of writing in 2013 fieldwork on the topic was excessively difficult to conduct. For now, with political stability and strategic policymaking elusive in these and in most other countries of the Middle East, food security and food sovereignty appear even further from reach.

2

HISTORIC FOOD REGIMES
AND THE MIDDLE EAST

Eckart Woertz

During the global food crisis in 2008, the current food regime failed. Global food markets faltered. Food exporters like Russia, Argentina and Vietnam announced temporary export restrictions as they were concerned about their own food security in the wake of price hikes. Middle Eastern countries became nervous as they import about a third of globally traded grain. Their reactions ranged from increased subsidies to price controls and the build-up of strategic storage of staple foods. They also announced international agro-investments to ensure food supplies from abroad.[1] Their policies have not only been informed by the changing fortunes of international food production and distribution, but also by their collective memory of past challenges to their food security—most notably, their food import dependence and their vulnerability to supply disruptions. Against this backdrop, this chapter analyses how different food regimes since the nineteenth century have affected Middle Eastern countries, and how these states have tried to adjust to changing realities. The focus here is on the Persian Gulf countries, the Mashreq and Egypt.

19

After outlining the theoretical framework, the chapter discusses the Middle East during the time of the first food regime, which lasted from the 1870s to the 1930s. Grain supplies from Australia, the United States, Canada, Russia and India to the UK and other industrialising countries in Europe were this regime's defining characteristics. Another important factor was the colonial export trade in tropical commodities like sugar, cotton and silk. While the Middle East in general was still self-sufficient in staple foods at that time, there was a need to level out regional imbalances. Some import-dependent regions like the Persian Gulf also took advantage of the grain trade with the peripheral settler colonies. The vulnerability to supply disruptions is then illustrated by discussing the Middle East's supply arrangements and agricultural policies during the two World Wars. In both cases, it was crucial for Arab leaders to maintain good diplomatic relations with powers that were in a position to guarantee the flow of food supplies and agricultural inputs.

After a period of crisis and adjustment in the wake of the Great Depression, the second food regime emerged after the Second World War. Subsidised agriculture in industrialised countries and surplus disposal to the developing world were at its core. By the 1970s, all countries in the Middle East were heavily dependent on grain imports. At the same time, the food regime faced a crisis with reduced grain stocks and diminished availability of food aid that ushered in the world food crisis of 1973–4.[2] Depending on their factor endowment, Middle Eastern countries had different options at their disposal to deal with the crisis. Oil- and cash-rich countries were obviously in a more convenient position, yet they faced threats of food embargoes in retaliation to their oil embargo.

With falling commodity prices in the 1980s and 1990s Malthusian fears of the 1970s subsided, but resurfaced in the wake of the global food crisis of 2008. It is an open debate whether we can speak of a third food regime that has developed since the 1980s with World Trade Organization-sponsored liberalisation and increased corporatisation of value chains in global food production. In the final section, the chapter discusses major implications for Middle Eastern countries and speculates how they might position themselves in the changing international political economy of food supplies.

HISTORIC FOOD REGIMES AND THE MIDDLE EAST

Historic food regimes—a theoretical framework

A food regime describes a system that allocates food resources via the two institutions that have shaped modernity—markets and states. Both are 'disembedded' spheres that are radically different from earlier social formations that were tied to face-to-face social relationships, as Karl Polanyi has argued.[3] Both require each other; the state pushed for the social change that brought about markets. Later, the state began regulating markets, because without regulation, markets undermine the social and environmental prerequisites that allow them to function. States in turn require a taxable economic base to sustain themselves, and use regulated markets to allocate resources. Despite fervent ideological debates, it is never about the market or the state, but always about the market and the state. Both have expanded their scope relentlessly and synchronically in modern times. Political lobbying, economic change and multilateral regimes influence their resource allocation.

If Middle Eastern countries today are heavily dependent on the long-distance food trade, it is important to stress how young this phenomenon is. It only took off in earnest in the nineteenth century. The UK repealed its protectionist Corn Laws in 1846 and made a conscious decision to rely on imported grains from settler colonies. The proliferation of steam power caused a dramatic decline in transportation costs from 1870s onwards and a concomitant increase in the transnational grain trade. The UK imported the majority of its grain by 1880.[4] In earlier times, the Roman Empire had relied on grain deliveries from corn provinces like Sicily and Egypt to provide for its armies and the city of Rome.[5] However, in general, self-sufficiency remained the rule. The long-distance grain trade was only a niche sector and was restricted to transport by sea. Even in the Mediterranean, with its long coastlines and accessible shipping routes, the long-distance grain trade was only a fraction of overall grain consumption, was only affordable for rich cities and was only possible after the needs of Rome had been served.[6] Once the Roman Empire declined, political security and the unity of currencies, measures and rules faded as well. The long-distance grain trade diminished and did not bear similar significance until the seventeenth/eighteenth century, before taking off in the nineteenth century.

In an influential 1989 article, Harriet Friedmann and Philip McMichael interpreted the development of commercial agriculture and food trade in the context of general capitalist development.[7] They identified two food regimes that had been in place since the nineteenth century. In the first food regime, from the 1870s to the 1930s, colonial export trade in tropical commodities provided industrial input factors. Family farmers in settler states like the United States, Canada and Australia produced grains to feed the workforce in the UK and other industrialising countries in Europe. In return, the settler states purchased manufactured goods and imported capital and migrants from those core countries. Colonies thus facilitated a process of wage-labour expansion.

After a period of crisis and reconfiguration, this food regime gave way to a process of intensification of accumulation after the Second World War. Consumption relations were restructured and became more important for the growth model. New consumer products like cars and white goods emerged. Diets underwent a process of 'meatification' in developed countries and consumption of packaged durable foods grew. Input factors for these food industries like soy-oil, corn syrup and other sweeteners were substitutes for colonial export crops and were produced in the centres, particularly in the United States, which overtook the UK as the main hegemonic power in the new food regime. During this time, synthetic fibres replaced cotton. Grain production was subsidised and moved back to the core countries. Steep productivity growth led to overproduction in the developed world and a resulting need for surplus disposal to developing countries in the form of food aid. Diets in developing countries were 'wheatified' and these countries became grain net importers. The respective governments were happy to take subsidised food deliveries as they hoped to use them as input factors for an expansion of their urban workforce and industrial development. Farmers in the developing world in turn could not compete with the subsidised grain imports. They had to leave the land, and, besides, they were attracted by the allure of the cities.

On the political side, the creation of agro-industrial integration and a world market between nation states superseded the vertical integration between colonies and mother countries. US control superseded British hegemony. Friedmann and McMichael interpret the second food regime as the completion of the state system and the transnational restructuring of the agro-sector with intensive meat production and the durable foods sector as central components.[8]

Since the 1970s, there has been an increasing shift from nation states to multinational companies as the most important actors controlling food regimes. Some interpret the concentration of retail chains, input supplies and financial services as a third food regime that has emerged since the 1980s.[9] Others disagree and hint that the collapse of the Doha round of talks in 2008 is an example that the old regime is in crisis, but still in place.[10] Still others have argued that the agricultural sector is different because of its peculiarities, and have criticised food regime theory for its top-down application of regulation theory and its industrial relations categories.[11]

This debate is ongoing and its outcome cannot be decided here. Yet, this chapter suggests that the broad categorisation of two distinct food regimes since the 1870s offers a helpful analytical framework for the Middle East. In the nineteenth century, the cultivation of colonial export crops proliferated in the Arab world. Governments in Syria, Iraq and Egypt were dominated by a class of private landowners, and the expansion of commercial farming led to the concentration of landownership. The post-Second World War decades then saw revolutionary change by military officers, land reform, the advent of oil-based economies, import substituting industrialisation and the rise of new urban middle classes.

The Western push for food surplus disposal coincided with a relative neglect of agriculture in the Middle East. In countries like Egypt, it was taxed to provide capital for industrialisation.[12] In Iraq and Iran, the oil boom led to Dutch disease and an import boom that affected domestic producers. This negligence effect was also observed in labour-sending countries such as Yemen and Egypt that witnessed a massive inflow of remittances from oil exporting countries.[13] Only Saudi Arabia, Libya, Jordan and Morocco subsidised wheat production in the 1970s.[14] Saudi Arabia was the most exceptional case. Its massive subsidisation of agriculture with the help of oil rents and non-renewable fossil water led to an unsustainable agricultural boom in the 1980s and 1990s.

The horizontal expansion of cultivation that had prevailed earlier was hampered as land became more scarce. Worse still, as the population grew, the Middle East as a whole lost its ability to grow its required food from renewable water resources by the 1970s.[15] There was a steep rise in grain imports after the Second World War and by the 1970s the region was a net importer. Middle Eastern countries like Egypt and Syria tried to counter the growing food gap in the 1980s and 1990s by implementing more supportive agricultural policies and by redressing earlier taxation.[16] The position of Middle Eastern countries in the globally prevalent food regimes was of crucial importance for their economic development, their food security and their legitimacy.

Geography and agriculture before the nineteenth century

The arid geography of the Middle East constitutes a challenge to agricultural production. Rain-fed agriculture in Iran, Anatolia and Syria show strong output fluctuation. Except for Egypt, irrigation is limited or difficult to manage, such as in Iraq where violent, salty floods and the slope of the valleys require more canals and care. Still, the Neolithic revolution started in the region and the historical existence of large cities and luxury consumption bear testimony to an agricultural surplus beyond subsistence production. Between the years 700–1100, countries in the Middle East showed remarkable agricultural development with investments in irrigation and the introduction of new crops from India, the Far East and Africa including rice, sorghum, cotton, sugar cane, lemons and eggplant.[17]

However, the Middle East fell behind Europe economically from the sixteenth century onwards. A relatively strong and uncontested Ottoman state did not have the same need for military innovation as the European states that were in constant rivalry with each other.[18] The Ottoman Empire also fell behind in overseas trade and prevented the independence of institutions like municipalities, universities and guilds. Water and wind power and their use in industry, grinding, water lifting and drainage was underdeveloped.[19] Furthermore, demographic factors favoured European development, a later marriage age and a trend towards smaller nuclear families kept population growth below the maximum and allowed more land to be used for woodlands and livestock husbandry.[20]

Despite this relative decline, the Napoleonic scientific mission to Egypt in 1798 found that agricultural productivity in the Middle East was on par with Europe or higher. The Ottoman Empire exported wheat from Egypt, Rumelia and Romania, livestock from North Africa and cotton from Cyprus, Greece and Syria. Silk was mainly re-exported from Iran.[21] Agriculture was the basis of the Ottoman state and its military expansion. The state owned most of the land since the fifteenth century and granted non-hereditary fiefdoms (*timar*) to its cavalrymen (*sipahi*).

This system was in crisis after the sixteenth century. Without productivity growth, stalling conquests put limits on the maintenance of the *sipahi*. At the same time, the proliferation of firearms greatly reduced the military advantages of a cavalry. The standing infantry army of the Janissary became more important and its support required cash income. The Ottoman state phased out the non-hereditary *timar* to the *sipahi* and, instead, increased tax farming (*iltizam*) of estates.[22] The right to tax was sold off to wealthy notables, who later turned into landlords once private landownership was introduced in the nineteenth century. The high concentration of land ownership and the rise of absentee landlords in Egypt, Iraq and Syria contributed to income inequality and were later blamed for the neglect of agriculture.[23]

Food security, land tenure and development during the first food regime: 1870s–1930s

In the nineteenth century, much of the Middle East was integrated into the world economy in a typically colonial fashion, although most parts of the region never formally became a colony. It provided primary commodities for industrialising Europe, which, in turn, spent great efforts to open up the Middle East as a market for its manufactured goods. In the capitulations, the Ottoman Empire lowered trade barriers for European imports, set impediments for the development of indigenous industries and granted extraterritorial jurisdiction to foreigners and minorities that were engaged in the colonial trade (Armenians, Maronites, Greeks and Jews). As a 'penetrated system,' the Ottoman Empire remained formally independent, but its sovereignty was compromised by military weakness and constant European interference in its internal affairs. Only competition between the European powers over its spoils enabled Constantinople to struggle along and manage a century of constant decline, before its formal demise after the First World War.[24]

Transport costs fell and market access increased with technological progress. Steamships proliferated from the 1830s, railways and the telegraph from the 1850s and the Suez Canal was built in 1869.[25] Besides subsistence farming, regional cereal markets and pockets of export cash crops developed. Egypt, Turkey and Iran were the centres of cotton cultivation in the nineteenth century. Later on, agriculture expanded in Sudan where Britain launched the Gezira irrigation scheme in the south of Khartoum in 1925. Wine was produced in the Levant, tobacco in Turkey and Syria, and silk in Mount Lebanon and Iran. The latter also was a major cultivator of opium, as was Turkey. Export crops yielded on average three times higher profit margins than wheat. About 80 per cent of crops were cereals. They were cultivated in extensive fashion and half to two-thirds of the land usually lay fallow. Half of the cereal production was grown for subsistence, while the other half was sold in local and regional markets. Olives constituted the bulk of fat supplies. Livestock production was also extensive, but fodder production for animals was only common in Egypt.[26]

The increased commercialisation of agriculture went hand-in-hand with changes in the system of land tenure. Egypt and Turkey introduced Western-style commercial codes to increase their tax bases. The new land tenure systems facilitated debt collection and allowed land to be owned, sold and mortgaged by private individuals. While Mesopotamia already knew private ownership before, the transformation to private ownership was most comprehensive in Egypt. Its economy became the most monetised of all the Middle Eastern countries and it witnessed a significant change from its former tributary system where the state was the landowner and refinanced itself by selling tax privileges.[27] Registration of tribal land under the name of village elders and the dynamics of capitalist agriculture led to the emergence of large, landholding families and a peculiar social stratification between them and smallholder peasants, sharecroppers and the landless population.

Agricultural output in the Middle East kept pace with population growth between 1800 and 1914. However, production growth was based on expanded cultivation of unused land or intensification of farming on existing plots. Apart from Egypt, productivity growth did not occur anywhere else in the Middle East. In these countries, there was little diversification of crops or improvement in agricultural methods. Such stunted growth was mainly due to conservatism, poverty, lack of knowledge and, most importantly, the land tenure system, which gave little incentive for enhanced agricultural productivity because of absentee landlords and the problem of land without secure title.[28]

The Ottoman Law Code of 1858 stipulated that land should be registered in individual ownership. In Iraq, this led to the transfer of large swathes of land to tribal sheikhs and occasionally city merchants and money lenders. For this reason, the law was later suspended. As a result, large amounts of land ended up without clear title.[29] Egypt was the only country with a complete cadastral survey and registration of landholdings. All over the Middle East, there was considerable confusion among five different types of landholdings that had emerged from the erstwhile Ottoman code. *Mulk* was land held in freehold ownership; *miri* was land originally held by the state, but which had been transferred by the Sultan for special services; *waqf* land was owned by a charitable trust for the benefit of certain persons or an institution; *matrukki* was land used for public benefit; and *masha* land was a form of communal ownership mainly in Syria and Transjordan, where a plot of land was reallocated every three years at the end of a crop cycle.[30]

While large landholdings of the *mulk* and *miri* category were held by absentee landlords whose main interest was rent collection; the other types of ownership were characterised by fragmentation of holdings and insecure land tenure. This discouraged productivity increases, while giving incentives to overwork the land and exhaust soils during tenure without consideration for the long-term consequences. In 1933, 1 per cent of the landlords in Egypt owned 40 per cent of the land, which they held in estates of 50 acres and more. The aftermath of the Great Depression led to a further concentration of landownership as tenants and sharecroppers were chronically indebted to landowners and usurers and often had to sell their land in times of crisis.[31]

A relatively weak bourgeoisie in the cities was only able to launch timid industrialisation drives, such as in Egypt in the 1920s under the Bank Misr.[32] When the Great Depression struck, regulatory reaction was limited, 'no Keynes or FDR burst upon the Egyptian scene in the 1930s to deal with the economic crisis'.[33] Hence, access to food was compromised by rural income inequalities, missing urban development and lack of government intervention. Domestic industries failed to give a strong demand impetus for agriculture and enhance its value chain.

On the eve of the Second World War, the dietary intake in the Middle East was richer than in other developing countries like India, but lagged far behind developed countries. Exact pre-war nutritional data does not exist and is completely absent for the Arabian Peninsula. Lloyd gives some approximations from Food and Agriculture Organization (FAO) food balance sheets after the war (see Figure 2.1). Bread grains dominated diets in the Middle East with 63 per cent and 70 per cent of caloric intake in Palestine and Egypt, respectively. Consumption of sugars and fats in the Middle East was only about a quarter of the United States' annual rate. For meat, fish and eggs it was only a sixth. Dairy products, fruit and vegetables ranked more prominently in the diet.

Figure 2.1: Pre-war diets in international comparison (approximations)

Item	Middle East	Italy	United States
Kilos per year:			
Grains, as flour	165	177	90
Roots, pulses and nuts	15–25	59	71
Sugar and syrup	11	7	49
Fats and oils	5	12	22
Meat, eggs and fish	15	33	85
Fruit and vegetables	100–200	84	184
Milk and cheese	50–100	42	177
Calories per day	2,200	2,689	3,164
Protein (gm. per day)			
Total	70	86	90
Animal	10–12	20	52

Source: Lloyd, E. M. H., *Food and Inflation in the Middle East, 1940–45, Studies on Food, Agriculture, and World War II*, Stanford, CA: Stanford University Press, 1956, p. 15; based on FAO, Food Balance Sheets, Washington D. C., April 1949 and FAO, 'Report of the Second Near East Meeting on Food and Agricultural Programs and Outlook', Bloudane, Syria, 28 August–6 September 1951.

The quasi-colonial export trade and the social structure it had generated characterised the Middle East. Apart from tropical commodities, like cotton or tobacco, exports also included grains. Iraq in particular developed into a food exporter in the second half of the nineteenth century by trading wheat, barley, dates and livestock. Between 1869–70 and 1912–13 its seaborne exports rose twelve-fold and its merchandise imports grew even faster.[34]

By 1935, wheat production in the Middle East recovered from the First World War and the Great Depression. The Middle East became a wheat net exporter again as it was before the war and traded about 4 per cent of its harvests across borders. Anatolia, Iraq, Transjordan and Egypt were major producers.[35] In the 1930s, Iraq exported considerable quantities of barley as feedstock to the UK.[36] It was thus part of the periphery-centre grain trade of the first food regime, albeit a minor player compared to countries like Australia or Canada.

HISTORIC FOOD REGIMES AND THE MIDDLE EAST

Food supplies and warfare

Provision of supplies and denial thereof are time-honoured means of warfare, and were used extensively in the two world wars.[37] Production declines and supply disruptions affected food security. Middle Eastern politicians engaged in dexterous diplomacy with the powers that were in a position to maintain or reopen supply lines. While the Middle East as a whole was a grain net exporter there were regional imbalances between surplus regions like Iraq, Egypt and inner Syria and importing regions like Palestine, Lebanon and the Arabian Peninsula. Regional dietary preferences also led to a substantial import of grains from the outside world. These vulnerabilities were exposed when the Entente forces put a naval blockade on the Ottoman Empire.

By the beginning of the twentieth century, on the coasts of the Arabian Peninsula, dates had been replaced by rice as a main staple, at least for the upper echelons of urban society. On the Red Sea coast, wheat and millet played an important role.[38] Cereals were mainly imported from India. After the maritime blockade of the Entente, no food reached the ports of the Mediterranean and the Red Sea, and trade routes into Kuwait were controlled. The effect was exacerbated by an inadequate Ottoman supply strategy, deficient harvests, inclement weather and hoarding by unscrupulous traders.[39]

By comparing the different effects of the blockade on Greater Syria and the Arabian Peninsula, interesting points can be made about the importance of diplomatic alliances and self-sufficiency. Greater Syria suffered from full-blown starvation by 1916 and half a million people perished up until the end of the war.[40] Mount Lebanon was particularly affected as it had reoriented its agriculture towards mulberry trees and silk exports. This had been a lucrative strategy during peacetime, but, during the war, the lack of meaningful cereal production proved disastrous. No grains reached the coast and the area lacked income from silk exports. Export-oriented agriculture exacerbated the crisis, not dissimilar to Mike Davis' account of the 'late Victorian holocausts' that took place in India in the late nineteenth century.[41] To make matters worse, the Ottoman army requisitioned food in inner Syria. Jamal Pasha, the governor in Damascus, outlawed grain exports to the coastal areas. The interior was struggling too and he wanted to prevent smuggling outside the Ottoman Empire via sea routes.[42]

In this situation Hussain, the Sharif of Mecca, turned to the British. Reopening of the grain trade via the Red Sea was a priority for him along with securing money and weapons. It was crucial for the legitimacy of his vulnerable, nascent polity. 'We shall not turn against her or aid her enemy,' he promised Britain at the beginning of the war, if she would only resume the grain trade.[43] The British reopened limited food exports to Jeddah in May 1915. After a year of coordination and the Hussain–McMahon correspondence, the Arab Revolt started in June 1916.

Contrary to the Hejaz, tribes in northern Transjordan only joined the uprising reluctantly, if at all. They had a degree of self-sufficiency and did not fully rely on grain imports. They also depended on the Ottomans who were in control of markets that were essential for their subsistence.[44] The Ottomans in turn gained the allegiance of the Transjordan tribes by diverting grain deliveries from Greater Syria, consequently exacerbating the famine there.[45] Since the maritime trade routes through the Red Sea were open, Transjordan and the Arabian Peninsula were both in a privileged position, and the British and Ottomans competed for their allegiance with grain supplies.

The importance of political alliances for securing food supplies would repeat itself in the Second World War. Shipping space for civilian supplies was scarce as a result of the war. The Mediterranean and the Red Sea were closed for Allied commercial shipping because of Italy entering the war, the initial success of the German submarine campaign and the British withdrawal from Greece in April 1941. Jeddah was shut off from supplies for some weeks in 1941. Trade routes in the Red Sea would only reopen in April 1941 after the defeat of Italy in Ethiopia. The Mediterranean remained closed for commercial shipping until the end of the war in North Africa in 1943, and the creation of effective counter measures against German submarines. Until then, supplies to the Middle East had to be rerouted around the Cape of Good Hope. This added six to seven weeks to the journey, and ships had to arrive at the ports in the south of the Suez Canal, which were less developed than in Alexandria on the Mediterranean and where there was less infrastructure for ground transportation after disembarkation.[46]

The Allied Middle East Supply Center (MESC) in Cairo fostered local procurement to save scarce shipping space. Regional trade in barley, mainly from Iraq, substituted pre-war imports of wheat from Canada and Australia.[47] The MESC pooled grain reserves, introduced rationing schemes and shifted acreage from cotton to cereals to make up for productivity declines that had been caused by supply disruptions of nitrate fertiliser from Chile.[48] The MESC also fostered inter-regional trade from East Africa. After a failed harvest in 1943, a famine in Hadramaut was only averted by bringing in emergency supplies of wheat and millet from Ethiopia.[49] The MESC also launched policies of import substituting industrialisation that would gain widespread popularity among Arab governments in the two decades after the war.[50] Middle East imports plummeted from 5.5 million tons in 1941 to 1.5 million tons in 1944. At the same time, intra-regional trade increased from 7 per cent of total trade in 1938 to 33 per cent during the war.[51] Food security was essential for political stability. J. M. Landis, the senior American representative to the MESC from 1943–5 said, 'A peaceful Islam was essential to the defense of Suez…[and] a peaceful Islam could not be assured if it were permitted to starve.'[52]

In the more developed areas of the Middle East like Egypt, Iraq and Syria, the challenge to ensure food security focused on combating inflation. A constant growth in military expenditure led to an increase in money supply without a concomitant increase in the availability of goods for civilian purchase. Fighting inflation was important in alleviating impoverishment of city dwellers and to entice the countryside to part ways with its agricultural production. The latter could only be achieved if there was some semblance of currency stability. To contain inflation and reduce excess liquidity, taxes were increased, and in countries with rudimentary capital markets, like Egypt, government loans were offered to the public. In Egypt, especially in the countryside, rather than making investments, savings were often translated into the hoarding of precious metals. Hence, there was an unconventional experiment with gold sales in 1943 and 1944, which aimed at reducing liquidity in paper currency. The Allies also hoped that a decline in gold prices would bring down the general price level and that the sales proceeds would limit the issuance of paper notes necessary for military expenditure.[53]

In the less developed Arabian Peninsula, Allied military expenditure was more limited and, therefore, inflation was too. With their high dependence on food imports and underdeveloped transport infrastructure, food politics in the Gulf countries took on a different turn. Ensuring food imports and affordable food for the population was indispensable for the Saudi king to safeguard the legitimacy of his rule, especially in areas that he had recently conquered like the Hejaz or the North. Ibn Saud was constantly lobbying the Allies for loans, the delivery of food and lorries to transport it.[54] Half of all food imports he distributed as charity and he used a quarter of imports for the palace and as payment for his administration. Only the remaining quarter was sold for money in the marketplace.[55] Ibn Saud also pushed for agricultural modernisation to cement his rule via sedentarisation and land distribution to cronies.[56] An agricultural mission from the United States visited the country in 1942 to evaluate its potential for enhanced food production.[57]

The experience of scarcity and dependence during the Second World War is still remembered today and provides an important motivation for current initiatives like the Qatar National Food Security Programme (QNFSP).[58] Food trade was used to further foreign policy goals in later decades, too. It was highly politicised in the 1970s and the United States mulled food embargoes on various occasions, either as a foreign policy tool to gain concessions, or in order to curb domestic inflation by export restrictions. A food stoppage against Arab countries was contemplated in retaliation to their oil embargo in 1973. It was only discarded for reasons of impracticability. The vulnerability of Arab countries was asymmetrically lower. They were much less dependent on food from the United States than the United States and its allies were in need of oil from the Middle East. With their limited population and ample oil revenues, Arab countries would have found alternative suppliers.[59] Barring a military blockade there was no way of preventing such trade diversion. The United States would learn this in 1980 during its failed grain embargo against the Soviet Union. Alternative suppliers like Argentina and some European countries happily picked up the slack left by the US embargo.[60] Yet with military enforcement and control of access points, embargoes could inflict a terrible toll, as the UN embargo against Iraq in the 1990s would show. Limited food and medical supplies caused a severe humanitarian crisis that finally led to a partial loosening of the embargo under the Oil-for-Food Program.[61] The embargo failed in achieving policy or regime change in Baghdad, but turned into a cause célèbre in the wider Arab world where it was perceived as unjust and cruel.[62]

The threats of food embargoes in the 1970s were cited as a motivation for subsidised wheat self-sufficiency in Saudi Arabia in the 1980s and 1990s. The oil-for-food episode in Iraq contained a lesson for Arab leaders as well. It prompted a self-sufficiency drive in Syria. Cereal production was increased by shifting acreage from cotton to wheat in the 1990s.[63] The geopolitical threat perception and scepticism regarding the reliability of world markets loom large to this day. Whatever the costs, Egypt and Iran have attributed renewed importance to some degree to cereal self-sufficiency in the wake of the global food crisis of 2008. Such concerns also apply to smaller and less well-endowed countries like Lebanon and Jordan.[64]

Subsidised agriculture in the centres and the second food regime: 1950s–1970s

With all the war-related supply problems, it is important to keep in mind that the Middle East as a whole was a grain net exporter before the Second World War. Its production had recovered from the ravages of the First World War and the Great Depression.[65] The food net exporter status continued quite some time after the war in the case of Iraq. As late as 1958, American officials pointed to Iraq's problems regarding the disposal of its exportable grain surpluses and advised assisting the country with marketing efforts before the Soviets would offer their help.[66] Iraq and Iran would only turn into food net importers by the 1970s. Oil revenues led to a relative neglect of agriculture. Productivity growth was found wanting, and population and income growth caused a spike in demand that outpaced production growth. The latter was predominantly based on expansion of land and faced natural limits.

The system of land tenure in the Middle East that had developed by the early twentieth century was widely seen as an impediment to development. Western experts identified disputed land titles and lack of technology as major problems, while Arab revolutionaries saw unequal land distribution as the main culprit for low productivity. Eric Hobsbawm has remarked that between 1945 and 1950 almost half of the world's population lived in countries that underwent land reform.[67] The Middle East was no exception and soon followed suit. Across the Middle East, regimes with starkly different ideological orientations— ranging from Nasser's Egypt, to the Baathist rulers of Iraq and Syria, and the Shah of Iran—used land reform as a tool of economic development. The presumption of Middle Eastern rulers was that a more equitable distribution of land would raise productivity, create higher incomes and increase purchasing power. Apart from the provision of raw materials for the development of nascent industries, this agricultural modernisation would thus create a rural middle class as a political base for the respective regimes.

Yet, lacking extension services, disincentives for agriculture and unclear land titles prevented success of the land reforms. In line with the mechanisms of the second food regime, imported food fed the growing urban population in the Middle East. Like elsewhere, local governments pursued strategies of import substituting industrialisation during the postwar decades. They welcomed subsidised food imports from the North to provide sustenance to a growing workforce.

The farm subsidies that the United States had put in place in the wake of the Dust Bowl farm crisis of the 1930s and increased mechanisation and fertiliser usage led to a production boom during and after the war. The United States was desperately looking for export outlets for its grain surpluses. To this end, Public Law (P.L.) 480 was introduced in 1954, which allowed for subsidised food aid deliveries. US diplomats actively lobbied for a 'wheatification' of diets in developing countries at the expense of traditional staple crops like cassava, rice, maize and beans. Bread is 'winning against chikwanga at the breakfast table,' the US agricultural attaché in Zaire cabled enthusiastically to Washington.[68] In Iran and Egypt, the United States and other wheat exporters competed for the expansion of market share. Egypt was the largest per capita recipient of US food aid worldwide between 1958 and 1965. Its wheat imports increased from 0.1 per cent of total imports in 1955 to 18.6 per cent in 1964 and became a serious drain on foreign exchange.[69] Securing food imports at preferential prices became a high priority of Egyptian foreign policy, and the United States was the only country that was able to supply required quantities. The share of P.L. 480 deliveries of total Egyptian grain imports rose from 24 per cent in 1959 to 66 per cent in 1960 and then to 91 per cent in 1964.[70]

Such dependence came at a price. The United States used food deliveries to entice political cooperation and reward clients. About half of P.L. 480 supplies in the Middle East went to Egypt and Israel in the 1960s. Roughly the same share went to Morocco, Algeria and Tunisia. Other countries in the region received less than 10 per cent.[71] In the case of Egypt, the United States hoped to lure Nasser away from the Soviet embrace. However, the Egyptian president did not abstain from radical posturing and acted against US interests, be it by intervening in the Yemeni civil war and the Congo conflict or by driving a course of confrontation with Israel. By 1965, President Johnson decided to put Nasser on a 'short leash' and suspended P.L. 480 deliveries.[72] Saudi Arabia had lobbied for such a step as it supported the royalist forces in the Yemeni civil war and felt threatened by its ideological rival in Cairo. P.L. 480 shipments to Egypt only resumed in 1974 under the condition that Egypt would enter peace negotiations with Israel. By 1978, the country was again the largest recipient of P.L. 480 food aid with 30 per cent of the total.[73]

Cheap food imports were badly needed in developing countries. Food prices rose alongside oil prices and ushered in the world food crisis of 1973–74. The United States reduced food aid in favour of commercial exports that now found ample takers. The new situation led to hunger and impoverishment in grain-importing developing countries. Only the oil exporters were in a comfortable situation, as they had oil revenues to pay for such imports. Yet, they were concerned about the threats of political food embargoes. This prompted plans to develop Sudan as an 'Arab bread-basket', but projects did not get off the ground or were not profitable due to a lack of political will, insufficient infrastructure, corruption and political instability. The expansion of rain-fed agriculture in central and north Sudan caused increased desertification and political conflict as holders of customary land rights were disenfranchised.[74]

After this failure, the agricultural visions of Persian Gulf countries turned inwards. Saudi Arabia cast its lot with a massive expansion of subsidised wheat cultivation and became self-sufficient by the 1980s. Global food prices came down in the second half of the 1970s. In the 1980s, the United States and the European Economic Community (ECC) again faced the old problem of surplus disposal. The secretary of agriculture during the Reagan administration, John Block, was anxious to re-establish the US reputation as a reliable supplier of food. He also travelled to Saudi Arabia and tried to convince the rulers to abandon their wheat programme and import US grain instead. However, trust was not easily regained.[75] The Saudi regime also used the wheat programme to redistribute oil rent and reward cronies.[76] Hence, there were powerful economic interests invested in it. The Saudi government started to reduce subsidies only in the 1990s. Finally, it decided to phase out wheat production from 2008 until 2016 as the mining of fossil water aquifers has become unsustainable.

*Pitfalls of a third food regime? Sliding into
the global food crisis*

Whether we can speak of a third food regime is a contested issue as has
been pointed out in the theoretical framework. In any case, there have
been significant developments over recent decades. If the 1980s and
1990s were a return to the post-war decades of surplus disposal and
export promotion they also signalled subtle changes that left their mark
during the global food crisis of 2008. China and other emerging markets began their ascent, which would result in a steep increase in demand
for meat and dairy products, with harmful environmental effects as
greater land would be needed for cattle grazing and fodder cultivation.
Trade in derivatives proliferated and commodity markets became 'finan-
cialised'. The Commodity Futures Modernization Act of 2000 deregu-
lated trade in Over the Counter Derivatives whose proliferation would
be at the heart of the global financial crisis in 2008. Increased speculation and additional demand by financial market participants like pen-
sion funds were important aspects of the global food crisis as they led to
increased volatility and overshooting of commodity markets.[77] Biofuel
legislation in the European Union and the United States in the 2000s
led to demand for agricultural resources that competed with food production.[78] The rise of packaged foods and the increased importance of
large corporations in input provision, food processing and distribution
that started in the second food regime have continued unabated.[79] In the
Persian Gulf countries, unhealthy diets have led to the highest obesity
and diabetes rates per capita worldwide.[80]

The deregulation of agriculture since the 1970s is an underreported
factor in the global food crisis.[81] It happened at three levels: the breakdown of international commodity agreements in the 1970s; the inclusion of agriculture in the Uruguay round of the General Agreement on
Tariffs and Trade (GATT) in 1986 that led to the establishment of the
World Trade Organization (WTO) in 1995; and the decoupling of farm
subsidies from price support schemes in the United States in 1996. In
the European Union, this decoupling took place in the wake of the
reform of the Common Agricultural Policy in 2003. Whatever the inef-
ficiencies of the old regulated system, the storage of staple crops for price
stabilisation disappeared and volatility of food prices increased. Food
self-sufficiency is unattainable for Middle Eastern countries because of

their lack of water, yet a purely trade-based approach to food security sits uneasily with them as the vulnerability to food supply disruptions during times of crisis is well remembered in the region.

The debate about the future of farming and food security is on and is a hotly contested issue. In the wake of Amartya Sen's seminal research about famines and entitlements, food security has come to be regarded as a political and social construct rather than just a technical challenge of marrying new technology with the best management practices.[82] Yet, a focus on technical fixes still prevails among technocrats in international organisations and in discourses of companies with ulterior motives of sales maximisation in seeds and pesticides.[83] Advocacy groups on the other hand have been accused of romanticising traditional rural life and underestimating the food supply challenges for the world's growing urban populations.[84] If technical fixes should not be the narrow focus of food security debates, they cannot do without them either. It is hardly conceivable to feed 7 billion people without such mundane innovations like mineral fertiliser.[85]

As the largest grain importers in the world, Middle Eastern countries are at the centre of the changing realities of the global food regime. The availability of an exportable surplus on a global level and domestic income to pay for imports are crucial for them. Yet, to focus on macro data and GDP per capita figures can be utterly misleading because of rising inequalities. Egypt witnessed solid GDP growth during the 2000s, while an increasing number of Egyptians faced impoverishment.[86] At the same time, the Ease of Doing Business Index (EDBI) of the World Bank lauded Egypt as the world's leading reformer in 2008, and, in 2010, the country had been among the top ten reformers of the EDBI for a record of four consecutive years.[87] Economic liberalisation and growth in the Middle East have often benefitted only a few people close to the respective regimes.[88] At times, economic reform has compromised the poor's access to land and resources, as the pushback of land reforms in Egypt has shown since the 1990s.[89] The developing world and the Middle East in particular are in need of new development paradigms.

Income plays a crucial role in improving food security. In largely urbanised societies, it is more important than access to agricultural production resources.[90] Middle Eastern governments will need to overcome their population's entitlement shortages with economic diversification and a growth agenda that includes poor people. The focus on rent-seeking needs to be replaced by more productive and labour-absorbing economic pursuits. As agricultural investors abroad, Arab governments need to bring local stakeholders on board, if 'win-win scenarios' are not to remain empty rhetoric. On a diplomatic level, Middle Eastern states will need to strengthen their institutional capacities to influence international regulatory regimes to their advantage and engage in bilateral dialogue with food exporters. At a time when their states and societies are in a period of rapid transition, these challenges are daunting.

3

AN ECONOMIC ANALYSIS OF NATIONAL FOOD SOVEREIGNTY POLICIES IN THE MIDDLE EAST

THE CASE OF LEBANON AND JORDAN

Jane Harrigan

The sharp rise in global food prices in 2007–08 refocused the attention of many countries on the issues of food security, and the Middle East and North Africa (MENA) region was no exception. Since the early 1970s there has been a steady growth of food imports to MENA stimulated by rapid population growth and changing patterns of food consumption based on rising incomes that favour higher valued foods. Ecological constraints on food production, however, are severe, due to the region's lack of arable land and its water scarcity.[1] As a result of these demand and supply factors most Arab countries now import at least 50 per cent of the food calories they consume and the region is the largest importer of cereal in the world.[2] The region's dependence on food imports is projected to increase in the coming two decades.[3] These projections, and the assumption that international food prices are likely to remain high and volatile for the foreseeable future,[4] mean that MENA governments have become acutely aware of the vulnerability caused by reliance on global food markets to meet domestic demand.

There are three traditional routes to national food security: domestic production, which contributes to self-sufficiency; commercial food imports; and international food aid.[5] Hence, a clear distinction needs to be made between self-sufficiency and food security, in that the former is only one possible route to food security at the national level.[6] However, since 2007–08, many MENA governments have started to consider greater levels of domestic food production as part of their national aggregate food security policies. Although from a political and strategic point of view such an approach may be justified in that it can help stabilise domestic food prices and reduce vulnerability to international markets and reliance on other countries,[7] it comes at an economic cost. This is because the resource endowments of most MENA countries— namely, water scarcity and lack of arable land—are not well suited to food production, particularly cereal production, and their comparative international advantages lie in other economic activities. Indeed, many of the international organisations involved in the MENA economies during the 1990s and the 2000s have advocated a food security strategy for most countries that relied upon diversification away from agriculture towards other activities, including manufacturing exports, with the resulting foreign exchange used to purchase food imports.[8] Within the agricultural sector there has also been emphasis on shifting resources into high-value crops that are most efficient in water use, such as fruits, vegetables, and tree crops, often with a focus on export markets instead of cereal production for domestic consumption.[9]

More recently, following the global food price shock, policy advice to MENA governments is becoming slightly more nuanced. For example, the World Bank stated that 'Policy-makers need to develop a comprehensive strategy that balances the risks associated with imports with the increasing costs associated with increasing domestic production.'[10] The overall purpose of this research is to assess the economic implications of increasing domestic food production, and to highlight the nature of the debate that is likely to take place between those who advocate greater reliance on domestic food production and those who continue to advocate a predominately trade-based food security strategy heavily dependent on food imports.[11] The former group invokes considerations that go beyond mere economic analysis and include political, social and environmental concerns, while the latter group mainly relies on the narrow neoclassical economic analysis of international comparative advantage. By articulating this debate and analysing its economic parameters we hope to be able to help policymakers develop the type of comprehensive strategy referred to in the quote from the World Bank. In order to do this, the chapter addresses the following research questions:

1. What was the economic impact of the global food price shock of 2007–08 on MENA countries?
2. Following the food price shock, to what extent are these countries re-orientating their food security strategies towards more domestic production?
3. What are the economic opportunity costs of such a strategy? In other words, how much does this involve violating international comparative advantage in the production process?
4. Within the agricultural sector of MENA countries, what production pattern and crop choice does international comparative advantage dictate, particularly in view of water scarcity?
5. What are the broader concerns beyond this narrow neoclassical economic analysis that will shape future approaches to food security and food sovereignty in the MENA region?

Answering the above research questions for all MENA countries cannot be done within the scope of the current research project. Hence, we adopt a country case study methodology. Two countries have been chosen for in-depth analysis, namely, Jordan and Lebanon. They have been chosen because both suffer from significant food insecurity according to a variety of different measurements in the MENA region (see Figure 3.1). Both are resource poor, non-oil exporting, middle-income countries with high cereal import dependency and fiscal and trade deficits.[12] Hence, international food price shocks threaten macroeconomic stability and may increase poverty. There are also important differences between Jordan and Lebanon which make a comparative country analysis interesting. Lebanon is unusual in the region in that it has more than a quarter of its land under cultivation or pasture (along with Syria, Sudan and Tunisia),[13] and is fairly well-endowed with water which means it can generate lessons for other countries similar in this respect (for instance, Iraq, Syria, Turkey, Sudan and Iran). Jordan is one of the least water-endowed countries in MENA[14] and hence can generate lessons for a separate country group, namely Libya, the Persian Gulf states and Palestine.

The first stage of the research methodology involved semi-structured interviews in both countries with government officials, academics and international organisations in order to address the first two and the last research questions. The second stage of the research addresses the third and fourth research questions, namely, what are the economic opportunity costs of greater domestic food production? To answer this question we took a narrow neoclassical economic approach which uses international comparative advantage as a benchmark of economic efficiency. Hence we asked, to what extent does each country's planned food security strategy deviate from the economic dictates of international comparative advantage? The first methodology employed to address this question was the calculation of Revealed Comparative Advantage (RCA).[15] For both countries we calculated RCA across a wide range of activities in both the agricultural and non-agricultural sectors. Although a useful first indicator of relative comparative advantage across different economic activities, RCA is based on actual trade shares which may be influenced by price distortions. To address this problem of distortions we employ a methodology known as the Policy Analysis Matrix (PAM).[16]

Section 2 of this chapter assesses the food security status of Lebanon and Jordan using a variety of different indicators. It analyses both countries' patterns of international trade in agricultural commodities in order to assess the extent to which international trade, as opposed to domestic food production, is used to achieve food security at the national aggregate level. Section 3 looks at the impact of the global food price shock on each country and asks whether this has led policymakers to reappraise their approach to national food security. Sections 4 and 5 carry out the RCA and PAM analysis for each country, whilst section 6 concludes the study.

The food security status of Lebanon and Jordan: the role of trade versus domestic production

It is often argued that MENA is one of the most food insecure regions in the world. This characterisation is based on the region's heavy reliance on food imports.[17] Lebanon and Jordan fit this pattern. However, food imports are only one dimension of food security. Other variables that help determine a region's food security status include wealth levels, income distribution and fiscal position. Although macro variables are important determinants of national aggregate food security, individual or household food security is a more meaningful concept. One internationally accepted measure that captures the individual dimensions of food security is the Global Hunger Index (GHI).[18]

Figure 3.1 summarises the food security classifications of Lebanon and Jordan derived from various studies on the food security status of MENA countries.[19]

Figure 3.1: Food security classifications for Lebanon and Jordan

Study	Lebanon	Jordan
Wilson and Bruins 2005	Low	Very low
World Bank 2009	Most vulnerable	Most vulnerable
IFPRI 2010	Food security challenged	Food security challenged
IFPRI 2012	Serious	Serious

Summarising the above studies, it seems that both countries face issues of food insecurity, with Jordan suffering more than Lebanon. The relative standing of the two countries is not surprising since, as pointed out in the introduction, Lebanon is better endowed than Jordan in terms of both agricultural land and water.

We now provide an overview of agricultural production and trade in Lebanon and Jordan in order to help assess the extent to which both countries rely on foreign trade versus domestic production to achieve national aggregate food security.

Lebanon: Food imports and domestic production

According to the World Bank 'agriculture is a small but stable part of the Lebanese economy.'[20] As a share of GDP it remained stable at around 6.8 per cent between 1994 and 2007, but had fallen to an estimated 4.7 per cent by 2010, with industry comprising an estimated 16.0 per cent and services 79.4 per cent.[21] Despite its modest contribution to GDP, the agricultural sector has considerable potential. Lebanon has ideal climate, soil, and water resources; the highest proportion of cultivatable land (around 25 per cent of total land area); and the most reliable rainfall and river assets in the Arab world.[22] Agricultural value added per square kilometre is higher than in many other neighbouring countries, partly due to the above factors and partly due to more intense production methods and the prominence of high value fruit and vegetables in the production pattern.[23] Until very recently, however, the sector has received low policy priority from the government, with less than 1 per cent of the budget allocated to the Ministry of Agriculture.[24]

Lebanon's varied climate means that there is considerable diversity in the range of agricultural activities. Vegetables (mainly potatoes, tomatoes and cucumbers) make up 47 per cent of production value, fruits (oranges, lemons, mandarins, grapefruits, grapes and apples) make up 35 per cent, and cereals (forage crops, wheat and barley) make up 15 per cent. Agricultural land is concentrated in the Bekaa Valley region (39 per cent), North (29 per cent) and South (20 per cent). Of the country's total agricultural land under cultivation, approximately 49 per cent is irrigated, mostly by inefficient furrow methods,[25] and the agricultural sector uses approximately 60 per cent of the country's water.

Despite the potential of the agricultural sector, its small size relative to GDP means that Lebanon is heavily reliant on imports to meet its food needs. According to the Minsitry of Agriculture, in any given year over 80 per cent of Lebanon's food supply is made up of imports.[26] Figure 3.2 shows imports as a share of total domestic food supplies for various categories of food between 1990 and 2007. As can be seen from Figure 3.2, Lebanon is fairly self-sufficient in fruit and vegetables, importing less than 20 per cent of domestic supplies throughout the period 1990–2007. In terms of oil crops, Lebanon relies on a fairly balanced combination of imports and domestic production to meet domestic needs. For cereals, wheat, pulses, and vegetable oils, Lebanon is very reliant on imports, which make up a large percentage of domestic supplies. From the mid-1990s onwards, around 90 per cent of domestic supplies of cereals have been met through imports (with the exception of 2006 when the import reliance dipped to 76 per cent). The most significant trend is in terms of pulses, where reliance on imports has dramatically increased from providing only 41 per cent of total domestic supplies in 1990 to providing 87 per cent of total domestic supplies in 2007.

In terms of the costs of imports, wheat imports are the second most costly of the top ten food imports after meat, with wheat imports costing $109 million in 2009.[27] In addition, wheat accounted for an average of 29 per cent of calorie intake in Lebanon in 2007.[28] It is therefore worth analysing in more depth the nature of Lebanon's reliance on wheat imports versus domestic wheat production and the features of the wheat market in Lebanon.

Figure 3.2: Lebanon import shares as percentage of total domestic supplies of major food groups 1990–2007

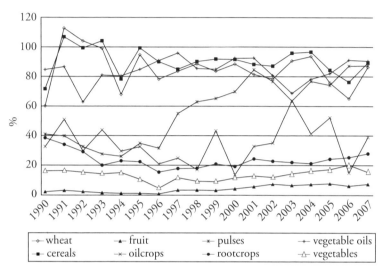

Note: Total domestic supply = domestic production + imports–exports + or–stock adjustment.
Source: FAOSTAT, Food Balance Sheet.

Lebanon's annual consumption of wheat for food is around 400,000 MT plus or minus 10 per cent.[29] Of this requirement, in an average year approximately 85 per cent is provided by imports. The private sector is largely responsible for importing and storing wheat. However, the government in the form of the General Directorate of Cereals and Sugar Beet (GDCS), which is part of the Ministry of Economy and Trade, often intervenes in the market and imports large quantities of wheat in order to keep the price of bread stable at 1,340 Lebanese Pounds (LBP) or $0.89 per kg.

In terms of domestic wheat production, the government guarantees to buy the annual wheat crop from farmers at a subsidised support price—in other words, a price that is usually above the world market price. According to the GDCS, in most years the government purchases the

Figure 3.3: Lebanon wheat sales to government 1993–2011 (MT)

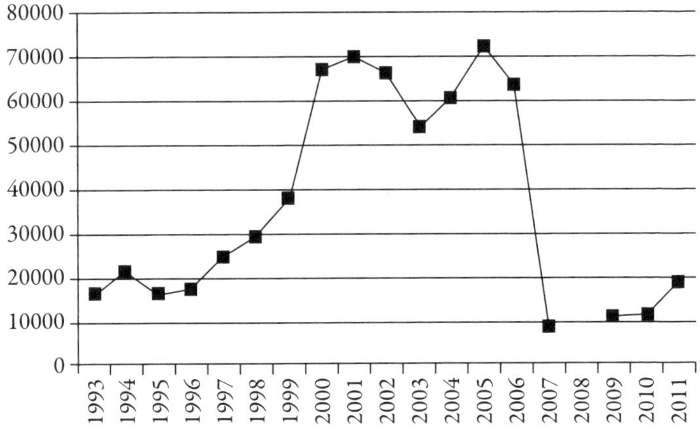

Source: General Directorate of Cereals and Sugar Beet.

bulk of the wheat crop.[30] Figure 3.3 shows purchases of wheat by the GDCS between 1993 and 2011. Since 2007, sales of wheat to the GDCS have fallen dramatically.[31]

Figure 3.4 shows that, according to Food and Agriculture Organization (FAO) data, wheat production increased between 2000 and 2006 by almost 50 per cent, whilst GDCS data shows that between 1993 and 2006 there was a steady and significant increase in wheat sales to the GDCS from 16,368 MT to 72,911 MT. However, increased domestic production does not seem to have had an impact on the country's import dependency ratio (Figure 3.2) which has remained high and with significant annual variation. This failure to impact on the import dependency ratio reflects increased domestic demand, especially for refined cereals.[32] The data also suggests a recent decline in wheat production—FAO data shows a sharp production fall in 2007 while GDCS purchases have fallen significantly since 2006.

Whether a renewed promotion of domestic wheat production (or cereals more generally) is a sensible future food security strategy, or whether an alternative strategy of promoting both non-agricultural exports and agricultural exports (such as fruit and vegetables) and using the resulting foreign exchange to import cereals makes more sense, will be the subject of analysis in the following sections of this chapter.

Figure 3.4: Wheat production data Lebanon 2000–11

Year	No. of farmers registered with GDCS	Area planted (Dunum) and registered with GDCS	Quantities received by GDCS (MT)	FAO production data (MT)	Subsidised price LBP/MT	Subsidised price $/MT	International price of Lebanese imports $/MT
2000	1,035	n/a	62,323	108,000	400,000	264	134
2001	1,418	n/a	70,417	140,000	400,000	264	142
2002	1,270	154,792	66,375	119,000	375,000	250	129
2003	1,207	161,080	53,669	116,000	375,000	250	146
2004	1,247	190,692	60,728	137,000	375,000	250	180
2005	1,276	158,953	72,911	144,000	375,000	250	157
2006	1,302	185,622	65,388	153,000	375,000	250	185
2007	1,069	162,735	8,345	116,000	375,000	250	280
2008	n/a	n/a	n/a	n/a	n/a	n/a	384
2009	688	130,595	36,690	n/a	475,000	316	203
2010	898	150,000	10,893	n/a	575,000	383	260
2011	939	140,000	18,000	n/a	550,000	366	270

Note: One dunum = approximately 0.1 hectares.
Source: General Directorate of Cereals and Sugar Beet and FAOSTAT.

Jordan: Food imports and domestic production

Jordan's agricultural sector only accounts for around 3 per cent of GDP, and its potential is severely limited by lack of water and arable land, as well as the fragmentation of arable land. Only about 4.3 per cent of the country's land area is suitable as arable land, of which 84 per cent is rain-fed. Most of the rain-fed area receives less than 100mm of rainfall a year and the country's severe scarcity of renewable water (less than 150 cubic meters per capita) limits the potential for irrigation.[33] Nevertheless, approximately 15 per cent of the population relies on agriculture as a source of income—around 80 per cent of the population is urban—and the agricultural sector uses 70 per cent of the country's water.

Limited agricultural potential means that Jordan is heavily reliant on imports to meet its food requirements. As of 2010, Jordan was self–sufficient in fruit, vegetables, poultry, and eggs. In the case of poultry and eggs, however, there is heavy reliance on imports for poultry feed. In terms of milk and dairy products, the country imports approximately 50 per cent of its needs. The bulk of the main cereals consumed is imported and includes wheat, maize, and barely—barley being mainly used for fodder.

Over the past three to four decades, Jordan's reliance on imports for its food requirements has been increasing. In the early 1970s, Jordan was self-sufficient in wheat production, generating around 300,000 MT per annum and occasionally exporting some of this. Since then, production has diminished rapidly, and now in a good year only around 20,000–30,000 MT is produced locally, mainly in the north of the country, while annual consumption is around 700,000 MT. Domestic barley production has also been declining from an annual average of 29,000 MT over the five-year period of 1995–8 to an annual average of 22,000 MT, with considerable yearly fluctuation. At the same time, imports of barley have increased sharply from 471,864 MT in 1994 at a cost of $43 million, to 850,895 MT in 2007 at a cost of $251 million.[34] Likewise, domestic production of legumes and pulses has declined over the past few decades.

Declining food production in Jordan is a reflection of the lack of a strong strategy for the agricultural sector over the past decades. This has been compounded by land-zoning policies under which agricultural land has been reclassified into residential and commercial land such that farmers in the cereal producing north, for example, can now sell a dunum of land for around $200,000, compared to an annual return for growing wheat of around $700 per hectare.[35] In addition, as land has become fragmented, partly due to inheritance laws, farmers have shifted out of cereal production into crops which do not have the same economies of scale—such as fruit, vegetables and tree crops, especially olives. Reduced rainfall and water availability, as well as declining returns to cereal production, have also contributed to the decline in production. As a result, in 2011 the country only produced around 7 per cent of its grain requirements.

In terms of vegetable and fruit production, in which Jordan is fairly self-sufficient, the main vegetables produced are tomatoes, potatoes, cucumbers and eggplant, and the main fruits are citrus, watermelon, apples, bananas, grapes and olives. Part of the produce is exported both to European and Persian Gulf markets, mainly by the larger farmers who are able to comply with international market standards.

Jordan's dependence on imports for food requirements, especially cereals, is predicted to increase over the next decade, with a population of around 6 million growing at a rate of 2.8 per cent per annum and limited potential in the agricultural sector. As in Lebanon, the orthodox policy advice is that Jordan's agricultural strategy should concentrate on crops that are more water efficient such as fruits, vegetables, and semi-arid crops like olives—rather than attempt to use scarce water to produce water intensive cereals—and should rely instead on a trade-based approach to secure cereal requirements.[36]

The limited cereal production in Jordan is supported by the government. The Ministry of Agriculture subsidises wheat and barley production with guaranteed prices to farmers (JD 275/MT for wheat in 2011 and JD 270/MT for barley), with barely being the larger of the two crops mainly grown under rain-fed conditions. However, the production subsidies are small in comparison to consumer subsidies. The Ministry of Trade and Industry is responsible for grain imports and both wheat and barley are sold at subsidised prices to consumers. Barley is sold as fodder at a subsidised price of JD 175/MT, which represents a subsidy of around 35 per cent. Previously, the subsidy was offered not just for the owners of the country's 3.2 million sheep, but also for cattle, poultry and camel feed. The sharp rise in the import price of barley in 2007–08 forced the government to increase the subsidised price from JD 150/MT to JD 175/MT and to restrict the subsidy to sheep fodder. The wheat subsidy largely takes the form of a heavy subsidy on the price of local bread, which has remained constant at 16 piasta per kg for the past seventeen years. Figure 3.5 shows the sharp rise in the cost of the consumer subsidies on barley and wheat as a result of the 2007–08 global food price shock, with the annual cost rising from JD 76.5 million in 2006 to JD 222.6 million in 2008.

Figure 3.5: Jordan annual cost of consumer subsidy on barley and wheat 2005–10 (JD million)

2005	2006	2007	2008	2009	2010 (first 6 months)	Total
70.0	76.5	201.0	222.6	142.0	105.0	817.1

Source: Ministry of Industry and Trade, Jordan.

The full impact of the global food price shock on Jordan, and whether Jordan should respond by attempting to boost domestic cereal production, are the subjects of the next two sections of this chapter.

The impact of global food price shocks

The global food price shocks of 2007–08 and 2011 are clearly illustrated in Figure 3.6 which shows the FAO Food Price Index. Headey and Fan provide a survey of the literature on the general economic and social consequences of the global food price shock on developing and emerging countries.[37] However, there is little robust work done on the impact on our two specific country studies and much of what we present below is descriptive in nature. We do, however, report the work of the International Monetary Fund (IMF) and Dessus et al,[38] which provide a more rigorous analysis of the impact on the balance of payments and reserve holdings in the former case and urban poverty in the latter case.

Impact and response in Lebanon

Because Lebanon imports such a large amount of its food requirements, the recent hike in global food prices has had several adverse effects. At the macroeconomic level, the rising price of food imports has pushed up the food import bill and contributed to the trade deficit as well as to domestic inflation, while also having an adverse fiscal impact as the

THE CASE OF LEBANON AND JORDAN

Figure 3.6: FAO monthly real food price index

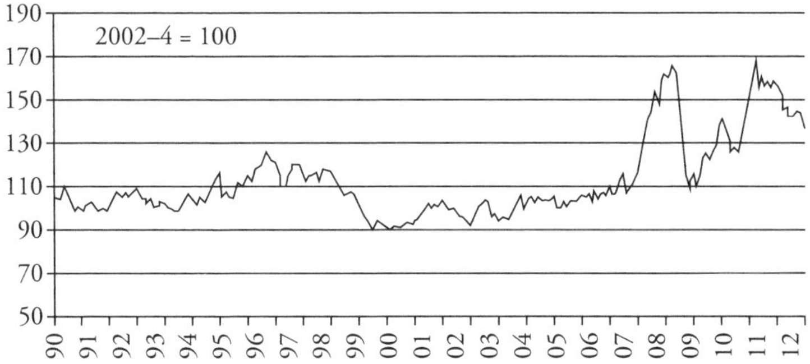

Source: FAO website.

government introduced measures to try to mitigate the effects of rising food prices. At the household level, the rising cost of food has had adverse effects on living standards, and has impacted on poverty.

Figure 3.7 shows the sharp increase in the amount spent on major food imports (excluding meat) as a result of the 2007–08 global hike in food prices. In 2008, Lebanon spent $165 million on wheat and flour imports, nearly three times the amount spent in 2006, with much of the increase driven by price increases as opposed to an increase in the quantity imported. As shown in Figure 3.8, the cost of Lebanon's wheat imports increased from $157/MT in 2005 to $384/MT in 2008. Likewise, the amount spent on oilseed imports doubled between 2006 and 2008 entirely due to price increase, while the amount spent on pulses nearly doubled largely due to price as opposed to quantity increases.

The sharp rise in the overall cost of agricultural imports is shown in the last row of Figure 3.7 and in Figure 3.8. The former shows that between 2004 and 2006 the total value of all agricultural products imported was fairly stable at just over $9,000 million. By 2009, this import bill for agricultural products had almost doubled to $16,600 million. Likewise, Figure 3.9 shows that between 2005 and 2008 the import unit value index increased by around 50 per cent.

Partly as a result of the fact that agricultural import prices rose more than agricultural export prices for Lebanon, the deficit in the balance of trade for agricultural products increased from $7,460 million in 2005 to $12,413 million in 2009 (see Figure 3.10) and this contributed to an increase in the overall trade deficit.[39]

Figure 3.7: Lebanon selected food imports 2000–9 (quantities and values)

Item	2000	2001	2002	2003	2004	2005	2006	2007	2008	2009
Quantity tonnes										
Flour of wheat	13487	15177	18559	16470	14838	7200	3	133	6514	9006
Wheat	407698	368984	372531	445282	485140	402576	321453	410443	418863	537692
Oilseeds –22 + (Total)	27839	40849	98375	148315	115025	75677	26270	37837	26958	35557
Pulses + (Total)	30508	38393	33183	28442	30823	29236	39958	41104	41800	36669
Wheat + flour, Wheat Equiv. + (Total)	426431	390065	398309	468159	505750	412577	321457	410628	427911	550201
Value $1,000										
Flour of wheat	3580	4083	5088	4629	5726	2909	3	95	4583	4887
Wheat	54666	52396	48052	65217	87200	63042	59325	114722	160785	108886
Oilseeds –22 + (Total)	20108	25399	30920	54196	58475	39533	23005	38973	47175	47697
Pulses + (Total)	20177	20100	17175	14874	16539	17793	25159	30319	41951	31172
Wheat + flour, Wheat Equiv. + (Total)	58246	56479	53140	69846	92926	65951	59328	114817	165368	113773
Total value all agricultural imports $millions	**6227**	**7291**	**6444**	**7168**	**9397**	**9339**	**9397**	**12251**	**16754**	**16600**

Source: FAOSTAT.

THE CASE OF LEBANON AND JORDAN

Figure 3.8: Lebanon's wheat import price ($ per tonne)

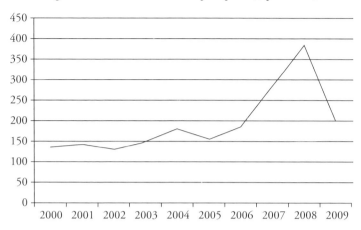

Source: FAOSTAT.

The above analysis of the impact of global food prices on trade balances is largely descriptive. The IMF has carried out more robust predictive work for a range of countries that includes Lebanon and Jordan.[40] The IMF takes actual global food and fuel price increases from January

Figure 3.9: Lebanon agricultural import unit/value index 2000–9 (2004–6 = 100)

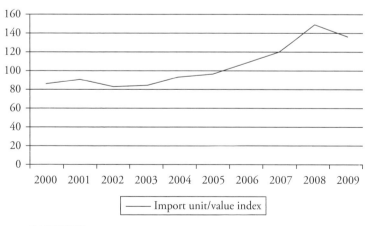

Source: FAOSTAT.

FOOD SECURITY IN THE MIDDLE EAST

Figure 3.10: Lebanon agricultural trade deficit ($ '000)

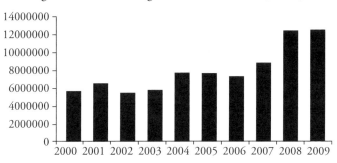

Source: FAOSTAT.

2007 to April 2008 and then adds in projected increases for 2008 and 2009 by taking the projected Spring 2008 World Economic Outlook baseline projections for 2008 and 2009 and assuming that food and fuel prices will be 20 per cent higher than the baseline predictions. It then estimates the effect of these projected price increases on the current account and foreign reserves of a number of countries (the results assume there are neither policy, nor behavioural responses to the price increases). The impact of the price increases is considered to be 'high' if it reduces reserves by more than 0.5 months of imports of goods and services coverage. Reserve coverage is also considered to be 'low' if it covers less than 3 months of the next year's import of goods and services. The results for Lebanon are given in Figure 3.11.

Figure 3.11: Lebanon predicted impact of food and fuel price increases on external position

Before shock		Oil price shock		Food price shock		Combined shock	
Current account	Reserves	Current account	Reserves	Current account	Reserves	Current account	Reserves
–10.2%	7.4	–12.9%	6.5	–11.2%	7.1	–14.0%	6.2

Note: Current account as percentage of GDP. Reserves are months of coverage of imports of goods and services.
Source: IMF, *Food and Fuel Prices–Recent Developments, Macroeconomic Impact, and Policy Responses*, Washington DC (2008), Table 1b.

As can be seen from Figure 3.11, the estimated effect of the global food price shock on Lebanon's external position was to increase the current account deficit from 10.2 per cent of GDP to 11.2 per cent and to reduce foreign exchange reserves from 7.4 months' cover to 7.1 months' cover—an effect not classified as 'high' according to the IMF criteria. The effect of the increases in oil prices, however, was significantly greater than the effects of food prices, but even after both effects are combined Lebanon continued to have adequate foreign exchange reserves predicted at 6.2 months' coverage—double the level classified as 'low' by the IMF.

The increase in the price of imported food contributed to domestic inflation. It is difficult to estimate the relationship between international and domestic food prices, which in any case is country specific. The extent to which global price increases are transmitted to the domestic economy depends on a variety of factors: the depth of international markets for different commodities; countries' exchange rate variations against the dollar; the degree of openness of the economy; the domestic policy response to the shock; and the country-specific nature of the food basket. In addition, domestic food prices may also be affected by other domestic factors such as the changes in the price of non-food goods.[41] Figure 3.12 shows that in 2008 the inflation rate for food and non-alcoholic beverages in Lebanon (which have a weight of 19.9 out of 100 in the consumer price index) was 15.1 per cent, contributing to an overall inflation rate of 3.9 per cent. Food and beverage inflation again increased to 5.5 per cent in 2011.

Figure 3.12: Lebanon inflation 2008–11

	2008	*2009*	*2010*	*2011*
Food and non-alcoholic beverages	15.1%	−0.9%	6.3%	5.5%
CPI	3.9%	3.3%	5.8%	4.8%

Note: 2008 covers January 2008 to January 2009; 2009 covers January 2009 to January 2010; 2010 covers February 2010 to February 2011 (no January 2011 data were published); and 2011 covers September 2010 to September 2011.
Source: www.cas.gov.lb/index

The rising cost of food imports to Lebanon and the negative effects on living standards were partially mitigated by a number of ad hoc government responses. By mid-2008, the government had started to import wheat and sell it at a subsidised price of $75/MT of wheat and $150/MT of wheat flour in order to keep the price of bread stable. By 2008, the government was subsidising over half the cost of a loaf of bread at a cost of $94.8 million, up from around $8 million in 2001–2.[42]

In addition, customs duties and tariffs were reduced or eliminated on basic foodstuffs such as red meat, poultry meat, fish, powdered milk, rice, pasta, sugar and vegetable oils, and public sector wages were increased.[43] These measures were fiscally costly—higher subsidies and public sector wages increased government expenditure, while tariff reduction reduced government incomes from trade taxes, such that by 2010 the budget deficit was 5.4 per cent of GDP.[44]

Despite introducing the above immediate measures in response to the global food price crisis, the government of Lebanon, in contrast to Jordan, has not formulated a comprehensive longer-term multi-agency food security strategy. Instead, its response has concentrated on giving greater priority to the agricultural sector as well as eliciting several statements that seem to indicate that domestic production of cereals will be promoted. According to FAO staff in Lebanon,[45] this was illustrated by the 2009 policy statement for the sector,[46] which recognised the institutionally fragmented nature of agricultural policy in Lebanon and the need to strengthen the Ministry of Agriculture by increasing its budget. It also committed to both increasing agricultural exports as well as domestic food production in order to reduce the agricultural trade deficit. More recently, the Ministry of Agriculture has stated that it intends to increase agricultural output from around 5 per cent of GDP to 8 per cent in the medium term.[47] According to an advisor to the minister for agriculture,[48] the ministry would like to increase local production of wheat and barley via both input subsidies and support prices, with the latter crop being seen as particularly appropriate for rain-fed areas. The stated aim is that in order to improve food self-sufficiency Lebanon should move from producing an average of 15–20 per cent of its grain consumption to producing 30–40 per cent via both yield and acreage increases. To quote the advisor: 'We definitely want to increase wheat production, vertically via better distribution of subsidised improved seed, and horizontally via extension advice which will include remote areas and small farmers'.[49]

Although the Ministry of Agriculture has indicated that it would like Lebanon to produce up to 40 per cent of its domestic cereal requirements, the target that has been set by the GDCS is for the country to produce and sell to the government 100,000 MT of wheat, which is equivalent to around 20–25 per cent of domestic requirements.[50] In order to achieve this, the government support price to farmers was gradually raised from $250/MT in 2007 to $366/MT by 2011 (see Figure 3.4). As a result of this price increase the number of farmers growing wheat increased between 2009 and 2011 (see Figure 3.4), although government purchases of 18,000 MT in 2011 fell well below the 100,000 MT target, with the GDCS claiming that many farmers exported or sold privately in the domestic market.

It is intended that part of the targeted increase in domestic cereal production will come about through yield improvements by encouraging the production of high yielding varieties via the use of certified seed, with plans to produce 5–6,000 MT of such wheat and barley seeds in 2012. To help achieve this, the subsidy at which wheat seed is sold to farmers was increased to around 30 per cent in 2011. Subsidies are also planned for pulses and chickpeas via subsidised seed and for forage crops such as barley, alfalfa and vetch in order to increase domestic production. The 2010/11 season was also the first in which the government supported barley production via the provision of subsidised seed and guaranteed sales of the crop to the government at a support price of $330/MT.

It is clear from the above that the government of Lebanon's response to the global food price increases of the past few years involves a strategy to increase domestic food crop production, particularly cereals, in order to increase domestic food self-sufficiency. The government's plans clash with the policy advice of many international organisations working in Lebanon. The World Bank, for example, in its 2010 paper on the agricultural sector,[51] clearly stated that in terms of agricultural policy the government should not move towards food self-sufficiency, but rather an intensified trade-based food security strategy should be pursued, with the export of high-value fruit and vegetables used to help cover the cost of cereal imports: 'Fresh fruit and vegetables are the most promising sub-sectors …Lebanon is relatively more competitive in fruits and vegetables than in cereals and livestock'.[52]

Making significant investments to reduce cereal import dependency may actually reduce food security by putting further strain on the Government of Lebanon's fiscal balance, thereby limiting its ability to respond to food price shocks.[53]

The World Bank has based its argument on the purely economic considerations of international comparative advantage, with the latter used as the yardstick by which to judge the efficiency of resource allocation. In this context, price support for cereal producers, and subsidies on inputs such as seed, are seen as price distortions which misallocate scarce resources to inefficient activities.

The next sections of this chapter explore the implications of the international comparative advantage arguments in more depth using two tools—Revealed Comparative Advantage (RCA) and the Policy Analysis Matrix (PAM).

Impact and responses in Jordan

Jordan, like Lebanon, being heavily dependent on food imports, was hit hard by the 2007–08 global food crisis. As shown in Figure 3.13, the cost of wheat imports rose from $79.8 million in 2006 to $381.8 million in 2008 largely due to price increases, while the cost of oilseed and pulse imports also rose sharply largely due to price increases. Overall, the cost of agricultural imports increased from $1,510 million in 2006 to $2,779 million in 2008.

Figure 3.14 shows the sharp rise in the cost that Jordan had to pay for its food imports, with the food import value index increasing from 104 in 2006 to 202 in 2008. This contributed to a large increase in Jordan's agricultural trade deficit, which increased from $750 million in 2005 to $1,742 million in 2008, as shown in Figure 3.15.

The results of the IMF's analysis of the predicted effects of global food price and oil price increases on the external position of Jordan are presented in Figure 3.16.

As can be seen by comparing Figure 3.16 with Figure 3.11, the estimated effect of the global food price shock on Jordan's external position was much greater than the effects for Lebanon. The global food price crisis increases the current account deficit from 13.4 per cent of GDP to 14.6 per cent and reduces foreign exchange reserves from 3.2 months' cover to 2.9 months' cover—an effect not classified as 'high' according to the IMF criteria but one which left foreign reserves at a level classified as 'low'. As with Lebanon, the effect of the increases in oil prices was significantly greater than the effects of food prices, and after both effects foreign reserves at two months' cover were significantly below the three months' level classified as 'low' by the IMF.

Figure 3.13: Jordan selected food imports 2000–9 (quantities and values)

Item	2000	2001	2002	2003	2004	2005	2006	2007	2008	2009
Quantity tonnes										
Wheat	584064	583028	618348	719975	795415	712899	591210	1063620	975749	519313
Oilseeds −22 + (Total)	26979	28835	24114	20259	23931	24772	26606	26757	21140	27451
Pulses + (Total)	34282	38602	38275	40167	43358	42849	46486	44063	50558	47956
Wheat + flour, Wheat equiv. + (Total)	601810	606627	634622	750083	814155	733042	612259	1081978	984126	537634
Value $1,000										
Wheat	92553	91793	86400	65544	150000	119858	79816	223492	381850	109317
Oilseeds −22 + (Total)	15690	16250	11692	13615	18756	19269	21594	25488	34105	33638
Pulses + (Total)	16337	18336	17006	17872	20142	22432	30091	32167	45681	37957
Wheat + flour, Wheat equiv. + (Total)	96199	97358	89645	71180	154220	124531	85041	228772	386594	116067
Agricult. products, Total + (Total)	840174	841832	866931	1019674	1379215	1402417	1509871	2011809	2779193	2341378

Source: FAOSTAT.

Figure 3.14: Jordan food import/value index (2004–6 = 100)

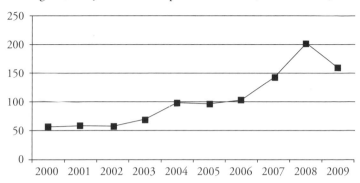

Note: Excludes fish.
Source: FAOSTAT.

Figure 3.15: Jordan agricultural trade deficit ($ million) 2000–9

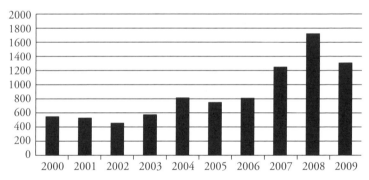

Source: FAO TRADESTAT.

Figure 3.16: Jordan predicted impact of food and fuel price increases on external position

Before shock		Oil Price shock		Food Price shock		Combined shock	
Current account	Reserves	Current account	Reserves	Current account	Reserves	Current account	Reserves
–13.4%	3.2	–17.7%	2.2	–14.6%	2.9	–18.8%	2.0

Note: Current account as percentage of GDP. Reserves are coverage in months of imports of goods and services.
Source: IMF, *Food and Fuel Prices–Recent Developments, Macroeconomic Impact, and Policy Responses*, Washington DC (2008), Table 1b.

THE CASE OF LEBANON AND JORDAN

The increase in the price of imported food contributed to domestic inflation, with food price inflation hitting 18.79 per cent in 2008, contributing to an overall inflation rate of 14.93 per cent (see Figure 3.17).

Figure 3.17: Jordan inflation 2007–11

	2007	2008	2009	2010	2011
Food	9.33	18.79	0.94	5.02	4.14
CPI	5.41	14.93	− 2.14	5.01	4.40

Source: FAOSTAT.

The increase in the price of food had a significant impact on the living standards of Jordanian citizens, particularly as it is estimated that the average Jordanian spends 32.4 per cent of their income on food.[54] The United Nations Economic and Social Comission for Western Asia (ESCWA) has estimated that the 2007–08 increase in global food prices increased poverty in Jordan by a head count of 30,000.[55] Dessus et al provide more rigorous empirical analysis of the effects of food price increases on the urban poor, and have included Jordan in their sample of seventy-two developing countries.[56] They estimate the cost of alleviating urban poverty brought about by the food price increase. This is approximated by the poverty deficit (PD), which is the variation in financial resources required to eliminate poverty under perfect targeting. They estimate three scenarios—a 10 per cent, 20 per cent and 30 per cent rise in domestic relative food prices—and use two different poverty lines, the $1.25 per day and $2.5 per day. The results for Jordan are shown in Figure 3.18.

As can be seen from Figure 3.18, food price increases do not have a great impact on the urban poor using the $1.25 per day measure of poverty. The upper scenario of a 30 per cent rise in food prices increases urban poverty from 0.9 per cent of the population to 2.0 per cent of the population, but has a negligible effect on the poverty deficit (in other words, financial resources as percentage of GDP needed to eliminate poverty). However, the results are more alarming when we use the $2.5 per day measure of urban poverty. The upper scenario of a 30 per cent food price increase raises urban poverty from 12.5 per cent of the population to 20.4 per cent, and raises the financial cost of eliminating urban

Figure 3.18: Jordan estimated effects of domestic food price rises on urban poverty and the poverty deficit

	Initial situation circa 2005		Final situation after price shock							
			Central scenario				Upper scenario		Lower scenario	
	Poverty rate	Poverty deficit	Poverty rate	Poverty deficit	New poor	Old poor	Poverty rate	Poverty deficit	Poverty rate	Poverty deficit
$1.25 per day	0.9	0.0	1.4	0.0	0.0	0.0	2.0	0.1	1.1	0.0
$2.5 per day	12.5	0.9	16.7	1.3	0.1	1.3	20.4	1.8	14.2	1.0

Source: Dessus et al 2008, Tables A1 and A2.

poverty from 0.9 per cent of GDP to 1.8 per cent of GDP. The results for the central scenario also show that most of the poverty deficit brought about by food price increases is due to the real income effect of those households that were already poor before the price shock, while the cost attributable to new households falling into poverty is negligible.

The increase in domestic food prices and urban poverty in Jordan contributed to food riots and general political discontent. The Jordanian government responded with a variety of short-term measures to cushion the impact, including increasing food subsidies (the bread subsidy rose considerably as a result of keeping bread prices stable, while subsidies on rice and sugar to the military also increased); reducing import tariffs on food imports; increasing public sector salaries by JD 20 per month (an increase of around 20 per cent for the lowest paid workers); increasing public sector pensions; increasing targeted transfers to the poor; and increasing other social transfers.[57] In addition, between 2007 and 2011 the minimum wage was increased from JD 100 per month to JD 150 per month. These fiscally costly measures contributed to a growing budget deficit which reached 8.0 per cent of GDP by 2009, the highest level in two decades. As can be seen from Figure 3.19, by 2007 food subsidies had reached around 1.8 per cent of GDP with the consumer subsidies on wheat and barley reaching JD 222.6 million in 2008.

Figure 3.19: Jordan food and fuel subsidies as percentage of GDP

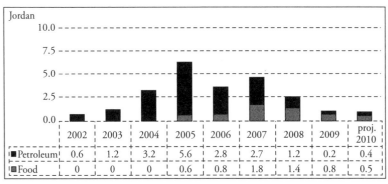

	2002	2003	2004	2005	2006	2007	2008	2009	proj. 2010
■ Petroleum	0.6	1.2	3.2	5.6	2.8	2.7	1.2	0.2	0.4
■ Food	0	0	0	0.6	0.8	1.8	1.4	0.8	0.5

Source: Ronald Albers and Marga Peeters, 'Food and Energy Prices, Government Subsidies and Fiscal Balances in South Mediterranean Countries', *Economic Papers*, No. 437, European Commission, Brussels, 2011, p. 18, Box 3.

Jordan's longer-term strategic response to the 2007–08 global food price crisis has been much more comprehensive than that of the Lebanese authorities, which is partly a reflection of the more interventionist nature of the Jordanian government. Prior to the crisis, Jordan already had a limited food security initiative in the form of a 2004 FAO-sponsored initiative. This was mainly concerned with improving household food security via a portfolio of projects designed to generate income, improve food production and cash crop production, and enhance water and soil conservation amongst 6,000 poor households, mainly via home garden projects. This limited project-based approach was immediately scaled up in the aftermath of the 2007–08 crisis. In 2007–8, a Framework for Food Security in Jordan was prepared by the Ministry of Agriculture and was launched in February 2009. Although multiple dimensions of food security were examined, this document took the form of a reactive urgent framework rather than a proactive longer-term strategy, and the outcome was a number of priority projects presented to the prime minister for urgent budgetary consideration. Some of the projects included an extension of the home gardens scheme and plans to increase the country's food storage capacity by increasing the size of the strategic grain reserve silos.[58] In addition, there were early signs that the government wanted to respond to the crisis by increasing domestic cereal production, and a scheme was launched under the Framework whereby wheat and barley farmers were paid JD 10 per dunum planted with these crops to encourage increased plantings. The Food Security Framework was complemented by a comprehensive study on nutrition and food security in Jordan carried out by the Ministries of Agriculture and Health, World Health Organization (WHO) and FAO, the output of which took the form of policy guidelines rather than specific projects.[59]

The above responses ran parallel to the 2002–10 National Agricultural Strategy which also addressed food security issues. A drawback of all these initiatives, however, was that food security was seen as a component of agricultural policy rather than the latter being regarded as an input to a more comprehensive approach to food security.[60] This was also illustrated by the fact that King Abdullah responded to the global food crisis by announcing that 2009 would be the year of agriculture in Jordan. All of the above responses lacked a comprehensive strategic approach to food security, and largely consisted of pulling together an ad hoc portfolio of existing projects with the addition of some new ones. They also illustrated the old way of thinking, namely that the Ministry of Agriculture was responsible for food security, despite the fact that the bulk of the country's food requirements are imported without the involvement of the Ministry of Agriculture.

These limitations were overcome to some extent in 2010 by the launching of an initiative in the form of 'Food and Nutrition Security in Jordan towards Poverty Alleviation 2010–2013'.[61] At the request of the Ministry of Agriculture, the United Nations Development Programme (UNDP) agreed to help with the development of a comprehensive, coordinated and coherent food security strategy involving both government and non-government stakeholders and based on a full situation assessment. A High Level National Committee on Food Security was established and a Comprehensive Framework for Action was adopted to bring together the various food security initiatives (actual and planned) of both the government and the UN agencies (UNDP, UNICEF, UNIDO and WFP). The aim was to improve food security in order to help reach Millennium Development Goal One—the eradication of extreme poverty and hunger—which was deemed to be off-target in Jordan.

The Food and Nutrition initiative has four main goals: 1) to produce a coordinated national response to food security issues, 2) to enhance sustainable smallholder production of food, 3) to ensure access to nutrition for all via improved social safety nets, and 4) to enhance livelihoods of the poor and food insecure.

Under the first goal, the government is to produce a five-year gender-sensitive National Food Security Strategy, led by the Ministry of Agriculture. The process of formulating this strategy is now underway, and amongst other things will involve an assessment of the extent to which Jordan should promote more domestic food crop production, including cereals, to reduce import dependence. Although strategy in this respect has yet to be formulated, there are already signs that the government will promote domestic food production, including cereals. This is shown by the fact that the second goal of the initiative is to enhance smallholder food production (although the types of food crops have yet to be specified) and by the recent introduction of the JD 10 per dunum incentive for wheat and barley producers. In addition, the UN has recently announced a Compensation Fund of $160 million to compensate Jordan for damage done to the north of the country caused by the second Gulf War. Initial indications are that the Ministry of Agriculture wants to use this to rehabilitate range land in the north with irrigation systems for barley production.[62] The questionable economic viability of barley production in the north is addressed in the section below.

Despite possible plans to expand domestic food production, Jordan is aware that food imports will continue to remain important in the future. Acknowledging this, efforts have been made to strengthen Jordan's position in international food markets. In 2008, a committee was set up with membership from the Ministries of Agriculture and Finance as well as the Central Bank to monitor global food prices and hedge in forward markets for wheat and barley. In 2010, the Ministry of Trade and Industry set up a unit to track grain prices and improve procurement. However, although the Ministry of Trade and Industry generally does a good job in procuring food imports at competitive prices, price monitoring and taking forward positions in global markets needs institutionalising. Despite this, the multi-agency Food and Nutrition initiative has specifically excluded import procurement and distribution from its mandate.[63]

The failure to acknowledge Jordan's position as a major importer of food by excluding procurement and distribution issues from the new approach to food and nutrition security is a major weakness of the initiative. In addition, the initiative has been criticised as still being somewhat ad hoc in approach and centred too heavily on the Ministry of Agriculture.[64] For example, operationalising the initiative has largely consisted of government and UN agencies bringing together what they were already doing under one umbrella,[65] but without any joint funding by the UN agencies. Although the initiative is a multi-agency one involving four UN agencies and four government ministries (Agriculture, Education, Health and Industry) as well as the Department of Statistics, the Ministry of Agriculture is the lead agency supported by UNDP. The technical unit supporting the initiative is located in the Ministry of Agriculture, and the High Level Committee is chaired by the minister for agriculture.[66] A freeze on civil service recruitment has also meant that the Ministry of Agriculture has been limited in its ability to improve capacity on food security issues. This has led some to argue that a truly comprehensive and holistic approach to food and nutrition security in Jordan requires the technical support unit and the High Level Committee to be located, not in the Ministry of Agriculture, but at the highest level of government such as in the Prime Minister's Office, with the prime minister as chair of the committee.

Despite the above criticisms, it is clear that the government of Jordan has taken the 2007–08 global food crisis seriously, and has responded in a variety of ways. The 2010–2013 Food and Nutrition Security Initiative will continue to deliver improvements in the country's approach to food security. Already a national institutional framework has been set up to guide and coordinate food security issues (despite its weaknesses) and, for the first time, a five-year National Food Security Strategy is being developed. Comprehensive data on nutrition and the food security status of the most vulnerable in the population is now being collected for the first time, and a thorough review of the country's social safety net programmes is being conducted by the government and UNICEF.

The analysis conducted in the sections below will potentially help the government in formulating the more macro dimensions of the National Food Security Strategy in terms of the balance between promoting domestic food production and relying on food imports, and in determining what types of domestic food crops are most economically viable.

Revealed Comparative Advantage

We have shown above that both Lebanon and Jordan have responded to the global food crisis of 2007–08 with decisions to increase domestic production of food, particularly cereals. Such an approach can be termed as a move towards 'food sovereignty', defined as a food security strategy that attempts to exert power and control over national food supplies by refusing to allow the strategy to be dictated by market forces alone. This rejection of market forces is often tantamount to neglecting the dictates of international comparative advantage in decisions about resource allocation.

One way in which a country's international comparative advantage in different production activities can be assessed is by calculating Revealed Comparative Advantage (RCA) for different activities. This involves using actual trade data to create a static snapshot of areas where the country seems to have an advantage in international trade. We do this below for Lebanon and Jordan.

RCA is calculated for exports from Lebanon and Jordan comparing all sectors of the economies, and sub-sectors within agriculture.[67] The RCA indicates the relative global importance of the country as a supplier of a commodity to the world market relative to the importance of the country's total exports.

It is calculated as follows:

$$RCA\ (i,w)j = (X(i,w)j/X(w,w)j)/(TX(i,w)/TX(w,w))$$

Where:

X(i)j is exports of commodity j by country i to the world (w)
X(w)j is world exports of commodity j to the world
TX(i) and TX(w) are for total exports by country i and the world respectively.

RCA values greater (less) than unity indicate comparative advantage (disadvantage) in the country's export share in the selected commodity import market is appreciably greater (less) than its overall export share in import markets for all commodities.

The results for all sectors are given in Figure 3.20, and show that both Lebanon and Jordan have a revealed comparative advantage in agriculture, food exports and chemicals for all years where data is available (for Lebanon data is only available from 1997 onwards). In comparison to Lebanon, Jordan has more sectors with export advantages and also a higher degree of advantage. In the period from 2000 onwards Jordan has an RCA in manufactures, pharmaceuticals and clothing, and in four sectors (food, chemicals, pharmaceuticals and clothing) the RCA was found to be greater than 2, indicating a particularly strong advantage. Following large increases in clothing exports from 2001 onwards, Jordan's RCA in that sector reached a peak of 8.5 in 2007.

These results suggest that if the two countries are to pursue a trade-based food security policy, then Lebanon should promote the export of food (predominantly high-value fruit and vegetables) and chemicals, while Jordan has the potential for a more diversified export base, including not just food and chemicals but also manufacturers, pharmaceuticals and clothing. Export earnings from these activities would then be used to import foods in which the two countries do not have an RCA, such as cereals and meat.

Figure 3.21 shows the calculations of RCA within the agricultural sectors of each country. It shows that comparative advantages were found for at least one time period for almost half of the agricultural sub-sectors across the two countries (15 out of 27). The RCAs within agriculture appear to have a greater variability than those for all sectors, although for both countries the RCAs for fruit and vegetables remain high for all of the three time periods.

Figure 3.20: Revealed comparative advantage values, period averages for all sectors

	Lebanon	Jordan		
	1997–2009	1980–9	1990–9	2000–9
Agriculture	1.64	1.36	1.58	1.68
Food	1.83	1.77	1.91	2.02
Fuels and mining	0.62	1.58	1.99	0.60
Fuels	0.01		0.01	0.03
Manufactures	0.85	0.76	0.72	1.02
Iron and steel	0.24		0.19	0.43
Chemicals	1.07		2.78	2.34
Pharmaceuticals	0.13			2.69
Machinery and transport equipment	0.34		0.29	0.38
Office and telecom equipment	0.08	0.06	0.07	0.28
Electronic data processing & office equipment	0.10			0.13
Telecommunications equipment	0.08			0.65
Integrated circuits and electronic components	0.02			0.02
Automotive products	0.09		0.33	0.37
Textiles	0.57	0.72	0.81	0.56
Clothing	0.95	0.59	0.54	6.93

Source: WTO database: http://stat.wto.org/StatisticalProgram/WSDBStatProgramHome.aspx

Considering each country in turn, Lebanon has a strong RCA (greater than 2) in fruit and vegetables, in pulses in earlier years and, more recently, in olive oil and tobacco. Some agricultural subsectors have seen a trend increase in their RCA values, from a position of disadvantage to one of advantage: beverages (concentrated in wine, bran, coffee, tea, cocoa and spices), and sugar and honey. Jordan does not exhibit such a frequency and strength of RCAs in agriculture as Lebanon. When compared to Jordan's more frequent advantage in other sectors, this may be due to its relative shortage of water resources. The highest RCA that Jordan experienced was for olive oil (5.7) between 1980 and 1989, although the variability in the RCA for Jordan's olive oil reflects a high variability in the value of olive oil exports from a high of $10,615,000 in 2006 to a low of $41,000 in 1997. More generally, Jordan displays advantages in fruit and vegetables in all three periods, in animal and vegetable oils since 1990, and in dairy and eggs since 2000.

The above analysis suggests that if RCA is taken as the guide to efficient resource allocation within the agricultural sector, then both countries should promote the production of fruit and vegetables for export. In addition, Lebanon should promote tobacco and niche products such as wine, bran, coffee, tea, cocoa and spices, and sugar and honey which have recently gained a comparative advantage, while Jordan should also promote oil and milk products. Export revenues from these agricultural activities where the two countries appear to have an international comparative advantage could then be used to import food items such as cereals and meat which Figure 3.21 shows are products in which both countries have strong comparative disadvantages.

While the above RCA methodology highlights the global importance of a country's exports in certain sectors and subsectors, it also contains a number of weaknesses. As the RCA calculations are based on the actual value of exports, the results are highly responsive to price changes and also reflect distortions in the local economy. For example, Lebanon's apparent RCA in tobacco is a reflection of a relatively high level of exports based on the producer price support scheme which pays farmers above the international tobacco price. If this price distorting scheme were dismantled Lebanon would no longer be able to export tobacco as it does not have a true comparative advantage in this product.[68] More generally, trade protection and domestic price distortions have the effect of encouraging water usage, compared to the usage in the absence of such interventions in the market, which distorts trade patterns.[69] In other words, the RCAs are actually capturing distorted comparative advantages, rather than pure comparative advantage. However, the RCA analysis can give some guidance to policymakers. We know, for example, that the fruit and vegetable market in Lebanon is not particularly distorted (apart from the small amount of support to transport costs for exporters offered under the previous Investment Development Authority of Lebanon scheme) and hence the RCA in this area probably is indica-

Figure 3.21: Revealed comparative advantage values, period averages agricultural sub-sectors

	Lebanon			Jordan		
	1980–9	1990–9	2000–9	1980–9	1990–9	2000–9
Fruit and vegetables	5.24	3.63	2.36	3.90	2.66	2.59
Beverages	0.28	0.63	1.26	0.23	0.25	0.58
Wine	0.10	0.82	1.13	0.00	0.01	0.01
Beer		0.20	0.41	0.36	0.06	0.27
Dairy products + eggs	0.66	0.20	0.27	1.02	0.78	1.25
Milk condensed + dry + fresh		0.13	0.09	0.11	0.32	1.73
Cereals and prep	0.15	0.15	0.58	0.47	0.17	0.23
Pulses	2.87	2.08	1.14	0.36	0.98	0.16
Rice	0.05	0.29	0.30	0.38	0.22	0.14
Wheat + flour, Wheat equivalent	0.01	0.07	0.35	0.75	0.12	0.06
Bran + milling prod		0.81	1.32	0.90		0.41
Groundnuts total shelled	0.16	1.33	0.28	0.20	0.33	0.31
Coffee + tea + cocoa	0.07	0.40	1.02	0.89	0.27	0.23
Fixed vegetable oils	0.06	0.91	0.91	0.49	0.62	0.38
Olive oil	0.14	3.44	2.70	5.70	0.76	1.31
Oilseeds	0.15	0.19	0.03	0.08	0.12	0.04
Animal vegetable oil	0.05	0.76	0.77	0.39	2.79	2.34
Meat and meat prepared		0.02	0.21	0.09	0.31	0.34
Bovine meat		0.02	0.18	0.08	0.56	0.60
Ovine meat			0.03	0.37	0.24	0.28
Pig meat		0.01	0.02		0.00	0.00
Poultry meat		0.05	0.56	0.24	0.47	0.56
Hides and skins	2.11	2.79	1.25	0.31	1.57	0.49
Sugar and honey	0.16	0.88	1.54	0.09	0.21	0.26
Textile fibres	0.17	0.08	0.02	0.03	0.24	0.06
Tobacco	1.49	1.34	2.68	1.46	0.32	1.87
Fodder & feeding stuff	0.47	0.11	0.34	1.50	0.75	0.81
Miscellaneous food	0.14	1.06	1.08	0.68	0.49	0.93

Source: FAOSTAT.

tive of a true comparative advantage. This is an area within agriculture therefore that Lebanon could promote as part of a trade-based food security strategy. In addition, despite the support given to wheat producers in Lebanon via seed subsidies and distorted producer prices, the country still has a strong revealed disadvantage in wheat and flour with an RCA of 0.35 for the period 2000–9, which suggests that if the economics of comparative advantage are used to guide efficient resource allocation wheat production is not an activity that should be promoted. This suggests that the recent Lebanese policy of increasing domestic wheat production does not make sense from a purely economic perspective which uses comparative advantage as the yardstick of efficiency— Lebanon would be better off concentrating on other agricultural activities and importing wheat and other cereals from countries that are more efficient producers of these crops.

Although we can derive some tentative policy prescriptions from the RCA analysis, the approach remains subject to the methodological weaknesses mentioned above. Some of these weaknesses are addressed in the second stage of the quantitative analysis using the Policy Analysis Matrix (PAM).[70]

The Policy Analysis Matrix (PAM)

The PAM is an analytical tool which shows the extent to which actual market prices for a commodity and its inputs diverge from efficiency prices, with the assumption that undistorted efficiency prices result in an optimal resource allocation. It is designed to measure market distortions and policy interventions in terms of their effect on a commodity production system. The PAM is based on a simple accounting identity, namely:

Gross Margin = Revenue–Variable Costs

In order to construct the matrix, costs are broken down into tradable inputs and non-tradable inputs called domestic resources or factors. Gross margins, revenue and the two types of costs are then calculated using both actual prices and efficiency prices. The differences between the actual and the efficiency prices are referred to as transfers and these transfers reflect the extent to which actual distorted prices diverge from efficiency prices. The general structure of a PAM is as in Figure 3.22.

The matrix is able to analyse a wide range of government interventions, including commodity specific policies such as taxes/subsidies on inputs and outputs; factor market policies such as minimum wages; and macroeconomic policies such as exchange rate policies. Its power as a policy analysis tool is its ability to examine the net effects of multiple policy instruments on different parts of a commodity system such as farm production.

Figure 3.22: A representative PAM

	Revenue	Tradable inputs	Domestic resources	Gross Margin
Actual prices	A	B	C	D
Efficiency Prices	E	F	G	H
Transfers	I	J	K	L

In order to construct a PAM for production of a particular commodity we need to construct farm budgets based on both actual and hypothetical efficiency prices—in other words, the prices that would prevail if all markets were perfectly competitive such that resources were optimally allocated. Since we cannot observe efficiency prices we need a set of proxies. The PAM uses the neoclassical concept of international comparative advantage to derive such prices. It uses farmgate import or export parity prices, based on border prices of actual and potential imports and exports (Cost, Insurance and Freight (C.I.F) and Free on Board (F.o.B)) plus local costs, to reflect the opportunity costs of resources used to produce the commodity and to price outputs at their scarcity value.[71] This approach rests on the assumption that a small open economy can maximise its production and consumption by producing the goods for which it has an international comparative advantage and freely trading in international markets. For domestic factors of production which are not tradable, such as land, labour and capital, the efficiency price is based on their domestic opportunity cost—in other words, what they would earn in their next best use with output from this next best use valued at its import or export parity price.

Having constructed a farm budget using both actual and efficiency prices, we can then enter the data into the PAM cells and the PAM can then be used to calculate various coefficients such as the following:

Nominal Protection Coefficient = A/E
Effective Rate of Protection = (A-B)/(E-F)
Domestic Resource Cost = G/(E-F)

The Nominal Protection Coefficient (NPC) indicates the net effect of distortions on output prices—the extent to which the output is implicitly subsidised or taxed as a result of government interventions in the market. An NPC greater than 1 indicates implicit protection and vice versa.

The Effective Rate of Protection (ERP) shows the net effects of distortions on both tradable inputs and outputs—in other words, it indicates the extent to which the overall production of a good is implicitly subsidised or taxed as a result of government interventions in both input and output markets. An ERP greater than 1 indicates implicit protection and vice versa.

The Domestic Resource Cost (DRC) indicates the opportunity cost of using domestic resources to produce a good when everything is valued at efficiency prices. In other words, it divides factor costs at efficiency prices (G) by the value added in efficiency prices (E-F). A DRC greater than 1 indicates that the cost of domestic resources used to produce the good is greater than the contribution of its value added at efficiency prices, meaning that the country has a comparative disadvantage in the production of this good which therefore represents an economically inefficient use of resources. By contrast, a DRC less than 1 indicates comparative advantage or that the commodity is making efficient use of domestic resources.

We will use PAM analysis to assess the economic efficiency of different production activities in Lebanon and Jordan. This will help us assess whether, for example, the Lebanese and Jordanian governments' response to global food price increases in the form of a strategy to increase domestic production of cereals (such as wheat and barley) is an economically efficient use of resources. Before doing this using current data, we will first review an earlier PAM exercise carried out by the ESCWA.[72] PAMs for a large number of crops in Jordan and Lebanon (as well as in the Palestinian Territories and Syria) were constructed and used to calculate NPCs, ERPs and DRCs for each crop. The results are reproduced in Figure 3.23.

The DRC calculations given in Figure 3.23 indicate that in the early 2000s Lebanon had a strong comparative advantage in the production of potatoes, cucumbers, aubergines, tomatoes, grapes, apples, citrus, bananas and watermelon (a DRC of less than 0.5 for all of these crops). Lebanon also had a weaker comparative advantage in the production of tobacco (DRC = 0.87) and olives (DRC = 0.60). On the other hand,

Lebanon had a comparative disadvantage in the production of wheat with a DCR of 1.20. In other words, according to the ESCWA calculations carried out in 2001, economically efficient resource allocation consists of concentrating on the production of a wide variety of fruit and vegetables and not on wheat production. However, the NPCs in Figure 3.23 show that the output of wheat (as well as sugar beet and tobacco) are all subsidised in Lebanon (an NPC greater than 1). In other words, despite its economic inefficiency, the government is subsidising wheat output. At the same time the economically efficient crops, namely fruit and vegetables, are all subject to implicit taxation (they have an NPC less than 1, such that in terms of producer prices their production is being discouraged). Figure 3.23 also shows the ERP—the net effect of interventions in the pricing of both tradable inputs and tradable outputs. Again it shows that wheat is heavily protected or subsidised with an ERP of 1.51 despite its economic inefficiency, whilst most of the efficient products (namely fruit and vegetables) are discouraged by low ERPs. Clearly Lebanese government policies and interventions in the early 2000s—such as taxes, subsidies, and an overvalued exchange rate—were not encouraging an economically efficient pattern of resource allocation in the agricultural sector.

A similar analysis applies to Jordan. Figure 3.23 shows that Jordan, like Lebanon, has a strong comparative advantage in the production of fruit and vegetables, as well as pulses (DRCs less than 1) and a disadvantage in the production of cereals such as wheat and barley (DRCs greater than 1). Despite this, Figure 3.23 shows that the Jordanian government was encouraging the production of inefficient crops, namely wheat and barley (with NRP and ERP coefficients greater than 1 for these crops) while discouraging the production of efficient crops such as pulses and most fruit and vegetables (NRP and ERP coefficients less than 1). The only two efficient crops being encouraged by government interventions in the input and output market in Jordan were watermelon and olives. It is particularly notable that both Lebanon and Jordan offered a very high level of effective protection for the production of wheat (ERP of 1.51 and 1.59, respectively) despite the fact that in both countries production of this crop represents the most inefficient use of domestic resources of all crops considered—it had the highest DRC.

Using the same data sources as ESCWA, Kubursi constructed PAMs for about eighty crops in nine agro-climatic zones of Lebanon.[73] We

Figure 3.23: NPC, ERP and DRC for selected crops in Jordan and Lebanon (2001 calculations)

Crops	Jordan			Lebanon		
	NPC	ERP	DRC	NPC	ERP	DRC
Wheat	1.08	1.59	1.26	1.25	1.51	1.20
Barley	1.01	1.14	1.07	–	–	–
Sugar beet	–	–	–	1.21	1.46	0.95
Tobacco	–	–	–	1.54	1.67	0.87
Potatoes	0.98	1.47	1.08	0.75	0.62	0.47
Pulses	0.53	0.48	0.17	–	–	–
Cucumbers	0.68	0.68	0.13	0.60	0.52	0.22
Aubergines	0.51	0.43	0.23	0.30	0.18	0.11
Tomatoes	0.53	0.49	0.12	0.96	0.95	0.27
Bananas	0.93	0.91	0.79	0.94	0.94	0.32
Grapes	0.98	0.99	0.48	0.45	0.40	0.25
Apples	–	–	–	0.54	0.48	0.33
Citrus	0.92	0.98	0.48	0.55	0.53	0.29
Watermelon	0.98	1.15	0.45	0.57	0.55	0.25
Olives	1.09	1.13	0.70	1.00	1.02	0.60

Source: ESCWA 2001, Tables 5–7.

summarise his results here for Zone 6 Zahle and West Bekaa, which is the zone we have chosen for our own PAM calculations. Kubursi's PAM results for Zone 6 are similar for the ESCWA results for Lebanon as a whole. He finds DRCs for most fruit and vegetables to be significantly less than 1, indicating a strong comparative advantage in the production of these crops, particularly tomatoes, which is one of the crops we analyse (see below). By contrast, the DRCs for wheat and sugar beet are above 1 indicating a comparative disadvantage in these two crops. Despite these results, government policies and interventions favoured the production of wheat and sugar beet whilst discouraging the production of fruit and vegetables. This leads Kubursi to conclude:

The Bekaa valley does not have a comparative advantage in wheat and sugar-beets. Wheat and sugarbeets appear to have very high rates of nominal and effective protection. Both of these products are a burden on the government being subsidised and with negative social profitability.[74]

We now proceed to use current data to carry out a PAM analysis for Lebanon and Jordan to see if the above conclusions based on earlier data still hold. It is beyond the scope of this research to produce PAMs for a large number of crops in each country. Instead, we have selected several key crops in each country, based on both historical and contemporary evidence regarding major crops in which the two countries have strong advantages and disadvantages.

In the case of Lebanon we have seen that, historically, according to the ESCWA PAM data of 2001, potatoes and tomatoes are two crops in which the country had a comparative advantage while wheat was the major crop in which the country had a comparative disadvantage (as shown by the respective DRCs). Contemporary analysis, although not based on rigorous data analysis, repeats this conclusion.[75] In addition, as we have seen in the section above, despite the policy advice of the World Bank, the Lebanese government has decided to promote the production of wheat as part of its response to the 2007–08 price shock. Hence, we have chosen tomatoes, potatoes and wheat as the three crops for our PAM analysis.[76]

In constructing PAMs for potatoes, tomatoes and wheat in Lebanon we need to produce a farm budget for the representative farmer for each crop.[77] Lebanon is divided into forty homogeneous agricultural zones contained within four regions—Bekaa (39 per cent of cultivated land), North (29 per cent), South (20 per cent) and Mount Lebanon (12 per cent).[78] Given the dominance of the Bekaa region in Lebanon's agriculture, particularly for cereal production, we have decided to use farm data for our three crops taken from zones within the Bekaa region. This data was supplied by the American University of Beirut study farm in the Bekaa valley. Appendix 1 gives details of the farm budgets for each crop based on actual prices and efficiency prices and assumptions used to produce these budgets. In the case of wheat, the main difference between actual prices and efficiency prices are that the actual prices include a subsidy on wheat seed and a support price for the wheat output, while the efficiency prices use a proxy price to reflect the true opportunity cost of using water. In the case of tomatoes and potatoes, the main difference between the two sets of prices is the use of the efficiency price for water.

Figures 3.24 and 3.25 use the data contained in the farm budget to construct the PAMs for both rain-fed and supplementary irrigated wheat, from which we can calculate the ERP, NRP and DRC. From the PAM for rain-fed wheat it is difficult to see why farmers in Lebanon would grow such a crop in that the gross margin they actually receive is negative, indicating a loss on this activity of $242 per hectare. This is despite the fact that the government offers a guaranteed price for their output which is above the import C.I.F. price. By contrast, wheat grown under supplemental irrigation is profitable for farmers, generating a return of $716 per hectare. We can see that for both crops the output is implicitly subsidised (revenue at actual prices is above revenue at social prices due to the guarantee support price), giving an NRP of 1.09 and 1.10 for rain-fed and irrigated wheat, respectively. In addition, input subsidies in the form of subsidised seed result in an ERP greater than 1, indicating that the combined effect of policies on tradable inputs and outputs offers a positive incentive to farmers.

Figure 3.24: PAM Lebanon rain-fed wheat 2011 ($ per hectare)

	Revenue	Tradable inputs	Domestic resources	Gross margin
Private (actual) prices	1,235	467	1,010	−242
Social (efficiency) prices	1,128	581	1,010	−463
Effects of divergence and policy (transfers)	107	−114	0	221

Rain-fed Wheat NPC = 1234/1128 = 1.09.
ERP = (1235–467)/(1128–581) = 1.40.
DRC = 1010/(1128–581) = 1.85.

Figure 3.25: PAM Lebanon supplemental irrigated wheat 2011 ($ per hectare)

	Revenue	Tradable inputs	Domestic resources	Gross margin
Private (actual) prices	2,470	467	1,287	716
Social (efficiency) prices	2,255	581	2,507	−833
Effects of divergence and policy (transfers)	215	−114	−1,220	1,549

Supplemental Irrigated Wheat NPC = 1.10.
ERP = (2470–467)/(2255–581) = 1.20.
DRC = 2507/(2255–581) = 1.50.

The DRC for both crops is positive, indicating that the activity does not have a comparative advantage and does not make efficient use of domestic resources, especially in the case of rain-fed wheat that has a DRC of 1.85. Clearly, in the case of both crops, the government is offering incentives to farmers to grow crops which do not make efficient use of scarce resources (although in the case of rain-fed wheat these incentives are not very attractive). This suggests that the recent policy to promote wheat production does not make sense from the point of view of economic rationality.

However, the above conclusions change significantly when we adjust some of the assumptions upon which the PAM analysis is based. We can use the PAM data to conduct a sensitivity analysis in terms of future predictions for yields and international prices of wheat. If the yields of the wheat crop in Lebanon were to double, the DRC changes dramatically, with a DRC of 0.51 for rain-fed wheat and 0.65 for irrigated wheat. It is unlikely that rain-fed yields would double, but it is feasible that irrigated yields, using improved seeds and good husbandry, could almost double. Interviews with the International Center for Agricultural Research in the Dry Areas (ICARDA) representative in Lebanon have suggested that under optimal irrigated conditions the yield could reach 9 MT/hectare, which is nearly double the yield used in our baseline analysis. If we also assume international wheat prices were to increase by 50 per cent (the PAM analysis used international prices as a proxy for efficiency prices), then the DRC becomes even more favourable at 0.41 for rain-fed wheat and 0.45 for irrigated wheat. Hence, under these scenarios, domestic wheat production, particularly irrigated production where the yield increases are possible, does represent an efficient use of domestic resources.

Figure 3.26: PAM Lebanon tomatoes 2011 ($ per hectare)

	Revenue	Tradable inputs	Domestic resources	Gross margin
Private (actual) prices	28,000	2,450	4,670	20,880
Social (efficiency) prices	28,000	2,450	9,792	15,758
Effects of divergence and policy (transfers)	0	0	−5,122	5,122

NPC = 1.00.
ERP = (28,000−2,450)/(28,000−2,450) = 1.00.
DRC = 9,792/(28,000−2,450) = 0.38.

Figures 3.26 and 3.27 present the PAMs for tomatoes and potatoes in Lebanon. The PAM analysis for tomatoes and potatoes indicates that at actual prices both crops are profitable, with a gross margin of

$20,880/hectare. for tomato production and $3,120 for potatoes. However, although the DRC indicates that Lebanon has a strong comparative advantage in tomato production—with a DRC of 0.38 indicating a very efficient use of domestic resources—the DRC for potatoes is 1.09 indicating that this is not a particularly efficient crop. Despite the efficiency of tomato production, the government does not offer any incentives to producers as shown by the fact that both the NPC and ERP are equal to unity.

Figure 3.27: PAM Lebanon potatoes 2011 ($ per hectare)

	Revenue	Tradable inputs	Domestic resources	Gross margin
Private Prices	10,500	4,310	3,070	3,120
Social prices	10,500	4,310	6,722	−532
Effects of divergence and policy (transfers)	0	0	−3,652	3,652

NPC = 1.00.
ERP = (10,500–4,310)/(10,500–4,310) = 1.00.
DRC = 6,722/(10,500–4,310) = 1.09.

Data availability on farm budgets for Jordan is much more comprehensive than for Lebanon, hence we are able to conduct a more thorough PAM analysis for Jordan. Given that we are interested in comparing the efficiency of grain production to that of high-value exportable crops, we have chosen to construct PAMs for the highland area in the north that produces the field crops of wheat, barley and maize and the nearby areas of Zizia, Mafraq, Baqaa and Qastal where cucumber, tomatoes and potatoes are produced. Appendix 1 provides details of the assumptions and data used to calculate the Jordan PAMs, and Figures 3.28 and 3.29 present the results. Figure 3.29 presents the NPCs, ERPs and DRCs derived from the PAMs for the various Jordanian crops.

The DRC coefficients from Figure 3.29 show that all the vegetable crops, apart from potatoes grown in Mafraq, make efficient use of domestic resources, with DRCs less than 1. Tomatoes grown under plastic houses are a particularly efficient crop. Despite this, the effects of divergences and policies currently prevailing in Jordan are such that there are strong disincentives to the production of these crops with NPCs and ERPs less than 1, indicating that output is implicitly taxed

THE CASE OF LEBANON AND JORDAN

Figure 3.28: PAMs for Jordan 2010–11 (Jordanian Dinar per dunum)

CUCUMBER ZIZIA

Items	Revenues	Cost of tradable inputs	Cost of domestic factors	Gross Margin
Private prices	3194.40	645.60	835.72	1713.08
Social prices	3799.09	715.67	1161.62	1921.80
Effects of divergence & policy	– 604.69	– 70.07	– 325.90	– 208.71

CUCUMBER MAFRAQ

Items	Revenues	Cost of tradable inputs	Cost of domestic factors	Gross Margin
Private prices	3620.32	744.66	746.35	2129.31
Social prices	4305.63	792.07	1142.90	2370.67
Effects of divergence & policy	– 685.31	– 47.41	– 396.54	– 241.36

CUCUMBER BAQAA

Items	Revenues	Cost of tradable inputs	Cost of domestic factors	Gross Margin
Private prices	3194.40	748.80	956.74	1488.86
Social prices	3799.09	802.92	1252.00	1744.17
Effects of divergence & policy	– 604.69	– 54.12	– 295.26	– 255.31

TOMATO BAQAA PH

Items	Revenues	Cost of tradable inputs	Cost of domestic factors	Gross Margin
Private prices	2272.32	442.00	1075.06	755.26
Social prices	3180.65	518.51	1423.00	1239.14
Effects of divergence & policy	– 908.33	– 76.51	– 347.94	– 483.22

TOMATO QASTAL PH

Items	Revenues	Cost of tradable inputs	Cost of domestic factors	Gross Margin
Private prices	2082.96	646.73	446.91	989.32
Social prices	2915.59	616.24	615.97	1683.38
Effects of divergence & policy	– 832.63	30.49	– 169.07	– 694.05

81

FOOD SECURITY IN THE MIDDLE EAST

POTATO MAFRAQ OF

Items	Revenues	Cost of tradable inputs	Cost of domestic factors	Gross Margin
Private prices	727.51	477.47	172.01	78.09
Social prices	1058.93	367.35	691.27	0.31
Effects of divergence & policy	– 331.36	110.12	–519.27	77.79

POTATO ZEZIA OF

Items	Revenues	Cost of tradable inputs	Cost of domestic factors	Gross Margin
Private prices	797.98	516.90	315.90	– 34.82
Social prices	1161.41	473.66	446.62	241.13
Effects of divergence & policy	– 363.43	43.24	– 130.72	– 275.95

WHEAT-HL

Items	Revenues	Cost of tradable inputs	Cost of domestic factors	Gross Margin
Private prices	180.00	36.32	134.57	9.11
Social prices	122.76	34.78	192.12	– 104.14
Effects of divergence & policy	57.24	1.54	– 57.56	113.25

BARLEY-HL

Items	Revenues	Cost of tradable inputs	Cost of domestic factors	Gross Margin
Private prices	100.00	34.77	122.00	– 56.77
Social prices	70.68	33.44	187.10	– 149.86
Effects of divergence & policy	29.32	1.33	– 65.10	93.09

MAIZE SUMMER-HL

Items	Revenues	Cost of tradable inputs	Cost of domestic factors	Gross Margin
Private prices	367.07	45.07	278.50	43.49
Social prices	481.97	43.74	457.42	– 19.18
Effects of divergence & policy	– 114.90	1.33	– 178.92	62.68

Note: PH = Plastic house, HL = Highland, OF = Open Field.

and that the net effects of policies on tradable outputs and inputs is implicit taxation. By contrast, the DRCs for field crops show that the production of these crops in the highlands does not make efficient use of domestic resources, with barley production being particularly inefficient with a DRC of 5.02 and wheat being inefficient with a DRC of 2.18. Despite this, the prevailing policy regime is such that production of both barley and wheat are strongly encouraged with an implicit subsidy on output (NPC greater than 1) and the combined effects of interventions in the markets for tradable outputs and inputs amounting to implicit subsidisation (ERP greater than 1). Ironically, maize is the only field crop that approaches efficiency with a DRC of 1.04, yet production of this crop is discouraged.

Figure 3.29: NPCs, ERPs and DRCs for selected Jordanian crops 2010–11

	NPC	ERP	DRC
Cucumber Zizia	0.84	0.83	0.38
Cucumber Mafraq	0.84	0.82	0.33
Cucumber Baqaa	0.84	0.82	0.42
Tomato Baqaa (plastic house)	0.71	0.69	0.53
Tomato Qastal (plastic house)	0.71	0.62	0.27
Potato Mafraq	0.69	0.36	1.00
Potato Zezia	0.69	0.41	0.65
Wheat Highland	1.47	1.63	2.18
Barley Highland	1.41	1.75	5.02
Maize Highland	0.76	0.73	1.04

The PAM results for Jordan lead to a similar conclusion as those for Lebanon: the Jordanian authorities' response to the 2007–08 global food price shock in the form of policies aimed at increasing grain production, particularly the intention to use the UN compensation fund to promote barley production in the highlands of the north, is not an economically rational policy response. However, this conclusion is based on the international price data and yield data for 2010–11 which have been used to construct the Jordan PAM. As with Lebanon, we have conducted a sensitivity analysis by varying the data used. For the three Jordanian field crops, if yields doubled and international prices increased by 50 per cent, the DRCs are as follows: wheat DRC = 0.58; barley DRC = 1.05; maize DRC = 0.33. This indicates that even if medium-term circumstances changed and Jordan was able to double its yields of these field crops and international prices for the import of these crops increased by 50 per cent, it would still not make economic sense for Jordan to produce barley as the DRC is still above 1—although wheat and maize become efficient crops under this scenario with DRCs significantly less than 1. It seems then, that the grains that the Jordanian government should focus on promoting in terms of yield enhancement under the assumption that import prices will rise are maize and, to a lesser extent, wheat, but definitely not barley. This is a worrying finding, given that it is the latter crop that the government seems intent on promoting.

Conclusion

The above analysis has shown that the 2007–08 global food price shock had a significant impact on both Lebanon and Jordan, leading to domestic food price inflation which put pressure on citizens' living standards, and increased agricultural trade deficits and fiscal strain as the governments tried to cushion the impact of rising food prices. In both countries, the crisis has prompted a move towards greater food sovereignty in the form of an emphasis on more domestic cereal production, which has involved a move away from the dictates of international comparative advantage in decisions about the allocation of scarce resources. In both countries, water is a critical scarce resource and the promotion of domestic cereal production is not an economically efficient use of this resource as shown by both the RCA analysis and the PAM analysis.

The two methodological approaches adopted in this research— namely semi-structured interviews in both countries and the more technical economic analysis, which employed the neoclassical methodology of RCAs and PAMs—show a clear disjunction. Semi-structured interviews with government officials and policymakers in both countries indicated a desire to move towards greater food sovereignty via the promotion of domestic cereal production using a variety of government interventions in the market, such as subsidised input prices and supported producer prices. However, the neoclassical economic analysis using RCAs and PAMs shows that from the very narrow perspective of economic efficiency, judged using the yardstick of international comparative advantage, this is not an economically rational use of scarce resources. This disjunction is a key finding of the research and highlights the nature of the debate that is now likely to occur between domestic policymakers in the MENA region and many of the international financial institutions such as the IMF and World Bank and other organisations such as the FAO and International Food Policy Research Institute (IFPRI). The disjunction arises because the former group of actors has a broad range of considerations that go beyond a narrow concern with economic efficiency and encompass social, political and environmental issues. As such, their decision-making is not just driven by the desire to maximise the economic efficiency of resource allocation. Food security issues in the region have moved beyond this and are captured in the broader concept of 'food sovereignty' which accepts that policymaking will be affected by issues that go beyond the purely economic and that, as a result, policies may legitimately diverge from the dictates of international market forces. For example, promoting domestic cereal production reduces vulnerability to the geopolitical need to maintain good relations with the world's main cereal exporters such as the United States and the EU. It also reduces vulnerability to both global price and supply shocks and potentially gives a country greater control over access to food and the terms of this access.

There are also important social reasons why the governments of countries like Lebanon and Jordan might want to promote domestic cereal production which cannot be captured by a purely economic analysis. For example, in both countries small poor farmers often do not have access to irrigated land and, as a result, rain-fed cereal production is their most viable activity. Linked to this is the fact that such production is often conducted as a risk minimisation strategy by poor farmers, who know that even if the rains are poor and their grain harvest fails they will be able to sell wheat straw as a by-product. Environmental factors are also important considerations in that cereal production is often part of a sensible crop rotation to help preserve soil fertility—in Lebanon, for example, wheat is an important part of the five-year crop rotation of many farmers.

Apart from the fact that the neoclassical methodology fails to go beyond narrow economic analysis, the methodology itself has a number of significant weaknesses. Most importantly, by using the concept of international comparative advantage as the yardstick by which to assess economic efficiency, it implicitly assumes that international food markets are themselves perfectly competitive. However, this assumption is far from true—both the United States and the EU heavily subsidise their own domestic food producers and restrict access to their domestic markets. Hence, if a trade-based food security strategy is to be advocated for the MENA region there is first a need to ensure that MENA producers of high-value fruit and vegetables destined for export have free and fair access to foreign markets, particularly the nearby European market. Export bans imposed by a number of major cereal exporting countries over the past five years are another indication of the imperfect functioning of international food markets with major implications for the importing MENA countries.

The RCA and PAM analyses are also predominantly static analyses. However, both domestic and global conditions change with time, and with strong policies countries are often able to reshape their dynamic comparative advantage. For example, our simple sensitivity analysis using the PAM has shown that if cereal yields were to significantly improve in both Lebanon and Jordan in the context of increasing global prices then, with the exception of barley in Jordan, cereal production becomes economically viable. This suggests that both countries, if they are intent on promoting increases in cereal production, need to accompany their planned move towards greater food sovereignty with strong efforts and policies to increase the productivity of domestic cereal production.

The methodologies used in this chapter, namely RCAs and PAMs, are only two of many tools in the box of neoclassical economics. There are other more sophisticated tools which could also be used to help decide whether or not a country should focus on domestic food production from an economy-wide and social point of view. These include computable general equilibrium models that link to household surveys, while public investment analysis can help decide whether investing in agriculture is a rational choice compared to investing in other sectors with respect to economic and social outcomes. However, the data for these more sophisticated types of analysis is often not available. There is an urgent need to improve data collection and dissemination in the MENA region, not just for its use in neoclassical analysis, but for use in all dimensions of work on food security. The Group of Twenty (G20) countries in their 2011 action plan on food price volatility argued that for the world as a whole there was an urgent need for more up-to-date and extensive country data on hunger.[79] ESCWA has also called for more relevant data and information on sustainable livelihoods analysis,[80] while

IFPRI identifies the need for state-of-the-art research approaches and data collection, including long-term panel datasets, gender disaggregated survey data, new impact evaluation techniques, participatory action research, and intra household analysis.

It should be clear from the above discussion that this research is not prescriptive, in other words, it does not advocate any particular food security strategy. Just because we calculate RCAs and PAMs based on international comparative advantage does not mean that we are advocating a trade-based food security policy—one where domestic resources are used to optimum economic efficiency to produce export crops that generate foreign exchange to purchase cereal imports. Although this may be what the PAM analysis shows as an economically efficient policy, there may be good reasons to override economic considerations for geopolitical concerns such as vulnerability to external food markets and a political desire for more food sovereignty. What this analysis does however show is the economic implications of such a strategy, even though policymakers may consider the cost worthwhile.

For both countries, even if they succeed in moving towards greater domestic food production, they will still remain heavily dependent on food imports—the Lebanese programme, for example, only plans to produce around 20–25 per cent of the country's wheat requirements. This means that even if domestic food sovereignty is promoted, there will still be a need for other supportive policies to enhance the trade-based dimensions of food security. These include policies to promote the production of high-value export crops such as fruit, vegetables and tree crops and to diversify the export base more generally towards manufacturing and service activities, as well as measures to improve both countries' positions in global food markets, especially for cereal imports. The latter can occur via reducing domestic transport, storage and general logistics costs of such imports; using forward options and hedging in international food markets; and developing strategic grain reserves (either physical or virtual).[81] In addition, both the promotion of domestic food production and the use of imports to achieve national food security need to be accompanied by measures to ensure individual food security. This involves not just strengthening social safety nets and reforming social welfare policy,[82] but also more generally promoting an inclusive pro-poor growth and development strategy. I have argued elsewhere that past polices in much of the MENA region have not been pro-poor and inclusive, but instead have generated a pattern of high economic growth over the past decade which has been accompanied by growing inequalities and unemployment.[83] The chapters on Yemen and Egypt in this book provide more detailed evidence of how past agrarian policies in both countries have often harmed rather than helped the poorest and most vulnerable groups in society. Hence, given the importance, not just of national food security, but of household and individual food security, it becomes impossible to divorce the concern for food security from a country's broader development strategy. In this respect, a holistic comprehensive multi-agency approach to food security is required, and although Jordan has moved further than Lebanon in this respect, there is still scope for improvement.

4

FOOD SECURITY IN EGYPT

Ray Bush

Food security has been a persistent and recurrent feature of Egypt's political economy since the 1950s.[1] One of the slogans used by protestors in the January 2011 Egyptian uprising was: *'Aish, Ḥuriyyah, 'Adalah Ijtima'iyyah*, which translates into 'bread, freedom, social justice'. High levels of malnutrition, poverty and inequality underpinned the spur for the uprising as well as persistent and recurrent worker strikes and demonstrations against the old regime. This chapter tries to broaden the debate about food insecurity in Egypt beyond the usual preoccupation with macroeconomic policy and its role in facilitating food, particularly grain imports to meet local patterns of consumption. Instead, by looking at some of the pitfalls of recent policy documents, I want to indicate how important it is to include a discussion of how food insecurity impacts rural development and farmer livelihoods that have been shaped by agricultural reform since the mid-1980s. This locates farmers, especially small farmers (those with less than five feddan), to the centre of the narrative about food security in Egypt. It thus contributes to the debate about agricultural modernisation, broadly defined, and how different strategies have been shaped not simply by government policy, but by patterns of capital accumulation in Egypt that have underpinned it. I want to explore issues that help us understand the politics of food insecurity in Egypt; the role that farmers and the rural landless played in the context in which the 25 January 2011 uprising took place; and how rural social classes may play an important part in the continuing struggles for democratic deepening in contemporary Egypt.

Looking at food security in Egypt in this broader way, including an understanding of the lives and livelihoods of food producers, I try to move away from focusing primarily on the issues of wheat dependency and food subsidies that have been central to mainstream debate about Egypt's food security. I want to nudge discussion about food security towards an understanding about the ways in which political and economic power have shaped the well-being of rural producers. I will argue that food security can only be understood by exploring how rural relations of production and reproduction are shaped by political and economic power, and patterns of land ownership, and how, ultimately, Egypt's agricultural sector is unevenly integrated into the world economy. Food security can thus only be properly understood as part of broader processes of accumulation and dispossession. I will identify continuity in the way in which Egyptian farming has been understood by the Government of Egypt (GoE) and international financial institutions (IFIs) over many years. In doing this there is an opportunity to raise questions about the class character of the Egyptian state in terms of which elements of the agricultural sector and which types of owners of land-holdings have benefitted from agricultural reform since the mid-1980s. This study will also provide a context for understanding the political space for modernising agriculture after the 25 January uprising.

Food security in Egypt

Egypt's agricultural sector contributed about 14 per cent of the country's GDP in the period 2006–8.[2] Accurate figures of the proportion of Egyptians employed or engaged in agriculture are difficult to determine. It is likely to be in the range of 20–30 per cent of the labour force that cultivates about 5 per cent of Egypt's total land area.

An indication of agriculture's contribution to the national economy is evident from Figure 4.1.

Figure 4.1: Egypt: selected key data

	2007[a]	2008[a]	2009[a]	2010[a]	2011[b]	2012[c]	2013[c]
GDP[d]							
Nominal GDP (US$ bn)	132.2	164.8	187.3	214.4	231.1	262.4	302.4
Nominal GDP (E£ bn)	745	896	1,039	1,207	1,372	1,603	1,851
Real GDP growth (%)	7.1	7.2	4.7	5.1	1.8	1.6	5.2
Expenditure on GDP (% real change)[d]							
Private consumption	8.8	5.7	5.7	4.1	4.5	4.3	5.2
Government consumptiom	0.2	2.1	5.6	4.5	3.8	4.2	4.7
Gross fixed investment	23.7	14.8	-10.2	7.7	-5.6	1.4	10.8
Exports of goods & services	20.2	28.8	-14.5	-3.0	4.6	6.2	14.2
Imports of good & services	30.5	26.3	-17.9	-3.2	4.6	6.2	14.2
Origin of GDP (% real change)[d]							
Agriculture	3.7	3.3	3.2	3.5	2.7	3.6	3.5
Industry	5.9	6.1	5.0	4.3	1.1	6.8	6.9
Services	20.2	8.2	3.8	6.0	2.8	-6.0	3.4
Population and income							
Population (m)	80.1	81.5	83.0	84.5	86.1	87.7	89.4
GDP per head (US$ at PPP)	5,060	5,433	5,656	5,910[b]	5,944	6,120	6,448
Recorded unemployment (av;%)	8.9	8.7	9.4	9.0[b]	12.2	12.7	11.9

a: Actual. b: Economist Intelligence Unit estimates. c: Economist Intelligence Unit forecasts. d: Fiscal year data ending 30 June. e: Includes prepayments of medium- and long-term debt in 2006–8.
Source: EIU, 'Egypt Country Report', February 2012.

Egypt's key agricultural products are wheat, rice, cotton, beans, fruit and vegetables, and livestock—see Figure 4.1 and Figure 4.5. Despite some of the highest yields for these products for any global producer, self-sufficiency for most crops is only about 50 per cent of consumption. For vegetable oils it is 30 per cent, but self-sufficiency for rice has recently been achieved and for red meat it is about 70 per cent.[3] Egypt is the world's largest wheat importer. Wheat production only meets between 50–60 per cent of consumption. More than half its wheat imports come from Russia; the rest originates from the United States, Australia, Argentina and Kazakhstan. It is estimated that 10 million tons of wheat was imported in 2010–11 with an additional 5.6 million tons of other cereals. Wheat production in Egypt in 2011 was about 8 million tons.

Egypt's dependency upon imported grains has placed a high cost on the country's balance of payments and made the economy vulnerable to shifts in the global price of food commodities, especially grains. This was felt acutely in 2008 when a combination of international factors such as conversion of land to bio-fuel production, climate change and food used as a commodity of speculation by global investors reduced the availability of grains on the world market. The price of wheat increased by 130 per cent and rice doubled in price in the first three months of 2008. A foreboding of trouble to come in Egypt was evident as struggles over access to food led to deaths in queues for subsidised bread in Cairo.[4] Wheat prices thus put enormous pressure on the GoE budget. Wheat prices rose by 32 per cent in 2010 and rice by 42 per cent,[5] contributing to inflation levels that in August 2008 had been 24 per cent but in early 2011 were down to about 11 per cent. While it is now more readily accepted that food security does not necessarily mean food self-sufficiency, vulnerability to often dramatic and sudden shifts in the prices of grain—determined often by the global grain merchants rather than government bilateral donors or trade per se—makes it very difficult for governments to plan or manage food security.

The 'trade-based' view of food security,[6] that economies not self-sufficient in food maintain food supply by ensuring there is enough revenue to purchase food on global markets, is dependent upon the viability and productivity of the national economy. And here is a paradox. On the surface at least there is an expectation that persistent and recurrent Egyptian per capita economic growth over the past ten years of 3 per cent per annum would, all things being equal, provide a sustainable and lasting platform for poverty reduction, economic diversification and food security. Yet, all the evidence suggests that while Egypt developed, Egyptians did not. To be more precise, neo-liberal economic reform, especially after the 2004 government of Ahmed Nazif, intensified poverty and exacerbated inequality. Poverty figures may be difficult to confirm with precision, but the number of Egyptians living on less than $2 per person a day is likely to be in excess of 50 per cent. Some commentators have argued that rural poverty may be as high as 80 per cent and that figure would suggest many parallels with the proportion of poor in Zimbabwe.[7]

One of the recurrent difficulties that confronted consecutive Egyptian governments is the challenge, or reluctance, to move away from an economy shaped predominantly by access to unproductive economic activity centred on the collection of rent. Rents from labour migrant remittances, now vastly reduced after the exodus of Egyptian workers from Libya and Iraq; rent from the sale of oil and gas; and payments from the Suez Canal continue to provide the mainstay of the economy. One of Egypt's food security challenges will be the need to diversify the national economy towards production based on improvements in labour productivity, and employment creation, rather than on limited and rather fragile natural resource extraction.

A further and linked challenge is the repeated anxiety expressed by the GoE and IFIs regarding the high financial cost of maintaining Egypt's food subsidies. The two food subsidy schemes are for the production and sale of *baladi* bread—universally available irrespective of income and which contributes to the high import requirement of wheat—and the provision of fixed monthly quotas of cooking oil, sugar, rice and tea to households using ration cards.[8] Food subsidies cost the Egyptian exchequer about 2 per cent of GDP in 2008–09 or LE 21.1 billion to $3.8 billion. This was up from 0.9 per cent of GDP between 1996 and 2001. The likely reasons for the increased recent costs are the already referred to increase in global commodity prices; the depreciation of the Egyptian pound; an increased range of items entering into the food subsidy basket; and greater numbers of people becoming eligible for ration cards.[9] Food subsidies were projected to increase in Egypt's draft budget presented to parliament in June 2012.[10] Food subsidies increased by 41 per cent with the subsidy for a loaf of bread in 2012–13 set to be 24.08 piasters (about

Figure 4.2: Egypt: selected agriculture indicators

		1990–2	1995–7	2000–2	2006–8	1990–2 to 1995–7 (%) annual	1995–7 to 2000–2 (%) change	2000–2 to 2006–8 (%)
Agricultural production major items								
Tomatoes	1000 MT	4241	5634	6631	8806	5.7	3.3	4.7
Rice, paddy 1000 MT		5055	5778	6962		2.7	3.1	
Wheat	1000 MT	4456	5769	6481	7877	5.2	2.3	3.3
Buffalo milk	1000 MT	1332	1624	2110	2363	4.0	5.2	1.9
Cow milk, whole (fresh)	1000 MT	988	1298	1751	2850	5.5	6.0	8.1
Major exports, share in agriculture								
Rice, milled	%	8.9	16.3	18.2	17.1	12.1	2.3	–1.0
Cotton, lint	%	24.6	23.6	33.9	10.7	–0.8	7.2	–19.3
Oranges	%	10.3	3.0	4.9	9.1	–25.0	10.1	10.4
Potatoes	%	9.3	14.9	5.2	7.9	9.5	–21.0	6.9
Major imports, share in agriculture								
Wheat	%	26.8	27.4	21.3	27.7	0.5	–5.0	4.4
Maize	%	7.4	10.9	16.4	14.0	7.9	8.0	–2.6
Oil of palm	%	4.8	5.5	2.1	6.7	2.7	–19.4	19.2
Beef and veal, boneless	%	0.0	4.5	5.4	6.4		3.6	2.8
Soybeans	%	0.0	0.9	2.0	5.8	57.8	16.1	17.9

Source: Adapted from FAO, www.fao.org

a quarter of LE 1). This was up from 19.8 piasters a loaf in 2011—a loaf is sold to consumers for 5 piasters.[11] Food subsidies have tended to favour urban areas and, in particular, Cairo, while the majority of the poor live in Upper Egypt. Between 2004 and 2009 it is estimated that 81 per cent of Egyptian households bought *baladi* bread, an increase from 76 per cent in 2004, and 87 per cent bought both *baladi* bread and *baladi* wheat flour. 68 per cent held ration cards in the same period, up from 58.5 per cent in 2004. The increased beneficiaries lived in Upper Egypt. The debate about the scale of food subsidies has focused on the financial cost and that there is inaccurate targeting of beneficiaries. One estimate is that 28 per cent of food subsidies in 2008 did not reach intended consumers. This 'leakage' was valued at LE 5.5 billion, and the World Bank estimates that improved targeting that excluded the country's richest 40 per cent could save LE 9.5 billion or 48.6 per cent of the cost.[12]

One of Egypt's structural difficulties is that while wheat imports remain central to a subsidised food system, the increase in the price of food commodities on international markets will directly impact the cost of imports. One measure of a country's ability to finance food imports from total export revenues is the ratio of exports to food imports, and Egypt's is measured at 6.9, considerably lower than either Tunisia or Libya, which both measure at 11.[13] As the World Food Programme (WFP) has noted, 'Egypt is considered to be among the North African countries most vulnerable to food-price shocks because of the relatively weak fiscal balance to cover the cost, taking into account the large wheat and bread subsidy programme.'[14]

Advancing the food security debate?

Two recent interventions have tried to advance the debate about food insecurity in Egypt. They are both symptomatic of the continued donor and IFIs' concern that Egypt's food strategy is untenable, too financially burdensome and may sustain persistent social and political unrest.[15] The WFP and the International Food Policy Research Institute (IFPRI) have both recently made important general observations regarding the need for Egypt to broaden and diversify its national economy to become less dependent upon food imports. They both refer to the need, although perhaps almost only in passing, to include poor farmers in the network of policy reform in order to advance food security. Both thus seem to fail to grasp the need for a transformation of policy where the views and expectations of small farmers might more directly and effectively be heard. After briefly exploring these two recent interventions we can see in what ways they may help in the analysis of food security. We can then look at the positions adopted by the GoE, what persistent continuities in policy have emerged, and why it is important to look more systematically at the class interests embodied in the state, and at the likely continued trajectory of rural development after the 25 January uprising.

The WFP's recent intervention gathered data during the uprising that toppled Hosni Mubarak. The WFP report highlights the structural dependence of the Egyptian economy upon services as a proportion of national income, including labour remittances, and it tries to find the missing element in the GoE's agricultural policy, namely to explore farmer and rural landless access to food. While the focus on the latter is not sufficiently explored, the report does seek to examine some of the interlinked factors that may inhibit food security. The WFP highlights the consequences and costs to Egyptians of 250,000 returning home during the uprising and NATO bombing that toppled Muammar Gaddafi in Libya. Coupled with a fall in Egypt's tourist income there was a dramatic increase in hardship for Egyptians who were dependent upon migrant labour remittances.

Possibly as many as 2.7 million Egyptians worked abroad in 2010. This is about 10 per cent of Egypt's labour force and the migrants are a mix of skilled and unskilled workers. By 2009, worker remittances were about $8 billion, almost equivalent to the country's Foreign Direct Investment and represented 5 per cent of GDP.[16] The return of migrants at a time of economic downturn jeopardised the ability of the GoE to address issues of food security and, in particular, to engage with reducing rural poverty. As the WFP notes:

The main underlying factors of food insecurity among Egyptian households are: low income, loss of purchasing power due to increased cost of living and unemployment, low agricultural production, lack of access to social assistance systems (including subsidized food), and low access to good quality water, sanitation and health services. Poverty is a critical structural factor of food insecurity.[17]

Although an overall reduction in levels of poverty can be seen—between 2005 and 2008, the poverty level dropped from 23 per cent to 19 per cent—a recent GoE household income and expenditure and consumption survey (HIES) indicated a return to 22 per cent of the population defined as poor in 2008–09. Moreover, extreme poverty—the inability to meet basic food needs—was 6 per cent of the total population, but 9 per cent in the countryside. Inequality was stark with 40 per cent of households controlling less than a quarter of the country's total income.[18] The majority of Egypt's poor, probably as many as 80 per cent, lived in the rural areas and most of these in Upper Egypt.

The WFP has well-established criteria for assessing household vulnerability to food insecurity. It includes an assessment of the education level of the household head, per capita food expenditures during the previous seven days in which data is collected, per capita income and per capita asset ownership. The WFP asserts that:

Typically, poor households have limited or no access to land, fragmented land plots, small livestock numbers, little or no education, no marketable skills, limited access to health and other social services, unstable employment (e.g. in construction or agriculture) and high dependency ratio.[19]

And on the basis of the WFP's criteria of income and asset ownership together with education levels, about one-fifth of households in Upper and Lower Egypt and major cities were 'highly vulnerable' to food insecurity in 2008. The GoE HIES survey during 2008–09 estimated that 22 per cent of rural households and 17 per cent of urban households consumed less than the minimum required 2,100 kilocalorie per capita. The WFP also notes that there is a paradox that needs further investigation. While aggregate national figures for kilocalorie per capita consumption is high, at about 2,780 kilocalories, there is both high under-nutrition among children and over-nutrition among young people and adults. More children under five years of age were stunted in 2008 than they were in 2005, which amounted to as many as 29 per cent of all children. There was also evidence of persistent micronutrient deficiencies, with more than half of women twenty to fifty years old and 40 per cent of children under five in 2010 suffering from anaemia.

The WFP concludes that Egypt needs to improve the nutritional quality of subsidies, create employment opportunities, develop human capacity and training, provide micro credit and improve access to agricultural inputs. In addition, it recommends that there should be 'facilitation of access to land and to extension services, school feeding, upgrading of water and sanitation systems and improved quality of health and education services'.[20] This might be an appropriate policy 'shopping list' but it would need a considerable rethink at the level of rural development strategy if it were to be seen as anything other than GoE rhetoric. One of the GoE's challenges partly recognised by the WFP is the difficulty in getting reliable and accurate data and evidence from Egypt in relation to food security. To this effect, the WFP suggests the need for more studies on the impact of returning labour migrants.

Assembling reliable data on food security is a major issue and Egypt is not an exception.[21] The issue of data collection and its reliability, however, seems not to be much reflected upon in Egypt. That may be because closer inspection of actual or locally perceived livelihoods would challenge GoE policy and would likely reveal higher levels of, among other things, rural and urban poverty than are currently recorded. Under-reporting for politically sensitive reasons or poor data collection is one thing, but we also know that using headcount poverty figures, for example, based on income or purchasing power parity cannot adequately grasp how poverty is created and reproduced.[22] To do this we need to inquire into how wealth is produced, who produces it, under what conditions of ownership and control, and who or which social classes access surpluses produced. There is also evidence that enumerators of food security and household income and expenditure surveys may not adequately investigate or record what they find.[23]

The need to improve data and capacity for evidence-based decision-making is one of three policy recommendations offered by the IFPRI's recent analysis of policy and investments for poverty reduction and food security in the Arab world.[24] The IFPRI also recommended fostering economic growth that enhances national and household food security along with improved and more efficient public spending. In facilitating this list of policy objectives, the IFPRI falls back onto the need for better governance in the Middle East. It also calls for a national dialogue about 'societies' joint vision and economic development strategies'. Implying that somehow the Arab world has been sleeping, the IFPRI notes: 'The Arab world is awake' and the:

Successful design and implementation of these strategies [for poverty reduction and food security] will require visionary leadership, sound laws and institutions, politicians who are accountable and listen to the voices of the people, and civil society that is patient and accepts the tenets of democracy.[25]

Citing the World Bank and International Monetary Fund (IMF) as well as a range of academic authors, the IFPRI asserts that for the Middle

East to prosper in the twenty-first century, policies of economic diversification are necessary. So too is market liberalisation, 'a pro poor growth focus, a stronger role for the private sector, an increased focus on improving income disparities, a shift from subsidies to targeted income transfers, and better governance'.[26]

Despite the lament regarding the difficulty of getting accurate food security data, the IFPRI is confident that its use of a 'unique and innovative combination of data sets'[27] ranging from UN agencies to the World Bank provides a comprehensive overview of key issues of concern. One issue consistent across most commentary on food insecurity is the shrinking of regional per capita spending on agriculture by 3.8 per cent annually. Figure 4.3 indicates that the deterioration in per capita spending on agriculture in Egypt has been running at almost twice the regional average decline. This decline is not a recent phenomenon. Gross investment in agriculture between 1980 and 1992 fell in Egypt by 31 per cent to 23 per cent. Thus, the so-called boom years of '*infitah*' and oil-led development were also years of agricultural neglect.[28]

Figure 4.3: Annual growth of public spending per capita, 2000–7 (%)

	Agriculture	Education	Health	Infra-structure	Social protection	Total	Agexp/AgVa
Egypt	– 6.1	0.2	0.2	– 2.2	76.6	5.5	8.5
FS	4.0	1.7	1.7	12.4	10.1	7.2	– 2.1
Arab-TI	1.1	2.4	9.0	– 0.1	12.8	5.4	0.6
LAC	– 0.8	10.9	24.6	1.2	11.5	10.4	4.7
SSA	6.6	6.7	11.8	4.2	12.9	5.4	– 3.7

Source: Breisinger et al., 'Beyond the Arab awakening', p. 24.
Key: FS, Food-secure Arab states; Arab-TI, Arab League countries plus Turkey and Iran; LAC, Latin America and the Caribbean region; SSA, sub-Saharan Africa.

In addition to declines in agricultural investment across the Arab world—the exception in the Middle East being Turkey and Iran—the IFPRI has stressed the need to establish a new framework for linking food security and poverty to economic and social development. Poverty and food security are closely linked because of the high vulnerability to 'food related "external shocks"'.[29] The IFPRI notes the need to understand that food security is shaped by macroeconomic and trade-related issues, specifically the share of food imports divided by total exports plus net remittance inflows. The IFPRI then uses the extent of child under-nutrition as a micro food security indicator.

Figure 4.4: Public spending by sector, 2007 (%)

	Agriculture	Education	Health	Infra-structure	Social protection	Total	Agexp/ AgVa
Egypt	0.8	3.7	3.7	0.5	7.3	26.9	5.8
FS	0.2	3.7	1.7	0.7	6.1	35.6	29.2
Arab-TI	0.7	3.0	2.5	0.9	4.8	27.3	7.0
LAC	0.3	3.6	2.7	0.3	1.3	15.7	4.7
SSA	0.8	2.8	1.2	0.6	0.8	17.5	2.6

Source: Breisinger et al., 'Beyond the Arab awakening', p. 23.
Key: FS, Food-secure Arab states; Arab-TI, Arab League countries plus Turkey and Iran; LAC, Latin America and the Caribbean region; SSA, sub-Saharan Africa.

A consequence of the 'Arab Awakenings' is likely to be increased expectations to meet food security needs, but the IFPRI indicates that Egypt is rated as having a persistent 'serious' condition of food insecurity as noted in Figure 4.5. The policy recommendations that follow from the IFPRI's analysis include a somewhat familiar checklist of more effective food targeting of subsidies for the poorest, employment creation through labour-intensive public works programmes, and improvements in women's health and education. Decision-making to ensure the delivery of these policies, moreover, will need to move away from historically determined top-down approaches and be based instead upon more inclusive measures for economic transformation. Successful decision-making must be evidence-based and a collaborative effort must be made between government, civil society, and the private sector.[30]

The struggle for democratic liberalisation was at the heart of the 25 January uprising, and both of the recent reports on food security just reviewed affirm the need for democratic deepening to run alongside macroeconomic policy and some rural development reform. Where both sets of analyses are limited in scope is in the failure to explore issues of land access and distribution as a factor in inhibiting or improving the lives of the majority of food producers, and thus advancing food security that can also promote the expansion of rural development broadly

Figure 4.5: Food-insecurity risk typology

	Food imports (% of GDP)	Total exports of goods and services (% of GDP)	Remittances (net inflows, % of GDP)	Macro food security (food imports/ total exports + net remittances)	Micro food security (% of stunted children)	Overall food security (average of macro and micro indicators)	Food security status
Egypt	3.2	31.1	5.3	8.7	30.7	19.7[1]	serious

Note:[1] = 2008.
Source: Breisinger et al., 'Arab awakening', p. 34.

defined. Access to land became a political weapon under the erstwhile regime of Hosni Mubarak. What emerged with effectively the blessing of the IFIs and U.S. Agency for International Development (USAID) as policy recommendations were for state withdrawal from the agricultural sector. In particular, by revoking Nasserist legislation that protected the rights of tenants, the now deposed National Democratic Party (NDP) rewarded a land-owning parliament with opportunities for wealth expansion. In contrast, landless and near landless Egyptian farmers were marginalised and impoverished as economic reform progressed. Investment went to large landowners in the newly reclaimed desert lands for promoting a trade-based view of food security and with it all the machinations of crony and corrupt land practices that became the hallmark of the Mubarak regime.[31] In contrast, investment and support for smallholders in the Delta was neglected.

Reforming agriculture and transforming livelihoods

Economic liberalisation in Egypt's agricultural sector began in the mid-1980s. Accompanying policy reform was a more open contestation over the terms and conditions of access to land. At the centre of the strategy was the promotion of market liberalisation, privatisation of input provision and expansion of horticultural production for export.[32] Decades of what were seen to be years of lamentable or, at best, stagnant agricultural economic growth were used as the rationale to accelerate a programme of 'de-Nasserisation' that had begun with President Anwar Sadat (1970–81). Gamal Abdel Nasser's regime had redistributed about one-seventh of the country's cultivable land from large landowners to the landless and near landless. For the first time he gave tenants, whose lives were wretched and impoverished before the revolution, rights in perpetuity, fixed rents in proportion to a land tax, and subsidised access to inputs and marketing outlets that were not controlled by a *pasha* class of large landowners.[33] Nasser reduced the ceilings on landholdings from 200 feddan in 1952 to 100 feddan in 1961, and he established agricultural cooperatives that were intended to further marginalise the political and economic power of large landowners.

Nasser's land reforms certainly contributed to improving rural livelihoods and boosting small farmer incomes,[34] but they failed to entirely break the power of the landlords or 'blue *galabia*' whose power was supported by Sadat's policies of economic liberalisation. *Infitah* began with the return of land to landowners whom Nasser had dispossessed. Law 69 of 1974 restored 147,000 feddan to former owners. Sadat also asserted that economic liberalisation would create a Cairo real-estate boom that would pull inward investment into construction and provide trickle-down benefit to the broader Egyptian economy. Yet, *infitah* increased foreign debt, led to food riots in 1977 and to Sadat's assassination in October 1981. Food insecurity during Sadat's presidency increased. Import of grains, especially wheat, increased following closer ties with the United States who were keen to reduce the Soviet Union's influence on Cairo.[35] And there was a sharp decline during the Sadat years, as noted earlier, of gross investment in agriculture.

Anwar Sadat abolished the Egyptian state's role as the custodian of land. It was easy for Hosni Mubarak to inherit the liberalising zeal that, among other things, returned land to owners, attacked tenant rights and undermined the possibility of strengthening the livelihoods of Egypt's smallholders. The policies that emerged were driven by the enthusiastic Minister of Agriculture Yusuf Wali. He was deputy prime minister and general secretary of the ruling NDP. Wali was also a large landowner and was stripped of his official positions in 2004 following allegations of corruption. He was again under investigation after the 25 January uprising for allegations of graft while he was minister of agriculture. Wali entrenched landowner interests and the power of a landowning parliament. In doing so, the agricultural counter-revolution created tensions between sections of the landed elite and NDP cronies. The latter had a range of cross-cutting economic interests in business and manufacturing, and the desire to develop the new desert reclaimed lands rather than consider modernisation and investment in the Delta and Upper Egypt.

There are two key issues that drove the agricultural reforms of the 1980s and 1990s and which have arguably impacted conditions for improving food security. The first was the view that an agricultural crisis of production had emerged because of too much state involvement and an absence of market efficiency in allocating resources in the sector. What followed was a reform of prices, cropping patterns and credit. The second key issue that drove reform was the fixation with returning land to landowners who had been dispossessed by Nasser's land reforms. This led to Law 96 of 1992, fully effective in 1997. This was to change the legal structures of land tenancy and to accelerate rural-social differentiation. It also created conditions whereby heirs of land that had been confiscated by Nasser's legislation emerged to reclaim lost assets. Claims emerged, backed by the illegal and widespread use of violence, to retake not only tenancies that were covered by Law 96, but also land-reform affected land and religiously-endowed land, or *Awqaf*. This politicised land immensely. Both these broad factors impacted on Egypt's food security as a trade-based theory of comparative advantage became entrenched and eclipsed the concern for farmer livelihoods and food sovereignty.[36] Agricultural reform created a legacy that shaped post–2000 policy and possibly also any prospect for radical agricultural transformation after 25 January 2011.

Prices, markets and commodities

Paralleling and then acting as a spur to Yusuf Wali's reforming zeal of the agricultural sector was a close relationship between the Ministry of Agriculture and Land Reclamation (MALR) and USAID. Reform of agriculture from 1986 predated Egypt's economic reform agenda adopted between the GoE and the World Bank in 1991. Agreement with the World Bank was part of the reward to the GoE for supporting the removal of Saddam's forces from Kuwait. Wali's reforms were accompanied by USAID's programme of Agricultural Production and Credit 1986–96, valued at $289 million, and the Agricultural Policy and Reform Programme that followed it. Since the mid-1980s USAID provided more than $1.26 billion for reform of the agricultural sector. USAID blamed excessive state intervention for poor agricultural performance of less than 1 per cent growth per annum in the 1960s and 1970s. The liberalisation of the agricultural sector, improved farmgate pricing and crop mix, and the expansion of wheat production and cultivable area were all explained as a result of the new market-driven opportunities.[37] Egypt's cultivated area increased from 6.2 million feddan in 1981 to 7.6 million in 1993, (compare figures in Figure 4.6) and there were increases in the production of wheat—that doubled between 1986 and 1992—maize and rice.

The programmes of reform, however, may not have been as successful as claimed by the GoE and the IFIs, and the rate of initial success does not seem to have been sustained.[38] Reformers focused on changes in production and cropping patterns that took place in the early phase of reform from 1986 until the early 1990s. Initial success was not sustained and it is likely that increased recorded output was not the result of economic liberalisation per se, but, rather, reduced reluctance that farmers had in revealing what was actually produced.[39] It is also likely that the decline in government subsidies and access to credit, seed and fertiliser, as well as the increase in costs of irrigation, added to rural unemployment and poverty. One estimate was that between 1990 and 1995, the agricultural sector lost 700,000 jobs.[40]

The clear emphasis from USAID and from the MALR was the adoption of a US farm model of extensive capital-intensive agriculture driven by market liberalisation and export-led growth. Figure 4.6 indicates the variations in growth of cropped areas and cropping patterns of Egypt's major crops from before economic liberalisation.

Figure 4.6: The cropped areas and cropping pattern of main crops

Crops	1980		1990		2007	
	1,000 feddan	%	1,000 feddan	%	1,000 feddan	%
Wheat	132	11.9	1955	16.1	2716	17.7
Maize	1906	17.1	1975	16.2	1848	12.1
Rice	970	8.7	1036	8.5	1673	10.9
Cotton	1245	11.2	993	8.5	575	3.8
Sugar beet	–	–	34	0.3	248	1.6
Total field crops	**9745**	**87.6**	**1091**	**83.7**	**12022**	**78.3**
Total vegetable crops	**1035**	**9.3**	**1123**	**9.2**	**2014**	**13.1**
Total fruit crops	**350**	**3.1**	**866**	**7.1**	**1310**	**8.5**
Total cropped area	**11130**	**–**	**12181**	**–**	**15346**	**–**

Source: Arab Republic of Egypt, *Sustainable Agricultural Development*, 2009, p. 39.

Despite some increases in cropped areas for the major crops, a persistent shortcoming of the agricultural reform project has been the failure to deliver export-led growth that was seen to improve Egypt's food security. A difficulty is that most agricultural imports to Egypt—wheat, edible oils and sugar—are of a low elasticity of demand. And the cost of wheat imports increased, for example, from $94 million 2002–03 to $215 million 2003–04. In contrast, Egypt's exports—rice, vegetables, and cotton—have high elasticity. The prices of cotton and rice both fell in the early 2000s when the GoE asserted that growth in horticulture could convert Egypt into another Mexico. The drive from USAID was for Egypt to promote agricultural export growth and to do so promoting comparative advantage. Yet, the rhetoric that Egypt could use its climate and productive soils to ensure three crops a year failed to explore a number of continuing concerns. First, regional competitors, Israel, Turkey and Palestine, were better equipped to deliver what Egypt's MALR tried to do. Second, there were persistent bureaucratic and transport limitations in Egypt and vulnerability to global shifts in demand linked to production of high-value and low-nutritious foodstuffs for European dinner tables. Evidence for the over-production of strawberries, for example, was everywhere on Cairo streets in the early 1990s as wasted fruit filled street gutters, which did not constitute a robust strategy for food security.

The second element of the Wali reforms was Law 96 of 1992. After a five-year transition period (during which the GoE had expressed fears that there might be fierce opposition to the legislation) Law 96 of 1992 revoked the rights to land-in-perpetuity that Nasser had given tenants. In the early 1990s, there may have been about one million tenant farmers. In fact, as with much other data, there was no exact figure for the number of tenants. The failure to know exactly how many would be affected by the legislation was a criticism at the time. The Shura Council, Egypt's upper house, for example, indicated that there were 2.5 million tenants in 1992 farming between 25–30 per cent of Egypt's cultivated area and the vast majority worked up to 5 feddan. The new legislation returned land to owners who were seen to have suffered from rent controls. During the transition period 1992–97, tenant rents increased from seven to twenty-two times the land tax. Rents in Dakahlia in the Delta, for instance, which had been about LE 200 per feddan before 1992, rose to LE 2500 in 1997 and were between LE 4800 and LE 6000 per feddan in 2007.[41]

Law 96 of 1992 has had two long-lasting consequences. One has been the re-politicisation of land where land as a commodity has more clearly become an arena of contestation. Struggles over access to land, its allocation and the values attached to it grew significantly during the Mubarak period on a scale that exceeded anything before in Egypt's history. It also led to heightened levels of rural violence and struggles against rural dispossession.[42] Violence was evident not only at the time of the implementation of the legislation, but continues to the contemporary period. The Sons of the Soil Land Centre in Cairo estimated that between 2009 and 2010, there were at least 499 deaths, 2,517 injuries and 3,020 arrests resulting from rural conflicts and struggles over ownership, tenancy, demarcations and irrigation.[43] The second long-lasting consequence of Law 96 of 1992 is the impact on rural-social differentiation. Rural violence, persistent struggles over land access, and the history of systemic and routine torture of farmers who resisted changes in their legal status as tenants, have been accompanied by the reduction in the size of the landholding category 'fully cash paid tenancies'.[44] Habib Ayeb has noted that perhaps as many as 45 per cent of tenant farmers abandoned their lands between 1992 and 1997.[45] The impact on tenancy, particularly on female-headed households, has been dramatic and unsettling for food security. Landowners it seems were reluctant to renew tenancies with women. They preferred to try and rent to male farmers who were from outside the village, who may therefore have had less local influence in mobilising opposition to the higher rents. Female-headed households were seen as possibly being unreliable in paying the new rents. The introduction of annual contracts rather than rights in perpetuity ensured farmers who did renew, or were able to access new tenancies, would not make long-term investments in the land. Law 96 of 1992 militated against long-term stable conditions for farmer investments that would enhance prospects for food security.

In addition to the pressure on tenants and the social relations of production that underpin the land-holding category of tenancy there has been an increase in the number of farmers that have fallen into the category of holding less than 1 feddan. According to calculations made by Ayeb from the 1990 and 2000 GoE agricultural censuses, it is likely that 44 per cent of farmers in 2010 had landholdings of 1 feddan or less. 68 per cent of farmers had less than 2 feddan and 93 per cent had less than 5 feddan. This meant that nearly 90 per cent of land was held by smallholder famers with less than 5 feddan, but 3 per cent of landowners controlled 33.5 per cent of agricultural land.[46] They have an average of more than 10 feddan each. Inequality in landholdings has intensified for those with more than 10 feddan compared with those of less than 5 feddan. Between 1990 and 2000, the number of farms of less than one feddan increased from 36.7 per cent of the total holdings to 43.5 per cent.

New rhetoric and old policy

The GoE strategy for food security has been to integrate Egypt's agricultural sector more effectively into international trade and to do so by promoting capital-intensive export agriculture. The period of economic adjustment led to the neglect of agriculture in the old lands in the Delta and it marginalised small farmers cultivating less than 5 feddan. It is even the case that the influence of 'social Darwinism',[47] where social differentiation in the countryside became more acute, impacted deleteriously what historically may have been seen as medium to large farmers with 5–20 feddan.

During the 1990s, Hosni Mubarak and the MALR had skewed agricultural spending towards large-scale scheme agriculture. The largest of these was at Toshka in the New Valley Governorate to the west of Luxor, and there were also large schemes in Sinai and the northern desert. Toshka covered an area roughly equal to 40 per cent of Egypt's land area with a budget of $86.5 billion 1997–2017. The scheme was initiated without an adequate environmental impact study and became effectively Mubarak's pyramid—something to establish his legacy. The scheme has been mired in controversy. There have been struggles to find adequate and sustainable investment resources, mostly from Saudi and the Gulf, and the water allocated to it from Lake Nasser has for years reduced the irrigation flows to the Delta. The scheme was intended as a boost for the export of horticultural products and to attract labour from an 'overpopulated' Delta, but it has achieved neither.[48]

In the 1990s and early new millennium, the GoE 'strategy' to invest resources in large-scale schemes served to shift the focus of Egypt's food security debate. The focus took on a new momentum of government action to deliver food security and reduce poverty. The strategy, however, remained focused on a trade-based perspective. Egypt's natural greenhouse was seen to be able to deliver agricultural growth that would generate higher levels of food self-sufficiency while also addressing the country's agricultural crisis. It is not surprising that the characterisation of Egypt's food and agricultural crisis as one of food import dependency determined the type of policy initiatives put forward. That dependency had to be reduced by promoting greater integration of Egypt's food system into the world economy. There has been a persistent refusal to prioritise issues of rural people's livelihoods and of the need to improve household access to land and work. There has also been a refusal to consider the long-term processes that shape the character of rural power and politics. These include the character of social differentiation and inequality and gender divisions of labour including the role that women play as heads of households and the particular difficulties that they are confronted with. The debate about food security has been substituted for rural development and agricultural modernisation that might instead have placed food sovereignty in the context of supporting the rural households that are both producers and consumers of food. There has been an almost total neglect of farmers with less than 5 feddan of land, the majority of whom struggle for access to food for self-provisioning.

The preoccupation with targeting larger landholders as the social category that will lift Egypt out of food import dependency was confirmed by a GoE policy document in 2009.[49] This may not be advanced by a new GoE, but, even if it is not, the continuity in policy statements that have emerged from the MALR since January 2011 have not suggested a dramatic change of priority.[50] The policy vision of the recent document is:

To achieve a comprehensive economic and social development based on a dynamic agricultural sector capable of sustained and rapid growth, while paying a special attention to helping the underprivileged social groups and reducing rural poverty.

And its declared mission is:

Modernizing Egyptian agriculture based on achieving food security and improving the livelihood of the rural inhabitants, through the efficient use of development resources, the utilization of the geopolitical and environmental advantages, and the comparative advantages of the different agro-ecological regions.[51]

The range of policy objectives issued by the MALR includes attempts to use Egypt's resources sustainably, to increase food security of strategic food commodities, to improve competitiveness in international agricultural markets and to improve rural living standards. The policy document is mindful of the food crisis from 2006 and, as a result, wants to improve Egypt's levels of food self-sufficiency in strategic commodities. The goal is to improve the rate of food self-sufficiency from 54 per cent to 81 per cent for wheat; from 53 per cent to 92 per cent for maize; from 77 per cent to 93 per cent for sugar; and dramatically increase levels for red meat and fish by 2030. The proposed mechanism for achieving enhanced food security is twofold. The first is to improve the agricultural policy environment. Evidently somewhat frustrated at limited success from twenty-six years of economic reform, the MALR asserts the need for stronger laws to establish a 'single entity' for the allocation of agricultural investments; a review of law and procedures for the allocation of land and land titles; and an improvement in the use of local assets as collateral so that farmers can have better access to credit. The second mechanism to enhance food security is to boost agricultural investment. The MALR estimates the need for an investment of LE 500 billion to achieve a growth rate of 4 per cent 2009–30 and LE 640 for a 5 per cent rate of growth. It therefore called for an increase in agricultural investment from LE 8.4 billion in 2008 to LE 13.4 billion in 2009.[52]

In the context of employing a more efficient policy environment to deliver reforms in order to boost agricultural production, the agricultural development strategy to 2030 has also indicated that: 'Improving the living standards of rural inhabitants is the core of the strategy vision and mission.'[53] The mechanisms for doing this are similar to both previous GoE policy initiatives discussed and those of the WFP and IFPRI. These are namely top-down initiatives established to improve agricultural production and marketing, and the promotion of small farmers' associations, especially in marketing and 'promoting the role of women' in the different fields of rural development.[54]

Bringing the farmers back in?

There has been a singular and overwhelmingly persistent feature in the debate about Egypt's food security, which is the substitution of meaningful debate and discussion about rural development by preoccupation with economic liberalisation. Underpinning the 'non-debate' within policy circles of the GoE and the IFIs has been an attempt to promote an agricultural strategy without farmers.

The foregrounding of the 1991 Economic Reform and Structural Adjustment Programme with agricultural reform from the mid-1980s could have led to a more nuanced approach to bolster rural incomes and livelihoods as a precondition to improve food security. Instead, the emphasis on the primacy of 'the market' and a trade-driven approach to food security concentrated on boosting the economic well-being of larger landholders, allocating resources to new land development and asserting that improvement in horticulture would provide stable income to help purchase the country's food needs. Thus, food sovereignty for the producers of food was substituted by an idea of food security for the nation. This was well captured by posters advocating the re-election of Hosni Mubarak in presidential 'campaigns' from 2000. In these posters, Mubarak was often portrayed standing among tall sheaths of wheat ready to be harvested, and was caricatured as a father of the nation advancing the country's food security. This was something deposed president Morsi also tried to emulate, especially in May 2013 when he asserted that Egypt would be self sufficient in wheat within four years—something quickly corrected by the MALR as an 'aspiration'.

The embrace of economic liberalisation, albeit in a partial and uneven way, breached a national consensus or corporatism that had been a central feature of Egyptian politics since Nasser. This was a consensus of reciprocity (not always adhered to) whereby the state would support farmers (and workers) in return for a degree of political compliance. The 'bargain' was not universally adhered to and peasants often reacted against challenges to their 'autonomy', but after Nasser's demise the attacks on the livelihoods of smallholder farmers became extensive. Policy reform of agricultural liberalisation dismantled the support structures that assisted small farmers. Although elements of the consensus remained, especially with the persistence of food subsidies since the mid-1980s, the GoE accelerated a process of rural dispossession that endangered small farmers' ability to feed their households. The uneven retrenchment of the state and its removal of subsidies for agricultural inputs and marketing; the lack of access to credit; and declines in extension service provision increased the risks confronting small farmers. In particular, smallholders were challenged by increases in rents and spiralling input prices for seeds, fertilisers and pesticides not met by increased farmgate prices for agricultural crops. In one small study of ten medium-sized landholding farmers in a village south of Minya, respondents were most vexed by fluctuations in market prices for their crops and high prices for inputs, especially seeds, fertilisers and irrigation. It was significant that while many had been critical of the corrupt practices of the previous agricultural cooperatives, they now lament their absence.[55]

In other studies, this time in Dakahlia in Egypt's Delta, ten case-studies of female-headed households indicated enormous stress and anxiety resulting from their marginalisation in the policies of agricultural modernisation, especially after the mid-1990s: they were very food insecure.[56] Each recounted tales of debt and impoverishment and immense concern for their own and their families' poor health. They were also worried about their children, the struggle to get them educated, the harsh conditions of day labouring that some forced to leave school had to endure and the difficulties associated with the daily grind of trying to access food.

When examining households that experience famine, it has long been one of the greatest ironies that it is the producers of food who are the first to suffer. Smallholder households eke out an existence and are not exempt from the fear and reality of slipping into starvation. This seems dramatic, but was evident in the villages in Dakhlia and near Minya and has become a crisis that challenges the rural social fabric. Food insecurity threatens rural conditions of existence. Female respondents would often recall strains in the community where the opportunity to try and socialise with neighbours had diminished. Their communities were also locations of increased crime, not least of which consisted of household thefts and thefts of crops from the fields. Theft and rural violence had increased as household debt soared and when there was little opportunity for work. In desperation for work, several women in the Dakhalia village recounted stories of how they had found employment as cleaners in a neighbouring town. This was hitherto unheard of—it was often against the wishes, and, in some cases, without the recognised knowledge of male household members. Yet, this was how they were able to feed their family. Village life is of course always in flux. These examples of tension are not to romanticise the village nor to suggest a traditional unchanging status within communities that has suddenly been affected by crisis. It is instead to report some important empirical themes that may well be generalisable and, if they are, will need to be examined closely in any food security initiatives.

The evidence seems to suggest a multifaceted rural social structure where it is impossible to talk only of smallholder farmers. The implication of the term 'smallholders' is that all they do is farm on their own or other people's land. But the matrix of relations that farmers engage with is complex and extensive. Talking about the complexity of tenancy relations in Upper Egypt, one commentator spoke of a tenancy web which involved a range of different ownership and farming practices.[57] It is clear that myriad social relations exist in farming communities and this raises the importance of understanding the different needs and aspirations of different categories of labour. These go beyond categories of ownership and non-ownership of land or simple tenancy or sharecropping relations. It also requires an exploration of labour migration and the different length and distances involved in migration as well as types of remittance. I have noted how social differentiation has been shaped by government policy and rhetoric about food security, but, to get a handle on who exactly is affected by shifts in the ability to access food, it is necessary to engage more precisely with the different types of agricultural modernisation efforts that have taken place in Egypt over the past thirty years. It is then necessary to look at the different types of rural labour that are evident and what kinds of relations of power and authority, and dominance and subordination, they may be part of in the transformation of rural life, and how these impact food production and strategies for the development of capitalism in agriculture.[58]

One of the consequences of agricultural modernisation that has pushed small farmers away from access to inputs, land and resources, has been the empowerment of larger landholders and merchants. Rural markets have not become more competitive. They are arenas for the rich and powerful to exact increased profits from farmers who have very limited access to alternative sources of farming, inputs or other income earning possibilities. Market reform has not created conditions for generalised and shared rural accumulation and increased productivity. It seems instead to have led to a stymied level of rural growth and considerable resentment by farmers against merchant monopoly. Resentment has also led to farmer resistance and struggles against attempts of landowners to reclaim land from the 1950s.

Small farmers have developed links with advocacy organisations and NGOs to advance the defence of their land. After 1997, for example, the Peasant Solidarity Committee (PSC) offered a radical interpretation for farmers to resist land loss and promote farmer solidarity. It also offered advice on farming techniques and knowledge of contrasting peasant experiences across Egypt.[59] The PSC also linked with networks of resistance that challenged GoE policy in the build-up to the 25 January uprising. Links were made with human rights organisations and with legal representatives that defended farmers who may have been dispossessed and who had been arrested and tortured in detention.[60] One of the most infamous cases of dispossession was in Sarandu as the large Nawwar landowning family pressurised tenants over dispossession after Law 96 of 1992. Many other struggles took place across the Delta, and beyond, as farmers resisted attempts by landowners to take advantage of changes in tenure to displace farmers from the land.

Independent peasant unions have emerged since 25 January. They have been spontaneous and linked to urban-based activists.[61] Rural struggles and contested fights over access to land continue, although the level of mobilisation by farmers in Cairo seems to have diminished after unprecedented numbers of farmers converged on the city in April 2011.

GoE policy has seen food security in terms of macroeconomic and large-scale farming techniques of managing income flows to enable the purchase of high volumes of wheat to meet the food needs of Egyptians, especially Cairene residents. Politically, this has been an essential element of maintaining urban peace. However, there continues to be pressure from local policymakers in the GoE and from the IFIs to reduce subsidies and wheat import dependency. This pressure has not yet created conditions for an innovative and imaginative or radical strategy for rural development. Food security debates will, however, need to more effectively embrace the needs of the producers of food in the Delta and in Upper Egypt if the slogans of the Egyptian uprising are to be delivered by the new president and government in Cairo.

5

PROSPECTS FOR FOOD SELF-SUFFICIENCY
IN IRAN IN 2025

Habibollah Salami, Toktam Mohtashami
and *Mohamad Saeid Noori Naeini*

Meeting the needs of the growing and increasingly urbanised population in Iran requires a substantial increase in food supply. Alleviating poverty and improving the level of food security depends, to a large extent, on sustainable agricultural development, as most rural communities depend heavily on the agricultural sector as their source of employment and income generation. In addition, enhanced domestic production of food commodities is a matter of cultural and political pride in Iran. Although domestic production of all food requirements might be hard to justify purely on the basis of economic principles, the full food-sufficiency strategy is supported both by the government and the people in Iran.[1] All governments in Iran after the 1979 Islamic Revolution have sought self-sufficiency in foodstuffs as a major objective in the overall goals of agricultural as well as economic development in the country. This strategy is backed by a variety of price and non-price support policies,

115

including subsidised credits and inputs; subsidised insurance against natural hazard; cheap foreign currency; guaranteed commodity prices; tax exemptions; and tariff protection to agricultural producers, specifically for foodstuff producers.

The role of agriculture in poverty reduction and income creation is an important element of food security. Prominent scholars conducting research in rural areas in developing countries have empirically demonstrated the links between agricultural development and poverty reduction.[2] The critical role of agriculture has been acknowledged in the eight Millennium Development Goals agreed to in 2000 by United Nations member states, particularly for its role in reducing hunger, fostering gender equality and maintaining a sustainable management of the environment.[3] It is also important to note that sustainable agricultural and rural development has been highly prioritised within 'The Strategic Framework for FAO 2000–2015'.[4]

This chapter provides a review of the conditions for food self-sufficiency in Iran, examining the past trends of self-sufficiency, and attempting to provide some critical analysis for what the future prospects of food self-sufficiency in 2025 look like for Iran.

Agriculture in Iran

From 162,855 thousand hectares of Iran's total surface area, roughly one-third is considered suitable for farming.[5] From this, only about 12 per cent is under cultivation. This is mainly due to poor soil conditions and inadequate irrigation water. The irrigated area is less than one-third of the cultivated area, and the rest is devoted to dry farming. Agriculture in Iran is dominated by small-scale, private producers. The contribution of agriculture in overall GDP based on the 2011 data is 11.2 per cent.[6] Agriculture also provides more than 20 per cent of employment, out of which 33 per cent is occupied by female workers.

The diverse geographical characteristics of the country and the multiplicity of climatic zones make it possible to cultivate a diverse variety of crops, including cereals (wheat, barley, rice and corn); fruits (dates, figs, pomegranates, melons and grapes); vegetables; cotton, sugar beets and sugar cane; pistachios; nuts; olives; spices like saffron; raisins; tea; tobacco; and medicinal plants. Wheat, rice and barley are the country's major crops. Iran is the twelfth leading producer of wheat in the world, with an average production of 14 million tons in 2011.[7]

Methodological framework

In this chapter, we aim to project the demand and supply of major food commodities in Iran for the year 2025,[8] and hence forecast both levels of national food self-sufficiency and food per capita consumption. Our projections are based on a policy simulation model specifically developed for Iran.

The Iranian policy simulation model is an integration of the multi-market partial equilibrium model, the Positive Mathematical Programming (PMP) model, and time series econometric models (see Appendix 2). Integration of these models was established in order to increase the efficiency of the model in impact analysis of various assumptions. The multi-market partial equilibrium model is the core of the model. It includes equations of supply and demand, trade, price transmission and market equilibrium.[9] The PMP method, which models provincial (regional) activities in the crop sector, maximises the regional total gross margin, given land and irrigation water availability constraints. Marginal cost functions in these PMP models estimated by maximum entropy and these regional models are then aggregated at national levels in order to estimate frontier cost function. Provincial PMP models are used to project supply of selected crops.[10] Results from these PMP models are integrated to the designed partial equilibrium model to reach equilibrium prices that in the next step again feed into the supply model until convergence is achieved. The outcome of this iterative process is equilibrium prices and quantities in the target year 2025.

Time series econometric models are used to forecast the initial prices to be fed into PMP models, the change in land productivity, the supply of horticultural products and demand for the selected food commodities. Demands for these commodities are estimated for urban and rural households separately.

The market model covers seven farm crops, including wheat, rice, cereals, sugar beet, oilseed, potato and onion, and four horticultural products namely, apple, orange, date and grape. In projecting supply of the crops, it is assumed that current agricultural and trade policies will continue in the future. However, the effects of some policy changes on food self-sufficiency, including fuel subsidy removals, projected water availability and land productivity, are simulated in the next steps.

Policy simulations are implemented by changing any constraint or technical coefficients in the model. The empirical model has been developed using data from thirty provinces of Iran, over fifteen crops consisting of wheat, barley, rice, corn, cereals, cotton, potato, onion, sugar beet, vegetables (tomato, watermelon and cucumber) and oil seeds (soybean, canola and sunflower). These crops contribute to 72 per cent of the total cropping sector production. We have calibrated the model to the pre-reform situation of 2007–8. All the required agricultural data was collected from published sources of the Agriculture Ministry (*Jahad-e-Keshavarzi*) of Iran. The database contains price and quantities of various crops produced in each of the provinces, cost per hectare of intermediate input utilised and the water requirement per hectare of each crop in different provinces.

The output of this model provides the information required to locate the supply curve in the market model. The location of the demand curve in the market model is specified by estimation of various time series models, each specified according to series statistical characteristics for each of the food commodities.[11]

Food consumption: prospects for 2025

This study has been divided into six periods corresponding to the years before economic, social and cultural development plans, the years of the first, second, third and fourth economic, social and cultural development plan, and the target year of 2025. Per capita food consumption for the first five periods is calculated based on the published data on food expenditure. Consumption for the target year 2025 is predicted by the model developed for this purpose.

The trend in per capita consumption of bread and potato has continuously decreased in Iran from the first to the fourth development plan. The reverse has happened for rice and pasta, which are considered as higher quality food commodities. As seen in Figure 5.1, it is predicted that this trend will continue and that in 2025, Iranian consumers will, on average, reduce their per capita consumption of bread to 140.7 kilogrammes and potato to 20.4 kilogrammes, and that they will increase their consumption of rice to 43.2 kilogrammes and pasta to 9.58 kilogrammes.

It is interesting to note that urban and rural households follow almost the same pattern in consumption of these commodities throughout the whole period. By comparing the urban and rural figures from the second economic plan to the target year (Figures 5.2 and 5.3), it is clear that the

Figure 5.1: Changes in per capita consumption at country level (kg)

Commodity	Years before plans	1st Devl. Plan (1989–3)	2nd Devl. Plan (1995–9)	3rd Devl. Plan (2000–4)	4th Devl. Plan (2005–9)	Target year (2025)
Bread	185	197.3	196.6	167.5	159.2	140.7
Pasta	3.5	5.62	5.5	6.45	6.68	9.6
Rice	34.4	36.2	40.4	42.2	42.9	43.2
Potato	33	30.8	23.2	23.8	22.3	20.4
Onion	19.6	16.3	13.9	14.9	13.5	10.1
Milk	79.4	81.3	77.5	80.6	94.5	120.6
Vegetable oil	10.4	11.3	12.3	17.6	19	25.3
Sugar	15.0	17.8	18.0	19.7	18.8	19.4
Egg	7.3	6.5	6.3	6.6	7.1	8.0
Red meat	16.2	11.9	10.1	9.6	9.8	9.0
Poultry meat	8.6	7.3	9.2	12.3	18.4	24.9
Pulses	7.3	8.3	7.8	8.6	7.9	6.2
Total meat	24.8	19.2	19.3	21.9	28.1	33.9
Apple	10.2	9.4	8.8	9.4	10.0	11.2
Orange	8.5	8.0	7.9	8.2	8.4	8.5
Grape	4.9	4.3	3.6	3.6	3.6	3.4
Date	1.4	1.3	1.3	1.4	1.6	1.8

Source: Calculated by the authors on the basis of data published by the Statistical Centre of Iran (www.amar.org.ir.) on food expenditure and population. For the target year 2025, consumption figures were predicted by the simulation model.

decline in per capita consumption of bread and the rise in per capita consumption of rice are higher for rural households. This is actually a promising sign of decreasing consumption disparities between the rich and the poor in the country.

Figure 5.2: Per capita consumption of bread, potato, rice and pasta (urban households)

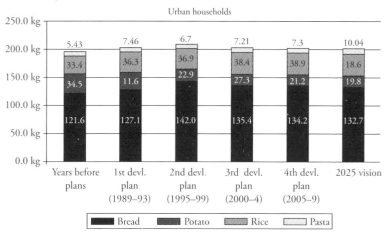

Figure 5.3 Per capita consumption of bread, potato, rice and pasta (rural households)

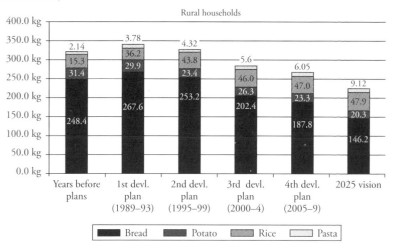

Data indicates a considerable increase in the consumption of milk in both rural and urban areas. Egg consumption is increasing as well, but not as substantially. We do not predict a significant increase in the consumption of eggs in the target year 2025. Our forecasts for per capita consumption of milk, vegetable oil and sugar for the target year are 120.6 kilogrammes, 25.3 kilogrammes and 19.4 kilogrammes, respectively. These figures show a considerable increase in consumption of these commodities as compared with those in the base year (Figure 5.1).

On average, the share of staples, such as cereals, and plant protein sources, such as pulses, is declining, while that of meat, dairy products and oil crops is rising. In addition, substitution of red meat for poultry is evident, which might be due to health considerations and a change in relative prices. Our forecast indicates that, on average, there will be a per capita consumption of 24.9 kilogrammes of poultry meat, 9 kilogrammes of red meat and 6.2 kilogrammes of pulses in 2025. Decrease in pulses and red meat will not be substantial for rural households, though their consumption of poultry meat will continue to increase to about 20 kilogrammes per person.

Our forecast on consumption of fruit during the study period indicates a small increase in per capita consumption of apple and dates, an insignificant decline in consumption of grapes and almost no change in the consumption of oranges.

Food production: prospects for 2025

Per capita food production can be considered as one of the main indicators of a country's food security status. Our forecast, based on the model described in the methodology section indicates that per capita production of wheat will be growing, while that of rice will be declining, as seen in Figure 5.4. Our prediction for the year 2025 indicates that the per capita production of wheat will increase to about 201 kilogrammes, while that of rice will decline to 25.4 kilogrammes. Given the increase in per capita consumption of rice in the same period, as seen in Figure 5.1, it is expected that the pressure to import this commodity will increase over time.

Per capita production of pulses is not expected to witness a significant rise. This is true for vegetable oil, despite the fact that Iran has experienced a significant increase in per capita production of vegetable oil in the past, which has doubled over the course of the four economic development plans. Per capita production of sugar and onions is expected to decline in 2025. This is mainly due to the high rate of water consumption in their production.

Per capita production of apple, orange, date and grape is predicted to increase. As all these products are export commodities, this provides an opportunity for increased food security through trade possibilities.[12] Also, per capita production of milk is expected to increase to about 135 kilogrammes in 2025.

From 1989 to 2009, the per capita production of eggs increased from 4.9 kilogrammes to 10 kilogrammes and is predicted to rise to 11.3 kilogrammes in the year 2025. Our prediction for the year 2025 indicates that Iranian agriculture lacks the capacity to produce the total amount of corn and soybean meal required as chicken-feed for producing eggs and poultry meat at the self-sufficiency level. Therefore, despite the fact that the capacity of production at the predicted level is already in place, if the feed supply deficit is not covered by imports, we will witness a reduction in the supply of poultry meat to 5.5 kilogrammes per person in the year 2025.

An increase in the per capita production of red meat is not predicted, which is not problematic as the per capita consumption of this food product will decline over the same period, as seen in Figure 5.1.

Food self-sufficiency in Iran: prospects for 2025

Assuming that all water collection projects achieve their target in Iran,[13] Figures 5.5 and 5.6 show food self-sufficiency in crops (wheat, rice, sugar, vegetable oil, onion, pulses, potato, corn), livestock (eggs, poultry meat), and fruit (apple, orange, grape, date). If this assumption is replaced by a continuation of the present situation, the outcome will be quiet different, as shown in Figure 5.7.

As Figure 5.5 indicates, Iran attained self-sufficiency in wheat production during the fourth economic, social and cultural development plan. Given the above assumption on water availability, we predict that the present self-sufficiency level will continue in 2025, but the balance is very fragile because the self-sufficiency coefficient is almost equal to 1. The forecast for rice production is that there will be some decline in the level of self-sufficiency—this has already been visible since 2000. The data indicates that rice self-sufficiency will continue to drop in the coming years, and will stand at a level of 0.57 by 2025.

Iran has never been self-sufficient in the production of sugar and vegetable oil, and there is little expectation that this will occur in the future. Iran's self-sufficiency status in vegetable oil will, in fact, worsen and by 2025 the ratio of supply to demand will have declined from 0.25 to 0.19.

The supply of onions, pulses and potatoes is greater than the demand for these products. The model predicts that this situation will continue and that self-sufficiency will increase for pulses, but will decrease for potatoes.

Corn is the main feeding input in poultry meat and egg production. Domestic production of corn has increased substantially over time in Iran. The self-sufficiency figure has increased by ten times from 0.05 in the years prior to 1989, to 0.5 during the second economic plan. However, there has been a small decline in this situation thereafter. We predict that this negative trend will continue and will reach 0.34 in 2025. This decrease will have a negative impact on self-sufficiency in the production of poultry meat in Iran.

If we allocate all domestically produced corn to egg production, a self-sufficiency of 1.73 will be reached in 2025, as seen in Figure 5.6. However, if the produced corn is totally allocated to poultry meat production, the country will reach a level of 0.31 self-sufficiency in 2025. In a different scenario, if the produced corn goes to egg production to achieve self-sufficiency, then the extra produced poultry meat will result in a self-sufficiency of 0.22 in the year 2025. Based on these figures, to meet demand for poultry meat in 2025, Iran has to import either 1,900 thousand tons of poultry meat or 3,100 thousand tons of corn to compensate for the deficiency in corn production in the domestic feed market.

Apple, orange, grape and date are exportable commodities in Iran. Iran achieved self-sufficiency in all these commodities (except oranges) long ago. We predict that oranges will reach self-sufficiency in 2025. Apples and dates will reach higher levels of self-sufficiency by 2025, while the self-sufficiency for grapes will decrease to some extent. Exporting the surplus of these products will help Iran's food security position by providing the required foreign currency for the import of deficit food stuffs.

Figure 5.4: Per capita production of major food commodities

	Years before plans	1st Devl. Plan (1989–3)	2nd Devl. Plan (1995–9)	3rd Devl. Plan (2000–4)	4th Devl. Plan (2005–9)	Target year (2025)
Wheat	142.1	156.8	170.2	173.6	185.1	200.8
Rice	32.7	38.9	40.8	35.2	31.8	26.4
Onion	15.5	18.3	19.5	19	19.2	17
Vegetable oil	2.0	2.6	2.9	3.6	4.5	4.6
Sugar	13.8	12.8	13.2	15.2	13.1	12.4
Egg	4.9	6.4	8.4	9.0	10.0	12.6
Red meat	10.4	10.8	11.6	11.4	11.4	11.3
Poultry meat	6.3	7.8	11.2	14.8	19.7	5.5*
Pulses	5.3	8.5	8.8	8.7	8.7	9.4
Apple	26.2	25.7	31.4	35.9	44.3	57
Orange	14.6	25.2	27.4	29.6	36.7	45.9
Grape	31.1	26.6	33.7	39	41.3	50.5
Date	9.0	10.2	14.1	13.7	15.7	20.5

Source: Calculated by the authors on the basis of raw published data. For the target year, production figures were predicted by the simulation model.

Figure 5.5: Production, demand and self-sufficiency coefficient in major crop products (unit: 1000 ton)

		Years before plans	1st Devl. Plan (1989–93)	2nd Devl. Plan (1995–9)	3rd Devl. Plan (2000–4)	4th Devl. Plan (2005–9)	Target year (2025)
Wheat	Production	6073.5	8745.1	10383.1	11600.9	13259.9	17070
	Demand	8078.5	10265.2	11783.7	12489.8	12905.6	17498.6
	Self-suff.	**0.75**	**0.85**	**0.88**	**0.93**	**1.03**	**0.93**
Rice	Production	1580.2	2166.5	2490.9	2464.7	2490.1	2110
	Demand	1785.4	2202.9	2557.15	3067.1	3303.4	3800
	Self-suff.	**0.88**	**0.89**	**0.97**	**0.80**	**0.75**	**0.57**
Onion	Production	776.3	1058.5	1274.8	1498.5	1677.8	1380
	Demand	1046.9	1035.9	1016.9	1138.9	1244.3	996
	Self-suff.	**0.74**	**1.05**	**1.24**	**1.31**	**1.34**	**1.38**
Vegetable oil	Production	94.21	146.5	177.1	242.9	342	395
	Demand	513.6	638.5	711.9	1142.6	1348.5	2111.2
	Self-suff.	**0.18**	**0.23**	**0.25**	**0.21**	**0.25**	**0.19**
Sugar	Production	662.8	716.1	805.4	1013.8	932.1	1056
	Demand	709.3	1070.7	1071.9	1307.3	1195.3	1373.7
	Self-suff.	**0.93**	**0.67**	**0.75**	**0.77**	**0.78**	**0.76**
Pulses	Production	257.2	473.9	536.6	579.1	581.4	804.8
	Demand	351.6	452.8	449.5	583.8	570.04	483
	Self-suff.	**0.74**	**1.04**	**1.19**	**0.99**	**1.05**	**1.58**
Potato	Production	1898.3	2618.1	3272.3	3912.8	4377.8	3270
	Demand	1980.1	2241.7	2111.6	2588.9	2575.6	2374
	Self-suff.	**0.96**	**1.17**	**1.55**	**1.51**	**1.68**	**1.40**
Corn	Production	83.6	329.9	867.45	1460.3	1903.4	1703
	Demand	1625	1396.6	1734.4	3014.6	4135.6	5015
	Self-suff.	**0.05**	**0.23**	**0.50**	**0.48**	**0.46**	**0.34**

Sources: Production and demand figures for study periods were calculated on the basis of published data. For the target year, data on Production and demand were predicted based on the simulation model.

Figure 5.6: Production, demand and self-sufficiency coefficient in major livestock products and fruits (unit: 1000 ton)

		Years before plans	1st Devl. Plan (1989–93)	2nd Devl. Plan (1995–9)	3rd Devl. Plan (2000–4)	4th Devl. Plan (2005–9)	Target year (2025)
Egg	Production	238.3	355	514.8	598.2	716.4	1146
	Demand	381.5	395.6	386.3	398.8	507.4	661
	Self-sufficiency	0.64	0.92	1.34	1.50	1.48	1.73
Poultry meat	Production	304.8	436	685.8	985.2	1407.6	760
	Demand	586.8	415.7	582.1	842.6	1333.2	2450
	Self-sufficiency*	0.53	1.05	1.18	1.17	1.05	0.31
Apple	Production	1264.9	1426.4	1920.5	2389.3	2831.3	4970
	Demand	1171.6	1292.8	1576.1	1933.7	2251.4	3730
	Self-sufficiency	1.07	1.10	1.22	1.24	1.26	1.32
Orange	Production	710.2	1402.6	1679	1968.6	2257.6	4047
	Demand	967.6	1543.7	1812.9	2100.8	2378.9	4018
	Self-sufficiency	0.73	0.90	0.92	0.94	0.95	1.00
Grape	Production	1502.2	1478.1	2063.2	2595.15	2945.6	4357
	Demand	1427.4	1409.9	1854.5	2271.3	2631	4000
	Self-sufficiency	1.05	1.04	1.11	1.14	1.12	1.09
Date	Production	433.8	563.9	861.9	913.6	1036.4	1760
	Demand	399.2	513.9	768	806.5	909.7	1490
	Self-sufficiency	1.08	1.10	1.12	1.13	1.14	1.17

* Self-sufficiency in the year prior to the target year is reached by importing corn.
Sources: Production and demand figures for the study periods were calculated on the basis of data on food expenditure and production of agricultural products published by the Statistical Centre of Iran and the Ministry of Agriculture and Jahad. For the target year, data on production and demand were predicted based on the simulation model.

PROSPECTS FOR FOOD SELF-SUFFICIENCY IN IRAN

Iran's Targeted Subsidy Plan and food self-sufficiency

In January 2010, Iran's parliament approved reform of the earlier subsidy programmes, and launched a new 'Targeted Subsidy Plan'. The goal of this new plan was to remove subsidies on food and energy (including various fuel products) and replace these price subsidies with direct cash transfers to Iranian households. As fuels are important inputs in producing food products, an increase in the price of fuels has important implications for changes in the relative prices of agricultural products, and hence on the relative supply of these food products. The effect of this increase in production of various food products depends on the fuel coefficient use of the commodities, especially regarding machinery and water energy requirements. The impacts of three different scenarios including removal of fuel subsidies, increase in land productivity and failure to achieve projected water storage (83,787 instead 95,290 million cubic metres) on the level of self-sufficiency in food production in Iran were measured through the simulation model. The productivity scenario that was simulated is based on the assumption that land productivity (average product) of the selected food products increases from the present level to 80 per cent of their potential levels. Figure 5.7 shows the current and simulated land productivity of selected products.

Figure 5.7: Current and potential yields of agricultural crops (kg/ha)

	Current yield (2008)	Potential yield (2025)	Growth %
Wheat	3560	7000	96.6
Rice	4225	6500	53.8
Corn	7338	8500	15.8
Sugar beet	34520	55000	59.3
Potato	26956	30000	11.2
Pulses	1361	2500	83.6
Oilseed	1922	3500	82.1
Onion	34778	50000	43.7

Figure 5.8 demonstrates the impact of each of the three scenarios on self-sufficiency in production of the selected food crops (wheat, rice, pulses, onion, sugar, vegetable oil, and potato) in 2025. The water constraint has the largest inverse effect on national self-sufficiency in pro-

duction of all food products in Iran. Removing fuel subsidies has the second largest negative effect on the self-sufficiency status of the country. Some of the inverse effects of the subsidy removal are compensated for if these crops experience land productivity at the level indicated in Figure 5.7.

Figure 5.8: Changes in self-sufficiency under different scenarios

	Wheat	Onion	Sugar	Veg. Oil	Potato	Rice	Pulses
Target year (2025)	0.97	1.38	0.76	0.19	1.4	0.57	1.58
Scenario no. 1	0.74	1.41	0.62	0.13	1.38	0.64	2.09
Scenario no. 2	0.95	1.6	0.7	0.3	1.4	1.04	2.5
Scenario no. 3	0.79	1.25	0.53	0.09	1.15	0.51	1.18

Scenario1: Fuel subsidy removal.
Scenario 2: Fuel subsidy removal and increase in yield.
Scenario 3: Current water storage.

Food security in Iran

The ratio of total food exports to imports (food trade balance) and food production per capita (potential of agricultural production) are the two main indicators used to measure food security of a country at the macro level.[14] The ratio of total food exports to imports is an indicator of the ability of a country to finance its food imports out of total export revenues. Figure 5.9 shows this ratio for Iran. This ratio has increased from 0.42 to 1.12 over the course of the four economic development plans. In addition, the ratio of agricultural exports to food imports over the same period increased from 0.51 to 5.12. These figures reveal a significant improvement in overall food security in Iran. Based on the per capita production criterion, as seen in Figure 5.4, there has been a positive growth for most of the food products in Iran. These indicators suggest an improvement in the level of food security in Iran over the past twenty-five years, and an expected enhancement in the future.

In addition to the above indicators measuring food security at the macro level, the FAO publishes regular data on food security indicators which can be used to assess a country's food security at the individual level.[15] These indicators have been used to see whether these measures support improvement of food security revealed by the other more general indicators. Figure 5.10 presents some of these indicators for Iran. These indicators were calculated to show the trends of food security from 1990 to 2008. Generally, these indicators show an improvement in food security in Iran over this period. For example, dietary energy supplies (DES) have increased from 2,970 calories per person in 1990 to 3,050 calories per person in 2008. The dietary quality has improved along with the share of animal protein, and the share of carbohydrates has decreased in dietary composition. The share of wheat flour in DES decreased from 46.6 in 1990 to 42.7 in 2008, while the share of rice increased from 7.5 to 9.3. The population growth rate declined from 1.7 to 1.1 per cent, which is an important determinant of food security as this decrease puts less pressure on the agricultural sector for food demand.

Figure 5.9: Changes in trade ratios

	Years before plans	1st Devl. Plan (1989–93)	2nd Devl. Plan (1995–9)	3rd Devl. Plan (2000–4)	4th Devl. Plan (2005–9)
Total export to agricultural import	0.42	0.73	0.72	1.04	1.12
Agricultural export to import	0.51	1.02	1.47	3.02	5.12

Sources: Computed on the basis of data on exports and imports published by Islamic Republic of Iran Customs.

Conclusion

Overall, food self-sufficiency, especially in major food staples of wheat, rice, poultry and red meat, forms the overriding political goal of agricultural development in Iran, particularly after the 1979 Islamic Revolution. Although this strategy might not be consistent with basic economic principles which encourage a more trade-based approach as opposed to a self-sufficiency one, the food crisis of 2008, as well as trade restrictions and non-economic market interventions by many governments based on national considerations, has provided some *ex post* justifications for such political considerations.

With a fairly high degree of confidence, we argue that Iran is very close to agricultural commodity self-sufficiency based on domestic sup-

Figure 5.10: Food security indicators for Iran

		1990–2	1995–7	2000–2	2006–8	1990–2 to 1995–7 (%)	1995–7 to 2000–2 (%)	2000–2 to 2006–8 (%)
I. FOOD DEPRIVATION AND CONSUMPTION INDICATORS								
Food deprivation								
Food deficit of undernourished population	Kcal/person/day	160	170	180	180	0.8	1.1	0.6
Proportion of undernourishment	%	<5	<5	<5	<5			
Number of undernourishment	millions	ns	ns	ns	ns			
Food needs								
Minimum dietary energy requirement (MDER)	Kcal/person/day	1700	1750	1810	1830	0.6	0.6	0.2
Average dietary energy requirement (ADER)	Kcal/person/day	2120	2210	2310	2350	0.9	0.8	0.3
Food supply for human consumption								
Dietary energy supply (DES)	g/person/day	2970	3040	3060	3050	0.5	0.1	–0.1
Total protein consumption	g/person/day	78.9	80.8	83.3	84.3	0.5	0.6	0.2
Animal protein consumption	g/person/day	17.1	18.3	19.1	23.3	1.4	0.9	4.9
Fat consumption	g/person/day	63.0	64.3	62.3	67.0	0.4	–0.6	1.5

Diet composition(share in DES)								
Carbohydrate	%	70.3	70.3	70.8	69.1	0	0.1	-0.5
Total protein	%	10.6	10.6	10.9	11.1	0	0.5	0.4
Animal protein	%	2.3	2.4	2.5	3.1	0.9	0.8	4.1
Fat	%	19.1	19.0	18.3	19.8	-0.1	-0.8	1.6
Major food commodities consumed (share in DES)								
1–Flour of wheat	%	46.6	44.3	47.0	42.7	-1	1.2	-1.9
2–Rice, milled	%	7.5	6.5	6.9	9.3	-2.8	1.1	6.1
3–Sugar, refined	%	8.7	8.7	8.2	8.3	0.1	-1.2	0.3
4–Oil of soybeans	%	7	5	5.3	4.9	-6.6	1	-1.3
5–Potatoes	%	2.6	2.8	3	3.6	1.2	1.5	3.3
II. FOOD PRODUCTION INDICATORS								
Role of production to consumption by major commodity								
1–Flour of wheat	%	102	101.7	102.1	102.1	-0.1	0.1	0
2–Rice, milled	%	98.4	100.2	80.2	47.4	0.4	-4.5	-10.5
3–Sugar, refined	%	53.5	58.6	105.2	111.1	1.8	11.7	1.1
4–Oil of soybeans	%	2.8	5.1	23.7	43.5	12.1	30.7	12.1
5–Potatoes	%	118.7	121.2	119.7	120	0.4	-0.2	0.1
III. FOOD TRADE INDICATORS								
Foreign food trade								
Exports								
Total merchandise	MLN $	19278	19711	26867	93070	0.4	6.2	20.7

		1990–2	1995–7	2000–2	2006–8	1990–2 to 1995–7 (%)	1995–7 to 2000–2 (%)	2000–2 to 2006–8 (%)
Share of crops and livestock products in total Merch. value	%	2.5	4.1	3.6	2.1	10	–2.6	–9.5
Share in total DES production	%	1.3	3.6	4.9	4.5	21.4	5.8	–1.2
Imports Total merchandise	MLN $	22265	14029	18417	50471	–9.2	5.4	16.8
Share of crops and livestock products in total Merch. value	%	9.9	20.8	11.8	8.7	14.9	–11.3	–5
Share in total DES production	%	39.8	47.5	53.7	41.2	3.5	2.5	–5.3
Net food trade (Food exp.—Food imp.) in total GDP	%	–1.5	–2.1	–1.1	–0.9	6.6	–12.8	–3.4
Ratio of imports to consumption by major commodity								
1–Flour of wheat	%	0	0.3	0	0	-	–165.4	–24.5
2–Rice, milled	%	1.8	0	21.1	53.4			19.6
3–Sugar, refined	%	57	51.1	3.3	16.1	–2.2	–54.9	31.8
4–Oil of soybeans	%	77.2	110.5	168.3	156.4	7.2	8.4	–1.5
5–Potatoes	%	0.3	0.6	0.5	1	11	–1.8	13.3

IV. MACRO AND SOCIOECONOMIC INDICATORS

Population								
Total population	1000	57983	63185	67698	7244	1.7	1.4	1.1
Share of urban in total population	%	57	61.1	64.8	68	1.4	1.2	0.8
Macroeconomic aggregates								
GDP at market prices (constant 2000 $)	MLN $	77317	88010	106395	149294	2.6	3.8	5.6
Share of agriculture value added in total GDP	%	18.8	16.3	12.9	10.3	−2.9	−4.7	−3.7

ns=not statistically significant.
FAO: FAO Statistical Yearbook 2012.

ply and demand for food. Major exceptions include rice, vegetable oil and meat production. The determining factor in red meat and poultry production is feed commodity production, especially corn and soybean. Analysis of different alternatives based on a specially developed simulation model reveals that, depending on varying production scenarios, Iran has the potential of being self-sufficient in one of these products.

Energy price will be a major policy instrument in food production and food security in Iran. On the one hand, as a major petroleum-exporting country, Iran has been using oil revenue to import its food deficits and maintain a high level of national food security. On the other hand, any increase in domestic energy price will have a major negative impact on food production in the country. Our analysis of the impact of the Targeted Subsidy Plan shows that it will negatively affect the food security of the country on the supply side. On the demand side, the impact is not clear. It might increase food security by increasing the purchasing power of the poor, but it might also have a negative impact on food security due to its inflationary trend.

Iran has great potential to increase its food security based on a strategy of producing exportable agricultural products, like fruit and vegetable, which have a comparative advantage. This is a long-term policy and needs political backing both in a policy setting and in trade regulations and considerations.

6

NEITHER SECURITY NOR SOVEREIGNTY

THE POLITICAL ECONOMY OF FOOD IN YEMEN

Martha Mundy, Amin Al-Hakimi and *Frédéric Pelat*

In the autumn of 2011, Oxfam warned of the narrow window of opportunity before food insufficiency gave way to famine for important sectors of the Yemeni population, calling on the 'Friends of Yemen'[1] to start the immediate provision of food aid.[2] In March 2012, the World Food Programme (WFP) stated that between one-fifth and one-quarter of the Yemeni population required emergency food aid and that no response had been forthcoming to Oxfam's call.[3] The levels of child malnutrition and emergent hunger are comparable to, or even worse than, those in Afghanistan where nearly half the children are underweight.[4] Thus, the WFP states that 'ten million Yemenis, nearly half of the population, are food insecure'.[5]

Yemen has its internal conflicts, but, unlike Afghanistan, has not been the object of international war and foreign occupation for over three decades. Agriculture and livestock production remain central to the livelihood of the Yemeni people.[6] How then to explain the starkness of the food crisis in Yemen?

This chapter seeks an answer to this question through an analysis of the background to the present food crisis. The crisis is much exacerbated by the shutting down of basic supplies (fuel, electricity and some food-stuffs) following the political contestation of 2011–12, but its core elements antedate the present political contestation.[7] We begin by a sketch of the wider political economy since the early 1970s. This forms the background to the patterns of change in agricultural policy, food production and the physical environment. Change in a food system is, by definition, simultaneously agricultural, social, environmental and political.[8] If the history with which we begin may strike some readers as unnecessary, we would respond that identifying the kinds of responses that could begin to reverse these secular trends requires understanding something of their historical development. Against this background we then sketch the changes in agricultural and livestock production. At the end we close with the kind of responses required to reconstruct the bases of production in Yemen.

The government of the economy in Yemen from the late 1960s

As we shall see below, smallholding agriculture has been severely reduced in terms of both the food staples it produces and the environmental conditions for continuing production. Understanding this process requires that we consider the location of food producers within the state and regional political-economic order as this has developed since the 1970s. Yemen is not unique in the marginalisation and impoverishment of smallholding agriculturalists in the face of large-scale capitalist farming, nor in the difficulty of politically representing physically dispersed agriculturalists, whether small landholders, landless cultivators or herders.[9] But for a country where such a high proportion of the population remains resident in small rural settlements, the silencing of their interests within the political order is stark by any measure. It can only be understood in terms of a progressive marginalisation within a governing polity constructed around international and national rent flows. Indeed, evidence suggests that many who remain on the land today may be better described as proletariat rather than farmers.[10] It is this difficult legacy that will need to be challenged for their livelihoods and for the environmental basis of Yemen itself to be insured.

By beginning with 1967 we do not mean to imply that this is the start of Yemen's 'modern' history: that extends across the arrival of the Idrisi in

Zabid in 1828, the British occupation of Aden in 1839, the 1869 opening of the Suez Canal, the Ottoman conquest of Sanaa in 1872 to the overthrow of the Imamate in 1962. Yemenis have migrated internationally and had links to the world market for a very long time. That said, 1967 was in Yemen, as in Palestine, a major political turning point. In society and economy, the year marked a shift from a world where population, production and justice in the countryside loomed large to one dominated by urbanisation, industrial import substitution and the circulation of oil rent. Yemen had its specificities—85 per cent of the population on the land, largely still sufficient in food production in the north—but did not stand apart from the wider Arab political economy.

1967 to the mid-1980s

The former Protectorate of South Arabia won independence from Britain in 1967, with the National Liberation Front taking power in what was to become, in 1970, the People's Democratic Republic of Yemen (PDRY). In the north, the Egyptian army withdrew and the political direction of the Yemen Arab Republic (YAR) was decided by the elimination of the socialist elements during the seventy-day siege of Sanaa, which took place between 28 November 1967 and 7 February 1968. The PDRY witnessed the engagement of urban and rural labour under socialist ideology and the exit of the Adeni trading capital to the YAR. From 1973 onwards, the YAR was to witness a wholesale migration of the male labour force to work in the oil-producing countries, primarily in Saudi Arabia. As Kiren Chaudhry has argued, this migration both weakened the local constituency for President Ibrahim al-Hamdi's centralising, pro-production vision of the polity and resulted longer term in the absence of labour as a political actor during the critical years of the developing state system of the YAR.[11] Lasting without break until 1986, the oil boom permitted a political marriage between a virtually unregulated private banking and trading sector and political representation by 'neo-traditional' leaderships in a country awash with cash.[12] Moreover, the rivalry between the socialist and capitalist blocks over the political direction of Yemen prompted Arab and international development organisations, and later NGOs, to invest heavily in projects in the YAR.[13]

Two characteristics of the political economy emerged that were to last beyond the boom years. First, international and Arab organisations and governments came effectively to be responsible for policy and provision with regard to agriculture and welfare. Second, at the popular level, experience of work and life in Saudi Arabia and the Gulf encouraged the returning men to multiply small-scale businesses and shops selling imported consumer goods and foodstuffs. Thus, at exactly the moment of a transition from widespread household-based subsistence agriculture to wage-labour, there appeared a divorce both socially and politically between employment in the oil states and food production left behind. This also took place at the level of households with a division between men who travelled and women who remained at home. Throughout these years, moreover, the doubly-subsidised price of imported wheat and powdered milk was so low that it flooded the market and, in comparative money terms, rendered local production derisible.[14] Men who migrated thus did not feel compelled, even if able, to participate in the maintenance of the terraces on which their parents, wives and children farmed, nor did they hire relatively expensive labour in their stead. So began a devaluation of the labour required to maintain the terraces which not only provide the surface for rain-fed grain production, but also are critical to watershed management throughout large areas of the country, especially along the western escarpment.[15] Simultaneously, the money circulating from labour in the oil-producing economies funded the first round of investment in lift-pumps throughout all the zones where they could be deployed, and the consequent obsolescence of upland irrigation systems dependent on surface streams or *qanat*. These investments occurred in the context of a near complete absence of state regulation of the economy and therewith of the deployment of pump technology. At the same time, however, from the early 1980s, as labour worked elsewhere, elements of a centralised security state began to be constructed in the north, just as important aspects of national economic management were delegated to international decision-makers.

Mid-1980s to the mid-1990s

In 1986, the oil price dropped ushering in recession and loss of employment by a significant number of Yemeni workers in the oil-producing states. As a response, the government of the YAR attempted to regain control over the flows of money into and out of the country. In the PDRY, the recession coincided with a bloody and delegitimising leadership conflict, corresponding to internal regional divisions. But in 1988, the first oil fields entered into production. Following the collapse of the Soviet Union in 1989, the YAR and PDRY merged in 1990 to form the Republic of Yemen.[16] The united Republic was then to see virtually all the Yemeni labour force expelled from Saudi Arabia in 1991—a generation of labour migration to Saudi Arabia came to an end in response to support by the Yemeni people for the Iraqi side in the Kuwait war.[17] Although Yemen's oil production did not lead to its taking a place 'among the richest countries' (as Vice-President Ali Salim al-Beidh promised at the time), its revenues came to provide resources to a leadership thereby little beholden to the labour force returning to the country. Struggle over the political direction of the Republic led the leadership of the former south under al-Beidh to attempt to pull out of the union in 1994, only for the south to be forcibly reconquered in a conflict that consolidated northern control of the security-military state. In retrospect, 1986, 1988 and 1994 saw the development of a much closer embrace of economic enterprise by the military and security structures of the state.[18]

1995–present

The years just following 1995 are characterised, on the one hand, by the roll-back of food and fuel subsidies under the IMF/World Bank aegis resulting in an increase in poverty and food insecurity,[19] and, on the other, by a consolidation of the military/security complex of the state. There are three aspects to the latter process under President Ali Abdullah Saleh that are relevant to our analysis.

First, the military and security budget represents a vast and unaccountable proportion of government expenditure. Estimates vary on the scale of the outlay and Saudi, United Arab Emirates and US support outside the state budget is also important. One study estimates the cost of the central military to be over 40 per cent of the state budget.[20] Compulsory military service, suspended in 2001, was reintroduced in 2007. Military and security work now represent an important, albeit largely unproductive—known more for destruction than construction of infrastructure—source of employment, with some 89,500 persons employed in the regular army and 71,000 in various security forces.[21] Another estimate judges the government budget for the military to be four times all expenditure on public services.[22]

Second, unlike the differentiation between political leadership and trading bourgeoisie in the 1970s and 1980s, the military-security state has become the broker of access to urban property, contracts related to oil rent and aid rent flows. Through informal and electoral representation via the governing party, its patronage network now binds rural leaders into the centre—since 1997, sheikhs have been granted salaries and special identity cards stating their rank on a four-point scale.[23] Political leaders, from former President Saleh on down, own shares in major trading companies, and state companies have near monopoly control in vital sectors of the economy. Peter Salisbury notes:

The importance of these elite commercial networks cannot be understated. A survey undertaken … shows that less than ten major groups from the tribes, military and business elite control 80 per cent plus of the country's import, manufacturing and processing businesses, local commercial banks (and hence credit), telecommunications firms, and most of Yemen's major transport companies. Most importantly … they control the commercial networks that import and supply basic goods crucial to households, while in many cases also controlling the state apparatus required to implement economic reforms.[24]

Oil revenues peaked in 2001, then began to decline markedly from 2005 leading to increased inter-elite contestation.[25] Inevitably, control over non-oil resources, such as land, water and agricultural produce, has loomed larger. Since 2007, as global financial speculation on food stocks pushed the price of grains, rice and sugar to unparalleled levels, international bodies began to examine the linkages between international prices and the structure of the market and distribution of food stocks inside Yemen. Their work suggests that linked to an international market dominated by only four great corporations is a mere handful of important companies in Yemen.[26] The top Yemeni company is reported to control 56 per cent of the market and it is vertically integrated from importing through milling and distribution of wheat and other grains.[27] In other words, there is today a close mesh between political leadership and business, and a quasi-monopolistic structure of the market.[28] Hence, the prices of basic food commodities in Yemen do not simply mirror shifts in world prices but, at times, amplify them.

Third, the valuation of male military employment and long-distance labour migration marries well with the wider ideological marginality of productive work inside Yemen, not least women's productive work. The ambient media culture of oil rent, with its omnipresent representation of the power of ready-made commodities manufactured elsewhere, dovetails with the investment in education and movements which valorise the roles of women as consumers and mothers, not as workers. In the 1970s and 1980s, the pro-natalist policies of the YAR were coherent with proletarisation and freeing of labour from agricultural production for manual labour in the oil-producing countries. But far from such policies being brought into question after the 1991 closure of almost all the Gulf labour markets, the unified Republic also rolled back the more pro-work and family planning programmes of the former south.[29] If there is still little valorisation of women's labour outside maternity, work more generally as a value in itself remains strikingly absent in state and cultural discourse. Workers figure positively as youth ready to travel elsewhere and to repatriate remittances to Yemen, or negatively as the mass of the poor and unemployed.[30]

Agricultural policy since 1962

It is not clear that we can speak of an 'agricultural policy' in the full sense of the word when the agricultural sector of North Yemen was opened to the world market during the civil war of 1962–71. It was, rather, in the 1970s that governmental and civil institutions concerned with agricultural development were established in both the YAR and the PDRY. The two young states were to pursue very different policies with regard to land tenure, infrastructural investment, crop choice and marketing. These earlier divergent policies continue to mark the two parts of the country unified from 1990.

Although its natural endowment for agriculture was even poorer than that of the north, the PDRY pursued land redistribution and forced cooperative association in agriculture, and dictated control of crop choice and marketing.[31] Notably, the government allowed the sale of *qat* only on Fridays and holidays.[32] After the 1990 unification of the YAR and the PDRY, agricultural policy was unified on the model of the north. The policies of land redistribution and socialised marketing of the PDRY were annulled, although farmers in irrigated zones in Hadramaut have resisted the wholesale dispossession required legally for the restitution of land to previous owners.[33] Conflict over land exists primarily over the appropriation of urban and common/state land by government officials from the north, allegedly illegally and sometimes forcibly, in the years after 1994.[34] Such practices—also described for other regions—are invoked today as one of the reasons for renewed calls by southerners for secession from the north.

In the north, with its much greater agricultural potential, economic and agricultural policy has remained fundamentally unchanged since the 1970s. The only brief departure was during the years of President Ibrahim al-Hamdi (1974–7) who promoted agricultural cooperative association and developmental collective action in rural communities. Aside from this period, the policy, planned or not, basically accepted that the rain-fed sector of Yemeni agriculture, exposed to water-shortage and with high labour inputs (largely outside the circuit of the market as domestically structured and heavily female), could be left to its own devices as a subsistence sector. The focus was on zones where predictable delivery of irrigation water could be assured for higher-value, market-oriented production. Even today, when the water deficit is among the most severe in the world,[35] this basic policy emphasis has barely changed, although the focus is now on lessening water loss in irrigated agriculture.[36] In terms of marketing, as we have seen, Yemen opened its market to imported foodstuffs, subsidised prices of imported grain and other basic foodstuffs on the local market, and refrained from regulating the marketing of produce, especially *qat*. Labour was encouraged to migrate to the oil-producing states, and it did in large quantities. In short, agricultural policy was effectively based on the premise that the arid and largely mountainous terrain of Yemen was incapable of producing high-quality grain, especially wheat, at prices competitive on the international market. Under the guidance of the international development agencies, the focus turned to increasing higher-value agricultural produce for the market in Saudi Arabia from the coastal *wadis* and in Yemeni cities more generally. This policy has been achieved successfully by and large. If there has been 'failure' in agriculture, this must be ascribed not to any tradition-bound rigidity on the part of farmers who have responded to the policy with myriad changes, but to the policy itself. Thus, it is reported that, between 1991 and 2003, areas planted in sorghum and barley declined, whereas those planted in *qat*, bananas, mangoes, citrus and apples increased,[37] and a 2009 UNDP report notes that the land planted in barley and maize was halved between 1961 and 2003.[38]

Change in forms of production

As part of the northern extension of the tropical climate area, Yemen experiences semi-arid to arid climatic conditions with most rainfall in summer. Climate and landscape vary according to elevation. At a gross level, Yemen can be divided into three main regions: coastal region, mountainous heights, and eastern plains. In all these zones, one can find rain-fed and irrigated agriculture and animal husbandry. Historically, however, the major zones of irrigated agriculture were in the lowlands and coastal plain; rain-fed terraced cultivation in the highlands; and pastoral animal husbandry in the eastern plains. The highlands are warm in summer, but on winter nights (October–March), the temperature can drop below 5°C, especially in the very high mountains. In the mountains, the average temperature ranges between 10°–22°C with rainfall between 200–600mm, except for higher rainfall in the area of Ibb city and parts of Mahweit, Hajja, Raima and Sanaa governorates, where average annual rainfall reaches over 1000mm/year.

Rain-fed agriculture

It is striking that sorghum, the primary cereal historically grown in Yemen, appears simply to be ignored in international development reports concerning agriculture in the region.[39] Sorghum was, however, central not only to diet but, as part of a grain-livestock household economy, the backbone of rural life over the centuries. As late as the mid-1970s, even in the capital city Sanaa, many houses kept a cow for home milk production. The cow lived in a stable-room on the ground floor of the tower house where it was patiently tended to and fed stalks of sorghum wrapped round with lucerne (a green fodder plant). The cow would be collected along with others of the quarter to drink at communal water sources in the city. Under the pressure of urbanisation, this house grain-livestock complex has disappeared in the city. So, too, following the fall in the water table, has vegetable production in the city's gardens that relied on irrigation from wells and supplementary grey-water from mosque ablutions. Even in the countryside the grain-livestock production complex has become much reduced depending as it did on a combination of sorghum and leguminous green-fodder production.[40] This household economy entailed the domestic, i.e. invisible to formal statistics, employment of senior women in the care of livestock inside the house and formed part of a structured division of labour between women in domestic food production.

Unemployment is an issue debated for men—Yemen's estimated official unemployment rate being 15 per cent, but perhaps more realistically it is at 40 per cent—but less remarked is the statistically invisible but very real under-employment of women in urban and peri-urban settlements. In the rural areas of the highlands, statistics indicate that the agricultural workforce is overwhelmingly female as women carry on with what remains of subsistence agriculture and livestock production in the face of male labour migration abroad (often illegally) and to Yemeni cities and smaller towns. There have been myriad small-scale international donor projects aimed at empowering women, but given that government research and investment in the whole of the agricultural sector remains marginal (2.8 per cent of the government budget), and the rain-fed sector neglected even within this,[41] we may assume that this neglect hits rural women workers particularly hard. And yet, it is this rain-fed sector which maintains the physical base for agriculture by terracing throughout the areas of northern Yemen receiving the highest rainfall.

The decline of rain-fed agro-ecosystems and local food systems

Terracing is a long-lasting process transforming mountainous escarpments into arable lands in order to reach a fragile ecological balance that impacts ecosystems far beyond terraced zones. Terracing affords adaptation to steep slopes, to erratic but substantial rainfall, to flash-flood runoff, as well as to high climatic and geographic variability. Harsh weather and topography never guarantee equal levels of food production across the years, and drastically limit the opportunities for intensification. Rain-fed production is dependent on low and extremely variable rainfall with consequently unstable and varying productivity. Hence, over the centuries, sustainability was the result of empirical selections of landraces adapted to very local conditions; practices of agro-biodiversity at field and farm levels; management of scarce natural resources; integration of animal and plant production; and community cooperation systems. Farmers' specific knowledge intervened in all these processes.[42] The human factor was at the core of the productive system in the areas which formed the primary home of the country's workforce in the country until the 1970s. When many male workers began to abandon rain-fed farming, the system lost important areas of land.

In Figure 6.1, we bring together statistics available on the source of water in cultivated areas for the years between 1975 and 2009. In spite of unreliable data, this shows clear trends: a decrease in rain-fed areas until 2000, then stabilisation and slight increase; a dramatic increase in lift-pump irrigated areas until 2000; a decline in spring-fed land; and slight increase in flood-irrigated lands.[43]

Figure 6.1: Agricultural land distribution according to type of water source 1975–2009 (1000 ha)

Year	Cultivated area (1000 ha)	Floods	Springs	Wells	Rain	Other (including dams)
1975	1515	120	73	37	1285	
1990	1121	101	25	310	685	
1995	1067	100	20	368	579	
2000	1144	126	46	457	515	
2001	1200	144	36	408	612	
2005	1202	137	34	393	609	29
2007	1485	148	29	454	753	101
2009	1306	235	34	366	614	57

Source: Yemen's Ministry of Agriculture and Irrigation (MAI) agricultural statistics for the period 1997–2009 and World Bank, 'Republic of Yemen Agricultural Strategy Note', Report No. 17973-YEM, 1999.

Thus, for rain-fed farming, substantial losses were recorded early: from 1975 to 1990, 627,000 hectares were lost, representing nearly 49 per cent of the 'original' expansion. But from 1990 the decline decelerated: the area of rain-fed farming in 2009 (614,000 ha) was close to that of 2001 (612,000 ha) and barely inferior to that of 1990 (685,000 ha).[44] These figures are comparable to those recorded in a land-use survey in 2002: 660,000 ha land are terraced, representing only 1.25 per cent of the national territory but still 45–50 per cent of the area cultivated today in the whole country.[45] By comparison, nearly 85 per cent of the land farmed in the mid-1970s was rain-fed.

Rain-fed land is cultivated largely in cereals and legumes. Figure 6.2 provides data on the distribution of these crops cultivated in rain-fed lands for years between 1970 and 2009.

Figure 6.2: Rain-fed and cereals/pulses area (in 1000 ha)

Year	1970	1975	1980	1990	1995	1996	1997	2000	2001	2005	2007	2009
Wheat	42		73	98	102	103	105	87	94	86	142	118
Barley*	126T	64T	47T	52T	64T	54T	49	37	41	35	43	32
Sorghum*	610T	921T	623T	491T	518T	411T	430	360	379	430	521	393
Millet							99	103	108	100	133	98
Maize*	13T	52T	52T	66T	58T	50T	40	32	35	39	52	37
GRAINS[46] group	1082		851	845	733	704	722	620	658	689	891	678
PULSES group	65	75		49	54	54	57	51	53	37	50	47
All rain-fed	1056	1285		685	579	579		525	612	609	753	614

Source: Yemen's Ministry of Agriculture and Irrigation (MAI) agricultural statistics for the period 1997–2009 and World Bank, 'Republic of Yemen Agricultural Strategy Note,' Report No. 17973-YEM, 1999.

* Note: The data available from the World Bank, 'Agricultural Strategy Note' give only total tonnage for 1970–96, not area, for barley, sorghum and maize. Furthermore, the data for 1970–96 combines sorghum and millet as if a single crop, entered in the sorghum row here. Nevertheless, this data has been incorporated here. The agricultural statistics published annually by the Ministry of Agriculture and Irrigation group crops into: grains, pulses, vegetables, fruit, qat, cash crops (excluding qat, fruit and vegetables).

Overall, the area planted in grains decreased by 27 per cent of land between 1970 and 1980. Since then, declines have slowed, but with differences across cereals. According to the World Bank, barley production was halved between 1970 and 1975 alone, from 126,000 tons in 1970 to 64,000 in 1975. Sorghum and millet, taken together, peaked in 1975 to decline until the early 1990s. Alongside the standardisation of diets and in the wake of governmental attempts to introduce highly water-demanding seeds of 'improved' varieties, wheat alone benefited from cropping transformations within the cereal group, gaining 56,000 ha between 1970 and 1990 when, overall, grains lost more than 230,000 ha. Nevertheless, sorghum has remained the first cereal cultivated, as it provides both grain for the family and fodder for livestock.

Animal production contributes some 28 per cent to the total production income for the agricultural sector in Yemen.[47] The most important types of animals raised in Yemen are cows, sheep, goats, donkeys, camels, horses and chickens. Local breeds have economic importance in different areas of governorates since they provide meat, dairy, eggs, leather, wool, fuel and fertilisers. In addition, they are considered the most efficient in their adjustment to the climatic and farming circumstances with the ability to produce and reproduce in tough conditions and to resist scarcity of rain and the cold weather conditions in the mountains. Due to the rapid changes in production systems and social and economic circumstances, the process of introducing foreign breeds of cattle and poultry with higher productivity threatens local breeds.

Following a policy which rapidly reduced the areas of cultivated rain-fed land nationwide and forced many households to abandon many of their tiny remote scattered fields within a few years, cropping statistics indicate that since the mid-1990s rain-fed farming has come to represent an economic refuge for many families. It is no longer a development strategy but a way of conserving some farmland to be brought back into cultivation when an 'urgent crisis' or an 'opportunity' takes farmers back to their fields. At this point, the farmers then face the consequences of a deteriorated situation: insufficient stocks of local seeds; forgotten knowledge; dislocated community cooperation; and degraded terraces. To what extent such farmers are today women rather than men likewise remains unclear. Yemen today imports more than 75 per cent of the cereals it consumes whereas in 1970 the figure was only 18 per cent.[48] The average consumption per person of food cereals is among the lowest in the world.

Irrigated agriculture

To speak simply, we may distinguish between two main types of traditional irrigated systems: spate-flow irrigated *wadi*s in lower lying areas and smaller areas of spring or *qanat* irrigation in the highlands. The results of increased control over water for irrigated agriculture differ between the areas of spate-irrigation and those formerly dependent on spring-fed sources. But farmers have throughout been responsive both to economic policies and to whatever technologies have been introduced through the market or through the international 'development community'.[49]

Spate-irrigated systems

Coastal agro-ecosystems were largely concentrated within the maximum limits of spate-irrigated *wadi* lands running down perpendicularly to the coastline and known for producing irrigated cereals, fruit, fodder, cotton, sesame or other cash crops. The feat of production in such systems resided in enabling agriculture under very dry natural conditions (temperatures ranging between 24°–35°C and rainfall between 10–100mm) and avoiding salinisation of the soil.[50] In the coastal plains, high-technology diversion structures have been built in the upstream sections of most of the major spate-irrigated *wadi*s along the Tihama. This has led to development of high-value fruit trees, and some vegetables, in the upper reaches of the *wadi*s. The downstream areas, by contrast, have quite radically lost access to surface irrigation water. In the 1970s, some of the farmers of these downstream zones were able to participate in the development of pump-irrigated farming and to increase their incomes, but with the dramatic fall in the water table (by 1 metre a year in 1980) exacerbated by the greater capture of water in the upstream areas in the spate systems, the alternative of shallow pump-farming in the coastal plain has become far more restricted. These developments are well reviewed by Frank van Steenbergen et al. in their 'Guidelines on spate irrigation', which compares work on such systems in Yemen, Pakistan and Ethiopia.[51] The authors single out for criticism the high-expense, upstream-engineering approach promoted by the World Bank in the Yemeni Tihama. They do this with restraint but on the basis of ample negative evidence, in terms of economic return on investment; social and economic equity; integration of livestock with agricultural production; and ecological impact in the former system as a whole. At the time of the planning of such structures, not all the international actors were in agreement. Thus, in the mid-1970s, the UK Ministry of Development sponsored a series of studies in one of the major systems, wadi Rimaʻ—these advocated medium-technology improvements in terms of the same four factors as above.[52] Socioeconomic surveys in Rimaʻ provided further evidence for this approach,[53] but the World Bank chose to accept a higher-technology foreign-constructed diversion structure at the head of the *wadi*.[54] In recent years, foreign technical assistance has taken the form of maintenance of secondary diversion-structures and of promoting the formation of water-user associations, the functioning of which has proved difficult in many cases given the sharp inequalities in land tenure between head and tail of the systems. There is no evidence, moreover, of these associations safeguarding farming women's access to water.[55]

Lift-pump irrigated agriculture

Prior to the introduction of lift-pump technology, there were no agro-ecosystems based primarily on groundwater irrigation in Yemen. The use of well-water was technically as well as naturally limited. In the past decades, wells have been drilled to irrigate flat and mechanisable lands located both on the coastal plains and on the plateaux below and beyond terraced escarpments. Large geographical areas have been transformed without building sustainable foundations. In the late 1970s, this development won praise from agricultural engineers. Thus, Yves Clouet lauded the initiative of some farmers who invested in well-drilling and motor-pumps in one Tihama *wadi*, which he thought a good initiative to mitigate the decline of national production already observed. This decline led the authorities to import massive quantities of cereals (140,000 tons in 1977) even though there was no problem of drought at that time. Twenty years later, however, the same Clouet questioned the sustainability of such agronomical and economic 'successes' as technologically inappropriate, totally unorganised and ecologically suicidal.[56]

As can be seen in Figure 6.1, between 1975 and 1990 irrigated lands expanded more than 13,700 ha annually, but whereas land irrigated by wells increased by 18,200 ha per year, land irrigated by spates decreased by 1,200 ha and that by springs lost 3,200 ha annually. In general, well-irrigation has allowed the expansion of production of cash crops in both coastal and highland agro-ecosystems. Figure 6.3 gives such data as is available for the major irrigated cash crops in the years between 1970 and 2009. Although the expansion of vegetable cultivation is less spectacular than that of fruit, today the areas planted in each are roughly equivalent. This reflects a recent restructuring of the pattern of fruit production wherein dates, grapes and orange plantations were halved in 2002–3, while surfaces planted in mango tripled. With regard to vegetables, potatoes and tomatoes represent between 45–55 per cent of all areas planted in vegetables since 1997. Fodder is also a dynamic group led by irrigated sorghum (essentially in Tihama) and linked to the increasing importance of rearing and fattening livestock for the market that represents an essential source of income for small farmers everywhere in Yemen. In 2009, overall surfaces cultivated with fodder crops were four times the level recorded forty years ago. Of this, sorghum represents 80 per cent, long before alfalfa and other feed crops. Fodder and *qat* are more profitable and reliable cash crops than coffee, sesame, cotton and tobacco. In the case of coffee, in spite of a policy to increase areas planted (+300 per cent from 1980 to 2009), total production is today only just returning to the levels of the late 1970s after a long decrease in the 1980s and 1990s.

As Figure 6.3 makes clear, in the highlands, the major response was to concentrate on a crop of very high value without an imported competitor; this crop was *qat*.[61] There, as well as in some intermediate *wadi*s, *qat* prevailed over all other crops with its area multiplying nearly nine times over the twenty-year period (+6,200 ha/year). Slowing slightly between 1980 and 1990 (+1,000 ha per year), and between 1990 and 2000 (+2,400 ha/year), *qat* expansion has accelerated again, with more than 5,500 ha added annually from 2000 to 2009. Today, 154,000 ha are cultivated with *qat*, and despite the existence of some purely rain-fed *qat*, only the expansion of irrigation in the highlands can explain such a craze. Even the decline in the area irrigated by wells since the early 2000s somehow has not slowed the *qat* race,[62] certainly helped by 'new' forms of irrigation such as dams and small tanks,[63] or possibly replacing other irrigated cash crops, such as grapes, fruit trees, coffee, vegetables and cereals.

In the 1970s and 1980s, the expansion of areas planted in *qat* in high-precipitation rain-fed and lift-pump agriculture afforded considerable cash income to a wide spectrum of farmers in the mountains. In many highland regions, but less so in Lower Yemen, rights to land were

Figure 6.3: Irrigated land and areas under major cash crops (in 1000 ha)

Year	1970	1975	1980	1990	1995	1996	1997	2000	2001	2005	2007	2009
Qat	8		70	80	89	91	93	104	109	124	141	154
Potatoes							15	17	17	17	19	21
Tomatoes							15	17	18	15	17	18
VEGETABLE group[57]	25		31	52	54	57	59	65	67	73	82	89
Mangoes							4	6	7	23	24	26
Dates							20	23	23	14	14	15
Bananas							9	10	11	9	10	10
Grapes							21	23	23	12	13	13
Oranges							13	14	14	7	8	8
FRUIT group[58]	14		44	57	75	79	81	91	95	83	88	93
Coffee			8	22	25	27	32	33	34	29	34	35
Sesame							29	32	33	19	22	23
CASH CROPS[59] group	32		40	65	67	75	86	97	99	73	83	87
Sorghum fodder							61	72	72	98	116	131
FODDER group[60]	40		50	61	85	94	101	116	118	122	147	163
Well irrigation	30	37		310	368	393		457	408	393	454	366
All irrigation	210	230		436	488	520		629	588	593	732	693

Source: Yemen's Ministry of Agriculture and Irrigation (MAI) agricultural statistics for the period 1997–2009 and World Bank, 'Republic of Yemen Agricultural Strategy Note', Report No. 17973-YEM, 1999.

reasonably widely distributed in association with communally maintained irrigation systems.[64] These were supplanted by water from pumps
either purchased collectively or, more commonly, by the more prosper-
ous farmers with the means to buy the requisite equipment to lift sub-
surface water from comparatively shallow depths. But, as the water table
dropped over the years, the cost of water in terms of deep-bore drilling
and pumping equipment escalated.[65] Thus:

> in some areas of Yemen a number of powerful landholding individuals have
> been able to capture the bulk of available resources that have been directed
> towards investment in 'modern' drilling and pumping equipment, controlling
> the benefits of these investments and directing them towards their own personal
> enrichment.[66]

Yemeni sociologists speak of a growing consolidation of water ownership and thereupon of land ownership in the hands of rural leaders who,
through political position and wealth in land, were able to invest in the
requisite equipment. Many cultivators have sold land to the water owners. They make do by working for the new 'pump-capitalists' by migrat-
ing abroad (an option in fact very restricted today) or by joining the
only very partially employed labour force in the Yemeni cities.

Environmental degradation: conditions emerging today

Yemen's agro-ecosystems[67]

Agricultural development over the past four decades was achieved without
an understanding of the ecosystems' ability to afford such interventions
in the long term and in a break with centuries of empirical knowledge
devoted to managing scarce natural resources efficiently. While Daniel
Varisco praised Yemeni farmers for 'altering the ecosystem centuries ago'
by 'transposing the harsh natural terrain of the mountains into productive
terrace systems',[68] Gerhard Lichtenthäler observed that for the people
witnessing 'with great surprise the new and unexpected groundwater
"miracle"' in the 1970s in the Sa'dah basin, the perception 'was that God
had mercifully rewarded them with the "gift" of water as he had blessed
the Saudis with the "gift" of oil'.[69] Although the illusion of removing
natural constraints forever was short lived, scarcity-driven relations to the
environment would be broken up everywhere in Yemen. On rain-fed
terraced slopes, ancestral cooperation systems vanished in the wake of

male outmigration,[70] while the absence of any traditional or modern form of regulation of groundwater irrigation played its part in an uncontrolled expansion of boreholes in plains and plateaux. Long-term collective interest gave way to private short-term investment.

In spite of a considerable increase in the volume of water extracted, access to groundwater was spatially restricted to aquifers in highland basins and to those in the coastal lowlands, where rainfall is very low and population densities are historically lower than on upland rain-fed slopes. Yet, pressure on the water resource kept growing during the past decades as regions experienced the consequences of technological investment in irrigated agriculture made by a minority, leading successive waves of rural migrants to try their luck as agricultural labour or to congregate in sprawling suburbs of cities. In rain-fed regions, water-harvesting structures were not maintained leading to waste of water and diminution of overall water availability.[71] Nationwide, losses witnessed in rain-fed farming have not been compensated by more irrigated farmland. Today, 125 cubic metres of water are available per year and per capita, from which more than 90 per cent is used in agriculture, and arable land covers only 3 per cent of the national territory, of which 68 per cent is effectively cultivated annually. In essence, Yemen remains a water- and land-scarce country. That said, the situation differs qualitatively and quantitatively between agro-ecosystems.

Ecological and climatic challenges

Ecological degradation

Dealing with climatic uncertainty and ecological variability has always been a challenge for Yemenis. Changes of such a magnitude have occurred since 1970; the degraded situation of natural resources in all agro-ecosystems of the country is certainly the greatest challenge to be faced today when planning future food policies and agricultural strategies.

Groundwater depletion is now well documented in Yemen. Running out of water, the city of Sanaa is an emblematic symbol as its population growth—10 per cent annually—increasingly competes with *qat* cultivation for the scarce resources of the aquifer.[72] Measures taken to save water are necessary but alone will not solve the national environmental problems. Rain-fed mountain areas were well-known for efficient management of surface-water in the past. But al-Ghulaibi reminds us that access to sufficient water for domestic purposes is today's first priority for many households, even prior to the maintenance of terraces.[73] Saving groundwater in upper plateaux may not rescue terraced systems, but preserving terraced systems would positively impact coastal lowlands directly connected to upper catchment areas. The different agro-ecological zones are interrelated as parts of watersheds. Effects of terrace destruction on erosion and runoff recharge below terraced units are now visible. Without quantitative assessment of the magnitude of the process,[74] it is now generally admitted that erosion problems have increased in the last forty years to become a major national problem.[75] At issue is soil erosion in the upper catchments associated with changes in agriculture, topography, hydrology (dried-up springs), terrace abandonment, and tree and shrub removal, especially in rangelands.[76] The 'domino effect'[77] of aggravated flash floods has caused 'destruction of economically viable terraces downstream and of *wadi*-bottom land'.[78] In some places, the phenomenon has reached such proportions that a major part of formerly highly productive spate-irrigated lands bordering *wadi* channels has disappeared. Thus, the collapse of the upland terraces threatens the entire watershed system, provoking ecological devastation downstream and reducing groundwater recharge, especially in major coastal *wadis*.

Climate change

Climate change has become a real threat for Yemen, adding an additional challenge to the list of its development problems, food insecurity and increasing poverty. Highland communities dependent on rain-fed agriculture are identified as the most vulnerable to the impact of climate change. The prognostics generated from three different scenarios agree on a general temperature rise, but propose divergent forecasts regarding rainfall.[79] In the worst case scenario with lowest precipitation, there would be immediate detrimental effects on rain-fed farming, with one study estimating that climate change could lead to a 50 per cent reduction in crop yields for rain-fed agricultural crops by 2020.[80]

A second more probable scenario where higher temperatures would be coupled with the same or more precipitation would provide the best conditions for the development of diseases, pests and weeds, creating new pressures on crop yields.[81] Whatever the prevailing scenario in the long term, more rainfall variability is to be expected with higher intensity in highlands. Extreme events such as droughts or flash floods, already recorded as having been on the rise in Yemen in the past decades,[82] will become more frequent in the future. The western highlands are at the top of the disaster-vulnerability list.

High weather variability and erratic rainfall, ranging for instance from 200 to 800mm from one year to the next, are, however, historical constraints in the northwest highlands and escarpments, where generations of farmers worked and maintained terraced fields. In a country where agricultural intensification based on short-term private profits has reached its limits within less than fifty years, the adaptive capacity of small farmers to overcome chronic environmental shifts by conducting sustainable agriculture relies on a capital of knowledge that needs to be recorded, strengthened and conserved to assure resilience of the farming systems. Thus, farmers have an essential role to play.

Cultivated lands represent 3 per cent of the surface area of Yemen today. Yet, as we have seen, the area farmed has decreased over the period 1975–2005. The causes for this decrease are complex. Natural, social and economic causes intermesh: the scarcity of water, the erosion of land, the collapse of terraces and desertification, the subdivision of landholdings and high population growth, and the lack of finance which has increased the price of agricultural inputs and poverty. In the face of this complex situation, the institutional response has been completely inadequate: poor agronomic institutional capacity, lack of agricultural research and guidance, absence of an effective agricultural policy, failure to register land and water ownership, and severely limited statistical basis of information about the agricultural sector as a whole.

Responses in the wake of 2011–12

In closing, we may return to the title of this chapter: 'neither security nor sovereignty'. At one level, 'no food security' is merely a statement of fact, the statistical evidence for which was cited earlier. But, at another level, the phrase points to the problematic effects of the international development industry that surrounds 'food security'. Over the decades surveyed, Yemen developed a division of labour wherein the Yemeni government directs military and political security and the international development agencies deal with welfare and agriculture. The latter interventions take different forms and some, such as programmes through the Social Fund for Development, are well targeted. But, overall, this division of labour has two effects. 'Security' is something any agency can deliver, and hence most apt for 'global governance' wherein poorly identified international bodies make policy, and bargain with state and regional power-brokers on the ground. Its terms silence citizens' claims against their own political order.

In a bizarre manner, even 'food sovereignty' is for now not apposite, since Yemen is neither politically nor economically sovereign given its dependence on political rent, aid and imported food.[83] In such a context, the idioms of 'food sovereignty' are little more than utopic slogans. The very productive base of land, labour, environment and knowledge is degraded and requires husbandry and rebuilding before the terms of food sovereignty can become relevant.

At present, the youth revolution is embroiled in the formation of political parties for electoral politics. There is little in the way of an economic development programme or awareness. Political rights are the order of the day with few calls for the economic rights accorded under the International Covenant of Economic and Social Rights to which Yemen is a signatory, and there is little social and political articulation of a project for rebuilding productive resources and ensuring their equitable distribution.

What steps need to be taken to move out from this impasse? At the level of policy and elite discussion, a start would be to review the past years of development intervention led by international organisations and NGOs in agriculture and livestock/pastoral production so as to make available that knowledge in coherent form and to learn from the errors and the successes of the same. In such a review, Yemeni specialists in the domain of food production and environment, many of whom left the public for the private sector, need to pool their experience and to formulate a response originating from their experience.

The technological and market-mechanical view of development espoused by the World Bank and related international agencies has contributed to massive environmental damage. This will have to be reversed in order to ensure productive livelihoods in Yemen. Such environmental degradation has been accompanied by the build-up of a dominant sector of unproductive military and security apparatuses, to which everyone is now tied. In any political settlement, local production under the control of local producers must once again be given priority, and their voices, including the voices of women, allowed to be heard. Rehabilitation of the productive base will require recuperating and building knowledge about the form of terraces, plant and animal species, the interdependence of crop and livestock production, water harvesting techniques and watershed systems. By foregrounding the need to hear and record local voices, we do not intend this as yet another knowledge-producing exercise for the international and national elite. Rather, Yemeni political institutions will need to be forged in order to plan and transmit information from the village to the city and back again. For any such process to be successful, rural labour can no longer be treated merely as the destitute to be swept aside by entrepreneurs, but will need to be seen as custodians and producers entitled to the land, water and biological heritage of Yemen.

7

URBAN AGRICULTURE AND FOOD SECURITY IN THE MIDDLE EASTERN CONTEXT

A CASE STUDY FROM LEBANON AND JORDAN

Salwa Tohmé Tawk, Mounir Abi Said and *Shadi Hamadeh*

Due to its heavy reliance on food imports,[1] the Middle East and North Africa region (MENA) is considered to be one of the most food insecure regions in the world.[2] Urban Agriculture (UA), a traditional practice in the MENA region, is an important source of income for many urban and peri-urban households. Urban agriculture is defined according to Mougeot as

> located within (intra-urban) or on the fringe (peri-urban) of a town, a city or a metropolis, and grows or raises, processes and distributes a diversity of food and non-food products, (re-)uses largely human and material resources, products and services found in and around that urban area, and in turn supplies human and material resources, products and services largely to that urban area.[3]

Studying the role of urban agriculture in the MENA region could provide a better understanding of its role in food security. The present study was conducted to investigate food security as related to peri-urban and urban agriculture in two peri-urban locations: Bebnine in Lebanon, where agriculture lacks support, and in Wadi el Seer in Jordan, where urban agriculture is being institutionalised. Our research is based on data collected from a representative sample of a total of 800 low-income producing/farming households as well as low-income non-producing/ farming households per location and serving as a control group, in addition to two focus group discussions with producers in each location. The findings indicate the prevalence of high food insecurity in both locations demonstrating that producers are more food insecure than non-producers, and that food security is strongly associated with poverty and the number of household members.

Food security in the Middle East and North Africa region

The MENA region faces tremendous challenges in achieving food security, and the gap in the Arab world, the difference between imports and exports of food products, will reach $71 billion in 2030[4] and will double by 2050.[5] On the demand side, the predicted increased reliance on food imports is due to strong population growth, income growth and urbanisation. The Arab world population will reach 545 million persons by the year 2030, at an increase rate of 63.3 per cent from the current rate.[6]

On the supply side, it is due to the region's low agricultural productivity, which is largely a result of factors relating to poor natural resource endowments. Projections for MENA show that by 2050, the availability of renewable water will fall to an average of 500 cubic metres per capita and that arable land will shrink to 0.12 hectares per capita.[7]

In MENA, 5 per cent of the population lives below the World Bank poverty line of $1.25 per day and poor families can spend as much as 65 per cent of their income on food.[8] The wave of political unrest that swept the region in the first half of 2011 was partly triggered by socio-economic factors such as declining real wages, increasing unemployment and rising food prices.[9] Inflation in the MENA region increased at more than twice the rate of world inflation in 2007–8,[10] Countries that relied heavily on food imports, but did not gain from higher oil prices, such as Jordan and Lebanon, saw a deterioration in their trade balance due to the higher cost of food imports.

A joint report by the World Bank, the Food and Agriculture Organization of the United Nations (FAO), and the International Fund for Agricultural Development in 2009 suggested three strategic approaches serving as pillars to strengthen safety nets:[11] 1) provide people with better access to family planning services, and promote education; 2) enhance the food supply provided by domestic agriculture and improve rural livelihoods by addressing lagging productivity growth through increased investment in research and development; and 3) reduce exposure to market volatility by improving supply-chain efficiency and by more effectively using financial instruments to hedge risk.

This research is undertaken in order to investigate domestic agriculture production in areas where urban economic activities are becoming increasingly important to the livelihoods in the surrounding areas, therefore addressing the second pillar in the report mentioned above.

Urban agriculture in the Middle East and North Africa region

Several researchers have tried to clearly distinguish between UA and rural agriculture. Criteria used to make such distinctions include closeness to the city centre, inclusion in the administrative municipal boundaries and type of products grown.[12]

The most important distinguishing feature of UA is the fact that it is an integral part of the urban economic, social and ecological systems. Further, it is strongly influenced by urban conditions such as policies, competition for land, and urban markets and prices, and makes a strong impact on the urban system.[13]

UA is an important source of income for many urban households. In addition to income from the sale of surplus agricultural output, farming households save on household expenditures by growing their own food. These savings can be substantial since the poor generally spend a sizeable part of their income (35–65 per cent) on food.[14] UA also encourages the development of microenterprises or related enterprises, both at the downstream and upstream ends of the production chain. For instance, agricultural inputs, processing, packaging and product marketing as well as the provision of services,[15] such as animal health services and transportation, are all related activities which are organised around UA.[16]

The contribution of UA to food security and healthy nutrition is probably its most important asset. Food production in the city is often the urban poor's response to a lack of purchasing power and to inadequate, unreliable and irregular access to food. In urban settings more so than rural ones, lack of income translates more directly into lack of food.[17]

Agricultural production in and around cities is integral to Mediterranean cultural landscapes and has been a long-standing traditional practice in the MENA region.[18] The Middle East has one of the highest urbanisation rates in the developing world, but, despite the increasing demand for land and water, crop cultivation and animal husbandry remain common throughout the region's cities. Fertile agricultural areas are still considerable and are expected to remain productive for years to come as they provide an important source of income and job opportunities. At the beginning of the twenty-first century, 6 per cent of MENA's population was involved in UA as compared to an average of 2 per cent in other regions.[19] Nevertheless, MENA's urban production suffers from a lack of recognition by city planners, agriculturists, policymakers, researchers and even its practitioners. Until now, the most successful instances of UA have been in cities and regions where conflict and extreme poverty has defined life, such as in Gaza, Palestine, and in refugee camps.[20] In these places, the need for survival has led communities towards UA as a solution to food insecurity.

Measuring household food insecurity

The FAO defines food security as existing 'when all people, at all times, have physical, social, and economic access to sufficient, safe and nutritious food that meets their dietary needs and food preferences for an active and healthy life'.[21] In addition to food availability and access, components of current food security definitions include social acceptability of the means employed to access food and adequate food utilisation. In 2008, the World Health Organization (WHO) elaborated on the concept by focusing on three pillars of food security: 'food availability' entails having sufficient quality of food on a consistent basis; 'food access' means having sufficient resources to obtain appropriate food for a nutritious diet; and 'food use' means having knowledge of nutrition and care, as well as access to adequate water and sanitation for cleaner food consumption.[22]

Traditional income and poverty measures do not provide clear information about food security, even though food insecurity and hunger often stem from constrained financial resources.[23] The full range of food insecurity and hunger is determined at the household level by obtaining information on a variety of specific conditions, experiences and behaviours that serve as indicators of the varying degrees of severity.

URBAN AGRICULTURE AND FOOD SECURITY

Household food insecurity is generally identified in one of three methods: 1) through a nutritional assessment of household members, including body-mass indices, dietary intake, and nutrient deficiencies; 2) through measures of income and food expenditures that identify whether households earn enough or spend enough on food; and 3) through direct or experiential measures of food security in which individuals are asked general questions about their (or more commonly, their household's) experience in accessing an acceptable quantity and quality of food.

Direct measures of food security around the world have been influenced by the successful development and implementation of a direct food security measure during the 1990s in the United States.[24] Direct measures of household food security are being developed and used in a growing number of countries,[25] as they are easier and cheaper to apply than the measures of nutritional adequacy and blood tests to determine nutrient deficiencies.[26]

While countries, regions and organisations may adopt different definitions of food insecurity and hunger, which often translate into different survey questions reflecting the circumstances and priorities of specific contexts, it has been the case that food security surveys only need to have three or four key questions in common for their results to be comparable.[27]

In the MENA region, direct measurements of food insecurity have been used in few surveys. In Yemen, a survey measured food insecurity according to four direct indicators: food availability (vulnerability to food insecurity); reduction in quantity consumed (moderate food insecurity); skipping meals (severe food insecurity); and when households report that one or more children are reducing meals (moderate food insecurity and severe food insecurity among children). The study showed that 42 per cent of Yemeni households which were found to be either food insecure or vulnerable to food insecurity were households having higher numbers of children, households relying more on temporary employment and households which were involved in non-agricultural activities. About 21 per cent of the households were found to be food insecure.[28] Food security in Palestinian refugee camps in Lebanon was assessed using four direct indicators: food availability (vulnerability to food insecurity); reduction in quantity consumed (mild food insecurity); skipping meals (moderate food insecurity); and when households

163

report that one or more household members did not eat for an entire day or went to sleep hungry (severe food insecurity). The study revealed that 55.7 per cent were considered vulnerable to food insecurity and 14.9 per cent were classified as severely food insecure. There was a strong correlation between poverty and food insecurity, where 76 per cent of the extremely poor were considered vulnerable to food insecurity.[29]

Studies relating food security to urban agriculture are non-existent for the MENA region. Surveying the role of UA in cities in the MENA region could provide a better understanding of the role urban production is playing in household food security.

The present study was conducted to describe agriculture activities and to investigate food security as related to peri-urban agriculture in two locations: Bebnine-Akkar in Lebanon—a large and poor peri-urban community located on the edge of Tripoli, the second largest metropolis, where agriculture is lacking institutional frameworks—and Wadi el Seer, a large poor peri-urban district of Amman, Jordan, where urban agriculture is being institutionalised. The study also aimed at identifying determinants of food insecurity in the MENA context.

Description of the study sites

Bebnine and Wadi el Seer share similar aspects as both locations are among the poor conurbations in their respective countries, and both are close to urban centres. Wadi el Seer is a district of Amman and Bebnine is located in the suburb of the second largest metropolis, Tripoli, and on the main international highway. The populations in both cities originate from rural backgrounds, and, although people in these areas are now living in the proximity of large cities, they continue to practice agriculture as one of their major livelihood strategies. The activities are well integrated in the economy of the city and its market.

The major difference between the two localities is the institutional and governmental support of agriculture. Peri-urban agriculture activities are poorly supported and not recognised by local authorities in Bebnine, while the same activities are being institutionalised in Amman through the urban agriculture bureau based in the municipality of Greater Amman. This bureau was initiated in 2007 as part of a regional project led by the Environment and Sustainable Development Unit of the American University of Beirut within the context of a 2007–9 project led by the Resource Centers Network on Urban Agriculture and Food Security Foundation to mainstream UA in the MENA region. The efforts to identify key action points culminated in the municipality of Greater Amman taking the initiative to establish the specialised urban agriculture bureau with dedicated human and financial resources.[30]

Bebnine-Akkar, Lebanon

Although the role of agriculture in Lebanon's economy is declining, it still occupies an important place, generating 6.7 per cent of Lebanon's GDP in 2004 and employing roughly 9 per cent of the labour force in 2003.[31] The country produces just 20 per cent of its food requirements, importing the balance mainly from neighbouring countries. This makes it one of the least agriculturally self-sufficient countries in the world.[32]

Bebnine is a town of 40,000 inhabitants in the province of Akkar situated on the edge of the second largest city Tripoli. Akkar, the second largest agricultural area of Lebanon, is one of the most deprived regions in Lebanon, with the highest overall poverty rate in the country.[33] In 1998, Akkar was home to 12.5 per cent of the country's poor, with 63.3 per cent of its families living in poverty, out of which 23 per cent were living in extreme poverty.[34] The region, which is characterised by a dense population and a high age-dependency rate, has the lowest average individual income level and the highest illiteracy rate in Lebanon. Bebnine, as well as the whole of Akkar, shows typical features of a poor community, including poor infrastructure and low-quality education and health services. Limited sources of income compound with limited support from the public sector to create a cycle of poverty.

Wadi el Seer, Amman, Jordan

Wadi el Seer, a town of 150,000 inhabitants, is one of the twenty-seven districts of Amman, the capital of Jordan. Almost 60 per cent of its 1700km^2 area is vacant and hence available for agriculture. Currently, 30,000 hectares of Amman is already being used in agricultural production, which generates 18.4 per cent of the kingdom's total crop yield and 19 per cent of its livestock despite the severe water scarcity in the country.[35] Amman accounts for 24.6 per cent of people living under the poverty line in the Kingdom of Jordan, and the incidence of poverty in Wadi el Seer is 12–16 per cent according to a census completed in 2006 by the Department of Statistics.[36] In Amman, 22 per cent of urban households are engaged in agriculture on a full-time or part-time basis.

Research methodology

Low-income households in both localities were targeted by the study. Low-income households are those who earn a minimum wage or less (equivalent to around $300 per month for both localities). The target population was identified based on available secondary data as well as primary data collection through interviews of key informants. A land use map—GIS maps based on aerial photographs—was developed along with field visits to define sub-regions or zones based on factors such as: urban density or built fabric (low-density and high-density urban fabric), water accessibility, topography and land availability. Sub-regions were delineated on the map. Nine sub-regions were selected in Wadi el Seer and twenty-four in Bebnine. A stratified random sample of 400 households was selected for each locality to reflect the proportion of producers versus non-producers in each locality: 300 agriculture households and 100 non-agricultural households in Bebnine, and 200 agricultural households and 200 non-agricultural households in Wadi el Seer. The sample is based on and reflects the relative proportion of the population (producers versus non-producers) to improve the accountability of the results.

The target population was surveyed on direct measures of food insecurity using a questionnaire based on the Household Food Insecurity Access Scale,[37] and on the International Network of Resource Centers on Urban Agriculture and Food Security questionnaire for the socioeconomic and farming systems information.

The surveys, conducted from August to October 2011, assessed varying degrees of the severity of food insecurity present within the households, and investigated the role of urban agriculture production in the two localities to determine whether or not UA mitigates food insecurity.

Nomenclature of the food insecurity status used in this chapter is based partly on a survey conducted in the Palestinian refugee camps in Lebanon.[38] The following three indicators were used:

– Vulnerable to food insecurity: a household which reported that, in the previous six months, family members could not afford to buy more food when food was insufficient.

– Moderate food insecurity: a household which reported that, during the previous six months, one or more household members skipped a daily meal because there was not enough food or money to buy food.

– Severe food insecurity: a household which reported that, during the previous six months, one or more children of the household did not eat for an entire day, or went to sleep hungry because there was not enough food or money to buy food.

In addition, an overall integrated food insecurity score was calculated by weighing each of the three indicators by attributing to them a score from 0 to 3. Accordingly, the surveyed population was characterised as 'food secure to moderately food insecure, with a score of 0 to 1', or 'severely food insecure, with a score of 2 to 3' (see Figures 7.5, 7.7, 7.8 and 7.9).

Various methods were used to gather information used in the compilation of this study. These included available secondary data and primary data collection. The primary data included household surveys and interviews with key informants and focus group discussions with producers. The key informants were producers, municipality officers, agricultural input suppliers and organisations working in the area.

Focus group discussions were conducted with male and female producers from the surveyed households to supplement additional qualitative information for contribution of agricultural production to food security and qualitative perceptions of agricultural practices and income effects.

Data analysis

Data based on 781 completed questionnaires in both localities was analysed using the Statistical Programme for Social Sciences Windows version 16. Food security indicators and the overall food insecurity score were compared according to location and to agricultural and non-agricultural activities using chi-square tests.

Multivariate regression analysis was used to model food insecurity indicators according to the following selected control variables that were shown to affect food security in several studies:[39] low purchasing power to buy food (self-reported by respondent); lack of access to shops to get food; lack of storage or provisions of food; number of family household members; income level; percentage of annual income from agriculture income; percentage of income spent on food; the total area planted reported by producers; land tenure of cultivated land; and whether farming is a primary or secondary job. Forward Wald logistic regression was used to test the significance of the model.

The likelihood ratio goodness of fit test of the model was described using chi-square goodness of fit statistics. Model performance on the testing sets was evaluated by calculating the area under the curve of receiver operation characteristics (ROC) plots. ROC values range from 0.5 to 1.0. Values above 0.7 indicate strong model fit, while those above 0.9 indicate a highly accurate model.[40]

Results and discussion

This section describes agricultural activities in Bebnine and Wadi el Seer. It presents food insecurity distribution according to location and involvement in agriculture and analyses the determinants of food insecurity according to the specific variables surveyed.

Agriculture activities in the two target localities

The land use map of Bebnine and the surface area of each type of land use (Figure 7.1) revealed that the area used for agriculture is relatively high compared to built areas (73 per cent versus 20 per cent, respectively). Only 2.6 per cent of the total land use represented urban sprawl on field crops, demonstrating that there has been little infringement of the built areas on agricultural lands over the past ten years. Interestingly, abandoned fields only accounted for a very small percentage of the total land area, demonstrating that producers are reluctant to change their economic activities. Olive plantations accounted for the highest percentage of land use, covering 24 per cent of the total land area in the locality. Plastic greenhouses were the second most common agricultural activity, accounting for 14 per cent of the total land use for vacant land. This is explained by the mild coastal climate suitable for such type of production in winter. Interviews with producers, field visits and focus group discussions, revealed that agricultural activities in Bebnine consisted of rain-fed olive orchards, rain-fed crops (chickpeas, wheat, fava beans and peas), and vegetables grown in plastic houses and in open fields. Producers reported that the main water source for irrigation was polluted by untreated sewage water and gas station wastewater, which limits production of summer crops during the dry season as farmers are forced to buy water in cisterns. Animal production was limited due to the high price of feed.

Figure 7.1: Land use types in Bebnine, Lebanon, and surface area of each type in square metres and in percentage of total area

Code	Land use type	Area (sq m)	%
111a	Dense urban fabric	38,973	1
112a	Medium-density urban fabric	335,453	5
112c	Low-density urban fabric	1,004,543	15
112d	Low-density informal urban fabric	3,571	0
121	Industrial or commercial area	7,429	0
	Total urban fabric	1,389,969	21
122	Port area	38,611	1
135	Urban vacant land	20,177	0
213	Abandoned agricultural land	51	0
220/112c	Urban sprawl on field crops	176,855	3
211	Field crops in medium to large fields	844,629	13
212	Field crops in small fields/terraces	280,720	4
221	Olives	1,613,669	24
223	Fruit trees	137,858	2
224	Citrus fruit trees	457,209	7
231	Open horticulture	475,906	7
232	Protected agriculture	957,174	14
	Total agricultural area	4,767,164	71
331	Scrubland	120,752	2
410	Dense grassland	193,332	3
630s	Sandy beach	16,442	0
722	Port basin	3,889	0
R1	Highway	24,511	0
	Total surface area	6,751,753	100.00

The Floor Area Ratio (FAR) varies from 40–80 per cent, which leaves space for cultivation. However, people illegally build on their lands, thus gradually encroaching on more and more fertile land. In comparison, in the nearby metropolis of Tripoli, the FAR can reach 100 per cent.

Land is highly fragmented due to inheritance, and land leasing/tenure was reported to be on an annual lease basis. It is important to note that medium-term land tenure of three to six years is essential to make investments in plastic house production structures worthwhile. Producers reported that they market their products in a wholesale market in Beb el Tebbaneh in Tripoli, which also provides the capital Beirut with fresh fruit and vegetables. They relied on middlemen who were also their credit suppliers, charging high interest rates (15 per cent) compared to banks (5 per cent). Producers reported that few cooperatives were active and that local authorities did not support the agricultural sector.

The land use map for Wadi el Seer and the area attributed to each type (Figure 7.2) showed that agricultural land is half the built area (19 per cent and 40 per cent, respectively). Fruit trees covered 15 per cent of the total land and are the main agricultural land use type.

Figure 7.2: Land use types in Wadi el Seer, Jordan, and surface area of each type in square metres and in percentage of total area

Code	Land use type	Area (sq m)	%
111a	Dense urban fabric	18,404,022	31
112a	Medium-density urban fabric	71,061	0
112c	Low-density urban fabric	3,150,168	5
121	Industrial or commercial area	1,996,364	3
	Total urban area	23,621,615	40
210/112c	Urban sprawl on field crops	332,098	1
220/112c	Urban sprawl on permanent crops	153,904	0
212	Field crops in small fields/terraces	2,376,507	4
223	Fruit trees	8,725,524	15
232	Protected agriculture	17,334	0
	Total agricultural area	11,119,365	19
310	Dense wooded land	1,168,709	2
320	Clear wooded land	5,003,115	9
331	Scrubland	15,208,930	26
332	Scrubland with some dispersed bigger trees	1,657,161	3
410	Dense grassland	45,584	0
610	Bare rocks	337,144	1
620	Bare soils	159,007	0
	Total area	58,806,632	100

Interviews with producers, field visits and focus group discussions revealed that the main crops planted are olive and fig trees that are rain-fed and irrigated in summer and during periods of drought. Vegetables (onions and aromatic herbs such as thyme) are mostly intercropped with olive trees and fig trees. The main water source for irrigation is a spring water source that is available all year round and that provides the producers in Wadi el Seer the benefit of year-round crop production, compared to the other dry regions in the rest of Amman.

Some producers reported that they owned the land and others reported that the lease was on a short-term basis (one to five years). They also reported that share cropping was common on a seasonal basis.

The FAR varies between 36 and 52 per cent, and Wadi el Seer has an area zoned for agriculture (around 15 per cent of total area) that provides areas for sustainable agricultural production. Customarily, any vacant land in Amman can be tended by any local farmer and the farmer has the right to remain on the land until he/she has harvested the crop, therefore offering an environment that is conducive to urban agriculture. However, producers are self-organised and only access lands to which they have family relationships. While no laws restrict raising animals in these areas of Amman, animal production is limited to goats and sheep that are raised in limited numbers, as well as chickens, pigeons and rabbits. Producers explained that rearing animals is limited due to the high costs and levels of care required.

Producers responded that they sell their products at a wholesale market in Amman. Similar to the situation in Bebnine, producers also relied on middlemen who collect produce at the farmgate. However, agriculture is supported by the Greater Amman Municipality, through the Urban Agriculture Bureau, which gives producers in-kind support such as agricultural inputs, including seeds and fertilisers, and extension services. In addition, the municipality and other interested and influential stakeholders adopted a city strategic agenda for developing urban agriculture in 2009. Pilot projects such as rooftop gardening have been implemented in poor neighbourhoods. The Urban Agriculture Bureau has worked diligently to include urban agriculture as a major component of greening and re-zoning initiatives in the city. Through such supportive and enabling urban policies, norms and regulations, urban agriculture can fulfill certain functions required for sustainable city development such as food supply, income generation and sustainable land management.[41]

How producers perceive urban agriculture

Two focus group discussions were conducted in each city, grouping twenty producers (ten men and ten women) per group. During these discussions, when producers were asked about the availability of food for consumption from their own production, the answers ranged from less than 10 per cent to above 50 per cent. Around 22.2 per cent of producers in Wadi el Seer reported that over 50 per cent of their consumption comes from homegrown food, whereas in Bebnine none of the focus group participants found that homegrown food contributed to over 50 per cent of the overall food consumed. On the other hand, a low contribution of homegrown food for own consumption (≤10 per cent) was reported in Bebnine (Figure 7.3). This reveals that the residents of Wadi el Seer have higher levels of household food consumption from their own production compared to those in Bebnine.

Figure 7.3: Availability of homegrown food for consumption among producers based on focus group discussion

Availability of home-grown food for consumption	No increase	≤10% increase	10–25% increase	25–50% increase	Over 50% increase
Wadi el Seer	0	0	45%	33%	22%
Bebnine	0	33%	45%	22%	0

Producers were also asked about the positive impacts of UA according to three given categories, including: availability of homegrown food; more diverse and healthier food; and more greenery and trees. In both localities (75 per cent in Bebnine and 90 per cent in Wadi el Seer), the highest level of importance was placed on 'availability of homegrown food' (see Figure 7.4).

Figure 7.4: Perception of the importance of the impact of urban agriculture among producers based on focus group discussion results

Importance of impact of UA	Wadi el Seer participants	Bebnine participants
Availability of homegrown food	90%	75%
More diverse and healthier food	60%	45%
More greenery/trees	15%	20%

Food insecurity distribution: Lebanon versus Jordan

High food insecurity levels ranging between 37 and 59 per cent for the overall food insecurity score were observed in both Bebnine and Wadi el Seer. However, food insecurity was more prevalent in Bebnine compared to Wadi el Seer (p>0.001).

The overall food insecurity score revealed that 51.6 per cent of households in Bebnine and 37 per cent of households in Wadi el Seer were food insecure (Figure 7.5). This was further confirmed by the three food security indicators. In Bebnine, 51.4 per cent of households compared to 37 per cent of households in Wadi el Seer reported that they were able to eat enough food, but not the desired types of food, or that they could not afford to buy more food when food was insufficient, demonstrating a vulnerability to food insecurity. Bebnine also had a higher percentage of households reporting that family members were forced to skip a meal during the past six months (47.6 per cent compared to 28 per cent in Wadi el Seer). Lastly, measuring levels of severe food insecurity, 25 per cent in Bebnine and 20 per cent in Wadi el Seer reported that children in their households were affected—either by not eating enough or by skipping a meal. This difference, however, was not significant (p<0.1).

Food insecurity levels found in this study are comparable to other reports from the region (see Figure 7.6). Overall levels of food insecurity

Figure 7.5: Frequency of food insecure households: Bebnine, Lebanon, versus Wadi el Seer, Jordan

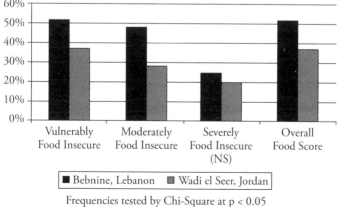

Frequencies tested by Chi-Square at p < 0.05

FOOD SECURITY IN THE MIDDLE EAST

among households in the five localities (Bebnine, Wadi el Seer, Palestinian camps and 'gatherings' outside the official camps in Lebanon, and Yemen) are quite similar, although Wadi el Seer demonstrates the lowest percentage of food insecure households. In terms of vulnerability to food insecurity, Bebnine demonstrates similar rates to the Palestinian camps and communities. The percentage of households vulnerable to food insecurity in Yemen is lower than the other areas, although this may be explained by the fact that the study was completed in 2004, before the 2007–08 food price shock that increased the number of undernourished people in the Arab region by an additional 4 million.[42] Bebnine has the highest number of households that are moderately food insecure, whereas Wadi el Seer has rates more similar to the Palestinian camps and communities. Bebnine and Wadi el Seer had the highest percentage of households that are severely food insecure. Observed differences in food insecurity could be explained by the specific contexts in which each of the areas are found— especially with regards to the food policies and subsidies, as well as support by the government for agricultural activities. Neither Lebanon nor Jordan has benefited from policies addressing the challenges found within the agricultural sector,[43] and both have been forced to increase their food imports since 2006.[44] An additional factor that might account for the differences lies in the indicators used to measure each category as well as the scope of the surveys whether local, national or regional. The present study targeted low-income households.

Figure 7.6: Degree of food insecurity in MENA reports

Households classified according to degree of food insecurity	Bebnine–Lebanon (2012)	Wadi el Seer–Jordan (2012)	Palestinian camps in Lebanon (2010)	Palestinian gatherings in Lebanon (2010)	Yemen (2004)
All food insecure households	51.60%	37.00%	59.20%	50.70%	42.40%
Vulnerable	51.40%	37.00%	59.20%	50.70%	20.80%
Moderate	40.60%	28.10%	32.30%	21.80%	13.80%
Severe	25%	20%	16.90%	12.00%	not applicable

As mentioned above, the Yemen study was completed prior to the food price shock, which likely accounts for the lower percentages of

174

households facing varying degrees of food insecurity. Recent reports by the World Food Programme noted that 22 per cent of the population requires external food assistance, which has almost doubled since 2009.[45]

Food insecurity among producers and non-producers

The overall food insecurity score differed between producers and non-producers (see Figure 7.7). It was found that 50.7 per cent of the producers (combined data for both Bebnine and Wadi el Seer) were food insecure compared to 32.7 per cent of non-producers ($p > 0.05$). In terms of all three indicators (vulnerability, moderate and severe), producers were always found to have a higher degree of food insecurity than non-producers. These results are similar to findings in rural areas of Lebanon where self-production of food was not significantly correlated with food security.[46] However, these results do not concur with other studies within the region—one, for example, reported that non-agricultural households in Yemen are less likely to be food insecure than agricultural households who rely on their own production as their main source of food.[47] Moreover, producers had higher food diversity scores than non-producers, suggesting that farming enabled the very poor to diversify their diet.[48] It is thus important to consider the context in which the communities are living, where agriculture activity in both target localities is declining. Additionally, 50 per cent of producers rely on agricul-

Figure 7.7: Frequency of food insecure households: producers versus non-producers across both localities

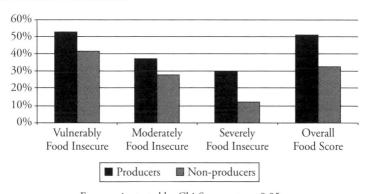

Frequencies tested by Chi-Square at $p < 0.05$

ture activities as their primary source of revenue. This represents an unstable income, as agriculture is a seasonal activity. In addition, as reported by producing households during interviews and focus group discussions, many producers are in debt to agriculture input suppliers and middle-men.

The contribution of off-farm income has been increasingly important in providing both rural and urban producers with a significant proportion of their income,[49] and, therefore, contributing to a better food security status. The share of rural income in the MENA region derived from non-agricultural economic activities was reported to be only 20 to 30 per cent and increased to 70 per cent in urbanising economies, showing the increased share of off-farm economic activities among urban producers.

Broken down by locality, the same trend is found in the Lebanese context, where producers are more vulnerable to all degrees of food insecurity than non-producers (p>0.05; see Figure 7.8). However, in Wadi el Seer the producers fared better than the non-producers in the overall food insecurity score as well as in the vulnerability to food insecurity score (p>0.05; see Figure 7.9).

When comparing producers across localities, those in Wadi el Seer fared better than the producers in Bebnine (p>0.05). The overall food insecurity score evidences that 55 per cent of producers in Bebnine are food insecure, compared to only 32 per cent of producers in Wadi el Seer. Similar trends are found when analysing the producers who are vulnerable to food insecurity (62.9 per cent of producers in Bebnine

Figure 7.8: Frequency of food insecure households: producers versus non-producers in Bebnine, Lebanon

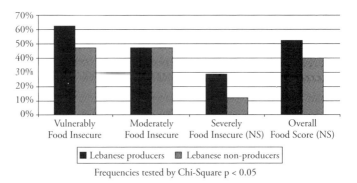

Frequencies tested by Chi-Square p < 0.05

Figure 7.9: Frequency of food insecure households: producers versus non-producers in Wadi el Seer, Jordan

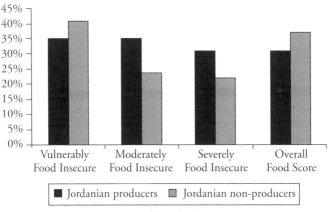

Frequencies tested by Chi-Square p < 0.05

versus 32 per cent of producers in Wadi el Seer), and those who experience moderate food insecurity (47.6 per cent of producers in Bebnine versus 34.9 per cent in Wadi el Seer). Severe food insecurity was similar in both areas (p<0.1). The different levels of food security found between these two areas may be due to the fact that urban agriculture is being institutionalised and supported in Amman, whereas no such support is provided in Bebnine.

Determinants of food insecurity

A logistic regression analysis was used to identify the variables determining the overall food insecurity score as well as each of the three levels of food insecurity (vulnerable, moderate, severe) in each location.

The analysis revealed that the following variables significantly contribute to food insecurity: low purchasing power to buy food (self-reported by respondents); no access to shops to get food; no storage or provisions of food; greater number of family household members; income; and higher percentage of income spent on food. Analysis of the overall food insecurity score, which included all food insecure households across both localities, revealed that the most important factors were the low purchasing power and the number of family members in the households

FOOD SECURITY IN THE MIDDLE EAST

(p>0.05). Families with four members or more were most likely to be affected (see Figure 7.10). Vulnerability to food insecurity was significantly determined by low purchasing power, lack of access to shops, lack of proper storage for food, number of family members in the household, and percentage of income spent on food. Families with seven members were most likely to be vulnerable (p>0.05; see Figure 7.11). Moderate and severe food insecurity were mostly determined by low purchasing power, the income level of the respondents and the percentage of income spent on food (p<0.05; see Figures 7.12 and 7.13).

Figure 7.10: Logistic regression on overall food insecurity score across localities

Variables	B	S.E.	Wald	Df	Significance
Low purchasing power to buy food (self-reported by respondents)	1.614	0.267	36.505	1	0.000
No. of family members			20.359	9	0.016
1 family member	19.930	2.842E4	0.000	1	0.999
2 family members	−0.759	0.681	1.241	1	0.265
3 family members	−0.066	0.550	0.014	1	0.905
4 family members	−1.060	0.537	3.897	1	0.048
5 family members	−0.887	0.538	2.719	1	0.099
6 family members	−0.503	0.523	0.925	1	0.336
7 family members	0.087	0.597	0.021	1	0.885
8 family members	1.027	0.616	2.778	1	0.056
9 family members	0.073	0.615	0.014	1	0.906
Constant	−0.341	0.447	0.583	1	0.445

Figure 7.11: Logistic regression on vulnerability to food insecurity

Variables	B	S.E.	Wald	Df	Significance
Low purchasing power to buy food (self-reported by respondents)	−0.736	0.252	8.553	1	0.003
No access to shops to get food	−1.725	0.426	16.420	1	0.000
No storage	−1.327	0.489	7.351	1	0.007
No. of family members			23.140	9	0.006
1 family member	−0.229	1.118	0.042	1	0.838

2 family members	0.274	0.671	0.167	1	0.683
3 family members	1.068	0.563	3.602	1	0.058
4 family members	−0.072	0.500	0.021	1	0.885
5 family members	−0.838	0.516	2.638	1	0.104
6 family members	−0.332	0.498	0.445	1	0.505
7 family members	−1.237	0.549	5.078	1	0.024
8 family members	−0.165	0.537	0.094	1	0.759
9 family members	−0.315	0.582	0.293	1	0.589
% income spent on food			30.180	6	0.000
0% spent on food	1.380	0.575	5.764	1	0.016
10% spent on food	−0.270	0.755	0.128	1	0.720
20% spent on food	0.659	0.578	1.299	1	0.254
30% spent on food	1.453	0.549	7.010	1	0.008
40% spent on food	1.306	0.588	4.930	1	0.026
50% spent on food	−0.069	0.536	0.017	1	0.898
Constant	−0.027	0.615	0.002	1	0.965

Figure 7.12: Logistic regression on moderate food insecurity

Variables	B	S.E.	Wald	Df	Significance
Low purchasing power to buy food (self-reported by respondents)	1.511	0.268	31.739	1	0.000
Monthly income			14.148	8	0.078
Income <$30	23.774	4.019E4	0.000	1	1.000
Income <$60	0.497	1.130	0.193	1	0.660
Income <$100	−20.107	2.707E4	0.000	1	0.999
Income <$150	−0.686	0.993	0.477	1	0.490
Income <$200	0.369	0.789	0.219	1	0.640
Income <$300	−0.320	0.727	0.193	1	0.660
Income >$300	0.947	0.638	2.205	1	0.138
Income do not know	0.290	0.761	0.146	1	0.703
% income spent on food			25.653	6	0.000
0% spent on food	−1.361	0.557	5.979	1	0.014
10% spent on food	0.030	0.686	0.002	1	0.965
20% spent on food	−1.072	0.597	3.223	1	0.073
30% spent on food	−1.917	0.571	11.261	1	0.001
40% spent on food	−0.399	0.561	0.507	1	0.476
50% spent on food	−0.246	0.503	0.239	1	0.625
Constant	−0.655	0.755	0.752	1	0.386

Figure 7.13: Logistic regression on severe food insecurity

Variables	B	S.E.	Wald	Df	Significance
Low purchasing power to buy food (self-reported by respondents)	3.954	0.427	85.827	1	0.000
Monthly income			14.889	8	0.061
Income <$30	20.450	4.019E4	0.000	1	1.000
Income <$60	−2.009	2.319	0.751	1	0.386
Income <$100	−21.170	4.019E4	0.000	1	1.000
Income <$150	18.831	1.553E4	0.000	1	0.999
Income <$200	−2.779	1.336	4.326	1	0.038
Income <$300	−2.687	1.129	5.660	1	0.017
Income >$300	−2.975	1.000	8.848	1	0.003
Income do not know	−0.608	1.143	0.283	1	0.594
% income spent on food			16.235	6	0.013
0% spent on food	−2.555	0.945	7.308	1	0.007
10% spent on food	−3.725	1.235	9.095	1	0.003
20% spent on food	−1.561	0.948	2.711	1	0.100
30% spent on food	−1.769	0.829	4.552	1	0.033
40% spent on food	−2.425	0.883	7.539	1	0.006
50% spent on food	−0.930	0.760	1.496	1	0.221
Constant	2.522	1.174	4.615	1	0.032

When broken down by locality, the logistic regression analysis of determinants revealed that low purchasing power and the number of family members in a household significantly determined severe food insecurity in Bebnine compared to low purchasing power and the percentage of income spent on food in Wadi el Seer (p>0.05; see Figures 7.14 and 7.15). The analysis of determinants for food insecure producers and non-producers revealed that low purchasing power was the major determinant for non-producers, in addition to the number of family members, and percentage of income spent on food for producers (p<0.05; see Figures 7.16 and 7.17).

All the above models explained 70 to 84 per cent of the variance among food insecure households, with a ROC value (0.7 to 0.9) indicating a strong fit of the models. These results clearly indicate a direct relationship between food insecurity and economic attributes, mainly income and purchasing power in poor households. The results are in agreement with past reports on the Palestinian camps in Lebanon which

Figure 7.14: Logistic regression on overall food insecurity score in Bebnine, Lebanon

Variables	B	S.E.	Wald	Df	Significance
Low purchasing power to buy food (self-reported by respondents)	1.452	0.339	18.383	1	0.000
No. of family members			17.682	9	0.039
1 family member	20.074	2.842E4	0.000	1	0.999
2 family members	−0.549	0.884	0.386	1	0.535
3 family members	.456	.661	0.475	1	0.491
4 family members	−1.013	0.629	2.598	1	0.107
5 family members	−1.068	0.651	2.696	1	0.101
6 family members	−0.361	0.603	0.358	1	0.549
7 family members	−0.076	0.758	0.010	1	0.920
8 family members	1.553	0.815	3.629	1	0.057
9 family members	−0.169	0.750	0.051	1	0.822
Constant	−0.323	0.513	0.397	1	0.529

Figure 7.15: Logistic regression on overall food insecurity score in Wadi el Seer, Jordan

Variables	B	S.E.	Wald	Df	Significance
Low purchasing power to buy food (self-reported by respondents)	1.411	0.569	6.139	1	0.013
% income spent on food			11.279	6	0.080
0% spent on food	−1.782	0.770	5.361	1	0.021
10% spent on food	−0.987	1.651	0.357	1	0.550
20% spent on food	20.921	4.019E4	0.000	1	1.000
30% spent on food	19.510	4.019E4	0.000	1	1.000
40% spent on food	−0.156	1.384	0.013	1	0.910
50% spent on food	0.095	0.827	0.013	1	0.909
Constant	0.282	0.775	0.132	1	0.716

demonstrate that 62 per cent of the poor and 76 per cent of the extreme poor reported experiencing some degree of food insecurity.[50] Similar results have been reported by other surveys.[51] However, Kabbani et al.,[52] in relating poverty to food insecurity in Yemen, suggested that food poverty is very much an outgrowth of poverty rates and should not be

FOOD SECURITY IN THE MIDDLE EAST

Figure 7.16: Logistic regression on overall food insecurity score among producers

Variables	B	S.E.	Wald	Df	Significance
Low purchasing power to buy food (self-reported by respondents)	1.397	0.329	18.068	1	0.000
No. of family members			21.110	9	0.012
1 family member	20.197	2.842E4	0.000	1	0.999
2 family members	−0.154	1.100	0.020	1	0.889
3 family members	0.758	0.645	1.381	1	0.240
4 family members	−1.158	0.617	3.520	1	0.061
5 family members	−1.066	0.625	2.905	1	0.088
6 family members	−0.209	0.565	0.137	1	0.712
7 family members	0.120	0.624	0.037	1	0.848
8 family members	1.128	0.662	2.909	1	0.088
9 family members	0.186	0.665	0.078	1	0.780
% income spent on food			15.197	6	0.019
0% spent on food	−2.310	0.862	7.187	1	0.007
10% spent on food	−2.475	1.063	5.419	1	0.020
20% spent on food	−0.785	0.715	1.205	1	0.272
30% spent on food	−0.520	0.690	0.568	1	0.451
40% spent on food	−0.454	0.740	0.376	1	0.540
50% spent on food	−0.255	0.683	0.140	1	0.709
Constant	0.128	0.766	0.028	1	0.867

Figure 7.17: Logistic regression on overall food insecurity score among non-producers

Variables	B	S.E.	Wald	Df	Significance
Low purchasing power to buy food (self-reported by respondents)	2.194	0.565	15.081	1	0.000
Constant	−0.767	0.336	5.226	1	0.022

taken on its own as a proxy for food insecurity. Indeed, non-poor households were also reported to show various degrees of vulnerability to food insecurity.[53] In 2005, Nord et al. reported that 20 per cent of US households classified as food insecure had midrange or high income levels, but were food insecure. This was due to transitory factors reflecting constrained access to food which were not reflected in annual income estimates, such as uneven incomes during the year.[54]

Our results indicate a strong association between food insecurity and number of household members: families with four members or more were likely to be more food insecure. A recent study on the rural areas of Lebanon found that households with eight or more members had greater chances of being food insecure than households with one member.[55] Kabbani et al. also associated food insecurity in Yemen with having a larger number of children.[56] All three studies showed that food insecurity is linked with large family sizes.

Variables related to production, such as the percentage of annual income from agricultural profits, the total area planted as reported by producers, land tenure of cultivated land and whether farming is a primary or secondary job, did not show any strong association with food insecurity in the present study. This correlates with our previous findings that show food insecurity to be more prevalent among producers than non-producers.

Conclusion

In summary, the present study indicates the high prevalence of food insecurity in the peri-urban areas studied within the MENA context. This prevalence was strongly associated with poverty and large families. In general, peri-urban producers were less food secure than non-producers. When the local policy environment was conducive to these activities, producers in such areas were more food secure than producers in areas where agriculture is not supported. Such is the case in Jordan where the government is supporting the development of agriculture within the districts of the capital, Amman.

These results are not meant to state that urban agriculture should not be considered as a viable economic activity for poor, local households. There is evidence that when the local environment is more conducive to agricultural production, producers are less food insecure. Continuing to support producers, therefore, is likely to bring about positive changes in the food security of their households. While some positive benefits have already been seen in Amman, the support for agriculture is relatively recent, and it is likely that further benefits will be evident in the future. Additionally, urban agriculture has likely provided a safety net for those families who have traditionally practiced agriculture by providing some additional income and extra food for household consumption.

The current study reveals the need for further research investigating the contribution of urban agriculture to the livelihoods and household consumption of producing families, as well as for the consumption of non-producing households in the area. Currently, there are no studies demonstrating the benefits and value of urban agriculture to these families. It is hypothesised that although the producing families are currently food insecure, if they were no longer producing they would likely face more extreme degrees of food insecurity, including hunger. This would also affect the availability of food in the region, linking back to the food availability and access issues mentioned by WHO in its three pillars of food security. Furthermore, it would be important to investigate whether these producing families in peri-urban areas have improved access to food diversity, therefore demonstrating the significant nutritional benefits derived through urban agriculture, which are not captured by the overall food security score.

8

FOOD SECURITY AND THE SUPERMARKET TRANSITION IN THE MIDDLE EAST

TWO CASE STUDIES

Karin Seyfert, Jad Chaaban and *Hala Ghattas*

Over the past decade, a number of developing countries have witnessed two food system transitions affecting their food security.[1] The first, known as the 'nutrition transition', is a shift from so-called 'traditional' diets—based on the consumption of foods high in fibre such as cereals, legumes, fruit and vegetables—to so-called 'modern' diets—which feature larger proportions of saturated fats, sugar and processed foods. This dietary shift has been facilitated by the second transition, in food procurement, known as the 'supermarket transition'[2] or the 'third and corporate food regime'.[3] This chapter focuses on changes in national procurement channels. The supermarket transition involves a shift from food production and processing in small units—whose output is sold to small retailers at wholesale spot markets—to one consisting of larger retail outlets trading with dedicated or contracted specialised wholesalers and food producers.

This transition is presently under way in Lebanon and Qatar, our two case study countries. Two reasons motivate the choice of Qatar and Lebanon as case studies. First, both are small, making them easier to analyse and therefore more apt for a comparative case study. Second, Qatar and Lebanon embody a key distinction among countries of the Middle East. Qatar is fiscally stable, relying on oil and gas exports but dependent on food imports, while Lebanon is fiscally unstable but possesses a productive agricultural sector by regional standards. Aspects of the Lebanese and Qatari political economies may slow or suspend the supermarket transition and, by extension, the corporatisation of their food supply chains. These impediments are not the product of orchestrated political resistance but are, rather, the unintended consequence of a marginally functioning state in Lebanon and of wholesale price controls in Qatar, introduced as a 'rentier bargain' policy aimed at protecting consumers from price volatility and obtaining their acquiescence.

The nutrition and supermarket transitions have had consequences for food security as they tend to affect the quality of the affected population's diet. Past studies on these transitions are reviewed in the first section of this chapter, with a particular focus on the procurement of fresh fruit and vegetables (FFV). The second section describes the methodology used in data collection. The third section discusses results and characterises the Lebanese and Qatari FFV procurement systems. The fourth section presents current policies in place as well as policy options, and the fifth and final section concludes the chapter.

Food system transitions: the nutrition transition

Food insecurity is often equated with under-nutrition resulting from calorie deficiency, however, in developed countries and increasingly in MENA countries, food insecurity manifests as poor quality diets rather than calorie deficient diets. Diets high in saturated fats, low in fibre and high in sugar and refined foods significantly contribute to increases in the burden of chronic disease in MENA country populations. Diabetes and cardiovascular disease rates in the Middle East are already among the highest in the world.[4] Sibai et al. observe high levels of adult obesity and metabolic syndrome, which are associated with a rise in total daily energy, protein and fat supply per capita over the past three decades.[5] Data from the region show that stunted children are more likely to be overweight,[6] and such a double burden of disease is likely due to the simultaneous occurrence of micronutrient deficiencies and calorie excess in the same populations, often referred to as 'hidden hunger'.[7]

Food consumption surveys in Bahrain and Damascus show low intake of fruit and vegetables with potential implications for micronutrient deficiencies.[8] Even in Lebanon, which has higher fresh fruit and vegetable consumption than less developed countries, these levels remain below the World Health Organization (WHO) recommended quantity.[9] Lebanon has high levels of overweight and obesity related to increased consumption of 'Western' diets,[10] consisting of fast-foods such as pizzas, sandwiches, French fries, sodas, meat, refined grains, pies, ice cream and sweets.[11] Similarly, Hassan and Al-Dosari reported high intakes of fatty foods by Qatari schoolchildren.[12] Although fresh fruits were frequently consumed as snacks, there was still a high prevalence of overweight and risk of becoming overweight among Qatari schoolchildren.[13]

Dietary guidelines from the developed world overwhelmingly advocate increases in fruit and vegetable intake. In countries experiencing a double burden of disease, fruit and vegetables have the potential to reduce both the burden of micronutrient deficiencies and the burden of chronic disease through the protective effects of fibres and antioxidants. Therefore, we focused in particular on FFV in the present study.

Socioeconomic factors influence FFV consumption

Socioeconomic factors influence diets. Low-energy density diets have been found to be more costly, and more sensitive to food price inflation, than high-energy density diets.[14] In Vietnam, consumption of FFV is 23 per cent lower in the poorest and 31 per cent higher in the wealthiest expenditure quartile.[15] In the United States, higher socioeconomic status is associated with adequate FFV consumption and dietary quality.[16] A study of university students in Lebanon found that those with higher socioeconomic status consumed more micronutrient rich foods such as vegetables and meats and lower amounts of carbohydrates.[17] Similarly, better education is associated with the consumption of wholemeal bread, low-fat dairy and low-sugar sodas.[18] At the lower end of the socioeconomic spectrum, researchers from the International Food Policy Research Institute noted that a common coping mechanism used by poor households to absorb price spikes in food is to shift to lower quality and less nutritious food.[19] A study of Palestinian refugees in Lebanon also found significant reductions in fruit consumption as well as in dairy and meat products as household food insecurity becomes more severe.[20] Hence, the price level of micronutrient-dense food groups such as fruit and vegetables are important considerations in ensuring food security.

Food shopping and diets

Food procurement patterns appear to influence dietary choices. Evidence from Guatemala shows that an increase in supermarket purchases increases the share that highly processed foods contribute to total caloric intake. This is at the expense of staple foods. In the same population, processed food consumption is associated with a higher Body Mass Index and contributes to the prevalence of obesity and overweight.[21] Evidence from Tunisia suggests that average calorie intake may rise when a supermarket is the first choice for food shopping, though the difference is not statistically significant.[22] Supermarkets, in this chapter, refer to large retail outlets, often part of a retail chain. Supermarket and retail chains are used interchangeably and are contrasted with grocers, in particular greengrocers, which are also sometimes called 'mom and pop' stores in the literature.

Food system transitions: the supermarket transition

In parallel with the nutritional transition in diets, a structural transition took place in the retail food procurement sector in many developed as well as emerging countries. The rise of supermarkets has transformed food procurement chains and the agro-food system. As with the nutrition transition, the rise of supermarkets occurs in tandem with urbanisation and rising household income, as well as, more specifically, greater participation by women in the labour force, higher levels of car ownership and improvements in infrastructure and refrigeration.[23]

The presence of a modestly affluent middle class is a prerequisite for the broader emergence of supermarkets. In Tunisia, supermarket use is associated with urbanisation, small households, higher socioeconomic status and easy access to food.[24] In Morocco, supermarkets are concentrated in the wealthiest neighbourhoods of large cities,[25] while survey data from Madagascar finds that its global retail chains sell at higher prices than those found at traditional retail markets.[26] In Vietnam, consumers' decisions to buy FFV from modern retail chains are heavily determined by wealth, as proxied by household expenditure.[27] Affluence allows for an increased ability to pay for product diversity, decoupling food supply from what is locally available and leading to an internationalisation of food procurement.[28]

Urbanisation and higher household income are associated with longer working hours and increased participation of women in the labour market. This leads to a greater emphasis being placed on reduced food preparation time, for which processed foods are often specifically designed. Devine et al. show that long and irregular working hours in the United States are associated with decreased food preparation time and increased consumption of processed foods.[29] Families are obtaining more food and meals, especially fast-foods, away from home. Stress may also play a role: sweetness and other sensory cues to high-energy density such as fatty texture can temporarily improve mood and mitigate stress.[30]

Supermarkets can better cater to this increased demand for processed foods at lower costs through scale economies. Processed food represents almost 80 per cent of supermarket shelf space.[31] Supermarket control over fresh foods has been slower and subject to greater international variety due to local habits and responses by local shops. Large retailers prefer to carry commodity fresh foods such as potatoes. Supermarkets' market share in fresh foods varies from 10 per cent in countries such as Guatemala to 50 per cent in Brazil and 75 per cent in France.[32]

The increased availability of refrigeration in homes and access to cars increases the amount of fresh food a household can store, leading consumers to make less frequent but larger purchases at locations outside their immediate neighbourhood.[33] However, in Tunisia, no statistical association with ownership of a refrigerator, freezer, or car was found.[34] From the supply perspective, technological changes have greatly improved procurement logistics and inventory management.[35]

Consumer preferences for supermarkets versus traditional outlets

Supermarkets may be unsuited to the preferences of some consumers. For instance, retail outlets in Japan remain the size of convenience stores and are less concentrated than elsewhere. Japanese consumers prefer freshness, small packet size and value health aspects. In addition, car ownership is low and living space small, limiting transport and storage capacities. This is combined with a willingness to shop in several locations.[36] Chinese consumers at present tend to prefer traditional wet markets, where fresh fruit and vegetables but also fish, meat and dairy products may be sold by traders on individual stalls, to supermarkets.[37]

Penetration of supermarkets in the Eastern Mediterranean is proceeding more slowly than in Latin America or South East Asia. FFV account for only about 3 per cent of supermarket turnover in Turkey and Morocco. Codron et al. attribute this to custom as well as constraints on Foreign Direct Investment (FDI).[38] In Vietnam and Hong Kong, freshness and convenience shape consumers' preference for traditional outlets,[39] while price played a key role in choosing shopping outlets for processed food products. Similar patterns were found by Goldman and Hino who compared Jewish- and Arab-Israeli shopping behaviour and found that the latter preferred traditional retail outlets, at least for fresh foods, while purchasing staples and processed foods in supermarkets.[40] The authors attributed this to both an Arab consumer's preference for service by a fellow Arab and a difference in material context: the lower rate of car ownership among Arab-Israelis, more constrained living conditions and lower participation of women in the labour market.[41] To draw in reluctant customers from the Eastern and Southern Mediterranean, supermarkets often focus on attributes like cleanliness, convenience, safety, consistency and product diversity while also selectively adopting 'traditional' displays that present produce in bulk, rather than packaging, allowing consumers to select and inspect.[42] Similar preferences for touching, feeling and smelling produce prior to purchase have been noted in Vietnam.[43]

The relative ability of modern and traditional food systems to offer cheap, high-quality food has important food security implications. Available evidence is conflicted as to which procurement system supplies superior quality foods at better prices. Reardon and Timmer argue that in the initial stages of supermarket penetration, local greengrocers have an edge in produce quality, freshness and convenience, but that this edge erodes as supermarkets are better able to cut costs and impose quality controls with local suppliers.[44] Investigations in Turkey and Morocco suggest that supermarket FFV products often fall short in consumers' expectations of freshness and taste, though sold at a premium over greengrocer prices.[45] In Vietnam,[46] Lusaka[47] and Delhi,[48] traditional outlets continue to outperform retail chains in price, quality, freshness or convenience. In Madagascar, however, Minten found that supermarkets supply superior quality produce when compared to local greengrocers.[49] The author stated that the quality is reflected in price differences, with greengrocers targeting lower-income segments. Evidence also points to Thai supermarkets selling higher quality at higher prices.[50] Due to their more extended control of the supply chain, supermarkets are in a better position to ensure food safety.[51]

A changing procurement channel

In their expansion, supermarkets must face price competition from traditional greengrocers while still maintaining product quality, safety and diversity.[52] Supermarkets profit through low margin, high volume sales. Since the 1980s, supermarket expansion in Western Europe and North America, through vertical and horizontal integration or coordination, has led to oligopolistic market structures. Retailers no longer buy what suppliers offer but stipulate what should be supplied. To supply supermarkets, suppliers must satisfy scale, quality and packaging demands and accept delayed payment. Suppliers also face repeated reductions in margins.[53] On a global level, Ploeg explains that 'food empires' are run on credit, requiring a large cash flow to serve interest on loans, which finance expansion. This requires agro-food corporations to exert permanent downward pressure on suppliers while maintaining upward pressure on prices paid by consumers. Ploeg shows how this has contributed to a widening gap between farmgate and consumer prices.[54] Furthermore, once in a supermarket, special offers as well as strategic product location may manipulate consumer choices.[55] A marker of the 'third food regime' is corporate control over food supply, where retailers are moving beyond distribution to influencing production and consumption.[56] These pressures and the power of supermarkets transform traditional procurements systems.

Reardon and Berdegué describe the 'traditional' procurement system as follows: each retail outlet procures its own stock; wholesale markets are the main procurement source; retailers rely on spot market prices rather than on contracts; and retailers rely on public quality and safety standards, if any.[57] Reardon et al. describe the modern procurement system conversely: retail outlets are supplied by centralised distribution centres; wholesalers specialise in certain products and quality standards; retailers deal with preferred suppliers through contractual agreements; and retailers set up private quality and packaging standards enforced upon suppliers by contract.[58] This is a characterisation of retailers and suppliers only. Regarding producers, and in reference to Ploeg as well as Lawrence and Burch, we would add that the abandonment of agriculture in marginal lands as well as the increased concentration of land ownership and industrial farming are also characteristics of the third food regime.[59] The two procurement channels are schematically represented in Figure 8.3.

These modern and traditional systems have different approaches to product sourcing, dissimilar wholesale sectors, different product quality regulatory regimes and different technological capacities. Each of these will be discussed below.

The demise of wholesale spot markets

Traditional procurement channels go through dedicated wholesale markets where produce is sold, sometimes at auction, and monitored by public authorities. In countries where the procurement system transition has taken place, wholesale markets are largely obsolete.[60] The demise of traditional wholesale markets is linked to the inability of wholesale markets to meet supermarkets' requirements for consistent quality and reliable quantities. Produce sold on wholesale markets are not graded by third parties, and quantities or volumes traded can be unpredictable. Dealing through numerous wholesale market brokers involves higher transaction and coordination costs than dealing with a few specialised wholesalers.[61] Though less critical than in the past, wholesale markets persist in the UK,[62] Mexico,[63] Turkey and Morocco.[64] Where such markets persist, their survival is usually ascribed to their relative efficiency.[65]

Supermarkets introduce a shift from wholesale spot markets to long-term supply contracts with specialised wholesalers to ensure quality and volume standards.[66] In the UK, exotic produce was initially bought entirely from wholesale markets but the largest supermarkets now work with dedicated importers.[67] This amounts to quasi-vertical integration wherein suppliers are assured a buyer for their produce and some security of revenue, and the supermarkets are assured of timely delivery and quality control. Full vertical integration is usually avoided by supermarkets and processors.[68] Wholesalers supplying supermarkets note that supermarkets, though low-risk clients, are more likely to impose fees, delay payments or demand discounts.[69]

In the traditional system, infrastructure such as packing houses, cold chains and supplier shipping equipment is usually basic and technologically unsophisticated. Supermarkets, however, demand that suppliers have the capacity to integrate into complex procurement systems and manage electronic inter-connections with supermarket inventory and billing systems.[70]

Consistent features of developing countries are poor regulatory institutions and monitoring of product quality. Channels that publicise market information are underdeveloped.[71] In traditional procurement channels, wholesale markets act as clearance houses for all produce. Evidence from Vietnam and Nicaragua shows that producers are not encouraged to sort or grade their produce since traditional wholesalers will always pay for all types of products, though their price may be highly discounted. Only damaged or extremely small produce may be discarded. Conversely, supermarkets routinely reject substandard produce altogether, and buy less than 100 per cent of a farmer's production. In the Nicaraguan case, the Wal-Mart chain tightly regulates product aspects such as variety, size, colouration, cleanliness, damage and weight.[72] Though a boon to consumers who benefit from food safety regulation in the absence of government monitoring, the implementation of these quality requirements make substantial investment demands on producers.[73]

The effect of the supermarket transition on growers

The supermarket transition can dramatically affect farmers. Evidence from Guatemala,[74] Kenya[75] and China[76] indicates that supermarkets and processors prefer large suppliers to small ones. Small farmers may find themselves unable to meet the high quality and low-cost demands made by supermarkets.[77] Amanor argues that market governance by retailers expressed in standardisation, grades and quality control may lead to the expansion of a small class of wealthy but still vulnerable farmers, leaving small farmers unable to compete.[78] McMichael adds that small groups of large-scale, high-input farmers are able to meet standards and minimum quantity requirements, while underprivileged, low-input smallholders cannot. The author points out that these two groups of farmers are not evolutionary stages of a sequence but co-exist simultaneously.[79] Ploeg adds that industrialisation of farming decouples yield from prevalent ecologies. Instead, yields depend on physical capital and chemical inputs with decreasing marginal investment costs. Since marginal production costs decrease with scale, producers are pressured to expand. Wherever possible, this involves land acquisition. Large-scale agricultural investments require infrastructure, labour and credit as well as political and economic stability.[80] However, as discussed by Tétreault, Wheeler and Shepherd in this volume, with respect to Persian Gulf investments in Ethiopia and Cambodia, land accumulation often harms long-term stability.[81] To the extent that profitable farming will require the adoption of the industrial model, Ploeg argues, farmland is likely to be abandoned wherever the industrial model cannot be implemented. This is likely to affect small-scale and marginal lands.[82] In chapter 6, Mundy, Al-Hakimi and Pelat observed the abandonment of terraces on mountain foothills in Yemen once the terraces' produce cannot be profitably sold at market rates.[83]

There is some evidence supporting an opposing argument, that small farmers are a safer supply source to supermarkets because they lack the options and bargaining leverage of larger producers, and because small farmers may be more willing to supply quality-increasing labour.[84] It may not necessarily be the largest farms that supply supermarkets, but those richest in physical and human capital. Small farmers specialising in branded products, such as those of a particular origin, or those organised in cooperatives, may fare better.[85]

Prices on traditional spot markets change hourly or within minutes, and sales transactions take place each time fresh produce moves hands.[86] In Vietnam, farmers selling through the traditional procurement system suffer from two price volatilities: a seasonal volatility and idiosyncratic fluctuations in demand at the wholesale market.[87] In Nicaragua, prices paid by Wal-Mart are significantly lower than those on the traditional market. However, the Wal-Mart contract also reduces price volatility.[88] Supermarkets in turn do not transmit price variations from suppliers to consumers, which dampens natural price volatility.[89] In terms of prices, supermarkets dampen price volatility but also pay lower prices. While reduced price volatility benefits all agents in a market, reduced prices benefit consumers but may harm farmers.

The impact of the supermarket transition therefore varies among agents in the FFV procurement chain. Supermarkets are increasingly replacing traditional greengrocers, which source their wares from wholesale spot markets. Supermarkets, on the other hand, keen to control prices and quantities, strive for vertical integration and prefer dealing with dedicated wholesalers or producers, independent of spot markets. Small farmers either struggle to meet the requirements of supermarkets or suffer price volatility from traditional wholesale markets. In what follows, we discuss the status of the supermarket transition in Lebanon and Qatar as well as to what extent agents within the FFV procurement channel are able to meet the challenges of the transition.

Methodology

Sample

Our sample within these two countries was set up as follows. First, we chose certain fruit and vegetables on the basis of nutritional considerations and common consumption among lower middle class families. A study on individual FFV intake in Lebanon[90] found that tomatoes, cucumbers, courgettes, potatoes, apples, oranges and bananas were among the most frequently consumed items.[91] For micronutrient considerations, we included peaches and cherries in our selection.[92] Second, Lebanon was divided into four main regions following the governorate boundaries of the North, the Bekaa, Mount Lebanon, and aggregating the governorates of the South and Nabatieh into one, which we will call the South. Qatar was considered as a single geographic unit. Our survey instrument included questions on firm size and characteristics, marketing channels used, and preferred product characteristics. Below we describe the data collection procedures used in Lebanon and Qatar.

Data collection in Lebanon

A survey was conducted in each of these areas with five categories of agents. 1) Wholesale market traders: twenty-five traders operating on a wholesale market in each of the four governorates were surveyed. A random walk through wholesale markets was used to select respondents. 2) Wholesalers operating outside the wholesale market: six wholesalers operating outside the wholesale market were interviewed. Respondents were chosen at random from Chamber of Commerce registers. The first six consenting traders were interviewed. Following the literature, these were presumed to have more modern characteristics than wholesalers operating on the wholesale market. 3) Traditional retailers: twenty-five retailers in one major city or town in each of the governorates were surveyed. Five neighbourhoods within each town were selected so as to represent varying socioeconomic strata. Within each neighbourhood, retailers were selected following a random walk algorithm. 4) Purchasing or sales managers of large retail chains: outlets of four major supermarket chains operating in Lebanon were interviewed. Retail chains were chosen with respect to their perceived size and the socioeconomic variety of targeted clientele. We initially targeted five respondents but were able to obtain consent from only four retailers. One of the retail chains involves only two, but large, stores. 5) Producers: in each governorate we interviewed between eight and eleven producers. We targeted producers of varying size that grew produce featured in this study. *Ex post*, we classified agents whose number of employees was in the ninety-fifth percentile or above as 'large'. Due to the small sample size for producers, we used the ninetieth percentile for that group. Retailers with more than seven employees, wholesalers with more than fourteen employees and producers with more than thirty employees were classified as 'large'. Agents in categories 1 and 3 were selected randomly, and the remainder purposively. We will assume that the selection bias resulting from the purposive sampling methodology is orthogonal to our variables of interest. Figure 8.1 provides an overview of sample sizes for each agent as well as key population characteristics.

The survey instrument also included a section where respondents and data collectors had the opportunity to leave comments and document observations. This is to allow for anthropological observations which do not fit a structured questionnaire. Data from this section is presented throughout this paper.

Data collection in Qatar

The Qatari sample is much smaller, reflecting the smaller population size of the country, as well as the more concentrated nature of the Qatari market. Three categories of agents were interviewed: 1) Wholesale market traders: ten traders operating in the Doha Central Wholesale Market

Figure 8.1: Description of the Lebanese sample

	Retail	Wholesale	Producer
Response rate	93.7	92.2	97.5
Valid sample	104	106	39
Lebanese ownership			
(otherwise non-Lebanese Arab)	87.5	98.1	100.0
proxy respondent: owner			
(otherwise sales, purchasing			
manager, accountant)	76.0	67.0	66.7
Avg. founding year	1991	1986	1972
(95% confidence interval)	(1989–95)	(1983–90)	(1965–88)
Governorate			
(location of wholesale and retail data collection)			
Mount Lebanon (Beirut)	29	30	10
North (Tripoli)	25	25	8
Bekaa (Zahle)	25	25	11
South (wholesale: Sour, retail:			
Nabatieh)	25	26	10

were surveyed. As in Lebanon, a random walk through the market was used to select respondents. 2) Wholesalers who also operate outside the wholesale market: two traders operating outside the Doha Central Wholesale Market were surveyed. We used an online survey to approach wholesalers in Qatar. Using online directories we were able to identify thirty-one FFV wholesalers. We contacted each listed company and could verify the existence of eighteen wholesalers, of which fifteen consented to receive an email containing details of our online survey. Only two wholesalers filled in the online questionnaire, which amounts to a response rate of 13 per cent, which is well below the average response for online surveys carried out with organisations.[93] Results for Qatar presented in the paper should be taken as indicative rather than representative. We sent potential respondents two follow-up emails and called each company twice. We exerted caution in the number of reminders, since some evidence indicates that, with organisations, reminders are associated with lower response rates.[94] 3) Purchasing or sales managers of retailers: we used the same online data collection method to survey Qatari retailers. A listing using online sources produced forty contacts, of which twenty-seven could be verified, and seventeen consented to fill in the online questionnaire. Only four retailers actually completed the online questionnaire, amounting to a response rate of 24 per cent, which falls within one standard deviation of the average reported by Baruch and Holtom.[95] Producers were excluded from the study since their role in Qatari fresh fruit and vegetable supply is marginal.

Figure 8.2: Description of the Qatari sample

Site	Retail online	Wholesale online	on wholesale market
Response rate	24%	13%	100%
Valid sample	4	12	
Qatari ownership (otherwise non-Qatari Arab or Asian)	2	12	
proxy respondent: sales or purchasing manager (otherwise sales, owner, accountant or director)	2	10	
Avg. founding year (*95% Confidence Interval*)	1992 (*1978–2007*)	2003 (*2002–4*)	
Location: Doha (incl. wholesale market)	3	12	

Wholesalers interviewed in the market and those responding online proved to be very similar in size and marketing operations. All but one indicated they also operate through the Doha Central Market. The two groups were hence combined. Responses to the questionnaires were supplemented by observations made during in-depth interviews with one Qatari wholesaler and one retailer as well as a field visit observing the daily auction at the Doha Central Market. The Qatari sample characteristics are summarised in Figure 8.2. Due to the small sample size, confidence intervals are likely to be large so instead we report the range of observations. Due to the small sample size of Qatari retailers, we present results as anecdotal observations within the main text.

In both countries combined, we interviewed 265 respondents, comprising 108 retailers, 118 wholesalers, and thirty-nine producers. Data was collected in Lebanon and Qatar between October 2011 and April 2012. Unsurprisingly, considering the comparatively recent emergence and growth of the Qatari economy,[96] wholesalers and retailers there have been established more recently than their Lebanese counterparts. Proxy respondents in Qatar were also more likely to be managers involved in FFV sales or purchases, rather than owners as had been the case in Lebanon. Lebanese FFV traders work closely with producers and production in Lebanon takes place year round, requiring minimal storage, hence Lebanese traders can operate with a relatively small capital stock and as small-scale owner-operators. This is not the case for Qatar, where produce is sourced globally, requiring sophisticated supply-chain management and storage. This implies that Qatari FFV traders are likely to have a much larger capital stock than their Lebanese counterparts. The survey evidence presented below validates this hypothesis. Hence, Qatari companies are likely to be larger, requiring more complex managerial structures.

The two case studies in detail

FFV procurement channels in Lebanon and Qatar have both traditional and modern features. We first discuss production, or level I (see Figure 8.3), followed by the wholesale sector, level II, and finally retail, level III.

Production

Qatar has a very small domestic agricultural industry, satisfying only 23–26 per cent of vegetable demand during the four- to six-month season, roughly from November to April.[97] For the remainder of the year, Qatar is dependent on imports of fresh fruit and vegetables, exposing it to the price volatility of the international market. Qatar faces a very concentrated suppliers' market, likely due to its mere 2.02 million consumers,[98] which may make it unattractive for a large number of suppliers to compete for market access. About 34 per cent of its cultivated land is devoted to vegetables, 9 per cent to fruit trees, while the remainder grows fodder crops.[99] Vegetables are the most commercialised. Commercial production began in conjunction with national oil exploitation and is capital-intensive, requiring soil and water treatment. This makes agricultural production in Qatar by default industrial, requiring

Figure 8.3: Schematic representation of the FFV channel in Qatar and Lebanon

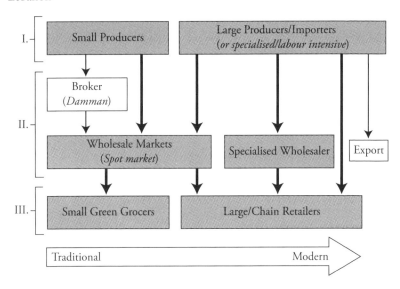

large amounts of inputs. The problem of marginalising small farmers does not arise, because, first, competition for land only arises to the extent that additional inputs are made available to render land arable, and, second, under the 'rentier bargain', farmers of any kind benefit from the patronage and protection of the state.[100]

In contrast with Qatar, Lebanon is a fruit and vegetable exporter.[101] In Lebanon, fruit trees and seasonal crops, such as vegetables and leafy greens, each cover just short of 50 per cent of cultivated land. Landholdings are unequal and fragmented. Though average plot size is 1.4 hectares, half of all producers' farm plots are of half a hectare or less, while 6 per cent of producers control more than half the available agricultural surface.[102] Data from the Ministry of Agriculture indicates that less than a quarter, and more likely less than a fifth, of Lebanese farmers make a living from farming.[103] Over the past decade, orchards have increasingly moved from terraces on hillsides onto the plains, where they have replaced cereals.[104] Lebanese farmers cannot grow wheat competitively at global prices,[105] a point discussed in more detail by Harrigan in this volume.[106] As a consequence, 20 per cent of usable agricultural land is abandoned, largely in marginal areas on mountain slopes rather than in the highly productive coastal plains.[107]

There is some indication, at least at the producer level, that the kind of product sold affects firm characteristics.[108] Though a somewhat crude classification, citrus and banana production tends to be undertaken by large-scale producers concentrated along the littoral, while rain-fed grapevines as well as apple, cherry and peach orchards tend to be managed by small to medium growers. The scale of vegetable production does not vary by product group, though more capitalised farmers will tend to grow vegetables under greenhouses and may be larger in size when compared to vegetables grown outside.[109]

Most agricultural production in Lebanon is characterised by traditional cropping patterns, while a few larger producers are highly capitalised.[110] Only 1 per cent of crops are under greenhouses.[111] Large producers may supply wholesalers or even supermarkets directly. About 15 per cent of supermarkets have contracts with big producers and do not go through wholesalers.[112] The political economy of Lebanese agriculture benefits large farmers with the capacity to undertake substantial investments. Despite Lebanon's comparable wealth of water resources, only one major public reservoir for water storage and irrigation exists, namely the Qaraoun Dam.[113] In rural areas, electricity cuts last from six to eighteen hours per day. This suggests that farmers need to use expensive generators to power irrigation pumps. Since drip irrigation requires stronger pumps and substantial capital investment, flood irrigation is often preferred, requiring merely gravity as a force but is more wasteful in terms of water use. The market for agricultural inputs is among the most concentrated in Lebanon, with five companies dominating trade in fertilisers, seeds, herbicides and pesticides, resulting in high input prices for farmers.[114]

The Lebanese rural economy is dichotomous. Small farmers do survive, if with difficulty, due to the lack of a modern state that would provide the infrastructure, public services and security necessary for modern, capital-intensive procurement channels that characterise the 'third food regime'. Instead, much agricultural production uses little capital and is semi-intensive. Farmers depend on their own resources to provide necessary infrastructure and services. Interestingly though, in Lebanon, change is brought about not by supermarkets or agro-food corporations, but by the country's increasing exposure to international trade in agricultural produce. This puts pressure on producers farming marginal and remote lands and forces production into the plains, which used to produce cereals at what would now be uncompetitive rates.[115] In the coastal plains, production is dominated by large-scale industrial farming where small-scale producers are sidelined.[116] The integration of Lebanese farmers into the world economy is uneven, similar to what Bush observes in this volume for the case of Egypt.[117]

Wholesale

In Qatar, as in Lebanon, nearly all wholesale buying and selling of fresh fruit and vegetables takes place through wholesale markets. The Doha Central Market is the sole wholesale market in Qatar, while eight wholesale markets operate in Lebanon. Lebanese wholesale markets are mostly supplied by local farmers. A major exception is the largest wholesale market, located in a Beirut suburb, which also clears imported produce and fetches the highest prices. The Doha Central Market is regulated by the Qatari government via its Consumer Protection Department (CPD), which has offices at the wholesale market. The Doha Central Market is supplied primarily by importers, along with some Qatari farmers between November and April. All FFV sold wholesale in Qatar has to go through the Central Market. In both countries, these spot markets are relatively more important for retailers than direct agreements between retailers and producers. In Lebanon, most retailers source their FFV from wholesale markets (see Figure 8.4). The branch manager of a large Qatari retailer stated that he regularly deals with two to three local wholesalers out of a total of six that he has on standby. In terms of volume, these are the sources of most of his FFV range. As for low volume and unusual varieties, such as star fruit or lemon grass, these are imported directly. He adds that most traders he deals with specialise in a small number of products.

While anyone can purchase produce from these wholesale markets, access for sales is restricted. In Qatar, wholesalers operate by licence from the CPD and the market is moderately concentrated. Similarly in Lebanon, produce can only be sold through the wholesale market if the trader has a stall in the market. Stalls are bought or inherited. Wholesalers in Lebanon do not own their stalls outright; they gain access to them by joining a syndicate, which administers the wholesale markets. At the Beirut market, the transfer of a stall between holders can be associated with a fee of between $150,000 and $300,000, according to various traders. Thus, access to the Beirut wholesale market is restricted, limiting competition. Access to lesser wholesale markets is less onerous but correspondingly less profitable. In total, between 632 and 918 fresh fruit and vegetable traders operate through the eight Lebanese wholesale markets.[118]

Interviews with wholesalers and retailers in both Qatar and Lebanon showed that wholesalers have habitual trading partners. Our results indicate that a third of wholesalers have not changed their suppliers in more than four years and only 17 per cent of wholesalers changed suppliers at monthly or shorter intervals. As for buyers, however, the distribution is two-humped, with nearly 60 per cent of wholesalers changing buyers daily or weekly, while 27 per cent indicate that they have not changed buyer in five years. Daily- or weekly-changing traders are primarily pedlars or small greengrocers shopping for the best deals, while traders with long-term clients probably indicate a certain degree of informal vertical integration and coordination between wholesalers and retailers. About 31 per cent of both Lebanese wholesalers and retailers have not changed suppliers in more than five years. Qatari wholesalers change suppliers somewhat more regularly, at least every year. Two-thirds of Lebanese producers interviewed stated that they had not changed suppliers in five years.

Figure 8.4: Suppliers of retailers and wholesalers

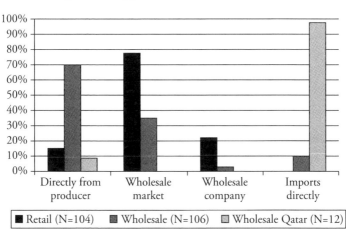

203

Wholesale price formation

In Lebanese wholesale markets, prices are individually negotiated with each potential buyer several times a day. Contracts or agreements are likely to be oral. Prices decrease significantly during the day and traders expect to make their daily profits from the first half of the day. One producer interviewed stated that the same variety and quality of apple may fetch five different prices on the same day. In Qatar, however, wholesale auctions were re-introduced in June 2011, following the food price crisis. The auction had been abolished in the framework of liberalising reforms.[119] Trading on the market starts at 6:00 am, when potential buyers bid against each other for certain products, with the highest bid winning the lot. CPD officials record the obtained prices. By 10:00 am, the CPD publishes a thus obtained price list for products traded that morning on the Doha Central Market, and all future transactions on the same day are bound by these prices. Retail prices are similarly fixed by the CPD through adding a small margin to wholesale prices. Price lists have to be displayed in all retail outlets in Qatar. The auction does not distinguish between different quality levels of the same produce.

In the Qatari as well as the Lebanese wholesale markets, most transactions with suppliers are by consignment, where producers remain the owners of the goods which they consign to the wholesaler or importer who takes a percentage from the sales price to cover handling and transaction costs. In Lebanon, this amounts to a margin of between 5–10 per cent. Unsold produce is not returned and the producer bears the risk of the loss. This type of transaction requires a significant amount of trust, since the producer has few means to verify the actual sales made by the importer or wholesaler. In Lebanon, interviewed farmers complained that they suspected wholesalers of underpaying them, selling their produce at low prices or falsely claiming it could not be sold at all. A trader in the Doha Central Market conjectured that 90 per cent of merchants trade on consignment.

Alternatively, produce can be purchased directly from the producer. Large retail chains in Qatar may import produce directly. In this case, if produce is bought which does not feature in the morning auction, it is not bound by any price controls. In Lebanon, this occurs mainly for imported or long-life stored produce,[120] in response to demand from a dedicated buyer, usually a large retail chain. A number of these dedicated wholesalers with established relationships to clients may operate outside the wholesale market. As of 2011, the Beirut Chamber of Commerce registered 552 traders that may or may not operate through the wholesale market, and the Lebanese Syndicate of Fresh Fruits & Vegetables Importers & Exporters lists eighty-eight members. In Qatar, using various online databases, we identified ninety-five fresh fruit and vegetable wholesale companies in Qatar, of which fifty-seven could be reached via telephone to confirm their existence.

Advance payments

Though prices on wholesale markets in Qatar as well as Lebanon are set daily, payments are not always made at the time goods change hands. There is some evidence that wholesalers may act as creditors to some of their suppliers, an observation also made by Tawk, Abi Said and Hamadeh in the previous chapter, with respect to North Lebanon and Jordan.[121] Wholesalers are much more likely to make advance payments (67 per cent in Lebanon and all Qatari wholesalers) to suppliers than retailers to wholesalers (2 per cent in Lebanon). Even large retailers state that they have not made advance payments in the past six months and only 7 per cent of Lebanese and no Qatari wholesalers state that they ever received an advance payment from a retailer. Of producers, 21 per cent confirm that they have received advance payment (see Figure 8.5).

Figure 8.5: Advance payments

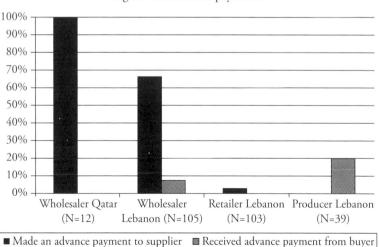

■ Made an advance payment to supplier   ■ Received advance payment from buyer

Though Lebanese retailers do not make advance payments, they do pay promptly. Three quarters (73 per cent) pay when exchanging the produce, compared to 20 per cent of wholesalers, most of which (71 per cent) pay their suppliers up to a month after having received their wares. Thus, Lebanese wholesalers extract liquidity from some suppliers, so as to be able to advance credit to others. The prompt payment of wholesalers by retailers seems to only be a feature of the Lebanese procurement channel. A Qatari retailer, for instance, delays paying suppliers by up to three months. Qualitative interview data with large suppliers dealing with supermarkets indicates that large retail chains in Lebanon similarly delay payments. This may limit wholesalers' ability to make advance payment to suppliers and is indicative of a transfer of power from wholesalers to retailers accompanying the transition from traditional to modern procurement channels.

The availability or absence of alternative trading partners is another measure of power within the supply chain. As discussed in the introductory section, the supermarket transition often entails supermarkets dominating supply chains to the extent that suppliers cannot find alternative outlets for their produce. This is not the case in Lebanon or Qatar. More than 80 per cent of retailers, wholesalers and producers in both countries state that they could have done business with another supplier or buyer had they wanted to. Though traders confirm that they have access to outside options, many prefer to build long-term relationships with suppliers (see Figure 8.6).

Quality certification

No third party quality controls exist either on the Qatari or Lebanese wholesale markets for local produce, though imported produce may have been graded in its country of origin. Basic distinctions do exist—in Lebanon, traders distinguish between three quality categories and in Qatar they distinguish between four. All quality determinations are done on the market following traders' inspection of external produce attributes. A notable difference between the Qatari and the Lebanese wholesale market is the varying importance of third-party certification. Though most traders admit that quality is vital or very important to their clients, Lebanese traders do not report that third-party certification is something they request. In Qatar, on the other hand, all interviewed

Figure 8.6: How often wholesalers change suppliers and buyers

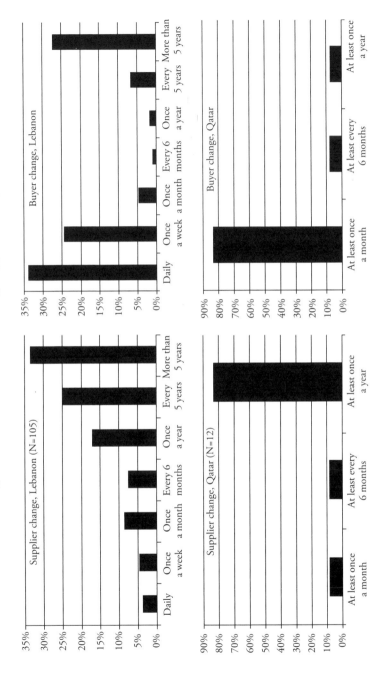

wholesalers stated that third-party certification is very important (see Figure 8.7). Such certification is a hallmark of modern procurement channels since it allows for standardised information about external product characteristics to be transmitted across long supply chains. This is more important when sourcing on a global level, rather than on a national one, as is the case in Lebanon.

Figure 8.7: The importance of third-party certification

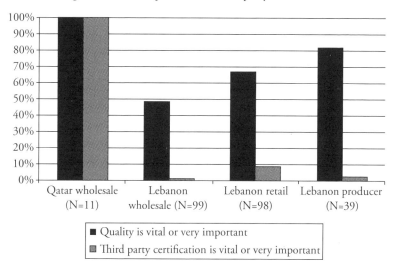

Standard of market facilities

Facilities at wholesale markets in both Qatar and Lebanon are rudimentary, in Lebanon more so than in Qatar. The markets themselves offer no closed cooling or storage facilities, though traders may operate warehouses outside the market premises. Loading and handling in Lebanon is done manually or using trolleys, while forklifts are employed in Qatar and trucks can be unloaded at ramps giving direct access to the marketing platform. Produce packaging at the Doha Central Market is more sophisticated than in Lebanon. This may be due to longer shipping and handling chains, which require adequate packaging to minimise losses as well as greater ability of the Qatari government as well as Qatari traders to make costly capital investments. Produce in Lebanon, on the other hand, can rarely be mechanically stacked, if stacked at all. This point is discussed in more detail below. Figure 8.8 illustrates the difference between packaging found at a Lebanese wholesale market (overfilled and un-stackable) and the packaging of imported goods sold in Doha.

Comparing Lebanese to Qatari wholesale markets, there are a number of common features. In both countries, wholesale trade is on consignment and FFV wholesalers face barriers to entry. From the perspective of traders, these barriers do not lead to a situation where they feel limited in their choice of trading partners. However, Lebanese wholesalers build longer-term relationships with suppliers than their Qatari counterparts. This is indicative of informal trust-based relationships playing a greater role in Lebanon than in Qatar, an observation further supported by the greater relative importance placed on third-party certification by Qatari traders compared to Lebanese traders. The Qatari government intervenes in the wholesale market by fixing daily prices through daily morning auctions, while in Lebanon prices vary throughout the day. The former reduces price volatility but does not allow

Figure 8.8: Packaging at Lebanese wholesale markets (left) and Doha Central Market (right)

enough variance to accommodate different degrees of quality, while the latter clears all products offered on the market but exposes producers to price risks. On the whole, Qatari wholesale is more formalised, due to its third-party quality certification, greater vertical integration and the higher incidence of advance payments to suppliers and delayed payments from retailers. The Lebanese wholesale market, with its higher incidence of ad hoc payments, its trust-based relationships and lack of certification, remains more traditional.

Retail

In Lebanon, supermarkets were introduced in the 1990s, similarly to Latin America and South East Asia but with lower rates of FDI. Supermarkets are still mainly owned by local investors and account for less than a third of the market.[122] Still, among all agents in the procurement chain, the incidence of foreign ownership is highest among retailers, with 13 per cent of Lebanese retailers interviewed being non-Lebanese owned. This echoes observations made in the literature that FDI is a driver of the retail transformation.[123] Food retailing in Lebanon is still dominated by the small-scale retailer, with only 137 supermarkets larger than 200 square metres in the country. Finding exact numbers for small grocers is difficult since Value Added Tax (VAT) records or company registers are not public. In addition, there are many informal traders selling food from carts.[124] The largest retail chains in Lebanon—Spinneys, TSC and Bou Khalil—each have between seven and nine outlets, while Charcutier Aoun has fourteen outlets. Registrations with the Chamber of Commerce in Beirut add seventeen further retailers to this list. Of these four, two chains have non-Lebanese owners. TSC is Kuwaiti, while the largest shareholder in Spinneys is Dubai-based private equity firm Abraaj Capital. Interestingly, many larger retail stores subcontract their fruit and vegetable sections, including Charcutier Aoun, as well as popular large supermarkets in Beirut such as Fahed, Fahd and Marche du Rond Point. These also offer consistently lower prices than TSC, Spinneys or Bou Khalil.[125] The FFV section in these supermarkets is operated by an independent greengrocer, which is different for each store of the same chain. These operate on a similar basis to the numerous greengrocers from whom most Lebanese residents source their fruit and vegetables.

The Qatari FFV retail sector is dominated by retail chains, rather than corner shop greengrocers. Smaller convenience or grocery stores make up a minority of the market. According to one retailer, there are approximately sixty major retail food outlets in all of Qatar. The four largest chains are the Al-Meera chain, with just above twenty stores; Lulu has five stores; and the Family Food Centre and Carrefour have three large stores each. The Qatari government is the main investor in Al-Meera, while Family Foods is registered in Qatar and privately owned. Lulu is owned by the Abu Dhabi-based EMKE Group and Carrefour has French ownership. Using various online directories,[126] we added another sixty-seven retailers to the list, bringing the total to above 120 retail outlets.

Dealing with large retailers in both Lebanon and Qatar is onerous. A wholesaler at the Doha Central Market stated that large retail chains demand a discount of 10 per cent on the prices of their purchase. A large producer in Lebanon stated that supermarkets will ask for occasional promotions, such as 'two for one' offers from their suppliers. Similarly, when TSC opened a new store in Beirut, suppliers were asked to pay a $1,000 fee for the privilege of trading with the new store. However, the same producer also stated that supermarkets offer a certain security and consistent level of demand. Supermarkets not only exert power upstream towards wholesales and producers but also downstream towards consumers. The purchasing manager of a large Lebanese chain stated that, during the food price crisis of 2008, the supermarket was able to pass on all price increases to consumers. There is some evidence that the CPD price policies may protect against price hikes. A trader at the Doha Central Market stated that officially sanctioned auction prices tend to go up less than global market prices. A large Lebanese retailer stated that his company adds between 14–17 per cent to the price of their produce, but margins vary across produce and to a lesser extent between stores.

During interviews with small retailers in Lebanon, we found that quality is adapted to an area's prosperity. In a poor area surveyed (Zarif), almost all retailers sold second grade produce. One store in the area was selling premium produce and traders were able to point him out. Greengrocers state that they set low prices to accommodate the economic needs of the neighbourhood but that customers still feel the need to haggle the price down even further.

Quality and price also differentiate shops. For example, one retailer, who also grows his own produce, operates two shops close to each other, with first grade produce in one and second grade produce in the other, at different prices. A small retailer may operate several stalls so as to better differentiate the produce and obtain varying prices which the retailer may not be able to charge in one shop. Some greengrocers will only sell bargains they found at the wholesale market. Other grocers prefer to buy from the wholesale market located closest to them, even if they think that the choice of produce there is limited, because transportation costs are prohibitive. When grocers do source from further afield, they tend to supply more than one shop. In terms of prices, research from a Beirut suburb indicates that greengrocers are able to offer lower prices than medium-sized mini-markets but finds no significant difference between prices charged by small greengrocers or large supermarkets.[127] Thus, the Lebanese retail sector is dichotomous with a few large retail chains juxtaposed with small greengrocers. Large chains are selling at higher prices than greengrocers and, presumably, serving clients from mainly affluent socioeconomic groups. Small greengrocers and pedlars source their wares daily or weekly at the local wholesale market, with quality and price levels targeted to their respective neighbourhoods.

Technical sophistication of the agent

A hallmark of the supermarket transition is the increased technical sophistication of agents. The analysis above points to varying sophistication and capitalisation of traders at all levels. Figure 8.9 illustrates that there is substantial skew among agents at all levels of the FFV procurement chain. Large segments do not have access to infrastructures that would indicate the degree of technological sophistication or capitalisation necessary to compete with emerging modern procurement channels. Indeed, two-thirds of wholesalers and 85 per cent of retailers have only their shop floors to store produce in, only 10 per cent of retailers and wholesalers have access to cold storage and 15 per cent or less engage in packaging. It is worth pointing out that nearly half of producers engage in packaging. However, observations at Lebanese wholesale markets indicate that much of farm-level packaging is rudimentary and not fit for long-term storage or transport.

Policy recommendations

Productions

In terms of food security, Lebanon and Qatar face different challenges and have used different policy approaches. While Qatar has the Qatar

Figure 8.9: Technical sophistication of agents

| | | Lebanon | | | Qatar |
		Retail	Wholesale	Production	Wholesale
Has access to storage/warehouse facilities (excl. cold storage)	per cent	14	25	14	100
	N	103	96	21	5
Operates packaging	per cent	4	16	49	33
	N	104	106	39	12
Operates cold storage	per cent	10	9	8	100
	N	96	103	37	4
Number of pick-ups, trucks, tractors	None	40	49	31	–
	1	47	24	21	–
	2	6	14	15	–
	3 or more	7	13	33	100
	N	106	104	39	10
Operates an electric scale/billing system/ inventory	Neither Electric scale/billing	54	42	n/a	–
	or inventory	26	46	n/a	–
	Two of the three	11	13	n/a	–
	All three	7	1	n/a	100
	N	106	104		12
Operates irrigation/ greenhouses	Neither Has	n/a	n/a	46	n/a
	irrigation/ greenhouse	n/a	n/a	33	n/a
	Both	n/a	n/a	21	n/a
	N			39	

National Food Security Programme (QNFSP), the Lebanese Ministry of Agriculture was only able to act in 2011 since it had gained access to EU funding. The strategic plan for agriculture had been written in 2009 and developed for the period of 2010–14.[128] Both countries have different political objectives that drive policy beyond what would be a best-case scenario. Qatari public policy will be made with the 'rentier bargain' in mind, while Lebanon has quite the opposite problem, with a government incapacitated by institutional gridlock and massive national debt. Indeed, the Lebanese government has not passed a budget since 2006. In the meantime, infrastructure in Lebanon is in a state of deterioration, public utilities are left unsupplied and companies themselves have to provide a large share of the public services their Qatari counterparts take for granted.

In terms of the food security challenges faced with respect to FFV procurement channels, in Qatar the main risk is price volatility to consumers, to which the official policy response is the re-introduction of its auction system. However, this does not tackle the underlying cause of price volatility, which is a highly concentrated supplier market. Its small domestic FFV production cannot offset international price variations. In addition, Qatar's small size makes diversification of supply sources difficult. In addition to price controls, current policy focuses on expanding national production. The QNFSP has been preparing a 'Master Plan', the publishing date of which has been repeatedly postponed.[129] One aim of this plan is to expand domestic production using technological innovations.[130] This may make sense from an emergency food security perspective but will be costly and possibly ecologically unsustainable. An alternative approach would be to buffer price fluctuations with the creation of strategic food reserves and food storage where possible. Strategic reserves of perishable items such as FFV are very difficult to maintain. The Qatari government could buy long-term futures in FFV, so as not to rely on international spot market prices, although even this will not fully protect Qatar against price fluctuations in FFV.

In Lebanon, one of the country's primary assets is the widespread availability of cheap, fresh fruit and vegetables all year round from nearby local production. Yet, this asset is threatened as small farmers give up farming and marginal land is abandoned. Increasingly, land concentration among fewer, highly capitalised farms is a likely future scenario, though Lebanon's size and rugged geography will set natural limits to the degree of concentration. Furthermore, increased concentration of supply, as the Qatari case illustrates, may increase price volatility. Investment in extension services, improved irrigation and infrastructure, as well as policy support for small-scale farmers and marginal lands, are non-existent and an unlikely policy scenario given government capacities. Additionally, the production sector in Lebanon operates very much along traditional lines and is under-capitalised. A number of shortcomings in basic government services, such as irregular electricity and water supply as well as insufficient road networks, keep alive traditional, non-intensive production methods. On the one hand, these shortcomings in public services in Lebanon favour large producers with the greater ability to replace government services with private ones. On the other hand, they resist small farmers' integration into a corporate food regime.

A frequently made policy recommendation to protect small farmers from fraudulent misreporting from wholesalers,[131] to whom they consign their produce, is price dissemination. Since 2003, the Beirut Chamber of Commerce collects weekly wholesale prices which are disseminated by email or SMS. Few of our respondents were aware of this programme, however 25 per cent of wholesalers and 20 per cent of retailers knew of the programme, while among farmers—those most in need of price information—only 6 per cent knew of it. In addition, of those who were aware of the programme, most believed that the reports were inaccurate. Our results further show that official sources such as newspapers, radio or television are used by less than 2 per cent of respondents. This suggests that price collection alone is not sufficient, and that the dissemination strategy of price information is crucial.

In Lebanon, there are tax exemptions on agricultural buildings and land, and agricultural industries. Though earnings are tax exempt, farmers pay many indirect taxes (VAT on inputs and import fees) and do not benefit from national social security because farm units are not registered as economic entities.[132]

Wholesale

In Qatar, price controls in combination with the consignment system act as disincentives for wholesalers dealing in premium produce or wishing to invest in storage and quality maintenance beyond certification, since wholesalers are not able to charge a premium for quality. The auction does not account for quality difference, which can make up 10–15 per cent of the price. If traders were to import high quality produce they would make a loss, since they cannot sell above CPD prices. This discourages investment in machinery and cold storage as well as packaging and labelling. In response, supermarkets looking for high quality produce will attempt to circumvent the auction by directly contracting with an importer. Sophisticated storage facilities could mitigate price fluctuations to some extent, especially for produce that stores well (bananas, oranges, apples, potatoes and onions for instance), but to a lesser extent cucumbers, tomatoes and leafy greens. Given Qatar's subsidised energy supply, it has an advantage in building sophisticated storage facilities, though consumer preferences may be strongly against stored produce.

Consignment pricing in Lebanon proves to be a similar disincentive for wholesalers to invest in technological or infrastructure capacity. One of the best attributes of the Lebanese wholesale sector is its ability to clear all produce, of all qualities. Its major shortcoming is its lack of technological sophistication, in particular with regards to handling and storage, which causes an unnecessary level of merchandise loss. Since merchandise does not seem to be scarce there is little incentive to look after it. Sales on consignment pose no risks to wholesalers, who have no interest in maintaining quality since it will not affect their margins. However, the consignment system does not offer enough opportunity for growers to trace their consigned produce and exposes them to price volatility, as wholesalers are the more powerful agents in the chain and producers are price takers. One recourse open to producers may be for them to circumvent the wholesale market and sell to large retailers directly. However, this would require substantial technology upgrades to satisfy supermarket quality and quantity demands, which most small farmers are unable to implement.

Though officially targeted at small farmers, Lebanese exporters were the ones benefitting from export subsidies under the Export Plus programme up until January 2012 when Lebanon shifted to Agriculture Plus to conform to WTO regulations. Agriculture Plus supports agricultural exports. However since small farmers rarely export and subsidies are paid on export, rather than support the process of becoming an exporter, the policy benefits mainly traders or large producers.

Retail

Lebanese retailers adapt the produce they offer to the socioeconomic capacities of their clients, and are able to offer fresh fruit and vegetables, albeit at low quality, to poor neighbourhoods. The insufficient penetration of supermarkets may mean that cheap low quality fruit and vegetables may not yet have to compete with cheap processed foods to the same extent as in Qatar. Because the availability of cheap, fresh produce depends on affordable transportation costs, poor populations living in remote areas of Lebanon may not enjoy the access to cheap fresh produce that other areas have. A study of Palestinian refugees living in the comparatively remote Bekaa valley in Lebanon found that they ate less fruit and vegetables.[133] A modern food procurement system dominated by supermarkets may not be able to cater for the FFV needs of poor households who may have sourced their fruit and vegetables from low margin greengrocers or pedlars offering lower quality produce. Preliminary unpublished research from Hala Ghattas and Nadine Sahyoun in Lebanon indicates that poor families wait until the middle of the season or until the end of the market day for the value of certain items to drop to affordable levels.[134]

In Qatar, an unintended consequence of price control policies is the exclusion of a premium quality FFV sector despite the fact that there is likely to be a brisk demand for premium produce. Another threat faced by Qatar is the easy access to processed foods that is concomitant with the rise of a modern retail system. There has been little research on the effectiveness of policies targeting consumer eating behaviour[135] and few countries have been successful in lowering the rate of obesity, which has increased while reductions in under-nourishment have stalled.[136] Among suggested policies are labelling campaigns, which advertise health benefits or dangers on product labels. The use of health claims seems to improve the quality of dietary choices.[137] Some evaluations indicate that when labelling campaigns are industry-driven they sometimes lack accuracy[138] and efficacy.[139] Attempts have been made to regulate or limit the consumption of unhealthy foods, such as the prohibition of soda vending machines in Qatari schools.[140] There have been further suggestions to restrict the marketing and advertising of unhealthy foods or to initiate nutrition education programmes.[141] Education programmes may be successful since evidence from the United States indicates that nutrition knowledge and beliefs affect diet. This is heavily mediated by socioeconomic factors, however, and education programmes have less of an impact among groups of lower socioeconomic status.[142] While most policy recommendations target individual behaviour, few consider procurement channels or the social and economic context of malnutrition.[143]

Conclusion

While the 'nutrition transition' is well underway in both Lebanon and Qatar, the 'supermarket transition' is not. Qatar is much more incorporated into the 'third food regime' than Lebanon.[144] This is not by policy design, but rather due to the complacency of the Lebanese government which does not furnish the infrastructure necessary to run standardised modern food procurement channels. In Qatar, agricultural production is by default industrial, requiring large amounts of input and benefiting from strong government support. The Lebanese agricultural economy is dichotomous. On the one hand, the complacency of the Lebanese government extends, if briefly, the lifespan of Lebanese small-scale farmers still under threat from global prices, while on the other, it does not stem the tide of land abandonment and concentration. In the long run this may seriously threaten the country's food sovereignty since its weak fiscal position makes it ill-positioned to purchase shortfalls in domestic production.

Contrary to the dictates of the supermarket transition, wholesale markets in both countries play a crucial role in FFV procurement and are likely to remain important sources of FFV for retailers. In Lebanon, they act as a clearing-house absorbing much of the coordination costs inherent in informal transactions, while in Qatar they are a key site of government intervention through the daily auction. Though the auction may reduce price volatility, it does not account for quality differences, discouraging traders from dealing in premium produce even if there may be a market for them. The Qatari wholesale market is more formalised and more vertically integrated than the Lebanese wholesale markets, which have a higher incidence of ad hoc payments and place greater importance on trust relationships.

While the Qatari retail sector is dominated by large retail chains, half of which are non-domestic, the Lebanese retail sector is dichotomous with modern and traditional elements. A few large retail chains in Lebanon, selling at higher prices, have so far not been able to compete with greengrocers. Lebanese supermarkets targeting lower socioeconomic classes effectively admit as much by outsourcing their FFV range to independent greengrocers. The continued availability of affordable FFV in Lebanon is an important outcome of the persistence of traditional procurement channels.

The fruit and vegetable procurement systems in both countries present a hybrid between traditional and modern characteristics, where Qatari supply channels have more modern features than Lebanese ones. However, as the re-introduction of the morning auction in Qatar indicates, this transition is not guaranteed nor is it likely to take the same shape in the two countries. Instead, procurement channels with recognisably modern and rational features are the idiosyncratic outcome of each country's negotiation between domestic policy objectives and constraints and international pressures concomitant to the third food regime.

Though strong pressures exist in both Qatar and Lebanon to integrate into a corporatised global food system, we believe that their full integration into this third food regime is not a foregone conclusion. In Lebanon, weak state capacity and the threat of political instability is likely to keep public and private investment low, thus maintaining traditional procurement channels. In Qatar—a strong state keen to protect consumers from price volatility, which is likely to increase—FFV procurement may evolve into a hybrid system, with a semi-traditional wholesale sector and corporate retail sector.

9

WIN-WIN VERSUS LOSE-LOSE

INVESTMENTS IN FOREIGN AGRICULTURE
AS A FOOD SECURITY STRATEGY OF THE ARAB STATES
OF THE PERSIAN GULF

Mary Ann Tétreault, Deborah L. Wheeler and *Benjamin Shepherd*

During the past few years, the Arab states of the Persian Gulf have
become involved in agricultural investments in developing countries. The
main drivers of this movement are demographic pressures, domestic agricultural production that imposes heavy demands on limited domestic soil
and water resources, and decreasing confidence in the reliability and price
stability of global food markets. Reflecting their strategic focus on food
security, three Gulf Arab oil-exporting states—Saudi Arabia, the United
Arab Emirates (UAE) and Qatar—are reported as being among the top
twenty countries engaged in the acquisition of foreign farmland.[1]

Saudi Arabia has dramatically altered its national food security policy
since the 2007–8 food price spikes.[2] Formerly, it had striven for self-
sufficiency in particular staples such as wheat and dairy products, but
now is seeking long-term, secure access to production capacity abroad

through the activities of the King Abdullah Initiative for Agriculture Abroad and its investment arm, the Saudi Company for Agro-Investments Abroad. These organisations are charged with signing contracts, supporting investors (diplomatically and financially) and launching specific projects which can then either be used as a model for Saudi private-sector investors to emulate in that market or as properties to be 'transferred' directly to a willing Saudi private-sector investor.[3]

Food security is important for all the Gulf Cooperation Council (GCC) regimes which operate according to a distributive social contract such that political stability is at least partly predicated on citizen well-being and prosperity.[4] This social contract was threatened by the surge in food prices in 2008, which heightened the interest of GCC governments in overseas land investment.[5] Yet, such investment increases the international vulnerability of states that already are highly exposed to strategic and economic pressures from globalisation.[6] In previous globalising eras, most GCC states experienced 'imperialism' in the form of unequal economic, political and social relations with relatively large, industrialised states. Since then, they have successfully asserted their sovereign rights over their oil and gas resources, but continue to face opposition to exercising autonomy with regard to their direct foreign investments in the West.[7] The exposure of these states to international scrutiny is itself a risk if human rights issues result from their investments. Regardless of negative reactions from 'the international community', host governments could use human rights as an excuse to expropriate GCC land investments. As we note below, such a strategy was hinted at by a Cambodian official, and is predicated on a narrative that puts the investor firmly in the wrong morally.

Moral arguments with regard to foreign investment in agricultural land can, are and indeed must be made against investment practices that lead to negative results for local populations.[8] That is not the intent of this chapter, however. Our aim is to identify the risks that such practices pose to investors, governments or agents of politically vulnerable GCC regimes which themselves possess natural resources like oil and gas coveted by other states.[9] We expect to demonstrate here that whatever moral arguments can be made, farmland investments as they are currently conceived and executed present risks for the investor as well as potential harm to host countries. Our intention in this chapter is not to dismiss the harm occasioned to communities in developing countries, but instead to show that this harm is not one-sided, and that the risks for investors also must be properly recognised, evaluated and managed if projects are to deliver the promised 'win-win' outcomes and avoid 'win-lose' or even 'lose-lose' scenarios. As things currently stand, the latter outcomes appear more likely than the former.

Direct foreign investment allows the investor to participate as an active agent in the design and operation of investment projects, and investment in developing countries tends to be more welcome and less regulated than investment in developed countries. That is not the only attraction for GCC policymakers, however. They also share the perspective of the former Western investors in Gulf hydrocarbons. Like the Western 'oil men' who saw their companies' exploration and development efforts as bringing needed human and economic resources to primitive host countries,[10] GCC states regard their land leases and investments not only as beneficial to themselves but also as a means for improving productivity and bolstering economic development in impoverished rural areas of less-developed countries.[11] Expectations on both sides in oil-exporter/developing-country investment partnerships tend to be high. Each side sees the other in idealised terms, but Kuwait's earlier experience investing in development projects in neighbouring countries illustrates the disillusionment that results. 'Kuwaitis faced the same problems investing abroad that developed country nationals encountered: poor infrastructure, political instability, popular resentment, and corruption.'[12] Host countries expected concessions while Kuwaitis expected praise for their willingness to risk scarce capital for uncertain returns. Domestic politics also affected the attitudes of foreign nationals towards Kuwaitis, whom they saw as outsiders. Few were aware of Kuwaiti efforts on their behalf.

A similar situation operates in GCC land investment, but GCC partners have more to offer than capital. As managers of major sovereign wealth funds, GCC land acquisition projects present an opportunity to set a new standard of international best-practice for foreign investment in agricultural land development. The interests of GCC investors are multiple and long term, encompassing goals in addition to simple profit-maximisation.[13] The desire to increase the productivity of the land, and thereby ensure adequate food supplies at reasonable prices for their own domestic populations, is one of them. Yet although one can envision a community of interests between home and host countries, foreign investments in agricultural land in developing countries have been the subject of significant criticism.[14] Investors and supporters of the deals argue that they can create 'win-win' outcomes that benefit the countries hosting the projects at the same time that they deliver returns to the investor.[15] Recent studies, however, show that although 'win-win' outcomes are possible in theory, evidence that investors achieve them in practice is hard to find.[16] Even so, some economists continue to argue that GCC investments, such as in agricultural land, present an opportunity to influence international best-practice precisely because investor interests are multiple and, even more important, these interests are long term,[17] affecting both risk assessment and risk management.

Each GCC home country making agricultural land investments has, in addition to its investment goals, its own unique culture, legal regime and economic structure. So does each host country in which it might invest. Ideally, every project should be analysed and assessed on its own terms. With regard to three of the GCC states mentioned earlier, we find no consistent implementation plan or policy framework to guide investment and development undertakings in the statements of policy-makers or on their websites.[18] Based on these sources, we conclude that policymakers assume with some validity that opportunities exist for the agricultural investor, but they also assume, we think less validly, that the risks are negligible. While they imagine that their investments will result in 'win-win' outcomes, Ben Shepherd's field investigations uncovered pathologies that could render them 'win-lose' or even 'lose-lose'.

Our aim here is to identify these pathologies, analyse their risks for investors and suggest strategies to mitigate them with a view to increasing the benefits from foreign agricultural investments for all involved. In particular, we set out to examine the social and political environments within which GCC member states are investing in foreign agricultural land and, as much as possible at this early stage of policy implementation, how these investments are playing out in local settings. We concentrate on the cases of Ethiopia and Cambodia because both recipients host sovereign investments by GCC states and others in the agricultural sector.[19] GCC investments are at the early stages in both countries, but each features well-established investments from other sources that exemplify the circumstances for investors and local communities. Both countries have water and fertile land resources, although whether they are truly available for foreigners' use is contestable due to already evident stress arising from climatic and population pressures in some regions. Both countries also have the capacity to increase production yields dramatically, and thereby the potential to produce surpluses for export after meeting domestic staple food needs. Among the conditions governing land investment investigated by Shepherd on field visits to Cambodia and Ethiopia were the host countries' regimes governing property rights and land leases to foreigners, the effects of foreign investment on local populations and, in light of these, the likelihood that these investments will eventually deliver food to GCC countries.

Key assumptions guiding our analysis are that pathologies are reduced when benefits are not monopolised by either host countries or investors and when some measures of equity exist among the several host-country interests affected by the investments. Another is that 'win-win' outcomes are more likely to be achieved when land transfers are governed by rule of law and are supervised by competent and accountable agents acting transparently and with fairness to all parties. Indeed, the harshest criticisms of overseas agricultural investment centre on corruption; expropriation of land from local populations who are often subject to forcible eviction with minimal compensation; and a lack of provision for the local people's livelihoods or even access to food after they have been evicted.[20] Among our aims in this chapter is to explain the land-acquisition regimes in Cambodia and Ethiopia in light of the assumptions of the win-win model.

Following this introduction, subsequent sections of this chapter compare and contrast the Cambodian and Ethiopian cases. We look first at the opportunity presented to GCC investors, property rights regimes and the mechanisms by which land transfers occur. Second, we discuss each country's political and social environments. Third, we recount how land deals are actually conducted and their impact on Cambodians and Ethiopians. The concluding section summarises the risks facing GCC states as investors in pursuit of food security objectives; notes how GCC investors are approaching them; and suggests other constructive approaches to consider, especially in terms of regulating the behaviours of the commercial enterprises managing these investments.

Property rights regimes and land transfers

Cambodia

Cambodia is potentially an ideal location for agricultural investments by GCC parties because of its small population relative to agricultural land.[21] Consequently, there is significant capacity to export surpluses; domestic needs in terms of aggregate production of staples can be relatively easily met. Cambodia is a largely agricultural country with fertile land, especially where the annual flooding of the Tonle Sap lake and the Mekong river renews nutrient-rich silt deposits. Despite this natural advantage, Cambodian agriculture is plagued by low productivity. This makes partnerships with investors who are able to bring technology and other productivity-improving techniques highly attractive to the country. The Cambodian government has established a framework for investment in land known as Economic Land Concessions (ELCs). These transfer long-term quasi-ownership of up to 10,000 hectares (ha) to local or foreign enterprises with lease terms of between seventy and ninety-nine years with the possibility of renewal. For foreign investors seeking land in Cambodia, ELCs are the primary mechanism by which land rights are obtained either directly in conjunction with a local partner, or by buying an already-awarded ELC from its current owner or from the government if the concession has been rescinded.[22] This last circumstance arises when the government determines that the developer has not adequately fulfilled the terms of the ELC.

Official data from the Ministry of Agriculture, Fisheries and Forestry (MAFF) in mid-2011 showed that 956,690 ha had been awarded as valid concessions to eighty-five different entities across sixteen provinces.[23] A further 379,034 ha are slated for contract cancellation. One human rights-monitoring NGO provided data gathered from some provinces and suggested that approximately 1.5 million ha are currently under concession in those areas alone.[24] This compares to the Food and Agriculture Organization of the United Nations' estimate of total arable land at 3.9 million ha.[25] An economist doing research on ELCs said that there were many more concessions than are publicly accounted for, but noted the lack of resources—and also the probable lack of desire—within the MAFF to maintain up-to-date records.[26]

One record missing from the public domain is a 130,000 ha concession granted to the State of Kuwait in Kampong Thom province. It appears on an internal MAFF spreadsheet from 2009 obtained by

Shepherd, but there is little additional public information about it. This concession far exceeds the 10,000 ha maximum for ELCs. The same spreadsheet also includes lines for Qatar and Israel as concession holders but no further information on these land grants is officially available. At least nine other concessions exceed the 10,000 ha size limit but most were concluded prior to the passage of the 2001 Land Law which stipulated this limit.[27]

The regulations governing ELCs are laid out in Sub Decree No. 146 issued under the 2001 Land Law. It outlines a process for obtaining an ELC which requires a number of steps that include submitting Environmental and Social Impact Assessments (EIAs and SIAs), prior consultations with affected communities and presenting a Master Plan showing how the land will be developed, including income-generating and infrastructure projects. The limits on land concessions include, in addition to the maximum legal area of 10,000 ha, a requirement that only 'state private land' can be transferred to an investor—in other words, that transferred land must be unencumbered by private or other (such as indigenous) title claims, and cannot be classified as land for public use, such as 'state public land' or protected lands. Finally, the law forbids involuntary resettlement of lawful landholders and demands that 'access to private land shall be respected'.[28] In theory, concession rights are not available on protected land that includes villages, villager subsistence farms or preservation areas, including freshwater courses.

In spite of these rules however, the Ministry of Environment (MoE) which oversees preserved and protected lands—which, in theory, are not 'state private land'—is apparently able, along with the MAFF, to issue ELCs. According to the *Cambodia Daily*, in July 2011, 'six land concessions have been granted since June 3, totalling 46,000 Ha in protected areas, to agribusiness companies'.[29] The Ministry of National Defense (MoND) also controls large amounts of land from the time prior to the passage of the Land Law and ELC sub-decrees, when the MoND was granting concessions. More recently, the MoND has been exchanging commercially valuable land for other areas designated for military use. In addition, while the Ministry of Land Management, Urban Planning and Construction technically has control over land use and planning, it actually has no control over land per se. Effectively, then, all these ministries compete for control over land whose extent and boundaries are often neither agreed upon nor clear.[30]

The process for awarding an ELC involves the highest levels of government. An investor seeking an ELC must send a request to the MAFF ELC secretariat. The secretariat sets up an inter-ministerial committee that includes representatives from the MAFF, the Council for the Development of Cambodia, the MoE, the Council of Ministers and local authorities. As described by a government official, 'the committee visits the proposed site … and … identifies any sensitivities'[31] before making a report to each ministry and the Council of Ministers. Once the Council of Ministers approves, the ELC is signed in person by the prime minister allowing the MAFF to issue a contract. After that, the concessionaire must implement the 'Master Plan'. Progress is reviewed on an annual basis. If the government decides that it is insufficient, the ELC may be rescinded and can then be resold to a new investor. The original investor has no remedy in the event of expropriation.

The regulatory limitations on ELCs do not necessarily reflect the reality of land transfers. Not one of the ELC projects Shepherd examined during two months of fieldwork in Cambodia conformed to the ELC sub-decree. A lawyer working on ELC-related matters stated that, 'It would not be outlandish to assume that no large-scale ELC has been granted in full accordance with the law.'[32] Other observers concurred with this view, especially regarding the procurement of accurate EIAs and SIAs and conducting proper community consultations prior to the awarding of a concession.[33]

Moreover, as some observers have noted, it appears that the regulations are merely a front for corrupt practices by a kleptocratic government.[34] They conceal what actually is transpiring not only from citizens who suspect what is going on, but also from investors. Investors believe that they will be paying the artificially small on-paper price reflected in their land contracts, but an investment adviser mentioned that new investors sometimes admit that they actually have to pay much more to obtain concessions.[35] If these deals fall through, there is no legal recourse. One foreign lawyer described the country's judiciary as 'corrupt, incompetent, and neither independent nor impartial'.[36] Observers believe that judicial appointments are purchased and made via political connections, and incumbents expect such investments to be recouped with interest.[37]

The corruption of the judiciary is evident in the decisions or non-decisions made by the courts in land-dispute cases. In the example of the

Udong conflict, which will be discussed shortly, courts at every level decided in favour of the concession-holder despite the villagers' clear and theoretically unassailable legal right to their land. Although there is no concrete evidence of money changing hands in this case, what is clear is that the court decision does not reflect the law. In other cases, decisions requiring state action simply were not made, leaving complainants without recourse while powerful corporations continued creating facts on the ground.[38] The problem for investors in Cambodia is not that they cannot buy a judge, but that they can—and they can just as easily be out-bought by a rival with more money or better political connections.

Ethiopia

The situation is quite different in Ethiopia whose business environment is probably the least dependent on bribery of any in East Africa.[39] Unlike in Cambodia, no one complains of having to make unofficial payments to make things happen in Ethiopia. Some investors use local intermediaries to facilitate their activities, but an established investor firm in Ethiopia reported that local go-betweens were unnecessary. One firm reported that it is able to deal directly with the minister of agriculture and pointed to the firm's willingness to be flexible and meet government desires as a key reason for its success.[40] Despite this apparent investor readiness to meet Ethiopian demands, the lease contracts that investors are making with the government place little obligation on the investors and little value accrues to the country from the transfer of land. For example, investors get tax holidays and are allowed to repatriate all their profits, while neither the government nor the population receives a direct financial benefit from the project. Furthermore, despite the considerable problem of hunger in Ethiopia,[41] the government offers incentives for investors to export their production.[42]

The need for rural development investment is acute. Ethiopia is one of the world's poorest countries, with a population of at least 82 million growing at 2.6 per cent—over 2 million persons—annually.[43] Of these, 84 per cent live in rural areas and are predominantly agrarian. The majority of rural Ethiopians exist in dire poverty—average per capita income is as low as 3 Birr (the equivalent of 17 cents) per day in some areas[44]—and have virtually no resilience to withstand exogenous shocks. Unfortunately, shocks such as poor harvests, bad weather and other natural disasters; violent conflicts; injury or death of working adults; and costly illnesses of other family members are common.

These conditions have helped make Ethiopia synonymous with poverty, widespread hunger and famine. While concurrent droughts in Australia, China or the United States cause hardship, the same phenomenon in parts of eastern Ethiopia result in widespread famine and death largely because the agrarian population has zero capacity—no alternative survival mechanisms—to compensate for such shocks. For the poor in these areas, once their crops fail there is no other source of income with which food can be bought, assuming that it is locally available at all. The government safety net programme; the strained and flawed emergency food aid; and humanitarian assistance systems are the only survival mechanisms for as many as 15 million Ethiopians.[45] The Ethiopian government recognises the need for development in the agricultural sector and is open to and willing—indeed pleading—for foreign investment to this end.

From the perspective of investors, Ethiopia's fertile soil and plentiful water hold the promise of achieving productivity improvements and higher incomes for rural Ethiopians along with profits. There are, however, obstacles to reaching these goals. For the foreign investor it is unclear how potential productivity improvements can deliver reliable food exports from Ethiopia before the dire food insecurity situation inside Ethiopia itself has been addressed.

On a practical level, even after that hurdle is overcome there are other constraints. Ethiopia is land-locked. Oil and transportation are expensive (which may be one source of the attractiveness of GCC investors to Ethiopia). The Somaliland port of Berbera provides a point of disembarkation for some consumer imports, but Ethiopia's main port for imports and exports is Djibouti. All shipments must be transported to the ports by road since the Addis–Djibouti railway is broken in many places and cannot operate.

The Ethiopian government can respond rapidly to investor requests in part because the federal government owns all the land. Land has long been used as a political tool by Ethiopian leaders, and is part of the foundation of the ruling party's power. During the feudal system under the monarchy, kings rewarded obedience and successful military campaigns by allocating large zones of land to their generals, who acted as feudal lords over the peasants on that land, demanding servitude and extracting wealth.[46] When the Derg deposed Haile Selassie on the back of the Marxist-inspired student uprisings on 12 September 1974, it appropriated the students' Marxist language—especially the phrase 'land to the tiller'—by designating all land as belonging to the state to utilise it in the service of the regime. The present government inherited this system and they use access to land both punitively, in the form of forcible eviction and exclusion from land and income, and as a reward in the form of long-term land leases (and other, less formal forms of access) that will generate high income in return for good political behaviour by the grantee. The ownership of land by the state also makes it uncomplicated to write a contract with investors, and explains how a senior government official could grant one million hectares to Saudi investors at a single meeting,[47] asserting that the land belongs to the government and not to the poor farmers using it.

The federal government controls the awarding of land leases to foreigners, but leaves the actual allocation of land to the *killil*—the state or regional government. These in turn delegate some of the activities to *woreda*—zonal officials. All levels of government are dominated by the ruling party, the Ethiopia People's Revolutionary Democratic Front (EPRDF). The land transfer mechanisms reflect the broader structure of the Ethiopian polity where centralised control and decision-making penetrate deeply into the rural and tribal fabric of the country. The Federal Democratic Republic state structure emphasises ethnic divisions which, along with land, constitute another element for controlling the population. The establishment of the federation divided the country into ethnicity-based *killils*. The EPRDF, under the leadership of Prime Minister Meles Zenawi (Mr. Meles), is a coalition of four ethno-centric parties, one each from Oromiya, the Southern Nationalities killil, Amhara and Tigray. The last, the Tigray People's Liberation Front, is led by Mr. Meles and is primus inter pares in the EPRDF. The EPRDF uses divide-and-rule tactics among the ethnic divisions,[48] effectively preventing the myriad opposition groups from cohering into a substantial or credible opposition.

The EPRDF is eager to attract foreign investors to Ethiopia. The federal government's effectively unfettered control over land is one of its key drawing cards and it places few obligations on investors seeking land. Officials at all levels of government appear to conduct little due diligence and have no procedure for assessing applicants or challenging prospective investors who might fall short. The application process for purchasing land requires the investor to submit a project proposal describing the project's objectives, the resources that will be invested, the equipment required, expected outputs, a schedule and time-line, a description of how the produce will be marketed, and a financial statement. The last states how the project is funded, what proportion is investor money, how much is borrowed and on what terms, and includes a profit and loss statement. There are, however, no rules or guidelines defining how these requirements are to be met for a project to be awarded.[49] The application process involves authorities at the national, *killil* and *woreda* levels and sometimes even reaches down to the *kebelle* or village. Local administrators identify specific lands to be awarded, determine whether it is 'available', and how much compensation is to be paid and to whom. Technically, these fees are supposed to be paid by the investor, not the state—although for some investors the government offers to deduct this cost from rent monies paid for the land.[50]

This federally-administered process replaced an older one where investors had to deal directly with the *killil* governments. One investor who has operated in Ethiopia since before this change was made explained that despite initial misgivings, the transfer of the company's relationships from *killil* to federal level was unproblematic. Another investor notes: '[we] only really have to deal with the top. … On the whole, the environment is good: government policies are favourable and the government is co-operative and easy to deal with. They are very responsive to our needs as investors.'[51] Another investor offered his advice to other investors, especially about being 'flexible':

Work with the government on where it needs your project… I know that some companies have come badly unstuck and have left the market because they either didn't really know what they wanted or they refused to be accommodating with the government and its needs. Work with the government. They are co-operative and very keen for the foreign investment. I think I could say that the government is even easier and better to work with than the government in your or my own country.[52]

The procedure described by these investors appears to side-step formal requirements and is not transparent and, as we discuss further below, such 'flexibility' allows the government to steer investment to accomplish multiple goals.

Infrastructure, equity and corruption

Cambodia

Cambodia's foreign investment regime is close to the neoliberal ideal. It is very favourable to investors at the expense of Cambodia and Cambodians. There are few regulatory constraints on investors other than Article 44 of the Constitution which limits land ownership to Khmer nationals. For the purposes of foreign investment, this requirement is formally satisfied by 51 per cent Khmer ownership but in practice, it is simply circumvented by foreigners taking land leases for terms as long as ninety-nine years with the option to renew. Investors may repatriate all their profits and production, and they enjoy income-tax holidays and tariff-free inputs to production.[53] If they set up operations in an analogue to a free trade zone, here called a Special Economic Zone,[54] they also can escape value-added taxes and benefit from expedited customs procedures.

These policies may be advantageous to investors in the short run, but they offer little or nothing to Cambodians. Companies provide little income-tax revenue, while their low wages and the absence of requirements to use local inputs, transfer technology or supply local markets at affordable prices makes no provision for contributing to the local economy.

Nevertheless, the promise of increased productivity from such investments has the potential both to increase output for the international market and to raise incomes for local producers. These would be achievable if the financial capacity of the investors is large enough to design and build irrigation systems and invest in processing and transportation infrastructure. However, doing business in Cambodia can be expensive and difficult. For example, Shepherd observed multiple instances of minor authorities like traffic police routinely 'taxing' commercial vehicles, which can add hundreds of dollars to the cost of taking a single load from its rural origins to the Sihanoukville port. Electricity is expensive, in short supply, and mostly imported from Thailand and Vietnam. Although Global System for Mobile Communications coverage is widespread, the lack of electricity coupled with rural poverty keeps internet penetration and connectivity very low. Credit is costly and nearly all inputs must be imported, although foreign investors are exempt from import duties—an advantage not granted to local farmers. The abject conditions of life for rural Cambodians extends to indiffer-

ent and graft-ridden healthcare facilities and very poor quality education.[55] This, in turn, limits the physical and mental capacity of the rural
workforce to meet the needs of investors as employers. Both the provision of material infrastructure and the support of the local workforce
require significant investor contributions and should be seen as integral
to any proposed project.

Commercial investment has the potential to improve the situation we
have described, but it is not clear that it can reduce the risks coming
from Cambodia's political and judicial systems. Despite the best efforts
of the United Nations to establish foundations of democratic governance,[56] there is no effective process for the transfer of power. Elections
are rigged; the opposition is harassed and intimidated, and Prime
Minister Hun Sen retains his position. Hun Sen appears to be grooming
his son to succeed him, but his cronies (*okhna*) are not uniformly enthusiastic. Because of the judicial corruption noted above, the courts are of
little use against the corruption that threatens investments.

Indeed, corruption extends throughout the Cambodian political
economy. Despite pressure from foreign aid donors who collectively contribute about half of the national budget,[57] it took fifteen years to get the
government to pass the 2010 anti-corruption bill. Since then only four
provincial officials have been charged under the law, giving credence to
analysts who observe that the anti-corruption appointees and procedures
are little more than institutions of the governing party, making any real
change unlikely.[58] The corruption already noted in such areas as healthcare
affects the labour force, contributing to Cambodia's infant mortality rate
(the highest in the region), low life expectancy and the high rate of poverty among its population.[59] Recounting his experience at a meeting
promoting investment in Cambodia, an investment adviser in Phnom
Penh told a story about a foreign representative who asked whether
refunds were available when payments to 'facilitate' a project failed to get
the desired result. The question was answered in the negative.[60]

The constant demand for payoffs is doubly problematic for foreign
investors in that it sullies their reputation when such corrupt acts become
matters of public knowledge.[61] Furthermore, payoffs contribute to the
anger that fuels growing political instability arising from disputed
resources and confiscated assets. Many of these payoffs are associated
with violations of the regulations for awarding ELCs. Some disputes
have become violent, further jeopardising the long-term security and

predictability of foreign investments in Cambodian agriculture. Disputes and contestations over ELCs and land grants to investors are common reactions to the corruption around titles and land tenuring that occurs regularly despite the 2001 Land Law. The government appears all too willing to seize land from farmers in order to sell it to wealthy investors, both foreign and domestic. Unlike domestic investors, however, foreigners tend to be more vulnerable to conflict and disputation because they are not integral to the ruling party as many domestic investors are. The government already blames such conflicts on investors:

these [conflicts]… arise only when companies or individuals do not accept what they are given, and are greedy and want to take over more, for example, take the whole 10,000 hectares even though there are areas excluded because of villages and villagers in some parts. Or … someone decides they want to make a political issue out of the ELC.[62]

Despite this dismissal of the extent and causes of conflict associated with investment, there are two to three reports every week in the English-language press dealing with court proceedings, protests, evictions and violence in relation to the commercial exploitation of land that Cambodians depend on for their lives and livelihoods.

During Shepherd's fieldwork, he witnessed a violent confrontation between villagers and some 300 regular police, military police and senior military officers in Udong village in Kampong Speu province. The security forces had come to forcibly evict villagers from land purchased by a company owned by a Taiwanese businessman. The company's title to the land had not come via an ELC but through an alleged back-room deal with the government for part of the land plus a company promise to purchase the rest from the villagers. According to the villagers, this promise had not been kept—payment was never forthcoming—but the company's claim to the land was nevertheless upheld by the provincial supreme court. This was the second confrontation between the security forces and these villagers. The first had included an assault against an elderly woman. This time, the villagers had armed themselves with stones, slingshots, machetes, poles, sharpened sticks, fury and desperation. The security forces, which included at least one relation of some of the villagers, backed off, but subsequent press reports claimed that the company and the authorities were preparing a third assault to evict the villagers by force. According to some local policemen, the legal and enforcement costs of the eviction were being paid by the company, along with the cost of bringing in earthmovers and heavy demolition equipment. This conclusion is more than plausible:

> At the end of February [2010], Cambodian Prime Minister Hun Sen kicked off a program creating partnerships in which businesses would provide donations for particular units of the Royal Cambodian Armed Forces. … The Cambodian military regularly guards large-scale private land concessions across the country, according to rights groups, and has been used to evict the rural poor for business developments. Hun Sen's new policy, says U.S.-based watchdog group Global Witness, is a step toward formalizing that process.[63]

The institutionalisation of government-corporate-military partnerships formed to evict Cambodian peasants from the lands they depend upon for survival should evoke second thoughts in investors. The potential for violence and sabotage of projects by the dispossessed is a risk likely to worsen over time, with its impact on labour availability, the project's likelihood of success and the investor's reputation. The legitimising 'win-win' discourse for this type of project envisions farmers as employees on the company-owned plantations. However, for the families 'relocated' to tiny parcels of inferior land on the (sometimes distant) periphery of projects, employment is rare and fails to compensate for the productivity of the lost land. These conditions were in evidence at the ELC projects visited by Shepherd. Corporate employers rarely provide work for women and are prohibited from allowing youngsters to work, so that the majority of people go unemployed—and unfed. Few of those interviewed by Shepherd in 2011 reported being able to grow enough for themselves and their (frequently large) families on their new parcels of land, even when resources are supplemented by the $2.50/day paid for the seasonal labour of an unskilled adult male. Travel between plantations and distant sites of relocation or to places where people can buy supplies imposes additional hardship. Cambodians who took Shepherd to the field in Amliang and acted as his intermediaries referred to these dispossessed persons as 'living ghosts', people without food, income or hope. They serve as a constant reminder to those still living on their land to resist government-orchestrated eviction and exile to tiny plots of land too small to live on. As the ranks of dispossessed farmers grow, their stories are starting to percolate into global consciousness.[64] This reflects on the reputations of foreign landholders. Investors also are vulnerable to further demands by the national government if they wish to retain possession of their land. Contribution to the public-private security-force partnerships is only one possible strategy devised by the national government for extracting such unforeseen payments from investors.

Ethiopia

As in Cambodia, field observations in Ethiopia showed scant evidence of the rule of law in awarding land concessions to investors or regulating their use. Political power is highly concentrated in the hands of the EPRDF and investor success is predicated on good relationships with key government figures. This introduces a level of uncertainty from the outset. In the event of a change of government, there is no guarantee that agreements reached with the previous office holders will survive intact. In addition, regulation can be sketchy and even when it is clear, may be indifferently applied. A common refrain of many of Shepherd's interviewees was that the legislation often is reasonable, but adherence and enforcement are problematic. As in Cambodia, the absence of the rule of law in Ethiopia goes to the heart of investment risk. This risk is not confined to contracts and regulation in Ethiopia as domestic food insecurity adds another dimension. If the Ethiopian government discovers that the trade-offs that it is making between the benefits it receives from foreign investors' projects and the domestic food security situation become untenable over the longer term, investors could find themselves in a position where the government decides that the value derived from their investment is no longer worthwhile. As a government official said: 'While regulation plays a role, remember at the end of the day, that if the government determines that the benefits of continued participation in the country outweigh the negatives, then the company has misman-aged its investment'.[65] At best, the result of such a scenario would be unanticipated additional costs and at worst, it could mean expropriation of the investment.

An additional complication for investors in Ethiopia is the dire situ-ation of the country's agricultural economy. Ethiopian agriculture can be generalised into two main types: lowland pastoral agriculture and highland rain-fed, crop-based agriculture. Both lowland and highland agriculture in Ethiopia are facing crises. In the lowlands, increasing population leads to larger livestock populations that strain the fragile lands. There is increasing competition over fresh water resources between local populations and commercial-industrial interests. One result has been enclosures of land and water frontages that disrupt pastoral movements. Indeed, many interviewees saw the government's 'villagisation' and settlement strategies as a signal that there is little future for pastoralism in Ethiopia. Increasing evidence of climate change, especially longer and more frequent droughts, are adding to already deleterious effects on traditional pastoral agriculture. Foreign investors seeking land add to the competitive pressures, including those that affect pastoralists. One further problem for pastoralists is that they rarely are included in agricultural statistics. On the one hand, nomadic pastoralism is difficult to incorporate into statistics relating to land use, such as plot sizes. Yet on the other hand, the effective 'disappearance' of pastoralists could reflect the denial of a future for pastoralism. It contributes little or nothing to GDP as conventionally calculated, and is pursued by populations whose peripatetic lifestyle makes them difficult to control. The disappearance also explains how the government can claim that farmers are not affected by large land leases, since affected pastoralists are neither defined nor recognised as farmers by the government. In the highlands, massive population growth combined with increasing competition for land from urban and commercial-industrial expansion is leaving agrarian families with smaller and smaller plots as one-third of the country's agrarian households live on just half a hectare or less.[66] This is not sufficient either to feed a large family directly or to generate enough income to support it.

In both Cambodia and Ethiopia, land-based investments, which are largely unregulated, deliver very little return to either the local or national economy; the rents are astonishingly low, as little as 82 Birr ($4.80) per ha for projects,[67] along with the long tax holidays mentioned earlier. What the government gets, according to a former official, is 'the importance of the project for the national economy'.[68] Further, the investors become complicit in the use of land deals by the EPRDF to further political objectives. The complex political interplay of ethnicity and land interests intersect when an empowered ethnic group uses the federal government's land policies to exploit old tribal rivalries, take vengeance upon ethnic opponents, or gain economic or political advantages over other tribes. Leasing land to foreigners offers additional opportunities to pursue these ends.

In the Gambela region of Ethiopia, an area of great ethnic diversity, where the federal government is allocating vast amounts of land to foreign lessees, there are two major tribes with a particularly long and sordid history of enmity, the Anuak and the Nuer. A Nuer tribesman told Shepherd that many of the administrators and police are Anuak, and that when they allocate land to foreign investors, they frequently evict Nuer and refuse to allow compensation to be paid to them.[69] Shepherd found, however, that both Nuer and Anuak communities are displaced in Gambela, from which we conclude that ethnic rivalry either works both ways or that administrators from the highlands are unfair to both these lowland tribes. Regardless, Nuer are convinced that Anuak are behind (at least some of) their evictions, which speaks to the success of the government in fostering ethnic rivalry to distract attention from its role in dispossessing people from many ethnic groups. Similar strategies are employed in the highlands. In Debre Zeit, Oromo authorities are allowing the agricultural land occupied (and depended upon for food) by an Amharic-ethnic community to be used as a dumping site for rubbish, including bio-hazardous hospital waste. Other parts of the same community's land was granted to investors without the legally required compensation being paid to the farmers.[70]

It should not be surprising that situations such as these underlie the paucity of goodwill between outside investors and communities affected by their projects. The resulting risk affects those whose activities are within the law as well as those who operate outside it. The lack of goodwill is magnified with regard to the impacts of development on land, water and the environment. These can have adverse effects on local communities and speak to the importance of investor sensitivity to their needs. As one government official explained:

Degradation of land and water resources is not productive for either the investor or the country. While there should be some regulatory controls around this, there is such a thing as responsibility that investors need to take heed of. They should be responsible for the impact of their activities both socially and environmentally. The first rule for an investor should be 'do no harm' and always act to leave the place no worse off than it was found.[71]

Sadly, given the impacts on communities to date, it seems that investment projects are falling short of fulfilling even this minimum.

In the absence of investors taking responsibility, the Ethiopian government itself does not demonstrate the capacity to ensure that its people are unharmed by foreign agricultural investment projects. Indeed, because in Gambela it has been forcibly relocating people in anticipation of making land leases to foreigners, the case can be made that the government is actively involved in harming these people. Preemptive relocations enable the government to tell investors that the land is empty of farmers as part of the positive inducement to take long-term leases. However, it demonstrates that investors cannot rely on the Ethiopian government to reduce the risks inherent in their investment projects because it is so deeply implicated in generating them. Instead, it seems incumbent upon investors to work harder at providing development opportunities to mitigate the future probability of bad outcomes on a large scale—commensurate with the scale of many of these deals.

We have already noted several infrastructural deficiencies in Ethiopia. As in Cambodia, education and healthcare are lacking in much of Ethiopia. For rural communities outside the Gambela township, these services simply do not exist. Schools and clinics are promised as part of investment projects—although there is no evidence of this happening—but access to them is anticipated to be free of charge only for employees and their families. The unemployed and those with no income will have to pay for services.[72] In the meantime, because much of the local population is unskilled, an investor who brings skilled labour from abroad is likely to exacerbate ethnic tensions. Other social dynamics of Ethiopian agriculture also involve risk. Large-scale commercial farming in an environment of smallholder—and deeply impoverished—agriculturalists has the potential to create bitterness and incite retaliation. Damage to newly created electrical power equipment was evident in a number of locations around the investment projects visited by Shepherd in the Gambela region. Cut power lines and felled poles give the appearance of being sabotaged, although the dispossessed groups Shepherd met all disclaimed any knowledge of how the infrastructure sustained its damage. Whether a particular investor is the direct source of a local problem is immaterial with regard to whether his or her project will be attacked. Aspects as pedestrian as location, as fortuitous as opportunity or as unjust as scapegoating are equally likely to influence the choice of target by a disaffected peasant.

One surprising difference between Ethiopia and Cambodia is how the bad outcomes for communities from foreign land investments in Ethiopia have not provoked visible violent conflict. Indeed, it is remarkable how 'passive' affected communities are even when family members are starving. If violent conflict did occur, it must have been quickly repressed. Few people in Ethiopia were willing to discuss violence (either as a reality or as a strategy) in reaction to 'land grabs', perhaps afraid of being seen as advocates for anti-government violence and suffering retaliation. One of the few observers who was not so inhibited said that local communities are increasingly willing to show their anger and frustration: 'Do not think that there have not been protests and revolts against authorities over this. There have been… they are just not reported.' He then added that, 'the government intervenes with its mighty hand forcing the people into silence'.[73]

The apparent lack of violence in Ethiopia as compared to Cambodia begs the question of whether this changes the equation for a food security land investor. Does it mean that Ethiopia is a less risky environment than Cambodia from a 'security' point of view? Perhaps. One could argue that given the corruption and violent conflict in Cambodia, project risks in Ethiopia are lower. However, the same primary risk factors are still in evidence in both places: dispossessed, impoverished, hungry and frustrated local populations in close proximity to the projects, and hostility among the communities expected to provide labour for them.

Innovative approaches to investments

Agricultural land investment is only one part of a broader food security strategy pursued by GCC governments, which also includes portfolio investment in global agricultural corporations, and what a senior member of the US diplomatic mission in Riyadh—who has worked closely with Saudis on food security—calls building 'grain ties' between their country and major exporters of agricultural products.[74] In addition to the United States, which exported 350 million tons of grain to Saudi Arabia last year,[75] GCC food-importers are also building ties with Latin American countries.[76] The diversification of food sources adds to the security of supply, and contract terms can contribute to price stability for consumers. Contracts can also protect populations in food-exporting countries where GCC members have invested in agricultural land. For example, contracts between Saudi Arabia and Ethiopia have been reported as specifying that 50 per cent of the yield from their operations must remain in Ethiopia to improve Ethiopian food security.[77] Such contract terms show goodwill towards achieving win-win outcomes even though, in practice, they are likely to depend heavily on the investor for compliance. Moreover, the investors are committed to improving the land and its productivity by applying modern farming methods, better seeds and other elements of the technology that has increased yields in the West. Such additional productivity would boost the amount of food available to people in Ethiopia under the terms of these contracts.

On our first visit to Qatar, we were told by the head of the Qatar National Food Security Programme (QNFSP) that Qatar was aware of the high risks associated with foreign land acquisitions, and had initially decided to take a different route.[78] This included making portfolio investments in major food-producing companies; encouraging these companies to locate their corporate headquarters in Qatar; and building diplomatic ties with major food-exporting countries, already touched on here. These strategies provide limited scope for investor autonomy, however. Direct investment does offer autonomy and the opportunity to avoid or ameliorate difficulties that we have shown have accompanied foreign land acquisitions in Cambodia and Ethiopia to date.

Adverse outcomes of land investments on the poor and vulnerable are similar in both countries, and add to investment risk. Risks from uncompensated population displacement range from a lack of competent and cooperative labour for the investors' farms to the potential for sabotage against farm installations and supporting infrastructure by desperate former owners. Some of these risks can be managed through contracts but success requires measures to ensure that contract provisions with regard to compensation are being adhered to. The nature of the political economy in both countries imposes risks that contracts cannot compensate for, such as the unpredictable costs of endemic corruption in Cambodia and the use of land as a political weapon in Ethiopia. In the investor's worst-case scenario, the consequences of host-country vulnerability and regime instability could ultimately result in expropriation of the investment, which happened to Saudi investors in Egypt after the fall of the Mubarak regime.[79]

Reputational risks are reflected in observers' concerns about the goals of GCC land investments, which the early stage of GCC projects does little to allay because so little is known about how they will be carried out in practice. Concerns arise from tensions over whether the principal aim of these projects is to grow crops for home-country markets as a way of sheltering them from price volatility; to increase production as a means of keeping global food prices low; or to engage in various speculative activities. The former risks abandoning host-country populations to continued food insecurity while a potential consequence of the latter is the risk of affecting world food prices in ways that are likely to be highly deleterious, regardless of the return it would bring to investors. Provisions to allocate a large proportion of production to host-country populations answers part of this concern, but the overall thrust of these criticisms highlights the tendency of some observers to question the legitimacy of policies few criticise when their own governments are the agents.

Some of the suspicion regarding farmland and other land-based foreign investment arises from judgements about the conduct of the most aggressive investor abroad, China.[80] Resentment at Chinese investment is mirrored by Chinese resentment at discrimination that shuts them out of desirable overseas opportunities. GCC investors had a similar experience when Dubai Ports World was granted permission by the British High Court to acquire the Peninsular and Oriental Steam Navigation Company, whose international operations included providing services to twenty-one US ports. Pressure from the US Congress forced Dubai to sell off that portion of its investment to US investors.[81] Similar pressures from Britain and the United States forced Kuwait to reduce or relinquish its investment in BP and Santa Fe, respectively.[82] The lament of a disappointed Chinese investor could have been uttered by GCC investors facing similar rejection:

'There are still double standards,' complained Huang Nubo, who had planned to build a massive tourist resort on a remote stretch of frozen heath [in Iceland]. 'The Western world asks us to open the Chinese market without restrictions, but when it's a question of their resources they close the door on us.'[83]

Turning state investments over to the private sector introduces another element of risk; that profit maximisation could trump national food security objectives,[84] with potentially further detrimental impacts on the local communities and their environment. Private investors rarely view investment opportunities from a long time horizon, and many are pressed by shareholders to seek short-term returns. The projects dealt with here, however, are supposed to raise agricultural productivity for the benefit of host- and home-country populations, a long-term undertaking. Agriculture by its nature is a long-term investment and building an enterprise for stable long-term returns requires a different set of behaviours from chasing a short-term windfall.

Two arguments are often made about commercial investment in developing country environments: the first is that the investment will bring economic benefits that create a rising tide that (eventually) lifts all boats. The second is that it is not the responsibility of commercial enterprises to deliver development outcomes at the expense of corporate success—this is the responsibility of the host-country government. The evidence presented here denies the first and makes a strong case for reconsidering the validity of the second.

The ethics of farmland investment are attracting concern. Critics call for investors to minimise the negative aspects of their activities and assume responsibility for their consequences.[85] Advocates focus on the possibility of positive development outcomes, particularly with regard to substantial productivity increases that would benefit all parties. Investment is essential for lifting the agrarian poor out of poverty. It seems, however, that most investors resist tailoring their investment strategies to address the well-being of the rural poor, preferring to make more payments to governments as the best guarantee of their security. They are quick to shirk responsibility for improving outcomes in spite of a 'development outcomes' mantra embedded in 'win-win' language in the discourses legitimising the projects in the first place. Nevertheless, without the cooperation and engagement of the rural communities, investments are unlikely to succeed. Further, given that the stability of these governments is far from guaranteed, an arm's-length relationship with them may well be the most prudent investment strategy in the long run.

Conventional investment wisdom says that good investments are ones with high returns and low risk. This is problematic when the high returns are generated by risky behaviour. The conditions under which the rural poor labour in both Ethiopia and Cambodia are largely the same: insecure land tenure; lack of access to capital; lack of access to inputs, technology and equipment; lack of infrastructure; and lack of access to markets. These are all things that investors can address by including smallholder farmers among the stakeholders in their enterprises. Re-framing investment strategies to focus on smallholder farmers provides an opportunity to mitigate reputational, financial and security risks.

The use of win-win language to legitimise investments is not enough to deliver 'win-win' outcomes. 'Win-win' investment strategies benefit from transparency and from incorporating what physician Paul Farmer calls 'a preferential option for the poor',[86] for example, by taking measures to support rural development for small-scale farmers by providing ancillary investment in processing. Especially if it is tailored for a wide catchment area, processing facilities would increase value added by providing currently unavailable services to local farmers while expanding investors' access to production beyond what comes from the land they control, reducing average operating costs. Helping farmers market their produce is another example, along with irrigation and grain-storage facilities. These would increase farmer incomes and make more of what is produced available locally and globally, reducing waste. In contrast, investment strategies centred on land acquisition alone create short-term cash gains for corrupt governments but offer little to citizens, while the resentment that results can destabilise investment environments and countries as a whole. These observations are supported by the findings of our study of already-operating agricultural projects in Cambodia and Ethiopia.

As we have noted, there are huge opportunities not only for social good but also for profitable gain in both countries. The profit potential comes from under-utilised resources: farmers in Cambodia and Ethiopia are producing much less than they could be. By producing more they could generate higher incomes to help lift them out of poverty. Still, there is a large unanswered question from the investors' perspective: could the surpluses that these farmers deliver with appropriate investment be sufficient to create reliable volumes for export? In Cambodia, the answer is almost certainly yes, but in the context of Ethiopia's acute poverty, hunger and population pressures it is difficult to be so sanguine in spite of efforts by GCC investors to address local food needs in their contracts with the host government. A favourable outcome in Ethiopia would be more likely if enough smallholder farmers could profit from the export of their surpluses to generate economic momentum sufficient to reduce the broader poverty and food insecurity problem.

Investment focusing on the capacities of the small-scale farmer is more likely to produce better outcomes than importing a plantation system based on the industrialisation of agriculture. The latter would both increase the exclusion and impoverishment of local farmers and reduce the diversity and quality of what could be produced on the land over the longer term.[87] Generally, family farms, even in developing areas, tend to be more efficient than industrial operations, particularly with regard to their use of resources.[88] Also, family farms along with farms combining characteristics of family and industrial operations, can fill lucrative market niches such as for organic vegetable and animal products for which there is a high demand in GCC countries, and return a higher rate on capital and labour investment than commodity production. Whether shifting investor focus to the smallholder is a sufficient solution, however, requires considerably more research and analysis.

Conclusion

To ensure reliable flows of agricultural staples, GCC governments need to understand the pathologies associated with overseas investments in farmland and to approach their projects with a view to managing their investments—and their agents—closely. The generation of insecurity and harm for communities is not only bad per se, but limits the likelihood of successful food security outcomes for the GCC states. Their multiple goals and long-term horizons allow GCC governments, and the private investors whom they invite to participate in these ventures, to consider and apply a range of strategies designed to limit the likelihood of 'lose-lose' and even 'win-lose' scenarios by pressing for equity across the several host-country interests affected by their investments. One such strategy would be to invest in developing the capacity of the farmers themselves instead of simply acquiring their land. This could include working more closely with those among their own domestic food producers who have long-term views on food security for their nations as well as interest in the success of their own enterprises.[89]

While host-country governments may be more focused on immediate benefits for their regimes, Gulf investors can use their advantages to commit resources to building local development, productive capacity and food security from the ground up. This would distinguish their projects from those that already have engendered hostility, thereby reducing risk and contributing to the achievement of long-term objectives. We are not alone in making this argument. The Center for Human Rights and Global Justice at New York University argues:

Small farmers in developing countries need infrastructure, such as roads and storage facilities. They need better access to credit. They need to be able to form cooperatives, and to improve their bargaining position in markets with better information about prices. Whether it is domestic or foreign, whether it is public or private, investment can help this to happen. However, what small farmers definitely do not need is investors acquiring from governments the land on which they rely for their livelihoods, robbing them of the single most important asset they have.[90]

GCC governments are uniquely positioned to shape their foreign investment in agriculture to produce 'win-win' outcomes. Thoughtfully designed constructive efforts to reshape foreign agricultural investment practice could bear fruit that would enhance both the value of their investments and the reputations of GCC states as supporters of responsible and sustainable agricultural and investment practices beneficial to themselves and their local partners. Given the new visibility of GCC states in foreign policy and as leaders in innovative approaches to sustainability in a variety of settings,[91] an inventive and humane investment policy in developing country agriculture would attest to their capacity to exercise soft power in multiple arenas, contributing greatly to their long-term security.

10

FOOD INSECURITY IN THE WEST BANK

Elisa Cavatorta and *Sam Waples*

This study explores the spatial patterns of food insecurity in the West Bank region of the Palestinian Territories, and how community-level factors, such as environmental aspects and resource accessibility, can explain these patterns.[1] It constructs an original dataset combining household survey data on food insecurity, census data on community level characteristics and environmental information extracted by elaborating Geographic Information System (GIS) surfaces. Unique in its approach, this study estimates a multilevel model of household food insecurity, including household, community characteristics and a spatial lag of surrounding community characteristics. We predict food insecurity incidences at the community-level for the entire West Bank and analyse the geographical patterns of food insecurity. The study finds strong influences of local environmental characteristics in explaining household food insecurity. It also finds evidence of distinctive geographical patterns of food insecurity, suggesting a role for geographically-targeted interventions. The policy scenarios hypothesised in the study highlight the responsiveness of food insecurity incidences to improvements in employment rates, removal of mobility restrictions and infrastructure development. The study is the result of an interdisciplinary cooperation between the authors and collaboration with Palestinian partners who shared knowledge and data. To collect the data, the authors engaged in an extensive data analysis, a number of visits to the Palestinian Bureau of Statistics and consultation with several Palestinian authorities and international bodies.

Socioeconomic development policies are often designed to address social disparities in particular types of geographical and economic environments. In the food security literature, there is recognition of the importance of environmental factors, such as market access or agricultural potential, to explain food insecurity, but these linkages are rarely assessed in an explicit geographical way even though, in certain contexts, these appear to be critical.

The West Bank region of the Palestinian Territories is among one of these cases where there is a direct link between geography and food insecurity. Plagued by an enduring political stalemate, Palestinian growth and development has been significantly affected by the lack of progress to peace and the legacies of this unresolved conflict. On the ground, access to market and resources is constrained by unequal development and hindered by mobility restrictions of people and goods. Israel retains control over security and planning on significant portions of land reserves as well as agricultural and grazing land. Employment possibilities are limited and livelihood opportunities depend on the surrounding environment. As a result, the West Bank demonstrates chronic levels of poverty and food insecurity. The Food and Agriculture Organization estimates that 22 per cent of the population of the West Bank was food insecure in 2010.

These linkages between the environment where individuals live and the risk of food insecurity have been overlooked in the literature. In fact, there seems to be a disciplinary partition between social scientists and environmental scientists. Social scientists usually explain food insecurity with household-level factors. Income, earnings, sectorial employment and family structure have been found to be influential determinants of household food insecurity.[2] In contrast to this, environmental scientists are generally concerned about district or country level factors, such as soil fertility depletion, agricultural sustainability and access to markets as crucial factors to explain food insecurity.[3] The 'third generation' of food security literature recognises that these factors are closely linked, and that multiple causes of food insecurity coexist at various levels: individual, household, community and national.[4] This literature places food insecurity in a broader framework, which includes the economic characteristics, demographics, educational attainment, and availability of services and community assets upon which individuals rely to manage their livelihood sources.[5] However, empirical works assessing these factors in combination are rare.

Environmental factors may be important to explain food insecurity incidence in certain regions, districts or communities within a country. For example, limited market access is a structural threat to food security especially for those people relying on purchasing food. Spatial factors explaining food insecurity can be accounted for by using regional-fixed effects in micro-level analysis, however this approach is silent about which environment factors are important.

This study aims to fill this gap between these two branches of literature in a context where taking into account the characteristics of the surrounding environments is crucial. For this reason, this study combines household survey data on food insecurity, census data on community level characteristics and GIS environmental information. It considers how both individual characteristics and aggregate environmental factors at the community-level are associated with household food insecurity. We build an econometric model including both household and community information to identify the effect of these factors on the household probability of food insecurity. The model allows us to predict the incidence of food insecurity across the entire West Bank and we analyse the spatial patterns that emerge. To shed some light on the consequences of possible policy interventions, we simulate changes in the probability of food insecurity that would arise under a number of hypothetical scenarios.

The analysis of the spatial distribution of the prevalence of food insecurity and environment factors across communities has a number of policy implications. First, it can help identify and quantify regional disparities in food insecurity behind the crude governorate statistics usually available from policy reports. Second, it may help identify the areas most deprived, which may inform policymakers about which areas to prioritise. Third, the analysis of the spatial distribution of food insecurity together with the spatial patterns of environmental factors, such as agricultural potential and market access, and their simulated changes, is able to show which environmental factors are most important. This may inform policymakers which interventions to prioritise for long-term improvement in food security: for example, if food insecurity in agricultural communities is associated with lack of access to markets, improving road density or public services may be an effective food security strategy. In order to show the geography of food insecurity in the West Bank, we make an extensive use of maps together with statistical analysis. Besides giving a more intuitive reading of the results, maps can be helpful in forming further research questions.

The context: the Palestinian Territories

The Palestinian economy has been significantly affected by the failure of the peaceful resolution of the Israeli-Palestinian conflict. GDP fluctuations, employment, and trade and aid flows are directly influenced by political developments within the Palestinian Territories and their relations with Israel. Thus, the political context has significant impacts on the well-being of Palestinians and their poverty and food security risk.

GDP fluctuations clearly reflect political changes: from 1994–9, the years after the Oslo Agreement, real GDP and per capita GDP showed positive rates of growth, reaching 12 per cent. These rates declined sharply with the unfolding of the second *Intifada* in 2000 and the intensification of Israeli restrictions that followed. The recovery has been slow: in the West Bank, real GDP per capita recovered to its 1994 level only in 2009, despite growth rates having been significantly worse than comparable countries with the same real GDP per capita in 1994.[6]

GDP figures for the whole Palestinian Territories conceal a wide divergence in macroeconomic conditions between the two comprising regions of the West Bank and Gaza Strip. Since 2007, the West Bank has experienced modest improvements, following public economic reforms and the relaxation of Israeli restrictions. The Gaza Strip economy remains devastated and it is mainly sustained by government spending, humanitarian assistance and a flourishing informal economy of private activities based on trade of goods smuggled through tunnels from Egypt.

In addition, the breakdown in negotiations in 2000 resulted in the division (originally planned as temporary) of the West Bank territory between area A (under Palestinian control), area B (under civilian

Palestinian control and Israeli military and security control) and area C (under full Israeli control). At the time of writing, these area divisions remain in place (see Figure 10.3 for locations of areas A, B and C). Nowadays, area C covers approximately 60 per cent of the West Bank land, including most land reserves and the majority of Palestinian agricultural land. Restrictive planning regimes, movement restrictions and Israeli settler violence make the development of these areas extremely difficult.

As a consequence of a stagnating economic environment and the restrictions on accessing the Israeli labour market, unemployment in the Territories remains high. Unemployment is estimated at 18 per cent in the West Bank (in 2009), while in Gaza it is estimated to be at 40 per cent.[7] Conflict and the closure regime have had a deep impact on the labour market. Economic downturns resulting from conflict and stalemate of political development have been followed by increases in unemployment and a continuous decline in labour force participation rates. Employment rates fell abruptly following the second *Intifada* and following the formation of the Hamas-led government in early 2006. In the West Bank, areas at the border with Israel which relied on Israel for employment opportunities have been severely hit by the construction of the barrier and the decline of granted work permits. Given the regimes of checkpoints and closures in place inside the West Bank, labour mobility is hindered, and employment possibilities are concentrated in government centres, especially in Ramallah.

Unemployment is highest among the youth. Average levels of education are high but this human capital does not translate into productive labour market outcomes. In addition, there is evidence of a declining trend in private sector growth, and de-industrialisation in manufacturing and agriculture.[8] The chronically high food insecurity rates are a direct manifestation of these economic difficulties.

In the West Bank, the predominant cause of food insecurity is lack of economic access to food. Thus, food insecurity is strictly linked to lack of purchasing power and, ultimately, poverty. The average share of expenditure on food in the West Bank is 34 per cent according to the Palestinian Central Bureau of Statistics (2010) and over 60 per cent in the lowest quartile of expenditure. Price disparities across the West Bank are stunning given its small size. Rising food prices reflect fluctuations in international food prices but are artificially inflated by controlled trade and internal mobility restrictions imposed by Israel. These trade and mobility restrictions increase transport costs.

The West Bank economy has been relatively isolated from the recent global financial crisis due to a lack of trade and financial links. However, in 2011 there was a decline in growth, slower easing of mobility restrictions and an uncertain political environment. Given the rather immobile agricultural sector and the trade dependency on Israel, self-sufficiency in food production in the West Bank is an unrealistic option. Thus, looking at the relationships between community characteristics, surrounding mobility restrictions and market access is crucial to understand possible clusters of high food insecurity incidence.

Data

The empirical evidence of this study is based on community-level data for 489 communities in the West Bank region of the Palestinian Territories.[9] The data collection involved much effort in gathering available secondary data from various sources, digitising information and computing variables from a GIS database to create a new comprehensive dataset of community information. A synthetic description of the data and their sources can be found in Appendix 3.

The primary source of socioeconomic and demographic variables at the community level is the Palestinian Population, Housing and Establishment Censuses 1997 and 2007. The Palestinian Central Bureau of Statistics allowed us to access aggregate proxy measures of wealth (for example, the availability of a kitchen, bathroom and toilet connected to water); sectoral employment (for example, the percentage of people employed in various sectorial activities including agriculture and types of agricultural holdings, manufacture, public administration and services); unemployment indicators (for example, dependency rates, gender unemployment rates, number of discouraged workers); demographic variables (for example, household size and demographic composition); educational attainment (for example, counts of illiterate people, population counts by completed levels of schooling); connection to service networks (for example, percentage of households connected to water, electricity and sewage networks); and fertility (for example, the number of births from which fertility rates can be derived). We collected information on the cultivated and uncultivated agricultural areas from the Agricultural Census 2010.[10]

We collected and elaborated water availability information from the Palestinian Water Authority such as the amount of water locally supplied and consumed, the average deficit from international World Health Organization (WHO) standards and average loss rates. We used existing GIS layers of the West Bank road system from the Office for the Coordination of Humanitarian Affairs and the Applied Research Institute-Jerusalem, to create a network to overlay existing information of mobility restrictions, such as various types of Israeli security checkpoints. This allowed us to compute measures of market access (measured by network distances to governorate capitals, which are more precise than simple Euclidean distances and crucial in a context, such as the Palestinian Territories, where mobility restrictions limit road access), access to services (measured by network distances to the nearest hospital), infrastructure (measured as the road density in the surroundings of each community) and measures of mobility restrictions, such as the number of checkpoints and road blocks in the surroundings of each community.

We digitised information of existing hospitals and clinics supplied by the Palestinian Ministry of Health. Information on land use and vegetation was extrapolated from available GIS raster files and used to compute measures of available crop land, distances to crop areas and a soil fertility measure. We extracted crop area data from the UMD Landcover Classification.[11] Soil fertility is measured as the mean annual value (1981–2000) of net primary production.[12] We also proxy land productivity by the mean annual value of the Aridity Index (1950–2000), computed as the ratio of mean annual precipitation to mean annual evapotranspiration.[13] All our communities fall within an arid to semi-arid climate class based on the United Nations Environment Programme (UNEP) 1997 classification.

Food insecurity information and individual level data comes from the Socio-Economic and Food Security Survey 2010, a nationally representative household survey conducted in tripartite partnership between the Palestinian Central Bureau of Statistics, the Food and Agriculture Organization and the World Food Programme. The survey contains information on household food insecurity for 3,875 households living in 125 communities within the West Bank.[14] Because of missing household information, the empirical sample is 3,853 households.

Various generations of food security literature have different definitions of food security. We adopt the definition contained in the Rome

Declaration on World Food Security (1996) and the World Food Summit Plan of Action which defines food insecurity as the situation 'when people do not have adequate physical, social or economic access to sufficient, safe and nutritious food which meets their dietary needs and food preferences for an active and healthy life'.[15] This definition includes four main components: adequacy of food supply or availability; stability of supply, without fluctuations or shortages from season to season or from year to year; accessibility to food or affordability; and quality and safety of food.

The literature suggests a number of food insecurity indicators, each capturing different aspects of food insecurity and food insecurity risk.[16] This chapter measures food insecurity by the Household Food Insecurity Access (HFIA) Prevalence. This is based on the frequency of occurrence of certain behaviours which result from an insufficient availability of food (such as being unable to eat because of lack of resources, eating a limited variety of food, going a whole day and night without eating); insufficient stability (such as having no food on certain days, going to bed hungry because food was not enough) and shortage (such as eating smaller meals than needed, eating fewer meals because food was not enough); and insufficient quality (such as eating food one prefers not to eat) and household anxiety about food being sufficient.[17] Households are categorised in four levels of food insecurity as they experience those conditions more frequently. At the household-level, this classification generates a categorical variable of food security with four groups: food secure; mildly food insecure; moderately food insecure, and severely food insecure. We focus on the category of severely food insecure households. The HFIA indicator is preferred over alternative indicators because it includes questions related to all aspects above and asks about anxiety regarding the availability of food, which is a direct reflection of the perception of risk of food insecurity.

Theoretical framework and empirical model

In our framework, household food insecurity depends on three sets of variables: a set of household characteristics, X'; a set of community characteristics, Z; and a set of surrounding community characteristics, $W'Z$, where W is a matrix of weights. The risk of food insecurity can be represented as a latent variable of which we observe a binary indicator, conditional on a threshold. The observed food insecurity indicator is thus defined conditional to the threshold c set by the HFIA categories.

The estimating model is thus:

$$y_{ij} = X_{ij}\beta + Z_j\gamma + W'Z_j\delta + u_{ij}$$

Here y_{ij} is a binary indicator equal to 1 when household i in community j is classified as severely food insecure; X, Z are defined above and W' is a matrix of distance weights. The weights are the inverse of the (Euclidean) distance between community j and community h and u_{ij} is the error term, which is assumed to follow a logistic distribution.[18] Due to missing observations, the empirical sample includes 3,853 households living in 125 communities in the West Bank. Our aim is to predict the food insecurity incidence at community-level throughout the whole country. We do so by calculating the mean of households' probability of being food insecure, conditional on a set of household and community variables, for each community. For the subset of communities for which we do not observe household characteristics, we assume a representative household with characteristics similar to its neighbouring communities.

More formally, the procedure develops in two steps. First we estimate the model based on the available information on 125 surveyed communities, say group A. We calculate the incidence of food insecurity as the mean of the households' predicted probability of being food insecure in a given community.[19] In the second step, we apply the parameters estimated from the first step regression to derive the imputed value of the probability of being food insecure in the non-surveyed communities, say group B.

Formally, the expected food insecurity in the surveyed communities A is

$$E[y_{ij}^A = 1 \mid X, Z, WZ] = Pr(y_{ij} = 1 \mid X, Z, WZ) = \Lambda(X_{ij}^A\beta + Z_j^A\gamma + W'Z_j\delta)$$

Here $\Lambda(.)$ is the cumulative logistic distribution. The predicted incidence of food insecurity in the surveyed communities, $\hat{P}_j^A$, given the estimated model is

$$\hat{P}_j^A = E[y_{ij}^A = 1 \mid X, Z, WZ, \hat{\beta}] = \frac{1}{n_j}\sum_{i=1}^{n_j} \Lambda(X_{ij}^A\hat{\beta} + Z_j^A\hat{\gamma} + W'Z_j\hat{\delta})$$

Figure 10.1: Models predicting food insecurity

	Dep. Var.: dichotomous, Yij = 1		
	X	X,Z	X, Z, W'Z
Household variables			
PCA wealth	−0.214***	−0.235***	−0.251***
	(0.021)	(0.022)	(0.025)
size	0.097***	0.108***	0.107***
	(0.017)	(0.018)	(0.016)
head schooling	−0.040***	−0.032**	0.031**
	(0.014)	(0.015)	(0.016)
dummy missing	−0.643***	−0.563***	0.571***
	(0.192)	(0.208)	(0.191)
spouse schooling	−0.027*	−0.029*	−0.026
	(0.015)	0.015)	(0.017)
dummy missing	−0.306*	−0.269	−0.233
	(0.173)	(0.175)	(0.195)
no. refugee	0.020	0.007	0.013
	(0.013)	(0.016)	(0.17)
manager	−1.208***	−1.261***	−1.259***
	(0.333)	(0.391)	(0.427)
professional	−0.526*	−0.566**	−0.517
	(0.269)	(0.255)	(0.302)
technician	−0.107	−0.354	−0.310
	(0.239)	(0.255)	(0.369)
agriculture	−0.429*	−0.354	−0.310
	(0.237)	(0.239)	(0.247)
sales	−0.412***	−0.445***	−0.411**
	(0.157)	(0.160)	(0.175)
craft	−0.202	−0.216	−0.249*
	(0.135)	(0.152)	(0.149)
cleric	−0.118	−0.105	−0.121
	(0.418)	(0.441)	(0.140)
unskilled	−0.224***	−0.252**	−0.246*
	(0.112)	(0.123)	(0.134)
Community variables			
pop 2007		0.000	0.001
		(0.002	(0.002)
agricultural hh %		−0.018***	−0.018***
		(0.005)	(0.005)
unemployment %		0.050***	0.038***
		(0.010)	(0.010)
non residential		−0.009	−0.008
		(0.011)	(0.010)

birth rate 2007		0.011***	0.009***
		(0.003)	(0.003)
rural		0.724***	1.110***
		(0.251)	(0.274)
camp		−1/077***	−0.572*
		(0.292)	(0.310)
restrictions		0.113***	0.023
		(0.031)	(0.032)
roadblocks		−0.027***	−0.009
		(0.008)	(0.008)
road density		−0.178*	−0.310***
		(0.100)	(0.102)
aridity index		−0.402	0.857
		(0.808)	(0.942)
aridity X area B		1.000***	0.202
		(0.331)	(0.371)
aridity X area C		1.475**	−0.003
		(0.597)	(0.685)
cultivated		0.007	0.019***
		(0.005)	(0.006)
hospital distance		0.052***	0.061***
		(0.010)	(0.011)
hospital X rural		−0.066**	−0.084***
		(0.015)	(0.017)
hospital X camp		0.048**	0.049**
		(0.020)	(0.021)
market 5–20km		−0.527***	0.356**
		(0.180)	(0.167)
market more 20km		−1.001***	−0.832***
		(0.211)	(0.211)
W unemployment			0.100
			(0.098)
W restrictions			1.313***
			(0.203)
W pop 2007			−0.001***
			(0.000)
constant	−0.996***	−2.039***	−3.150***
	(0.205)	(0.773)	(0.855)
N	3875	3853	3853
Corrected Predicted	60%	65%	67%
MLL	−1937.0	−1834.1	−1804.2

Notes: The dependent variable is a binary variable equal to 1 if the household is food insecure (HFIA definition), 0 otherwise. Standard errors (in parenthesis) are bootstrapped with 300 replications. Excluded categories are unemployed household head, unban location, area A, market within less than 5km.

Here n_j is the number of households surveyed in community j and $\hat{\beta}$, $\hat{\gamma}$, $\hat{\delta}$, are the estimated coefficients.

The predicted incidence of food insecurity in non-surveyed communities, $\hat{P}_j^{\,B}$, is predicted using the estimated coefficients by

$$\hat{P}_j^{\,B} = \Lambda\,(\hat{\bar{X}}_j^{\,B}\hat{\beta} + Z_j^B\hat{\gamma} + W'Z_j\hat{\delta})$$

Here $\hat{\bar{X}}_j^{\,B} = W\bar{X}^A$ is a weighted average of the household characteristics in nearby communities. This is equivalent to assuming a representative household from community $j \in B$ has similar characteristics of those households in nearby communities. The matrix W is a matrix of weights, where the weights are the inverse (Euclidean) distance between community j and community h. Thus, community j's nearby communities will have a stronger influence on determining food insecurity in community j.[20]

Empirical results: explaining the geography of food insecurity

The data collection effort leads to fifty indicators characterising each community and which cover several aspects of each communities' livelihoods: the social and economic structure; its demographic composition; its human capital; its accessibility to markets and services (including restrictions of movements); and its physical capital such as access to water and soil fertility. Some of these indicators are strongly correlated, thus we had to make a selection among the correlated indicators. We selected the covariates with greater explanatory power based on Information Criteria. We estimated the probability of being food insecure using a Logit Model. The estimated coefficients are shown in Figure 10.1. Adding community covariates and weighted averages of surrounding communities improves the fit of the regressions (columns 2 and 3). The full model specification, including household characteristics X, community characteristics Z and the nearby communities' factors $W'Z$, has the best fit. The Logit specification has the advantage of bounding predictions between zero and one. The full Logit model has a reasonable rate of correct predictions (67 per cent) and we base our predictions on this specification (column 3).

The household covariates include household wealth (measured as the first principal component on household assets), household size, the household head and spouse's years of schooling, the number of regis-tered refugees in the household, and the profession of the household head. As expected, household wealth has a strong and negative effect on the probability of being food insecure. Larger households are more likely to be food insecure. Household human capital, captured by levels of schooling, is significantly and negatively associated with food insecurity. Household head employment decreases the probability of food insecu-rity across all sectors with stronger decreases for high-skilled professions, an indicator of higher income status. Despite refugee families usually being among the more disadvantaged, there is no evidence to support the view that refugee families are more food insecure than non-refugee families. This result may reflect the improving conditions of refugees which, together with the UN Relief and Works Agency assistance, have been progressively more integrated into the labour market.

The community covariates include a set of socioeconomic variables measuring community size, the prevalence of agricultural households, unemployment rates, the percentage of non-residential buildings as a proxy of economic development, and birth rates. We include dummy variables for the types of community: urban, rural and refugee camp. Restriction of movement is captured by the number of checkpoints and road blocks in the surroundings of the community. Infrastructure avail-ability is proxied by the road density in the surroundings of the com-munity. Agricultural productivity is proxied through the Aridity Index where low values indicate more arid soil and thus are less fertile. The availability of land is proxied by the extension of cultivated land in each community. Access to services and markets is measured by the distance to hospitals and distance to the governorate capital. Finally, in column 3 we include a selective number of neighbouring communities' character-istics, such as unemployment rates of nearby communities, number of checkpoints and population size.

Among these factors, topographic and geographical indicators can be considered exogenous, while socioeconomic variables may be endoge-nous. For example, in terms of population size—a predictor of food insecurity incidence—if low food insecurity communities attract migrants, so that the size of these communities increases, population size in the model is an endogenous variable. For these factors we can reason-ably assume exogeneity only in the short run. Using an instrumental variable approach is theoretically possible, provided a variable correlated with the endogenous covariate and uncorrelated with the regression error exists. However, it is difficult to think about valid instruments which are precisely measured at community-level. This of course limits the causal interpretation of the coefficients.

Among the most interesting results from the set of community variables is that unemployment rates are strongly associated with household food insecurity. High rates of unemployment are present along the border in areas where a significant share of the population goes to work in Israel. With the tightening of border regulation and permits following the second *Intifada*, these areas have seen unemployment rising, which may also reflect limited availability of jobs in these areas.

Households living in rural communities are more likely to be food insecure. Holding locality-type constant (for instance, rural, urban or camp), the probability of food insecurity is lower for those communities with a higher share of agricultural households. This might point to the fact that home-production may be an important source of food, but we do not have information on the share of food produced and consumed at home to test this hypothesis. Mobility restrictions in the forms of checkpoints are positively associated with food insecurity. The result is stronger when controlling for nearby community mobility restrictions.

Restrictions on movement fragment space and increase transaction costs. In particular, delays at checkpoints increase transport costs and the cost of fuel. It is not surprising in this regard that transportation costs make up the second highest share of households' budgets after expenditure on food according to reports by the Palestinian Central Bureau of Statistics. Changes in checkpoints may also affect unemployment rates and unemployment.[21] Further analysis to identify the effects of checkpoints on unemployment and transport costs and how these feed back on food insecurity risk is the topic of ongoing work.

There is some evidence in column 2 that more fertile soil (higher values of aridity index) is associated with lower food insecurity. Fertility of the soil however may have a different effect in areas A, B, or C; one reason could be the different administration of land. We capture this with interaction effects between the aridity index and the location of communities in areas B and C. There is some evidence that the effect is different in areas B and C.

Finally, distance to main hospitals is associated with higher risk of food insecurity. The distance to markets shows that major urban centres have a high food insecurity risk. The results showing that food insecurity is associated with low agricultural communities, low soil fertility and proximity to large urban centres suggest that food insecurity is also a phenomenon related to urbanisation. Fast urbanisation without sufficient economic dynamism in labour markets may increase inequality and precarious income opportunities, which may explain the high food insecurity rates in these communities.

Using the results from the full model Figure 10.1, column 3, we predict the food insecurity incidence for 489 communities in the West Bank. For those communities for which we observe community information from the Census 2007 but do not observe individual characteristics, we assume the values of a representative household with characteristics equal to the mean of nearby communities. We plot these prediction quintiles in Figure 10.2.

One characteristic feature of the geography of the West Bank is that the area along the Jordan River is not populated. This can be explained by several factors. First, the adverse local climate, warm and dry, due to the low altitude declining to 400m below sea level. Second, the river, shallow and modest in flow and draining into the Dead Sea, does not offer the benefits for trade and commerce that rivers usually bring about. Third, all the area is classified as area C and as such under full Israeli control.

There are clear geographical clusters emerging from Figure 10.2. Highest predicted values of food insecurity are concentrated in the northwestern communities along the border with Israel and clustered around the main towns of Hebron and Bethlehem. The cities of Qalqylia and Jenin, on the northwest border with Israel, are mostly agricultural areas. The construction of the wall, physically separating the West Bank from Israel, severely affected farmers' access to their land in these areas as part of these fields are now located behind the wall and are only accessible with permits.

Hebron is the largest population centre, with a history of large industries in stone cutting, manufacturing and agricultural produce. Despite a potentially large market access, in the past decade, the city's economic activity has declined. Israeli settlers have taken over part of the city and there are frequent episodes of violence between religious settlers and Palestinians. The city has become poorly connected with the rest of the West Bank due to a high concentration of checkpoints within the city and in its surrounds as seen in Figure 10.5. This may explain the high concentration of food insecurity incidence around the city.

The city of Bethlehem has also been affected by mobility restrictions and the construction of the wall, which completely cuts off its connection with the Jerusalem Municipality (East Jerusalem) and Ramallah. A journey from Bethlehem to Ramallah of about 32km can take almost two hours via Palestinian routes. Bethlehem is surrounded by area C and

Figure 10.2: Quintiles of predicted food insecurity

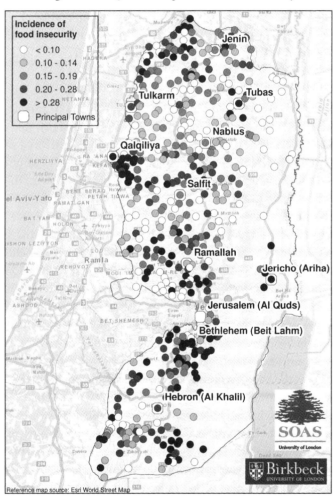

the city is one of the most compelling cases where, despite a high rate of university education, the unemployment rates are among the highest in the West Bank.

The political division of land between areas A, B and C has resulted in an unequal pattern of development. Industries and people are relocating to area A, mostly urban areas, where real estate and the construction sector is booming. Figure 10.3 overlays these area divisions with the

Figure 10.3: Food insecurity incidence and land division

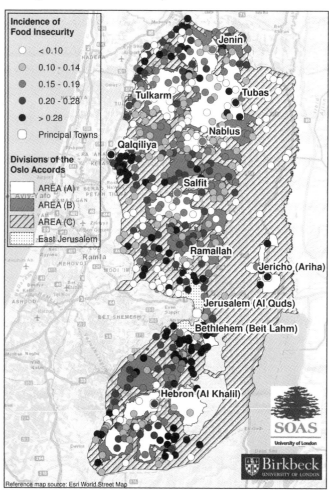

incidence of food insecurity. By a visual inspection, there is evidence that the most severe food insecure communities are located in area C.

Figures 10.4 and 10.5 display food insecurity incidence with unemployment rates and mobility restrictions. To ease visualisation of the relationship between the factors mentioned above we created surfaces of food insecurity, a method of approximating food insecurity in areas where it has not been measured. This is achieved by using a distance weighted average of the nearest localities where a measurement is available.

Figure 10.4: Food insecurity (surface) and unemployment rates

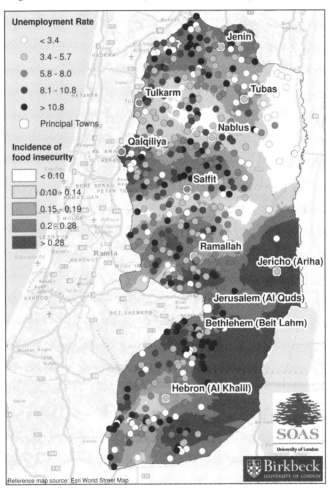

FOOD INSECURITY IN THE WEST BANK

Figure 10.5: Food insecurity (surface) and mobility restrictions

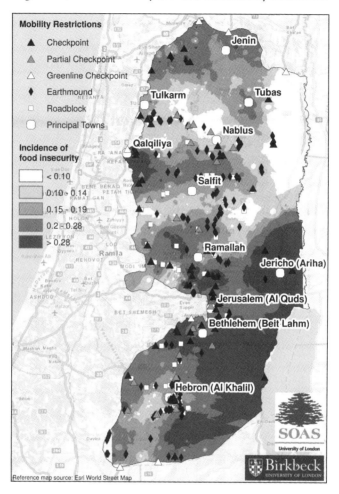

There is substantial variation in unemployment rates even across nearby localities. The data refers to residents' unemployment which only partially reflects where job opportunities are available. There are increasing patterns of migration from all parts of the West Bank towards the main cities, especially Ramallah. Figure 10.4 visually represents the positive association between high unemployment rates and food insecurity. Although proximity to large cities is usually associated with higher economic dynamism and job opportunities, this pattern is less clear in the West Bank. One potential explanation is the rapid urbanisation while labour markets remain thin and inflexible.

It is visible from Figure 10.5 that security checkpoints are located around the main towns, while earthmounds and road blocks are more dispersed and located further away from the main city centres (with the exception of Hebron). Clusters of high food insecurity incidence (the upper quintile) appear together with a higher presence of checkpoints, as the statistical analysis has shown. Overall, natural barriers, the political division of land and mobility restrictions in the West Bank explain spatial differences in food insecurity incidence across the West Bank.

Policy scenarios

Based on the results from Figure 10.1, we simulate a number of policy interventions and predict the changes in probabilities of food insecurity that would occur under such scenarios. This is an illustrative exercise as some of the variables are endogenous in the model. Figure 10.6 shows the average predicted changes in probability by the governorate. The first scenario we consider is an increase in household wealth in a specific community (column 1). We simulate this change by an increase of one standard deviation in our proxy for household wealth. For example, take the city of Jenin in the north of the West Bank. The estimated probability of food insecurity in Jenin is 0.12. Under the wealth increase scenario, the probability of food insecurity in Jenin falls to 0.07. Hence, there is a 5 percentage point change in food insecurity incidence. The model predicts an average reduction of food insecurity risk of about 8 percentage points. On average, the reduction is particularly pronounced in the governorates of Salfit and Jericho.

The second scenario is a decrease of one standard deviation in unemployment rates in a specific community (column 2). This change is equivalent to a decrease in unemployment of about 4 percentage points. The governorate averages show a homogenous decrease in the probability of food insecurity of about 3 percentage points. The third scenario represents a total removal of mobility restrictions in the form of checkpoints (column 3). The model predicts reductions in food insecurity ranging from a modest 1 percentage point in Tubas to 11 percentage points in the heavily controlled areas of Jerusalem and Bethlehem.

Finally, the fourth scenario (column 4) shows the changes in probability associated with an increase in road density of one standard deviation (equivalent to 0.7km/km²). The effect is modest but significantly important given the relatively small policy change. The effects are more visible in the underdeveloped areas of Salfit and Jericho and in the governorate of Hebron. These predictions are based on hypothesised policy changes in the community. The probability changes including the feedback from policy change in the surrounding communities will be amplified.

Figure 10.6: Changes in probabilities under different scenarios

Governorate	One std. dev increase in wealth	One std. dev. decrease in unemployment rates	Removal of checkpoints	One std. dev. development in road density
Jenin	0.063	0.020	0.030	0.011
Tubas	0.085	0.031	0.018	0.014
Tulkarem	0.070	0.027	0.056	0.012
Nablus	0.076	0.030	0.071	0.015
Qalquiliya	0.073	0.029	0.067	0.013
Salfit	0.087	0.034	0.037	0.019
Ramallah	0.063	0.024	0.047	0.016
Jericho	0.108	0.030	0.042	0.016
Jerusalem	0.063	0.025	0.0104	0.012
Bethlehem	0.093	0.035	0.110	0.016
Hebron	0.072	0.026	0.048	0.028
Total	0.073	0.026	0.058	0.016

Notes: Average changes in the probability of positive outcome when a regressor changes and the others are kept constant. Probability is calculated at the mean values of X_{ij}.

Conclusion

This study analyses the spatial patterns of the incidence of food insecurity in the West Bank region of the Palestinian Territories, and the effect of community-level factors, such as environmental factors and resource accessibility, in explaining them. To this aim, the study constructs an innovative dataset combining household survey data on food insecurity, with census data on community-level characteristics and environmental information extracted by elaborating GIS surfaces. It uses a multilevel model, including both household and community characteristics, to identify the effect of community-level factors that explain food insecurity incidence. Using the model, the study predicts the incidence of food insecurity at the community-level for the entire West Bank and it analyses its spatial distribution in relation to key variables. Finally, it predicts changes in food insecurity that would occur under various policy scenarios.

The study finds that community-level factors have important influences on household food insecurity and hence on the prevalence of food insecurity at the community-level. Specifically, we find that the community-level of economic development, employment rates, agricultural potential and access to markets are important predictors of food security. Plotting predicted food insecurity incidence for the entire West Bank, we find distinctive geographical patterns of food insecurity. The dual influence of household characteristics and the local environment points to an important role for policy interventions aimed at specific areas. The study highlights the responsiveness of food insecurity levels to improvements in employment rates, removal of mobility restrictions and infrastructure development. Further analysis will build on these emerging spatial patterns to investigate the positive spillover that policy interventions in specific communities may generate into neighbouring areas.

In conclusion, our results show that food insecurity is a combination of individual factors and environmental factors and, most importantly, food insecurity in the West Bank has distinct geographical patterns. The results indicate that potential policies not only impact upon incidence of food insecurity with varying levels of effectiveness but also that the response to policy varies geographically too. Thus, geographically targeted interventions and ultimately a political solution in Palestine will have a large impact on erasing food insecurity in this part of the world.

11

THE NUTRITION TRANSITION
AND OBESITY IN QATAR

Tahra ElObeid and *Abdelmonem Hassan*

Qatar is one of the most food import-dependent countries in the world, and net food imports are anticipated to rise even further in the future. About forty years ago, Qatar had very limited food choices due to the arid nature of the country. The main components of traditional diets at that time consisted of rice and seafood, and, due to historic migration patterns, local cuisine was strongly influenced by the Persian and Indian kitchens. In this chapter we discuss the issue of a nutrition transition and food security in Qatar, and how this transition has led to the increase in the prevalence of obesity and non-communicable diseases (NCDs) among the different sectors of the society.

Qatar Statistics Authority Report for 2012 reported that Qatar is now one of the leading countries in the world in terms of oil and natural gas production and has had sharp economic growth during the past few decades. With this economic boom, food imports have increased and now account for more than 90 per cent of national food consumption. This high dependence on imported food can be attributed to both

271

demand- and supply-side factors. The demand-side factors are comprised of the rising population due to the immigration of people from different parts of the world for employment purposes, and the change in food habits of the Qatari society due to higher income and the incorporation of Western foods into their diet. The supply-side factors include limited natural resources such as arable land and water. Wealth, globalisation and immigration of people from different parts of the world to Qatar have led to a nutrition transition in the country. The levels of overweight and obesity have increased significantly in Qatar. As a consequence, the prevalence of obesity-related health complications is increasing among the Qatari population. Change in local food habits due to the evolution of traditional diets to more Westernised meals, and the introduction of unhealthy, high caloric fast-food is a primary cause of the increasing prevalence of obesity. The movement towards urbanisation from a typically rural or nomadic lifestyle has also aggravated the problem of obesity in Qatar. Economic progress and wealth has led to the adoption of a more sedentary lifestyle, with greater dependence on labour-saving technology in people's daily activities.

The World Food Summit of 1996 defined food security as existing 'when all people, at all times, have physical and economic access to sufficient, safe and nutritious food to meet their dietary needs and food preferences for an active and healthy life'.[1] Generally, the concept of food security includes physical and economic access to food that meets people's dietary needs and preferences. Food security itself has three dimensions and the third dimension related to this chapter is food security through utilisation of food via an adequate diet. The new definition of food security now includes the understanding that food is relevant to pursuing healthy and active lifestyles. Available food should be adequate both in terms of quantity and quality, allowing people to be physically active and healthy. In the case of Qatar, there is the problem of over-consumption as well as unhealthy food choices for both the higher income sector of the society as well as the lower income population, who face the same consequence of obesity and its related complications due to their consumption of 'cheap high fat, high carbohydrate, low nutritive value filling foods'.[2] What Qatar is facing can be explained by the concept of 'the double burden of disease', which is a term used to describe the situation in most developing and booming economies, where under-nutrition and malnutrition occur alongside diseases that may be due to over-consumption of food and eating unhealthy food.

THE NUTRITION TRANSITION AND OBESITY IN QATAR

During the past four decades, Qatar, Bahrain, Kuwait, Oman, Saudi Arabia and the United Arab Emirates have gone through a revolution in their socioeconomic status which has led to changes in their food habits, consumption patterns, lifestyles and health status.[3] The dietary patterns which have recently appeared in this region are characterised by the high intake of meat, trans fats and carbohydrates, coupled with the low intake of vegetables and fruit, which are the main risk factors for obesity.[4] The sedentary lifestyle together with an obesity-promoting diet has led to the marked increase in levels of overweight and obesity among Qatari children, and this is the only sector of the Qatari society studied for prevalence of overweight and obesity.[5] Several studies in the Gulf Cooperation Council (GCC) countries indicate that obesity in the general population and especially among children is considered a public health problem.[6]

Data on dietary patterns and the prevalence of obesity in Qatari society is scarce when compared with data available on diet and dietary patterns reported in other regions similarly going through a nutrition transition. Only a few studies have been published on the prevalence of overweight and obesity in Qatar.[7]

The nutrition transition and food security

'Nutrition transition' is a term used to describe shifts in diet, physical activity, health and nutrition. A nutrition transition can usually be traced to changes in economic status, the impact of the media and food marketing, and a range of changes in the nature of work and leisure. The nutrition transition in Qatar has shifted from a traditional diet towards a Western diet, accompanied with lower levels of physical activity generally leading to higher body weight. An economic boom in some countries has led to a rapid growth in household incomes, leading to a shift towards animal-source foods, more refined foods and to other less healthy dietary practices that lead to obesity and non-communicable diseases. Although there is a significant economic advancement in many countries, there are several communities and countries where low- and high-income households have similar problems associated with obesity, micronutrient deficiencies and non-communicable diseases. Alongside the problem of a shift in food habits in the higher-income households, there is an additional problem of high marketing and widespread availability of low-cost, high-calorie dense foods, such as edible oils and processed, refined carbohydrate-rich foods, which have also affected those with limited income. It is important to note that processed foods and calorie-dense foods are more attractive to the low-income populations due to the relatively lower price of foods high in fats, oils, sugar and animal-sources. Lower-density, highly nutritious foods such as fresh fruit and vegetables are usually more expensive.

Individuals of different generations may also respond differently to social and economic changes, with the younger generation adopting new dietary patterns more quickly, while the elderly continue to eat in more traditional (and sometimes healthier) ways.

The total population of Qatar is approximately 2 million inhabitants. The population is cosmopolitan and is comprised of several nationalities from various parts of the world. In the 1930s, the typical Qatari diet consisted of rice and fish, with a few other animal source foods, fruit and vegetables. During that era, the diet of the Qatari population was directly influenced by the Indian and Pakistani cuisines. Along with the economic boom, there was a drastic change in quantitative and qualitative aspects of the diet and in the food consumption patterns in Qatar. The structure of the traditional diet has moved towards a high-energy-density diet with more fat, saturated fat and sugar in foods accompanied with low intake of complex carbohydrates, dietary fibre, fruit and vegetables.[8] In all the GCC countries, the total per capita energy intake exceeds 3,000 kcal, and fat represents 25–35 per cent of total energy. However, animal fat represents 40–52 per cent of total per capita fat intake in the region.[9] There is no data on the per capita intake of any of the macronutrients in Qatar. However, data from Food and Agriculture Organization Food Balance Sheets indicate that, in the GCC countries, the daily per capita availability of red meat and poultry during 2003–5 ranged from 106–63 grams compared to 2–73 grams in other countries in the Middle East, with a slight increase in fish intake during 1990–2005. The consumption of fruit and vegetables by people in the GCC was reported as being below the recommended daily allowance. A World Health Organization/Regional Office for East Mediterranean (WHO/EMRO) report stated that more than 85 per cent of adults in the GCC consumed less than five servings of vegetables and fruit per day.[10] Studies in the UAE found that 53 per cent of adult men and 59 per cent of adult women consumed fruit and vegetables daily, whereas consumption for men and women was approximately 77 per cent in Oman and 54 per cent in Bahrain.[11]

Although literature on Qatar is lacking, studies from within the region show that the consumption of vegetables and fruit has increased in the GCC, where the main contribution to fibre intake comes from vegetable-based foods (31 per cent), cereals and their products (26 per cent) and fruits and their products.[12] Up-to-date data on food consumption patterns in Qatar is absent, and most of the literature is based on research conducted in other parts of the region, such as Bahrain and Saudi Arabia. The traditional diet of GCC countries is very similar, with minor national differences. However, food consumption habits across the region have not been studied in an in-depth manner.

On the international level, access to new food production technologies such as low-priced edible oils and refined carbohydrates/'empty calories', food distribution and marketing, and the more efficient flow of goods and services are changing diets in many countries regardless of the economic status. Supplementary to this are issues related to food security and global access to food that is adequate to meet the quality and quantity of nutrients. Generally, the nutrition transition has drastically changed the price, quality and availability of foods, and has created new patterns of food consumption linked to obesity in both high- and low-income sectors of society.

Overweight and obesity

Qatar's contemporary nutrition patterns and changed dietary practices have had both positive and negative health consequences. Although local diets have diversified and now incorporate more healthy fruit and vegetables, there has also been a shift towards more energy-dense, nutrient-poor foods that contain high levels of sugar and saturated fats. This change to traditional diet combined with reduced levels of physical activity has led to an epidemic of overweight and obesity in Qatar. While genetics could play an imperative role in determining a person's weight gain, the strong linkage between increased fat intake and obesity has been shown in multiple studies.[13] Overweight and obesity among adults is commonly assessed using the body mass index (BMI), defined as weight in kilogrammes divided by the square of height in metres (kg/m^2). A BMI greater than 25 is defined as overweight, and a BMI greater than 30 is defined as obese. In the World Health Organization–NCD

FOOD SECURITY IN THE MIDDLE EAST

Country Profiles for 2011, the BMI of Qatari males and females was 28 and 29, respectively.[14]

Information on the prevalence of obesity and dietary patterns in Qatar is scarce in comparison to data available for other countries going through a similar nutrition transition. Out of this limited pool of available data, one study reported in 2008 that 73 per cent of Qatari males and 70 per cent of Qatari females were overweight. Another study conducted in 2005 reported that among the adult Qatari population, overweight and obesity levels for males was 34.4 per cent and for females 33 per cent.[15] These two studies indicate a sharp increase in the prevalence of overweight and obesity over a period of three years. There have also been a few studies on the prevalence of overweight and obesity among Qatari schoolchildren.[16] One of these studies reported that among Qatari children aged 6–12 years old, 37.5 per cent of boys and 41.6 per cent of girls showed prevalence to overweight and/or obesity whereas about 40 per cent of Qatari schoolchildren aged 9–12 years old were overweight and/or obese. However, the same study showed that among adolescents (12–17 years old) this percentage dropped to 23.6 per cent and 36.5 per cent among females and males, respectively.[17] This percentage sharply increases when these adolescents grow into adults, where the prevalence of overweight and obesity among males and females is 73 per cent and 70 per cent, respectively.

The main factors that are responsible for this increase in the levels of overweight and obesity is the increased consumption of high-energy-density foods, along with certain lifestyle choices like long hours of watching television or using the internet, which is a sedentary lifestyle that is becoming prevalent in Qatari society.[18] Studies on food habits conducted on Qatari schoolchildren reported that, on average, only 8 per cent of the students had fruit juice included in their breakfast, whereas 90 per cent had eggs and cheese, and an average of 81 per cent had breakfast cereals. Although there was a high consumption of potato chips (81 per cent), there was also a high consumption of fruit (90 per cent), but a low consumption of milk at 35 per cent.

The influx of people from different parts of the world, as well as the introduction of fast-food chains in Qatar, introduced a large variety of foods and gradually led to a change in dietary habits and lifestyle among the Qatari population. This change in dietary pattern and lifestyle among the Qatari population is associated with increased prevalence of diet-related chronic diseases such as cardiovascular disease (CVD), diabetes mellitus, hypertension, obesity, cancer and osteoporosis.[19] Non-communicable diseases are the main causes of death in Qatar. Health statistics reveal that, in 2010, the total deaths in Qatar among the different age groups due to NCDs was approximately 50 per cent.

A 2006 World Health Survey reported that diagnosed diabetes in Qatar ranged from 12 per cent (Qatari and non-Qatari) to 17 per cent (among Qataris), with another 10 per cent characterised as 'pre-diabetes', which is when individuals have a higher than normal level of glucose in their blood but not high enough to be considered diabetic.[20] In another study conducted in 2009, the prevalence of CVDs among Qataris was 23 per cent and diabetes was 20 per cent, whereas a third study found that the prevalence of diabetes mellitus (DM) among the adult Qatari population was 16.7 per cent, with reported figures for DM demonstrating that it is higher among Qatari women (53.2 per cent) than Qatari men (46.8 per cent). This variation in results makes it difficult to assess the actual prevalence of DM in Qatar. However, all studies agree that obesity, family history and low physical activity are the main contributors to DM among the Qatari population. A study conducted by Bener et al. in 2009 reported that 93 per cent of Qatari women with DM were obese, with an average waist circumference of more than 88cm—the normal waist circumference should be less than 88cm.[21] Obesity, especially abdominal obesity, is a potent risk factor for the high percentage of type 2 diabetes which is the chronic form of diabetes with very high levels of glucose in the blood. A sedentary lifestyle, which is one of the main contributing factors to overweight, obesity and CVDs, is prominent in Qatar where only 50 per cent of males and 40 per cent of females exercise on a regular basis.[22] These statistics may be questionable as there are no studies that indicate the level of physical activity in Qatari society, nor is there an exact definition as to what physical activity means.

Bener et al. reported that the prevalence of hypertension (high blood pressure) in Qatar was 32.1 per cent among the Qatari nationals.[23] However, in the 2006 World Health Survey Report on Qatar, it was reported that CVDs were the leading cause of death in Qatar, the second cause being road accidents, followed by cancer and diabetes. In this report, 13 per cent of Qataris were found to be hypertensive, however, with an increase in the number of obese and overweight people, hypertension and other NCDs should have drastically increased. The risk of obesity increases among adolescents and young women who become pregnant, as they will have a higher risk of complications related to gestational diabetes and hypertension. Maternal obesity, even without gestational diabetes, increases the risk of having a child who will become obese through a pathway related to fetal over-nutrition.

The role of fast-food

Traditional Qatari cuisine includes the use of high-fat ingredients such as fatty meats and cooking oil, as well as refined carbohydrates, such as polished rice. These ingredients are risk factors for obesity. The appearance of Westernised fast-food chains in Qatar has also led to the dissemination of unhealthy eating habits. Several studies have assessed the association between regular fast-food consumption and weight gain.[24] A study in the United States found that over a period of fifteen years, frequent fast-food consumption can lead directly to weight gain and to the risk of insulin resistance.[25] People who ate at fast-food restaurants more than twice a week gained 4.5kg more weight than those who ate less than one fast-food meal per week. Studies on physiological mechanisms recognise that there are some main features that explain why fast-food consumption results in overweight and obesity and these are: outsized portion sizes; increased energy density due to high fat content; limited use of energy dense vegetables, fruit and whole grain products; high consumption of sugar-rich soft drinks; and a high content of industrially-produced trans fatty acids.[26] The high glycemic index of carbohydrates used in fast-foods may also contribute to weight gain and obesity. However, clinically controlled trials do not support this hypothesis.[27] A daily intake of 5g trans fat is associated with an approximately 30 per cent increase in the risk of coronary heart disease.

Over the past few years, the portion size of most fast-food items has increased from 'normal' to 'large' to 'extra-large' and, therefore, the amount of calories consumed by an individual has also increased to two or even four fold.

Recent research studies have reported that fast-foods can be addictive.[28] The objective of various studies was research on food addiction to highly palatable foods. Fast-foods fall into the category of addictive foods and the presentation, packaging, marketing strategies and pricing of these foods aggravate the problem even further. Most of the calorie-dense fast-food meals are usually consumed with soft drinks resulting in increased intake of refined carbohydrates. A growing body of research has found a correlation between the frequent consumption of fast-food and soft drinks and obesity.[29]

Salt and sugar consumption

The relationship between sweetened drinks, obesity and diabetes has also been well-documented in various studies at both regional GCC and international levels.[30] Over the past forty years, the per capita consumption of refined carbohydrates has increased significantly, and parallel to this has been the increase in metabolic syndromes, which include insulin resistance, overweight, hypertension and dyslipidemia.[31]

Foods high in salt and sugar are heavily consumed in the GCC. The food composition of traditional foods and dishes common in the GCC countries show a high content of sodium and sugar.[32] The major factor for the elevated consumption of sodium and sugar is the use of table salt, spices and pickles, along with the high consumption of fast-foods. Many studies on the region have also pointed out that foods high in fructose, corn-syrup, glucose and sucrose are consumed in great quantities by children and adolescents.[33]

Total calorie supply per capita per day in Qatar

In general, dietary energy measured in kcals per capita per day has been steadily increasing in many regions of the world. Globally, the percentage increase in per capita energy availability was 19 per cent between 1964 and 1999, increasing from 2,358 to 2,803 kcal over the period of thirty-five years. This change has varied across the different regions of the world. The per capita energy available in the Near East and North Africa (which represents all Eastern Mediterranean Region countries) has increased by 716 kcal in the periods 1964–6 and 1997–9, and is projected to reach 880 kcal in 2030. The per capita availability of energy for the period 2003–5 exceeds 2,000 calories in all countries of the region.

Although there are high levels of over-nutrition and obesity in Qatar, there are also problems related to under-nutrition and micronutrient deficiencies. In Qatar, stunting in children is 8.1 per cent for both boys and girls. According to the International Bank for Reconstruction and Development, iron deficiency anaemia is 26 per cent among children and 30 per cent among pregnant women.[34] A cross-sectional study on the prevalence of vitamin D deficiency among 458 male and female Qatari children under 16 years of age revealed a high prevalence of vitamin D deficiency (68.8 per cent). The deficiency was found to prevail mainly in the 11–16 year age group and was more common among girls.[35] Therefore, this problem should also be addressed in the different sectors of the society bearing in mind that a large sector includes migrant workers and labourers with relatively low income.

It is important to integrate the various stakeholders as the different institutions can play a major role in assessing and studying these areas in order to have a positive input towards the national strategy. The Qatar National Food Security Programme (QNFSP) is also working on assessing the nutrition situation in Qatar. Under this project the QNFSP is to compile a comprehensive report on the nutrition situation in Qatar and to identify which institutions (whether governmental or private) are working on different aspects of nutrition, compiling reports of activities and events related to nutrition for future reference and sharing of information, providing a nutrition analysis for Qatar based on recent and available data and making data available to different stakeholders. The last and most important component of this effort is the identification of activities that the QNFSP can capitalise on in order to assist in the alleviation of the nutritional problems in Qatar.

Forces of change in Qatar

Obesity mirrors an energy imbalance—the fact that more calories are consumed than are expended. Accordingly, the key areas for intervention should be directly related to dietary intake and energy expenditure: in other words, increased physical activity. Technologies and mechanisation, various means of transportation and reduced housework have all produced industries that are less physically taxing and less dependent on human labour, thus leading to an overall reduction in the level of physical activity. This energy imbalance has intensified many of the health problems in Qatar, which is emblematic of a country that showcases the problems that high-energy intake and reduced physical activity can lead to. In Qatar, this energy imbalance is manifest in high rates of obesity and NCDs.

Recognising the need to address this public health crisis through focused policy efforts, and to find ways to increase physical activity across all age groups in Qatar, the 'Qatar Vision 2030', which is the national strategy of Qatar up until 2030, has included within its mandate the need for increasing human energy expenditure through physical activity. Although physical activity is of great significance in weight reduction, dietary modification is also an essential component of lowering the prevalence of obesity. Residents of Qatar and Qataris have witnessed an ongoing increase in state-led efforts to encourage physical activity through increasing the number of outdoor venues for walking and exercising, along with an addition to the number and quality of fitness centres in many parts of Doha. However, there is yet to be a study which determines whether this evident increase in physical activity is a feature of the expatriate population or the Qatari nationals.

In October 2009, the WHO-EMRO presented Qatar's Supreme Council of Health with a proposal for a national 'Nutrition Strategy and Action Plan'. The WHO-EMRO Nutrition Strategy stated that Qatar has undergone a major nutrition transition that has resulted in high levels of overweight and obesity as well as micronutrient deficiencies in certain subgroups of the population. This bears in mind that unhealthy diet and physical inactivity are among the leading causes of the NCDs such as cardiovascular disease, type 2 diabetes and certain types of cancer, and contribute substantially to the global burden of disease. Despite government attempts to put nutrition on the primary healthcare map, the situation is not that optimistic. Currently, nutrition and diet have still not been effectively incorporated into the national development planning agenda in Qatar, nor have they been adequately prioritised. Qatar is still struggling to balance the needs of various key challenges in its fight against obesity. In order to manage the public health crisis around obesity, strategic interventions are needed to address some of the following key challenges (Figures 11.1 and 11.2):

1. A delay in the translation of political commitment expressed by the state to address nutrition into tangible action. To date, Qatar has no unified strategy or nutrition action plan.
2. Inadequate policy frameworks and institutional capacity to plan, implement and monitor sustainable nutrition programmes that respond to the multi-sectoral dimensions of nutrition programmes.
3. Increased obesity among children and adolescents.

4. Inadequate technical capacity in nutrition in most health and educational institutions such as primary healthcare and schools.

5. The limited health budgets being allocated to support preventive healthcare strategies and plans such as nutrition and NCDs.

6. The replacement of more nutritious traditional foods with fast-foods that reduce dietary diversity and increase rates of obesity and NCDs.

7. Unclear lines of coordination and mechanisms for cooperation between concerned national authorities delay the development of efficient monitoring and evaluation systems, and lead to the lack of a functional surveillance system.

8. Inadequate health and nutrition training given to the communities, especially among mothers and schoolchildren.

9. Weaknesses of consumer protection laws and institutions, and inadequate monitoring of food supply chains.

10. Increased micronutrient deficiencies, especially vitamin D and iron, among children, women and elderly people.

The WHO-EMRO proposed 'Qatar Nutrition Strategy and Plan' of October 2009 was not endorsed by the Supreme Council of Health as it required more input from the different stakeholders who were working on nutrition in Qatar. Accordingly, the Supreme Council of Health formulated a task force in 2011 called the 'National Nutrition and Physical Activity Committee' which was given the mandate to reduce obesity and increase physical activity in all the sectors of the society and which had set defined outcomes to overcome the high obesity levels in Qatar (see Appendix 4 for more on the Action Plan).

The National Nutrition and Physical Activity Committee acknowledge that obesity and NCDs have adverse effects on the whole community of Qatar. Quality of life and health are directly affected by obesity and lead to various conditions such as respiratory difficulties, musculoskeletal problems, skin problems and infertility, as well as to more severe diseases including non-insulin-dependent diabetes, gallbladder disease, hypertension, strokes, coronary heart disease and cancers, all leading to an increased risk of premature death. Obese women are two to six times more likely to have hypertension, diabetes and raised serum cholesterol, whereas, for severely obese individuals, the risk of mortality is twelve fold in 25 to 35 year olds when compared with normal weight

THE NUTRITION TRANSITION AND OBESITY IN QATAR

Figure 11.1: Nutrition-related diseases in Qatar

Disease/disorder	Prevalence	Group	Reference
Stunting in	8.1%	Children	(Int. Bank for Recon. Develop)
Iron deficiency anaemia	26% 30%	Children Pregnant women	(Int. Bank for Recon. Develop)
Obesity	30%	Adults	(Int. Health Surv., WHO, 2006)
Overweight obesity Children	37.5% 41.6%	Females, children Males, children	The CCC study, 2009 Kerkadi, Hassan, Altayeb, 2008
Overweight obesity	23.6% 36.5%	Females, adolescents Males, adolescents	Bener, 2006
Diabetes mellitus	16.0%	Adults	(WHO-EMRO database)
Hypertension	13%	Adults	(Int. Health Surv., WHO, 2006)
Vitamin D deficiency	68.8%	Children <16y	
Taking folic acid pre-conceptual	12.6%	Pregnant women	Hassan and Alkharusi, 2008
Leading types of cancer	Breast, Colon, Lung, Bladder		(WHO-EMRO database)

Source: WHO-EMRO, 'Regional data on non-communicable diseases'.

individuals. From a psychological perspective, there are negative attitudes towards the obese which may lead to discrimination in many areas of life. Furthermore, it can also lead to lowered self-esteem and clinical depression. The stakeholders that partner with the Supreme Council of Health in the National Nutrition and Physical Activity Committee include Primary Health Care, Hamad Medical Corporation, Ministry of Municipality and Urban Planning, Ministry of Environment, Qatar Media Corporation, Qatar University, Qatar Olympic Committee, Qatar Women's Sports Committee, Qatar Museum Authority, ASPETAR (Qatar Orthopedic and Sports Medicine Hospital) and Qatar National Food Security Programme.

Figure 11.2: Indicators related to NCDs and their risk factors in Qatar

NCD indicators

Mortality due to diseases of circulatory system (2007)	21.5 per 100,000
Mortality due to cancer (2007)	13.9 per 100,000
Prevalence of type 2 diabetes	6%
Prevalence of pre-diabetes	10%
Prevalence of hypertension	9.9%
Prevalence of obesity (adults)	28.8%
Prevalence of overweight (adults)	39%
% who consume at least five servings of fruit and vegetables per day	18.3%
% who do at least 150 minutes of moderate physical activity per week	44%
Prevalence of overweight among children under 5 years old	28.7%
Prevalence of overweight among females aged 14–19 years	13.4%
Prevalence of overweight among males aged 14-19 years	33.1%

Source: State of Qatar, Supreme Council of Health, 'Qatar National Health Accounts'.

Conclusion

Qatar has become one of the leading nations in promoting athletics through government-sponsored initiatives, and has successful institutions which educate and promote athletes such as Qatar's Aspire Sports Academy, Qatar Private Primary Schools Sports Association and the Sport Science programme at Qatar University. In 2022, it will host the FIFA World Cup. In line with this, the awareness of the importance of physical activity has also risen and it is covered intensively by the media. As part of this strategy, Qatar hosts a multitude of sports events including high-profile tennis, football, swimming and volleyball tournaments, among other sports promotional activities. Qatar is making serious attempts to solve the problem of obesity and its related complications, but this is a task that will require much effort and intervention from all the different stakeholders. Many other countries have tried to reduce levels of obesity and NCDs through various national plans with little success. Qatar has a strong chance of success due to the relatively small population and adequate financial resources that will help in the implementation of the different areas in the action plan.

The benefit of regular planned physical activity in promoting health is well documented. During the past few years, Qatar has created opportunities for physical activity, including the establishment of recreation facilities such as parks, fitness centres and outdoor play areas for children, and is working on providing more green spaces. It is important to note that physical activity acquired during childhood and adolescence has a higher chance of being maintained through a person's lifespan. The Ministry of Education in Qatar has initiated a campaign to increase schoolchildren's awareness of the importance of health, diet and physical activity.

In line with the 'Qatar Vision 2030' and the 'National Health Strategy 2011–2016', the Supreme Council of Health is working towards the alleviation of obesity and NCDs and to increase the awareness of the importance of nutrition and physical activity in Qatar.

APPENDICES

APPENDIX 1

ASSUMPTIONS AND DATA USED TO PRODUCE FARM BUDGETS AND PAMS FOR LEBANON AND JORDAN

Lebanon wheat

In the wheat farm budget presented in Figure A.1.1, the yields and actual price data are those for a representative farmer in the Bekaa Valley for 2011, based on data supplied by the American University of Beirut (AUB) farm located in the valley. The actual wheat output price of $366/ MT is the government guaranteed price for registered growers and the actual seed price is based on a subsidised price of $330/MT. No other inputs or output taxes/subsidies exist. Efficiency costs of all inputs are difficult to calculate. For tradable inputs, the only divergence between actual and efficiency prices is for seeds, where actual prices are subsidised. We base the efficiency price for seed on the import parity price as given by the import C.I.F price paid by the government for wheat seed in 2011, namely $900/MT. Since Lebanon is a dollarised economy, we do not need to use an equilibrium exchange rate to calculate the efficiency prices of tradable inputs. We have assumed for all non-tradable inputs, other than water, that efficiency prices are equal to actual prices given that shadow prices are not available for land and labour in Lebanon and given that our data source does not separate out the costs of machinery hire from the labour used to operate the machinery. However, for water

Figure A.1.1: Lebanon rain-fed and supplemental irrigated wheat farm budget 2011

1 Ha. Wheat $		Actual cost	Efficiency cost
TRADABLE INPUTS			
Seed	200kg (Ministry of Agriculture price—$330/ton)	66.00	180.00
Fertilisers	250kg of DAP—planting time	216.25	216.25
	300kg of Urea (46% N)—in Feb	159.00	159.00
Herbicides	1.75lit. 2,4D + MCPA	26.00	26.00
TRADABLE INPUT TOTAL		467.25	581.25
NON-TRADABLE INPUTS			
Land rent		500.00	500.00
Tractor and machine expenses inc. labour			
Land preparation (fuel)	Tractors and implements	200.00	200.00
Planting	Tractors, graindrill or broadcaster	50.00	50.00
Chemical application (fertiliser, herbicide)	Boom sprayer, fertiliser broadcaster	20.00	20.00
Harvesting	Combine harvester, baler, trailer	200.00	200.00
Trucking	Tractor, trailer	40.00	40.00
NON-TRADABLE INPUT TOTAL		1,010.00	1,010.00
Supplementary irrigation if required (fuel)		250.00	250.00
Water	Water requirements: 1,648m³/Ha		1219.52
Casual workers to install and remove sprinklers	1.5 day @ $18.00	27.00	27.00
Total operating expenses			
	Rain-fed	**1,477.25**	**1,591.25**
	Irrigated	**1,754.25**	**3,087.77**
REVENUE			
Expected yield	Rain-fed: 2.5 tons seed		
	2.0 tons straw		
	Irrigated: 5 tons seed		
	4 tons straw		
Price (Actual price)	$366.00/ton seeds & $160.00/ton Straw		
Price (Efficiency price)	$323.00/ton seeds & $160.00/ton Straw		
Revenue (Yield x price)	Rain-fed	1,235.00	1,127.50
	Irrigated	2,470.00	2,255.00
GROSS MARGIN (Total revenue—operating expenses)			
	Rain-fed	**–242.25**	**–463.75**
	Irrigated	**715.75**	**–832.77**

APPENDIX 1

Figure A.1.2: Lebanon farm budget tomatoes 2011

	1 Ha. Tomato $	Actual cost	Efficiency cost
TRADABLE INPUTS			
Seed	10,000 seedlings	1,000.00	1,000.00
Fertilisers	1,000kg NPK for		
	planting	700.00	700.00
	Soluble	300.00	300.00
Pesticides	Fungicides, insecticides, foliar		
	fertiliser	300.00	300.00
Mulch		150.00	150.00
TRADABLE INPUT TOTAL		2,450.00	2,450.00
NON-TRADABLE INPUTS			
Land rent	Irrigated	1,000.00	1,000.00
Tractor and machine expense incl. labour			
Land preparation (fuel)	Tractors and implements	200.00	200.00
Planting	Casual workers	130.00	130.00
Irrigation water			5,122.28
Irrigation (fuel)		1,200.00	1,200.00
Harvesting	Casual workers	2,000.00	2,000.00
Trucking	Tractor, trailer	120.00	120.00
Repair and maintenance		20.00	20.00
NON-TRADABLE INPUT TOTAL		4,670.00	9,792.28
Total operating expenses		**7,120.00**	**12,242.28**
REVENUE	**80MT at $350/ MT**	**28,000.00**	**28,000.00**
GROSS MARGIN (Total revenue—operating expenses)		**20,880,00**	**15,757.71**

it is possible to calculate an efficiency price. We employ a methodology used in other PAM studies such as that used by Al-Karablieh et al. 2011, namely, basing the efficiency price of water on the cost to deliver water to urban consumers. The average water tariff for the public network is $0.37/cubic metre, but it is estimated that in order to fully cover costs a price of 0.74/cubic metre would be needed (World Bank 2009), and hence we use the latter as a proxy for the efficiency cost of water. In terms of the efficiency prices for output, the efficiency price for the wheat seed is based on the average import C.I.F. price for wheat in 2011

Figure A.1.3: Lebanon farm budget potatoes 2011

1 Ha. Potato $		Actual cost	Efficiency cost
TRADABLE INPUTS			
Seed	2,500kg Tubers	3,250.00	3,250.00
Fertilisers	1,000kg NPK for planting	700.00	700.00
	300kg Urea (46% N)	150.00	150.00
Herbicides	Metribuzine	60.00	60.00
Pesticides	Fungicides, insecticides	150.00	150.00
TRADABLE INPUT TOTAL		4,310.00	4,310.00
NON-TRADABLE INPUTS			
Land rent		1,000.00	1,000.00
Tractor and machine expenses incl. labour			
Land preparation (fuel)	Tractors and implements	200.00	200.00
Planting, herbicide and fertiliser application	Tractors, sprayer, planter, broadcaster	200.00	200.00
Irrigation (water)			3,651.90
Irrigation (fuel)		1,000.00	1,000.00
Harvesting	Tractor, cultivator	100.00	100.00
Collecting, bagging	Workers, jute bags	550.00	50.00
Repair and maintenance	Incl. salaries of workshop staff	20.00	20.00
NON-TRADABLE INPUT TOTAL		3,070.00	6,721.90
Total operating expenses		**7,380.00**	**11,031.90**
REVENUE	30MT at $350/MT	**10,500.00**	**10,500.00**
GROSS MARGIN (Total revenue—operating expenses)		**3,120.00**	**–531.90**

which was $322/MT (customs.gov.lb). The wheat straw is sold locally and we assume the efficiency price is equal to the actual price.

We have not included any overhead costs and depreciation because the machinery is usually hired in. The only overhead that should be added is the cost of installing and depreciation of the irrigation system. A drip irrigation system costs $3,500 per ha and a sprinkler system $10,190, but most farmers buy one-fifth of the system and share it with others by moving the pipes after each irrigation, hence the costs spread over say a ten-year life span are not high and we have not included them.

Lebanon tomatoes and potatoes

The market for tomatoes and potatoes in Lebanon is largely undistorted, such that the farm budgets at actual and efficiency prices are the same, apart from the fact that an efficiency price is used for water, based on the same assumptions as for wheat. All other assumptions are also as for wheat.

Figures A.1.4 and A.1.5 are the farm budgets using private prices— the prices actually faced by farmers. Price data for outputs and inputs are for 2010 and are derived from FAOSTAT. Yield data are based on farm surveys carried out by University of Jordan staff in 2011. Quantity and cost of non-tradable inputs (land, water and labour) are taken from Al-Karablieh et al. 2011. Depreciation costs are based on the assumption that plastic sheets last three years, plastic house frames fifteen years, irrigation equipment five years and the interest rate is 7 per cent.

Figures A.1.6 and A.1.7 are the efficiency farm budgets for the various crops. The efficiency prices for tradable inputs and outputs are based on farmgate export and import parity prices (all inputs as well as maize, wheat, barley and potatoes are treated as imports while tomatoes and cucumber are treated as exports). A shadow exchange rate is also used to convert into Jordanian Dinar. Figures A.1.8 to A.1.10 show how the farmgate import and export parity prices and the shadow exchange rate were derived. In terms of non-tradable inputs we base the social price of water on the price that the Jordanian Water Authority charges its consumers and we assume that the social price of land and labour is the same as the private price.

It should be noted that the methodology used for the PAM calculations for Lebanon and Jordan differ slightly. The gross margin calculations for Lebanon include land rental as part of the production costs in the calculation of the gross margins whereas for Jordan land costs are not included. This reflects the different methodologies generally used in the two countries. This does not, however, affect the arguments presented in this chapter since the purpose is to compare PAMs for different crops within each country and not to make comparisons across countries.

Figure A.1.4: Jordan farm budget private prices for vegetables (Jordanian Dinar)

(One Dunum)

Summer

Items	Cucumber-Zizia Input/output	Price/cost	TOTAL	Cucumber-Mafraq Input/output	Price/cost	TOTAL	Cucumber-Baqaa Input/output	Price/cost	TOTAL	Tomato-Baqaa-PH Input/output	Price/cost	TOTAL	Tomato-Qastal-PH Input/output	Price/cost	TOTAL	Potato-Mafraq-Open Field Input/output	Price/cost	TOTAL	Potato-Zezia-Open Field Input/output	Price/cost	TOTAL
Crop produce (output) (kg)	12.00	266.20	3194	13.60	266.20	3620	12.00	266.20	3194	14.40	157.80	2272	13.20	157.80	2083	3.10	234.70	728	3.40	234.70	798
Tradable inputs			**646**			**745**			**749**			**442**			**647**			**477**			**517**
Seeds/seedlings (kg/no)	30.00	8.00	240	30.00	8.00	240	30.00	8.00	240	4.00	5.00	20	16.00	8.00	128	250.00	0.60	150	250.00	1.10	275
Seed transplantation (Dunum)	1.00	30.00	30	1.00	30.00	30	1.00	30.00	30	1.00	30.00	30	1.00	30.00	30	1.00	30.00	30	1.00	30.00	30
Chemical fertiliser						0			0			0			0			0			0
–Nitrogen (Urea)(kg)	80.00	0.46	37	120.00	0.46	55	120.00	0.46	55	120.00	0.46	55	136.00	0.46	63	38.00	0.46	17	35.00	0.46	16
–DAP (kg)	80.00	0.36	29	116.00	0.36	42	100.00	0.36	36	80.00	0.36	29	116.00	0.36	42	69.00	0.36	25	30.00	0.36	11
–Potash (kg)		0.25	0.0		0.25	0.0		0.25	0.0		0.25	0		0.25	0		0.25	0		0.25	0
–Compound	122.00	1.00	122	200.00	1.00	200	170.00	1.00	170	180.00	1.0	180	176.00	1.00	176	45.00	1.00	45	71.00	1.00	71
–Micro-elements	4.00	6.00	24	4.00	6.00	24	4.00	6.00	24	4.00	6.00	24	4.00	6.00	24	21.00	5.00	105	4.00	6.00	24
Plant protection chemicals (Dunum)	1.00	65.00	65	1.00	60.00	60	1.00	90.00	90	1.00	60.00	60	1.00	60.00	60	1.00	45.00	45	1.00	35.00	35
Mulch (kg), THREADS	16.00	1.50	24	22.00	1.50	33	22.00	1.50	33	16.00	1.50	24	16.00	1.50	24		1.50	0	16.00	1.50	24
Machinery																					
–Land preparation (hr)	4.00	5.00	20	4.00	5.00	20	4.00	5.00	20	4.00	5.00	20	4.00	5.00	20	4.00	5.00	20	4.00	5.00	20
–Sowing/planting (hr)	0.00	0.00	0	0.00	0.00	0		0.00	0	0.00	0.00	0		0.00	0		0.00	0	0.00	0.00	0
–Husbandry (hr)	0.00	0.00	0	0.00	0.00	0	0.00	0.00	0	0.00	0.00	0	0.00	0.00	0	0.00	0.00	0	0.00	0.00	0
Fuel	100.00	0.55	55	74.00	0.55	41	92.00	0.55	51	110.00	0.55	61	146.20	0.55	80	73.00	0.55	40	20.00	0.55	11
Non-tradable inputs			**836**			**746**			**957**			**1075**			**447**			**172**			**316**
Water requirement (CM)	600.00	0.50	300	600.00	0.40	240	700.00	0.60	420	800.00	0.60	480	400.00	0.60	240	500.00	0.02	8	250.00	0.50	125
Manure (ton)	2.00	30.00	60	1.50	25.00	30	1.50	30.00	45	1.50	30.00	45	2.00	30.00	60	2.00	30.00	60	2.00	30.00	60
Manual labour			0			0			3			2						2			
–Land preparation (hr)	12.00	0.15	2	12.00	0.15	2	21.00	0.15	3	12.00	0.15	2	5.00	0.15	1	12.00	0.15	2	12.00	0.15	2
–Sowing/planting (hr)			0			0			0			0			0			0			0
–Husbandry																					
–Harvesting (hr)	1500.00	0.24	360	1500.00	0.24	360	1500.00	0.24	360	1800.00	0.24	432	240.00	0.24	58	240.00	0.24	58	300.00	0.24	72
Interest (%)		0.07	114		0.07	115		0.07	129		0.07	116		0.07	89		0.07	45		0.07	57
PH depreciation			150.0			150.0			150.0			150.0			150.0						
Plastic sheets depreciation			60.0			60.0			60.0			60.0			60.0						
Irrigation network depreciation			10.0			10.0			10.0			10.0			10.0						
Land rent (Dunum)	1.00	40.00	40	1.00	40.00	40	1.00	40.00	40	1.00	40.00	40	1.00	40.00	40	1.0	40.00	40	1.00	40.00	40

Total fixed costs	260	260	260	260	260	40	40
Total variable costs	1481	1491	1706	1517	1094	649	833
Gross margin	1713	2129	1489	755	989	78	–75
Net profit	1453	1869	1229	495	729	38	–35
Return to water (JD/cm)	3.35	3.949	2727	1.544	3.073	0.171	0.361
Virtual water (Liter/kg)	50	44	58	56	30	161	74
Total costs excl interest	**1627**	**1636**	**1837**	**1661**	**1265**	**644**	**816**

Figure A.1.5: Jordan farm budget private prices for field crops (Jordanian Dinar)

Items	Wheat-HL			Barley-HL			Maize-summer-HL		
	Input/output	Price/cost	TOTAL	Input/output	Price/cost	TOTAL	Input/output	Price/cost	TOTAL
Crop produce (output) (kg)	0.6	300.00	180	0.4	250.00	100	1.8	203.93	367
Tradable inputs			**36**			**35**			**45**
Seeds/seedlings (kg·no)	12.0	0.25	3	10.0	0.17	2	10.0	1.20	12
Seed transplanting Dunum)	0.00	0.00	0	0.00	0.00	0	0.00	0.00	0
Chemical fertiliser		0.46			0.46			0.46	0
–Nitrogen (kg)	12.5	0.46	6	2.0	0.36	1	2.0	0.36	1
–Phosphorus (kg)	5.4	0.36	2	5.4	0.25	1	5.4	0.25	1
–Potash (kg)	2.5	0.25	1	2.5	1.00	3	2.5	1.00	3
–Compound		1.00	0		6.00	0		6.00	0
–MICR-elements		6.00	0			0			0
Plant protection chemicals (Dunum)	1.00	20.00	20	1.00	20.00	20	1.00	20.00	20
Mulch (kg) THREADS		1.20	0		1.20	0		1.20	0
Machinery		5.00	5		5.00	5		5.00	5
–Land preparation (hr)	1.00	5.00	5	1.00	3.50	4	1.00	3.50	4
–Sowing/planting hr)	0.00	0.00	0	0.00	0.00	0	0.00	0.00	0
–Husbandry (hr)	0.00	0.00	0	0.00	0.00	0	0.00	0.00	0
Non-tradable inputs			**135**			**122**			**279**
Water requirement (CM)	150.00	0.50	75	150.00	0.50	75	400.00	0.50	200
Manure (ton)	1.0	20.27	20	1.0	20.27	20	2.0	20.27	41
Manual labour									

–Land preparation (hr)	12.00	0.15	2	12.00	0.15	2	12.00	0.15	2
–Sowing/planting (hr)		0.50	0		0.50	0		0.50	0
–Husbandry (hr)	0.00	0.50	0	0.00	0.50	0	0.00	0.50	0
–Harvesting (hr)	40.00	0.50	20	30.00	0.50	15	30.00	0.50	15
Interest (%)		0.07	18		0.07	10		0.07	21
PH depreciation									
Plastic sheets depreciation									
Irrigation network depreciation									
Land rent (dunum)	1	20		1	20		1	20	
Total fixed costs			20			20			20
Total variable costs			171			157			324
Gross margin			9			–57			43

Figure A.1.6: Jordan farm budget efficiency prices for vegetables (Jordanian Dinar)

(One Dunum) — Summer

Items	Cucumber-Zizia			Cucumber-Mafraq			Cucumber-Baqaa			Tomato-Baqaa-PH			Tomato-Qastal-PH			Potato-Mafraq Open Field			Potato-Zezia Open Field		
	Input/output	Price/cost	TOTAL	Input/output	Price/cost	TOTAL	Input/output	Price/cost	TOTAL	Input/output	Price/cost	TOTAL	Input/output	Price/Cost	TOTAL	Input/output	Price/cost	TOTAL	Input/output	Price/cost	TOTAL
Crop produce (output) (kg)	12.00	316.59	3799	13.60	316.59	4306	12.00	316.59	3799	14.40	220.88	3181	13.20	220.88	2916	3.10	341.59	1059	3.40	341.59	1161
Tradable inputs			**716**			**792**			**803**			**519**			**616**			**367**			**474**
Seeds/seedlings (kg/no)	4100.00	0.09	369	4100.00	0.09	369	4100.00	0.09	369	3500	0.05	175	3500.00	0.05	175	250.00	0.60	150	250.00	1.10	275
Seed transplantation (Dunum)	1.00	30.00	30	1.00	30.00	30	1.00	30.00	30	1.00	30.00	30	1.00	30.00	30	1.00	30.00	30	1.00	30.00	30
Chemical fertiliser			0			0			0			0			0			0			0
–Nitrogen (Urea)(kg)	80.00	0.34	27	120.00	0.34	40	120.00	0.34	40	120.00	0.34	40	136.00	0.34	46	38.00	0.34	13	35.00	0.34	12
–DAP (kg)	80.00	0.41	33	116.00	0.41	48	100.00	0.41	41	80.00	0.41	33	116.00	0.41	48	69.00	0.41	29	30.00	0.41	12
–Potash (kg)		0.53	0.0		0.53	0.0		0.53	0.0		0.53	0		0.53	0		0.25	0		0.25	0
–Compound	122.00	0.75	91	200.00	0.75	149	170.00	0.75	127	180.00	0.75	135	176.00	0.75	132	45.00	0.75	34	71.00	0.75	53
–Micro-elements	4.00	0.34	1	4.00	0.34	1	4.00	0.34	1	4.00	0.34	1	4.00	0.34	1	21.00	0.34	7	4.00	0.34	1
Plant protection chemicals (Dunum)	1.00	65.00	65	1.00	60.00	60	1.00	90.00	90	1.00	60.00	60	1.00	60.00	60	1.00	45.00	45	1.00	35.00	35
Mulch (kg), THREADS	16.00	1.50	24	22.00	1.50	33	22.00	1.50	33	16.00	1.50	24	16.00	1.50	24		1.50	0	16.00	1.50	24
Machinery																					
–Land preparation (hr)	4.00	5.00	20	4.00	5.00	20	4.00	5.00	20	4.00	5.00	20	4.00	5.00	20	4.00	5.00	20	4.00	5.00	20
–Sowing/planting (hr)	0.00	0.00	0	0.00	0.00	0		0.00	0		0.00	0		0.00	0	0.00	0.00	0	0.00	0.00	0
–Husbandry (hr)	0.00	0.00	0	0.00	0.00	0	0.00	0.00	0	0.00	0.00	0	0.00	0.00	0	0.00	0.00	0	0.00	0.00	0
Fuel	100.00	0.55	55	74.00	0.55	41	92.00	0.55	51	110.00	0.55	61	146.20	0.55	80	73.00	0.55	40	20.00	0.55	11
Non-tradable inputs			**1162**			**1143**			**1252**			**1423**			**616**			**691**			**447**
Water requirement (CM)	600.00	1.00	600	600.00	1.00	600	700.00	1.00	700	800.00	1.00	800	400.00	1.00	400	500.00	1.00	500	250.00	1.00	250
Manure (ton)	2.00	30.00	60	1.50	25.00	38	1.50	26.00	38	1.50	30.00	45	2.00	30.00	60	2.00	30.00	60	2.00	30.00	60
Manual labour			0																		
–Land preparation (hr)	12.00	C.15	2	12.00	0.15	2	21.00	0.15	3	12.00	0.15	2	5.00	0.15	1	12.00	0.15	2	12.00	0.15	2
–Sowing/planting (hr)																					

–Husbandry			0			0			0			0			0			0			0
–Harvesting (hr)	1500.00	0.24	360	1500.00	0.24	360	1500.00	0.24	360	1800.00	0.24	432	240.00	0.24	58	240.00	0.24	58	300.00	0.24	72
Interest (%)		0.07	140		0.07	144		0.07	151		0.07	144		0.07	98		0.07	72		0.07	63
PH depreciation			150.0			150.0			150.0			150.0			150.0						
Plastic sheets depreciation			60.0			60.0			60.0			60.0			60.0						
Irrigation network depreciation			10.0			10.0			10.0			10.0			10.0						
Land rent (Dunum)	1.00	40.00	40	1.00	40.00	40	1.00	40.00	40	1.00	40.00	40	1.0	40.00	40	1.0	40.00	40	1.00	40.00	40
Total fixed costs			260			260			260			260			260			40			40
Total variable costs			1877			1935			2055			1941			1232			1059			920
Gross margin			1922			2371			1744			1239			1683			0			241
Net profit			1662			2111			1484			979			1423			–40			201
Return to water (JD/cm)			4.203			4.951			3.492			2.549			5.208			1.001			1.965
Virtual water (litre/kg)			50			44			58			56			30			161			74

Figure A.1.7: Jordan farm budget efficiency prices for field crops (Jordanian Dinar)

Items	Wheat-HL			Barley-HL			Maize-summer-HL		
	Input/ output	Price/ cost	TOTAL	Input/ output	Price/ cost	TOTAL	Input/ output	Price/ Ccost	TOTAL
Crop produce (output) (kg)	0.6	204.61	123	0.4	176.70	71	1.8	267.76	482
Tradable inputs			**35**			**33**			**44**
Seeds/seedlings (kg/no)	12.0	0.25	3	10.0	0.17	2	10.0	1.20	12
Seed transplanting (Dunum)	0.00	0.00	0	0.00	0.00	0	0.00	0.00	0
Chemical fertiliser		0.34			0.34			0.34	
–Nitrogen (kg)	12.5	0.34	4	2.0	0.34	1	2.0	0.34	1
–DAP (kg)	5.4	0.41	2	5.4	0.41	2	5.4	0.41	2
–Potash (kg)	2.5	0.53	1	2.5	0.53	1	2.5	0.53	1
–Compound		0.75	0		0.75	0		0.75	0
–MICR-elements		0.34	0		0.34	0		0	0
Plant protection chemicals (Dunum)	1.00	20.00	20	1.00	20.00	20	1.00	20.00	20
Mulch (kg) THREADS		1.20	0		1.20	0		1.20	0
Machinery									
–Land preparation (hr)	1.00	4.00	4	1.00	3.50	4	1.00	3.50	4
–Sowing/planting (hr)	0.00	0.00	0	0.00	0.00	0	0.00	0.00	0
–Husbandry (hr)	0.00	0.00	0	0.00	0.00	0	0.00	0.00	0

Non-tradable inputs	192			187			457		
Water requirement (CM)	150.00	1.00	150	150.00	1.00	150	400.00	1.00	400
Manure (ton)	1.0	20.27	20	1.0	20.27	20	2.0	20.27	41
Manual labour									
–Land preparation (hr)	12.00	0.15	2	12.00	0.15	2	12.00	0.15	2
–Sowing/planting (hr)		0.50	0		0.50	0		0.50	0
–Husbandry (hr)	0.00	0.50	0	0.00	0.50	0	0.00	0.50	0
–Harvesting (hr)	40.00	0.50	20	30.00	0.50	15	30.00	0.50	15
Interest (%)		0.07	0		0.07	0		0.07	0
PH depreciation									
Plastic sheets depreciation									
Irrigation network depreciation	1	20	20	1	20	20	1	20	20
Land rent (dunum)			20			20			20
Total fixed costs			20			20			20
Total variable costs			227			51			462
Gross margin			-104			-149			-19

Figure A.1.8: Calculation of shadow exchange rate (Jordanian Dinar to $)

	2008	2009	2010	Average
Taxes	306.9	290.3	284.8	294
Exports	4431.1	3579.2	4216.9	4075.733333
Imports	12060.9	10107.7	10935.5	11034.7
SCF	0.980915			
OER	0.708			
EER	0.72			

Figure A.1.9: Calculation of farmgate import parity prices (Jordanian Dinar)

Item	Nitrogen	Compound	Potash	Maize	DAP	Potato	Trace elements	Wheat	Barley	Maize
CIF Aqaba Gulf ($/ton)	435	1000	700	324	500	400	400	211	171	295
Equilibrium exchange rate (JD/$)	0.721775	0.721775	0.721775	0.721775	0.721775	0.721775	0.721775	0.721775	0.721775	0.721775
CIF Aqaba Gulf (JD/ton)	313.9723	721.7754	505.2428	233.8552	360.8877	288.7102	288.7102	152.2946	123.4236	212.9237
Handling charges (JD/ton)	0.625	0.625	0.625	0.625	0.625	0.625	0.625	0.625	0.625	0.625
Clearance fees (JD/ton)	0.171429	0.171429	0.171429	0.171429	0.171429	0.171429	0.171429	0.171429	0.171429	0.171429
General fees (JD/ton)	1.8	1.8	1.8	1.8	1.8	1.8	1.8	1.8	1.8	1.8
Losses 0.5% of total costs	1.582844	3.621859	2.539196	1.182558	1.817421	1.456533	1.456533	0.774455	0.6301	1.077601
Distance between port and warehouse (km)	350	350	350	350	350	350	350	350	350	350

Transport rate between warehouse to port (JD/km)	0.027143	0.027143	0.027143	0.111429	0.111429	0.111429	0.111429	0.111429	0.111429
Transportation cost between port and warehouse (JD/ton)	9.5	9.5	9.5	9.527143	39	39	39.11143	39.11143	39.22286	39.33429
Import parity price at warehouse (JD/ton)	327.4801	737.3222	519.707	246.9896	404.1301	331.5917	331.7031	194.6055	165.7015	255.7606
Transport cost from warehouse to farm (JD/kg)	10	10	10	11	10	10	10	10	11	12
Import parity price at farmgate (JD/ton)	337.4801	747.3222	529.707	257.9896	414.1301	341.5917	341.7031	204.6055	176.7015	267.7606
Import parity price at farmgate (JD/kg)	0.33748	0.747322	0.529707	0.25799	0.41413	0.341592	0.341703	0.204605	0.176702	0.267761

APPENDIX 1

Figure A.1.10: Calculation of farmgate export parity prices (Jordanian Dinar)

Item	Tomato–Baqaa	Cucumber–Zizia
FOB at Saudi-Arabia border ($/ton)	391	524.8996
Equilibrium exchange rate (JD/$)	0.721775	0.721775
Unadjusted price of produce (JD/ton)	282.2142	378.8596
Handling and clearance charges (JD/ton)	10	10
Distance between border and exporter packaging centre (km)	350	350
Transportation rate (JD/km/ton)	0.11	0.11
Transportation cost from packaging centre to border (JD/ton)	38.5	38.5
Unadjusted price of produce at exporter packaging centre (JD/ton)	233.7142	330.3596
Marketing costs (JD/ton)	19.08605	21.01896
–2% of cost of produce for Amman municipality	4.674283	6.607192
–75JD per truck, certificate of origin (Truckload 17 tons)	4.411765	4.411765
–Transport from wholesale market to packaging centre	1	1
–Post-harvest labour	5	5
–Post-harvest materials	4	4
Unadjusted price of produce at Amman wholesale market (JD/ton)	214.6281	309.3406
Transport cost from farm to Amman wholesale market (JD/ton)	6.25	7.25
Export parity price at farmgate (JD/kg)	0.220878	0.316591

APPENDIX 2

EQUATIONS

As mentioned in the theoretical section of this chapter 5, the multi-market partial equilibrium model is the core of the model. It includes equations of supply and demand, trade, price transmission and market equilibrium. The equations are as follows:

Equations of market model:

$$Supply_i = as_i + \sum_j bs_{i,j} ppr_j$$

$$Demand_{is} = bd_{is} + \sum_j ed_{js}\, cpr_{js} + c_{is} Y_s + g_s mr_s \qquad s = urban, rural$$

$$ppr_i = arm\,2\ p_i + PSE_i$$

$$cpr_i = arm\,1\ p_i - CES_i$$

$$arm\,1\ p_i = \frac{IMPW_i imp_i + dsale_i pmk_i}{arm\,1_i}$$

$$arm\,1_i = Demand_{ih} + Dwaste_i + Dfeed_i + Dseed_i$$

$$= asp\big[sm\ IMPW_i^{-rhoc} + sdom\ Sale_i^{-rhoc}\big]^{-1/rhoc}$$

$$arm\,2_i = Supply_i = csp\big[sx\ EXPW^{-rhot} + sdoms\ dSale_i^{-rhot}\big]^{-1/rhot}$$

$$arm\,2\ p_i = \frac{exp_i\ EXPW_i + dsale_i\ pmk_i}{arm\,2_i}$$

$$imp_i = pmk_0(1 + tarif_i)\,EXR$$

$$\frac{IMPW_i}{dsales_i} = \frac{sdom}{sm}\left(\frac{pmk_i}{imp_i}\right)^{\frac{1}{1+rh01}}$$

$$\frac{EXPW_i}{dsales_i} = \frac{sdoms}{sx}\left(\frac{pmk_i}{exp_i}\right)^{\frac{1}{1+\phi_1}}$$

$$Demand_{is} + Dwaste_i + Dfeed_i + Dseed_i =$$

$$Supply_i + IMPW_i - EXPW_i$$

Variable/ parameter	Variable description	Exogenous/ endogenous	
Supply	Quantity of supply	endogenous	
Demand	Quantity of demand	endogenous	
ppr	Producer price	endogenous	
cpr	Consumer price	endogenous	
arm1p	Demand price of composite commodity	endogenous	
arm1	Total demand of composite	endogenous	
arm2	Total supply of composite	endogenous	
arm2p	Supply price of composite commodity	endogenous	
Imp	Import price	endogenous	
IMPW	Import quantity	endogenous	
dsales	Domestic supply	endogenous	
EXPW	Export quantity	endogenous	
Pmk	Domestic equilibrium price	endogenous	
Pmk0	World price	exogenous	Predicted by IMPACT
PSE	Producer subsidy equivalent	exogenous	Calculated by the authors
CSE	Consumer subsidy equivalent	exogenous	Calculated by the authors
Dwaste	Quantity of wasted crops	exogenous	From literature as a share of total output
Dfeed	Demand for feeding	exogenous	Estimated by the authors
Dseed	Demand for seeds	exogenous	Estimated by the authors
Y	Total consumer expenditure	exogenous	Predicted for target year
sm/sdom	Shares of domestic/ import in aggregate demand	exogenous	Calculated by the authors
sx/sdoms	Shares of export/ domestic demand in aggregate supply	exogenous	Calculated by the authors
csp	Supply shifter	exogenous	
asp	Demand shifter	exogenous	
exp	Export price	exogenous	Predicted by IMPACT
as	Supply curve intercept	exogenous	Through calibration
bd	Demand curve intercept	exogenous	Through calibration
bs/ed	Slopes of supply/demand	exogenous	From elasticities

APPENDIX 2

PMP model

The PMP method used in estimating models involves three stages. The first stage is defined by determining n ($n=1\ldots 30$) linear programming (LP) models, one for each province of Iran and an additional LP model for the entire country. The n provincial LP models have the same structure and maximise gross margins of each activity in a province, subject to a series of resource endowments. In this stage, calibration constraints add to the model, which force the optimisation model to observed output level in the base year. The n-*th* regional LP model has the following structure:

$$(1) \quad \max_{x_n \geq 0} (\acute{p}_n x_n - \acute{c}_n x_n)$$

Subject to

$$(2) \quad A_n x_n \leq b_n \quad (y)$$

$$(3) \quad x_{nj} \leq x_{Rnj}, \quad (\lambda) \quad \text{for } x_{Rnj} > 0,\ j = 1, \ldots, J_n$$

In which, constraints (2) are structural constraints while constraints (3) indicate calibration constraints. The vector of λ_n corresponds to the calibration constraints and contains all non-explicitly specified costs that affect production decisions. p_n is the vector of output prices faced by the n-*th* region, c is a vector of production cost per unit of output, A_n is a matrix of fixed technical coefficients involving limiting allocable inputs, b_n is a vector of available inputs and x_{Rn} is a vector of realised output levels for all crops produced in the province. Each province is endowed with i allocable inputs (land and water are two main constraints) and j ($j=1, \ldots, J_n$) products. If the vector of realised land allocation decisions indicated by h_{Rn}, the n-*th* matrix A_n of technical coefficients is defined as $A_n = [a_{nij}]$, where $a_{nij} = h_{Rni}/x_{RnJn}$. The additional (N+1)-*th* LP model for the entire country is defined over all provinces' resources and crop activities. The land availability and crop activities of all provinces are summed up in vector $\bar{b}$ and $\overline{X}_R$. Prices and accounting costs are averaged over these provinces and the matrix of technical coefficients for the entire sample is defined as the ratio of acreage of each crop divided by the total quantity of outputs for that crop at country level. So, the LP primal model is presented as:

$$(4) \quad \max_{x \geq 0} (\overline{p} x - \overline{c} x)$$

Subject to

(5) $Ax \leq \overline{b}$

(6) $x \leq \overline{x}_R,$

Where $\overline{p'}$ and $\overline{c'}$ are vectors of average price and variable costs of each crop at country level, A is technical coefficient matrix and $\overline{b}$ is total land available for cultivation.

In the second stage of PMP, the dual values are used to specify a non-linear variable cost function such that the variable marginal cost of the activities (mc(x)) equals to the sum of the known cost c and non-specified marginal cost (λ), that is mc(x) vector of the n-*th* province is given by ($\lambda_n c_n$) and the mc(x) marginal cost vector for the entire sample is presented by ($\overline{\lambda} + \overline{c}$). Following Paris and Arfini's 2000 article 'Frontier Cost Functions, Self-Selection, Price Risk, PMP and Agenda 2000', it is assumed that there exists an overall cost function for all crop produced in all provinces. Then, the cost function in each province is deviated from the aggregate cost frontier an error vector (u) that reflects a province's specific preferences and environment. A quadratic functional form in output, that is $C(x) = x'Qx/2$, is assumed for the cost function, where the Q matrix is symmetric and positive semi definite. Then, marginal cost function at the national level can be represented by $mc(x) = \overline{\lambda}_{LP} + \overline{c} = Q\overline{x}_R$, while marginal cost function of the n-*th* province is represented by $mc(x) = \overline{\lambda}_{LP} + \overline{c} = Q\overline{x}_R + u_n$. To recover the marginal cost function, the maximum entropy method is utilised.

The third step of the PMP methodology consists of assembling non-linear models and reproducing the primal and dual solutions of the first stage LP models. The final n-*th* quadratic programming models are defined as follows:

(8) $\displaystyle \max_{x_n \geq 0} \left(\overline{p}'_n x_n - \frac{x'_n Q x_n}{2} - \hat{u}_n x_n \right)$

Subject to

(9) $A_n x_n \leq b_n$

(10) $g_{nj} x_{nj} \leq \overline{bw}_n$

Constraint (10) represents water limitation of each province in which $\overline{bw}$ is total cubic metres of water available in each province for the

APPENDIX 2

cropping sector from underground and surface sources. g is water used per kilo production (technical coefficient) of irrigated crop j in the province n, which is based on the water requirement of each crop adjusted by irrigation efficiency in each of the provinces. For the frontier model as a whole, the following quadratic programming model reproduces the total output and allocation decisions:

(11) $\displaystyle\max_{x \geq 0} \left(\overline{p}x - \frac{x_n' Q x_n}{2} \right)$

(12) $Ax \leq \overline{b}$

(13) $g_{nj} x_{nj} \leq \overline{bw}_n$

APPENDIX 3

DATA AND VARIABLE DESCRIPTIONS

Variable	Description	Proxy	Source
AgriHH	no. agricultural HH/total HH	Sectorial Employment	PCBS Census 2007
Plant	% of types of agricultural holdings (plant, animal, mix)	Sectorial Employment	PCBS Census 2007
Animal	% of types of agricultural holdings (plant, animal, mix)	Sectorial Employment	PCBS Census 2007
Mix	% of types of agricultural holdings (plant, animal, mix)	Sectorial Employment	PCBS Census 2007
Primary	% workers in primary extractive industry (agricult, fishing, mining)	Sectorial Employment	PCBS Census 2007
Public	% workers in public services (education, health, community services)	Sectorial Employment	PCBS Census 2007
Manu	% workers in manufacturing	Sectorial Employment	PCBS Census 2007
PublicA	% workers in public administration	Sectorial Employment	PCBS Census 2007
Consum	% workers in consumption industries (construct, wholesale, hotels)	Sectorial Employment	PCBS Census 2007
TraUti	% workers public utilities (transport and communication, electricity)	Sectorial Employment	PCBS Census 2007
BusSer	% workers in business services (financial institutions, real estate)	Sectorial Employment	PCBS Census 2007
dep	dependency rate	Employment	PCBS Census 2007
Urever	unemployment rate	Employment	PCBS Census 2007

Variable	Description	Category	Source
Urnever	% of discouraged workers	Employment	PCBS Census 2007
Fempr	% female employment	Employment	PCBS Census 2007
UR9707	percentage point change in unemployment (1997–2007)	Employment	PCBS Census 1997 and 2007
over65	% over 65	Demographics	PCBS Census 2007
less5	% under 5	Demographics	PCBS Census 2007
Pop9707	% change in population (1997–2007)	Demographics	PCBS Census 1997 and 2007
HHsize9707	change in HH size (1997–2007)	Demographics	PCBS Census 1997 and 2007
hh size	HH size	Demographics	PCBS Census 2007
Illiterate	% illiterates	Education	PCBS Census 2007
RW	% Can read and write	Education	PCBS Census 2007
Second	% at least a secondary education	Education	PCBS Census 2007
Sch Yes	% attending school	Education	PCBS Census 2007
aveSch	average yars of schooling	Education	PCBS Census 2007
NoSch	% of over 10s with zero years schooling	Education	PCBS Census 2007
Births	no. of live births	Fertility	PCBS Census 2007
BR07	fertility rate	Fertility	PCBS Census 2007 and authors' calculations: rates are computed over all women population aged at least 10 because female 15–44 unavailable)
nonres	no. establishment/no. building (proxy for economic development)	Economic activity	PCBS Census 2007
Estab9707	% change in establishment (1997–2007)	Economic activity	PCBS Census 1997 and 2007
WMR	% HH connected to water network	Access to services	PCBS Census 2007
NetElec	% HH connected to electricity work	Access to services	PCBS Census 2007

Variable	Description	Proxy	Source
NetSewa	% HH connected to sewage system	Access to services	PCBS Census 2007
Kitc2w	% availability of kitchen with water	Access to services	PCBS Census 2007
BR2w	% availability of bathroom with water	Access to services	PCBS Census 2007
Toi2w	% availability of toilet with water	Access to services	PCBS Census 2007
water cons pc	water consumption per capita (m3)	Water availability	PWA and authors' calculations: the available information covers 70 communities for a total of 80% of domestic water supplied. Quantities in remaining communities are derived by the residual water quantity and weighted by the residual population. This methods imposes the assumption that in remaining communities within the same governorate consumption (and supply) per capita are equal.
water supply pc	water supply per capity (m3)	Water availability	PWA and authors' calculation: see above cell
water deficit	water deficit from international WHO standards	Water availability	PWA and authors' calculations: the residual from the total water supplied and the recommended WHO standards (100 litres/capita/day)
water loss	Water loss rates	Water availability	PWA and authors' calculations: loss rates are available for 70 communities. The remaining communities loss rates are derived by weighting averages, where weights are the water quantity supplied, so that the total loss rate equal the average loss at governorate level published by PWA
dist Ramalah	distance from community centroid to Ramallah (km)	Access to markets	Authors' calculations
dist hospital	distance from community centroid to the nearest hospital (km)	Access to services	Authors' calculations

dist markets	distance from community centroid to main governorate town (km)	Access to markets	Authors' calculations
checkpoints	number of checkpoints	Mobility restrictions	OCHA and authors' calculations; number of checkpoints within 5 km buffer from community
Green Line	number of Green Line checkpoints	Mobility restrictions	OCHA and authors' calculations: number of Green Line checkpoints within 5 km buffer from community
partial checkp	number of partial checkpoints	Mobility restrictions	OCHA and authors' calculations: number of partial checkpoints within 5 km buffer from community
road blocks	number of road blocks	Mobility restrictions	OCHA and authors' calculations: number of road blocks checkpoints within 5 km buffer from community
road gates	number of road gates	Mobility restrictions	OCHA and authors' calculations: number of road blocks checkpoints within 5 km buffer from community
dist to crop	distance to nearest crop land (km)	Access to land	Authors' calculations: euclidean distance from community centroid to nearest crop land cell from GIS land-use raster file
cultivated crop	percentage of cultivated land	Land availability	Agricultural Census 2010 (PCBS)
road density	road density (km/km2)	Access to services	Authors' calculations from GIS road network (ARIJ-OCHA)
NPP	Net Primary Production (mean value)	Soil fertility	Authors' calculation from GIS remote sensing data: NPP is the production of organic compounds from atmospheric or aquatic carbon dioxide, principally through the process of photosyntesis and, to a less extent, chemosynthesis.
Aridity Index		Agricultural potential	Authors' calculations from GIS remote sensing data: the Aridity index is the ratio of rainfall to evapotranspiration

APPENDIX 4

QATAR NATIONAL NUTRITION AND PHYSICAL ACTIVITY STRATEGY (AS FROM THE ACTION PLAN)

The fundamental goal of the 'Qatar National Nutrition and Physical Activity Action Plan' (hereafter, the 'Action Plan') is to reduce morbidity and mortality attributable to chronic non-communicable diseases in the State of Qatar. This is in line with part 3.2 of the National Health Strategy goals related to preventive healthcare and its objective. The main objective is to establish comprehensive initiatives related to improved nutrition and physical activity for those sectors of the population with a prevalence of obesity. The 'Action Plan' was designed with goals in mind that can be achieved through a series of activities and programmes, each with specific objectives. The 'Action Plan' is meant to be implemented, upon approval, through eight action areas covering the main themes important to achieving the overall aim of reducing morbidity and mortality attributable to chronic NCDs in Qatar. These action areas are:

1. Area 1: National policies and legislation.
2. Area 2: National coordination mechanisms.
3. Area 3: National nutrition programmes.
4. Area 4: National physical activity programmes.
5. Area 5: Promotion and advocacy.
6. Area 6: Surveillance, monitoring and evaluation.

7. Area 7: Capacity-building.
8. Area 8: Partnership with academic institutions and the private sector.

Expected outcomes

1. The rates of obesity and overweight are reduced by 1 per cent yearly (5 per cent within five years).
2. The rates of physical activities are increased by 1 per cent yearly (5 per cent within five years).
3. The proportion of the population consuming five servings of fruit and vegetables daily is increased by 10 per cent in five years.
4. The proportion of the population suffering from high blood cholesterol levels is decreased by 2.5 per cent in men and 0.05 per cent in women in five years.
5. The level of public awareness on nutrition and physical activity is increased by 25 per cent in five years.

NOTES

1. FOOD SECURITY AND FOOD SOVEREIGNTY IN THE MIDDLE EAST

1. Holt-Giménez, Eric and Loren Peabody, 'From food rebellions to food sovereignty: urgent calls to fix a broken food system', *Institute for Food and Development Policy*, vol. 14, no. 1 (Spring 2008), p. 1.
2. The World Bank, *Improving Food Security in Arab Countries*, Washington, DC: The World Bank, 2009, pp. xi-xii.
3. Larson, Donald et al., 'Food Security and Storage in the Middle East and North Africa', *World Bank Policy Research Working Paper 6031*, Washington, DC: The World Bank, 2012, p. 2.
4. Ibid., p. 3.
5. See, for example, Adoni, Lamis and Jillian Schwedler, 'Bread riots in Jordan', *Middle East Report*, no. 201 (October–December 1996), pp. 40–2.
6. Larson, et al., *Food Security and Storage in the Middle East and North Africa*, p. 4.
7. Ianchovichina, Elena, Josef Loening and Christina Wood, *How Vulnerable Are Arab Countries to Global Food Price Shocks?*, The World Bank Policy Research Working Paper 6018, Washington, DC: The World Bank, March 2012, p. 5.
8. Lampietti, Julian A. et al., 'A strategic framework for improving food security in the Arab countries', *Food Security*, vol. 3 (2011), p. S9.
9. Headey, Derek and Shenggen Fan, 'Reflections on the global food crisis: how did it happen? How has it hurt? And how can we prevent the next one?', *Research Monograph* no. 165, International Food Policy Research Institute, 2011, p. 3.
10. Pinstrup-Andersen, Per, 'Food security: definition and measurement', *Food Security*, vol. 1 (2009), p. 5.
11. Food and Agriculture Organization of the United Nations (FAO), 'Food security', *Policy Brief* no. 2 (June 2006), p. 1.
12. Ibid. See also, Tweeten, Luther, 'The economics of global food security', *Review of Agricultural Economics*, vol. 21, no. 2 (Autumn-Winter 1999), pp. 475–6.
13. Dilley, Maxx and Tanya E. Boudreau, 'Coming to terms with vulnerability: a critique of the food security definition', *Food Policy*, vol. 26 (2001), p. 230.
14. Shepherd, Benjamin, 'Thinking critically about food security', *Security Dialogue*, vol. 43, no. 3 (2012), p. 196.

15. Ibid., p. 206.
16. Tweeten, 'The economics of global food security', p. 485.
17. Godfray, H. Charles J. et al., 'Food security: the challenge of feeding 9 billion people', *Science*, no. 327 (12 February 2012), p. 812.
18. Patel, Raj, 'What does food sovereignty look like?', *The Journal of Peasant Studies*, vol. 36, no. 3 (2009), pp. 663–706.
19. Wittman, Hannah, Annette Desmarais and Nettie Wiebe, 'The origins and potential of food sovereignty', in *Food Sovereignty Reconnecting Food, Nature and Community*, Black Point, NS: Fernwood Publishing, 2010, p. 2; Windfuhr, Michael and Jennie Jonsen, *Food Sovereignty, Towards Democracy in Localised Food Systems*, Warwickshire: ITDG Publishing, 2005, p. 11.
20. For more on this see 'International campaign for the immediate release of WTO prisoners', La Via Campesina, available at: http://viacampesina.org/en/index.php?option=com_content&view=article&id=47:food-sovereignty&catid=21:food-sovereignty-and-trade&Itemid=38 (last accessed 18 Feb. 2014).
21. Pinstrup-Andersen, 'Food security: definition and measurement', p. 5.
22. FAO, *The State of Food Insecurity in the World*, Rome: FAO, 2011, p. 25.
23. Headey and Fan, 'Reflections on the global food crisis', p. 3.
24. World Food Programme, *The Status of Food Security and Vulnerability in Egypt, 2009*, Rome: WFP, 2011, p. 5.
25. Breisinger, Clemens et al., 'Food security and economic development in the Middle East and North Africa: current state and future perspectives', *International Food Policy Research Institute Discussion Paper No. 00985*, May 2010, p. 4.
26. Ibid.
27. United Nations, *Millennium Development Goals Annual Report 2012*, New York: UN, 2012, p. 11.
28. Ibid.
29. McMichael, Philip, 'Food, the state and the world economy', *International Journal of Sociology of Food and Agriculture*, vol. 1 (1991), pp. 71–85.
30. Ibid. p. 75.
31. Friedmann, Harriet, 'The political economy of food: a global crisis', *American Journal of Sociology*, no. 88 (1982), p. 248–86.
32. McMichael, Philip, 'A food regime genealogy', *The Journal of Peasant Studies*, vol. 36, no. 1 (2009), p. 139.
33. Campbell, Hugh and Jane Dixon, 'Introduction to the special symposium: reflecting on twenty years of food regimes approach in agri-studies', *Agriculture and Human Values*, vol. 26, no. 4 (2009), p. 263.
34. McMichael, 'Food, the state and the world economy', p. 80.
35. Pechlaner, Gabriela and Gerardo Otero, 'The neoliberal food regime: neoregulation and the new division of labor in North America', *Rural Sociology*, vol. 75, no. 2 (June 2010), pp. 180–1.
36. Ibid. p. 183.
37. Moltzen, Kelly, 'Subsidies and "specialized" crops: an analysis of the current state of US agricultural policy', unpublished manuscript, Fall 2009, p. 1–2; and Burfisher, Mary E., Sherman Robinson and Karen Thierfelder, *Farm Policy Reforms and Harmonization in the NAFTA*, U.S. Department of Agriculture, Regional Trade Agreements and U.S. Agriculture/AER-771, pp. 1–9.
38. Ibid. p. 81.

39. Woertz, Eckart, Samir Pradhan, Nermina Biberovic and Christian Koch, 'Food inflation in the GCC countries', *Gulf Research Center Report*, 2008, p. 13.
40. World Hunger Education Service, '2013 World Hunger and Poverty Facts and Statistics', available at: http://www.worldhunger.org/articles/Learn/world%20hunger%20facts%20 2002.htm#Number_of_hungry_people_in_the_world (last accessed 18 Feb. 2014).
41. Institute for Food Policy Research, *Global Hunger Index 2011, The Challenge of Hunger: Taming Price Spikes and Excessive Food Price Volatility*, Washington, DC: IFPRI, 2011, p. 11.
42. United Nations, *Millennium Development Goals*, p. 12.
43. Ibid.
44. Breisinger et al., 'Food security and economic development in the Middle East and North Africa', p. 4.
45. Ibid. p. 3.
46. Egypt alone is the largest wheat-importing country in the world. For more on this, see: Weigand, Chad, 'Wheat Import Projections Towards 2050', U.S. Wheat Associates, 2011.
47. Lampietti et al., 'A strategic framework for improving food security in the Arab countries', pp. S7–8.
48. 'TABLE-The world top ten wheat importers and exporters', Reuters, 2009, available at: http://in.reuters.com/article/2009/07/13/wheat-trade-idINSP49082020090713 (last accessed 18 Feb. 2014).
49. Lampietti et al., 'A strategic framework for improving food security in the Arab countries', pp. S7–8.
50. Larson et al., *Food Security and Storage in the Middle East and North Africa*, p. 5.
51. Woertz, Eckart, 'Arab food, water, and the big landgrab that wasn't', *The Brown Journal of World Affairs*, vol. 18, no. 1 (2011), p. 128.
52. Breisinger et al, 'Food security and economic development in the Middle East and North Africa', p. 4.
53. Ibid. p. 3.
54. Bakshi, Gitanjali, 'In search of hidden water: GCC nations and food security', Strategic Foresight Group, 2009.
55. Qatar National Food Security Programme, 'Agriculture', 2012.
56. Breisinger et al, 'Food security and economic development in the Middle East and North Africa', p. 4.
57. Lampietti et al, 'A strategic framework for improving food security in the Arab countries', p. S11.
58. World Food Programme, 'Yemen: price and food security update', January 2012, p. 3, available at: http://documents.wfp.org/stellent/groups/public/documents/ena/wfp244909.pdf (last accessed 18 Feb. 2014).
59. World Food Programme, 'Food security survey to reveal alarming levels of severe hunger in Yemen', March 2012, available at: http://www.wfp.org/news/news-release/food-security-survey-reveal-alarming-levels-severe-hunger-yemen-0 (last accessed 18 Feb. 2014).
60. Ibid.
61. Godfray et al., 'Food security: the challenge of feeding 9 billion people', p. 813.
62. Shetty, Shobha, 'Water, Food Security and Agricultural Policy in the Middle East and North Africa', *The World Bank Working Paper Series No. 47*, July 2006, p. ii.
63. International Food Policy Research Institute, *2011 Global Food Policy Report*, Washington, DC: IFPRI, 2012, p. 2.
64. Godfray et al., 'Food security: the challenge of feeding 9 billion people', p. 812.

65. FAO, *The State of Food Insecurity in the World*, p. 11.
66. Tweeten, 'The economics of global food security', p. 477.
67. Shetty, 'Water, Food Security and Agricultural Policy in the Middle East and North Africa', pp. 13–5.
68. Bezemer, Dirk and Derek Headey, 'Agriculture, development, and urban bias', *World Development*, vol. 36, no. 8 (2008), pp. 1342–64.

2. HISTORIC FOOD REGIMES AND THE MIDDLE EAST

1. See chapter 9 in this volume: Tétreault, Mary Ann, Deborah Wheeler and Benjamin Shepherd, 'Win-Win versus Lose-Lose: Investments in Foreign Agriculture as a Food Security Strategy of the Arab States of the Persian Gulf'.
2. Rothschild, Emma, 'Food politics', *Foreign Affairs*, vol. 54, no. 2 (1976), pp. 285–307; Shaw, D. John, *World Food Security: A History since 1945*, New York: Palgrave Macmillan, 2007; Wallerstein, Mitchel B., *Food for War-Food for Peace: United States Food Aid in a Global Context*, Cambridge, MA: MIT Press, 1980.
3. Polanyi, Karl, *The Great Transformation*, New York: Farrar & Rinehart, 1944.
4. Morgan, Dan, *Merchants of Grain*, New York: Viking Press, 1979, p. 36.
5. Erdkamp, Paul, *The Grain Market in the Roman Empire: A Social, Political and Economic Study*, Cambridge: Cambridge University Press, 2005.
6. Ibid., p. 203 and following. Exact data for Roman times is not available. For the sixteenth century, Fernand Braudel estimates that the long-distance grain trade was only 8 per cent of overall grain consumption in the Mediterranean. See Braudel, Fernand, *The Mediterranean and the Mediterranean World in the Age of Philip II*, trans. of the 2nd revised ed., 1966 ed., 3 vols, London: The Folio Society, 2000, p. 62.
7. Friedmann, Harriet and Philip McMichael, 'Agriculture and the state system: the rise and decline of national agricultures, 1870 to the present', *Sociologia Ruralis*, vol. 2, no. XXIX (1989), pp. 93–117. For a revaluation of the theory twenty years later, see McMichael, Philip, 'A food regime genealogy', *Journal of Peasant Studies*, vol. 1, no. 36 (2009), pp. 139–69, doi: 10.1080/03066150902820354.
8. Friedmann and McMichael, 'Agriculture and the state system', p. 105.
9. Burch, David and Geoffrey Lawrence, 'Towards a third food regime: behind the transformation', *Agriculture and Human Values*, vol. 4, no. 26 (2009), pp. 267–79, doi: 10.1007/s10460–009–9219–4; McMichael, Philip, 'A food regime analysis of the "World Food Crisis"', *Agriculture and Human Values*, vol. 4, no. 26 (2009), pp. 281–95, doi: 10.1007/s10460–009–9218–5.
10. Pritchard, Bill, 'The long hangover from the second food regime: a world-historical interpretation of the collapse of the WTO Doha Round', *Agriculture and Human Values*, vol. 4, no. 26 (2009), pp. 297–307, doi: 10.1007/s10460–009–9216–7.
11. Goodman, David and Michael Watts, 'Reconfiguring the rural or fording the divide?: Capitalist restructuring and the global agro-food system', *Journal of Peasant Studies*, vol. 1, no. 22 (1994), pp. 1–49, doi: 10.1080/03066159408438565.
12. Richards, Alan and John Waterbury, *A Political Economy of the Middle East*, 3rd ed. Boulder, CO: Westview Press, 2008, p. 160 and following.
13. See chapter 6 in this volume: Mundy, Martha, Amin Al-Hakimi and Frédéric Pelat, 'Neither Security nor Sovereignty: the Political Economy of Food in Yemen', and chapter 4 in this volume: Bush, Ray, 'Food Security in Egypt'.
14. Richards and Waterbury, *A Political Economy of the Middle East*, p. 162.

15. Allan, Tony, *The Middle East Water Question: Hydropolitics and the Global Economy*, London: I.B. Tauris, 2001.

16. Richards and Waterbury, *A Political Economy of the Middle East*, p. 162 and following.

17. Issawi, Charles Philip, *The Middle East Economy: Decline and Recovery: Selected Essays, Princeton Series on the Middle East*, Princeton, NJ: Markus Wiener Publishers, 1995, p. 42.

18. Parker, Geoffrey, *The Military Revolution: Military Innovation and the Rise of the West, 1500–1800*, 2nd ed., New York: Cambridge University Press, 1996; Pawelka, Peter, *Der Vordere Orient und die Internationale Politik*, Stuttgart: W. Kohlhammer, 1993; Kasaba, Reşat, *The Ottoman Empire and the World Economy: The Nineteenth Century*, Suny Series in Middle Eastern Studies, Albany, NY: State University of New York Press, 1988.

19. Ashtor, Eliyahu, *A Social and Economic History of the Near East in the Middle Ages*, Berkeley, CA: University of California Press, 1976; Issawi, *The Middle East Economy*, p. 66 and following.

20. Issawi, *The Middle East Economy*, p. 69.

21. Ibid., p. 60 and p. 82; Braudel, *The Mediterranean and the Mediterranean World*, vol. 2, p. 205 and following; Owen, Roger, *The Middle East in the World Economy, 1800–1914*, London: I.B. Tauris, 1993, chapter 2.

22. Matuz, Josef, *Das Osmanische Reich: Grundlinien seiner Geschichte*, Darmstadt: Wissenschaftliche Buchgesellschaft, 1985, pp. 104–37; Issawi, Charles Philip, *An Economic History of the Middle East and North Africa: The Columbia Economic History of the Modern World*, New York: Columbia University Press, 1982, pp. 134–49.

23. Lloyd, E. M. H., *Food and Inflation in the Middle East, 1940–45, Studies on Food, Agriculture, and World War II*, Stanford, CA: Stanford University Press, 1956; Richards and Waterbury, *A Political Economy of the Middle East*, pp. 156–60.

24. Brown, Carl L., *International Politics and the Middle East: Old Rules, Dangerous Game, Princeton Studies on the Near East*, Princeton, NJ: Princeton University Press, 1984.

25. Issawi, *An Economic History of the Middle East*, p. 6; Owen, *The Middle East in the World Economy*, p. 113. Egypt built its first railway in 1851, before Sweden or Central Poland. Major railways in the heartlands of the Ottoman Empire like the Baghdad and Hejaz railways were built in the 1890s and 1900s.

26. Issawi, *An Economic History of the Middle East*, pp. 118–29.

27. Issawi, *The Middle East Economy*, p. 97.

28. Batatu, Hanna, *The Old Social Classes and the Revolutionary Movements of Iraq: A Study of Iraq's Old Landed and Commercial Classes and of its Communists, Ba'thists, and Free Officers, Princeton Studies on the Near East*, Princeton, NJ: Princeton University Press, 1978; Tripp, Charles, *A History of Iraq*, 3rd ed., Cambridge: Cambridge University Press, 2007; Hinnebusch, Raymond A., *Peasant and Bureaucracy in Ba'thist Syria: The Political Economy of Rural Development, Westview Special Studies on the Middle East*, Boulder, CO: Westview Press, 1989; Waterbury, John, *The Egypt of Nasser and Sadat: The Political Economy of Two Regimes, Princeton Studies on the Near East*, Princeton, NJ: Princeton University Press, 1983.

29. Issawi, *The Middle East Economy*, p. 148 and following.

30. Lloyd, *Food and Inflation in the Middle East*, p. 8 and following.

31. Ibid., p. 9 and following.

32. Davis, Eric, *Challenging Colonialism: Bank Misr and Egyptian Industrialization, 1920–1941, Princeton Studies on the Near East*, Princeton, N.J.: Princeton University Press, 1983; Bahadir, S. A. and Eckart Woertz, 'Von der Kolonisierung zur Globalisierung. Das Scheitern des nationalen Entwicklungsstaates in Ägypten', in *Von der Weltwirtschaftskrise*

zur Globalisierungskrise (1929–1999). Wohin Treibt die Peripherie?, Feldbauer, P., G. Hardach and G. Melinz (eds), Frankfurt, Vienna: Brandes & Apsel, Südwind, 1999.

33. Waterbury, *The Egypt of Nasser and Sadat*, p. 233.
34. Issawi, *The Middle East Economy*, p. 148. As prices fell by about 20 per cent over the same period the growth in real terms was even higher.
35. Schatkowski-Schilcher, Linda, 'Die Weizenwirtschaft des Nahen Ostens in der Zwischenkriegszeit: Der Einfluß der Ökonomie auf die Politik am Beispiel Syriens', in *Der Nahe Osten in der Zwischenkriegszeit, 1919–1939. Die Interdependenz von Politik, Wirtschaft und Ideologie*, Schatkowski-Schilcher, Linda and Claus Scharf (eds), Stuttgart: Franz Steiner, 1989, p. 247 and following.
36. Lloyd, *Food and Inflation in the Middle East*, p. 171. Between 1934 and 1939, average annual barley exports from Iraq to the UK were 200,000 tons.
37. Collingham, E. M., *The Taste of War: World War Two and the Battle for Food*, London: Allen Lane, 2011; Ellings, Richard, *Embargoes and World Power: Lessons from American Foreign Policy*, Westview Special Studies in International Relations, Boulder, CO: Westview Press, 1985; Hufbauer, Gary Clyde, Kimberley Ann Elliot and Barbara Oegg, *Economic Sanctions Reconsidered*, 3rd ed., Washington, DC: Peterson Institute for International Economics, 2008.
38. Steinberg, Guido, 'Ecology, knowledge and trade in central Arabia (Najd) during the nineteenth and early twentieth centuries', in *Counter Narratives: History, Contemporary Society, and Politics in Saudi Arabia and Yemen*, Al-Rasheed, Madawi and Robert Vitalis (eds), New York: Palgrave MacMillan, 2004, pp. 77–102 and p. 82; Ochsenwald, William, 'The commercial history of the Hijaz Vilayet, 1840–1908', *Arabian Studies*, no. 6, 1982, pp. 57–76 and p. 67 and following; Lloyd, *Food and Inflation in the Middle East*, p. 66; for austere, date-based diets of Bedouins in the post-war period, see Thesiger's account of his travels in the Empty Quarter 1945–1950 in Thesiger, Wilfred, *Arabian Sands*, 1st ed. New York, NY: Dutton, 1959.
39. Schatkowski-Schilcher, Linda, 'The famine of 1915–1918 in Greater Syria', in *Problems of the Modern Middle East in Historical Perspective: Essays in Honor of Albert Hourani*, Spagnolo, John (ed.), Reading: Ithaca Press for Garnet Publishing Ltd., 1992: pp. 229–58, p. 234.
40. Schatkowski-Schilcher, 'The famine of 1915–1918'.
41. Davis, Mike, *Late Victorian Holocausts: El Niño Famines and the Making of the Third World*, London, New York: Verso, 2001.
42. Schatkowski-Schilcher, 'The famine of 1915–1918', p. 236.
43. Teitelbaum, Joshua, *The Rise and Fall of the Hashimite Kingdom of Arabia*, London, New York: Hurst, New York University Press, 2001, p. 71 and following.
44. Tell, Tariq, 'Guns, gold, and grain: war and food supply in the making of Transjordan', in *War, Institutions and Social Change in the Middle East*, Heydeman, Steven (ed.), Berkeley, CA: University of California Press, 2000, pp. 33–58, p. 43 and following.
45. Schatkowski-Schilcher, 'The famine of 1915–1918', p. 239.
46. Wilmington, Martin W., 'The Middle East Supply Center: a reappraisal', *Middle East Journal*, vol. 2, no. 6 (1952), p. 153; Lloyd, *Food and Inflation in the Middle East*, p. 138; Hunter, Guy, 'Economic problems: The Middle East Supply Center', in *The Middle East in the War*, Kirk, George (ed.), London; New York; Toronto: Oxford University Press, 1953, pp. 169–93, p. 180.
47. Collingham, *The Taste of War*, p. 129 and following; Jackson, Ashley, *The British Empire and the Second World War*, London; New York: Hambledon Continuum, 2006, p. 166.
48. Hunter, 'Economic problems', p. 180.

49. Lloyd, *Food and Inflation in the Middle East*, p. 65.

50. Heydemann, Steven and Robert Vitalis, 'War, Keynesianism and colonialism: explaining state-market relations in the postwar Middle East', in *War, Institutions and Social Change in the Middle East*, Heydemann, Steven (ed.), Berkeley, CA: University of California Press, 2000, pp. 100–45, p. 103 and p. 121.

51. Wilmington, 'The Middle East Supply Center', p. 147; part, but by no means all, of this increase could be attributed to a decrease in total foreign trade.

52. Landis, J. M., 'Anglo-American co-operation in the Middle East', *Annals of the American Academy of Political and Social Science*, no. 240 (1945), pp. 64–72 and p. 65.

53. Lloyd, *Food and Inflation in the Middle East*, pp. 208–17.

54. Woertz, Eckart, *Oil for Food: The Global Food Crisis and the Middle East*, Oxford; New York: Oxford University Press, 2013, chapter 2.

55. Stonehewer-Bird, General Distribution, 5 February 1940, and Jeddah to Baxter/FO London, 31 December 1943, in Tuson, Penelope, and Anita Burdett (eds), *Records of Saudi Arabia: Primary Documents 1902–1960*, vol. 7, Slough, UK: Archive Editions, 1992, p. 192 and p. 353.

56. Jones, Toby Craig, *Desert Kingdom: How Oil and Water Forged Modern Saudi Arabia*, Cambridge, MA: Harvard University Press, 2010.

57. Fakry, Ahmed Omar and Karl Saben Twitchell, *Report of the United States Agricultural Mission to Saudi Arabia*, Cairo, 1943.

58. Personal interview with Fahad al-Attiya and Sheikh Hamad bin Ali bin Jassim al-Thani, Chairman and Vice-Chairman of Qatar National Food Security Programme, Doha, 15 November 2011.

59. US Congress, *The United States Oil Shortage and the Arab-Israeli Conflict*, Report of a Study Mission to the Middle East, 22 October to 3 November 1973, Pursuant to House Res. 267, Committee on Foreign Affairs, U.S. Government Printing Office: Washington, DC, 1973.

60. Paarlberg, Robert L., 'Lessons of the grain embargo', *Foreign Affairs*, vol. 1, no. 59 (1980), pp. 144–62.

61. Gordon, Joy, *Invisible War: The United States and the Iraq Sanctions*, Cambridge, MA: Harvard University Press, 2010.

62. Lynch, Marc, *Voices of the New Arab Public: Iraq, Al-Jazeera, and Middle East Politics Today*, New York: Columbia University Press, 2006.

63. Westlake, Michael, 'The economics of strategic crops', in *Syrian Agriculture at the Crossroads*, Fiorillo, Ciro and Jacques Vercueil (eds), Rome: FAO, 2000; Daoudy, Marwa, *Le Partage des Eaux Entre la Syrie, l'Irak et la Turquie: Négociation, Sécurité et Asymétrie des Pouvoirs, Moyen-Orient*, Paris: CNRS, 2005, p. 81; personal interviews.

64. See chapter 3 in this volume: Harrigan, Jane, 'An Economic Analysis of National Food Sovereignty Policies in the Middle East: The Case of Lebanon and Jordan'.

65. Schatkowski-Schilcher, 'Die Weizenwirtschaft des Nahen Ostens in der Zwischenkriegszeit'.

66. Rountree to Dulles, Washington, 27 December 1958, US Department of State, *Foreign Relations of the United States*, Near East Region, 1958–1960, vol. XII, p. 203.

67. Hobsbawm, Eric, *The Age of Extremes: A History of the World, 1914–1991*, 1st American ed., New York: Pantheon Books, 1994, p. 354 and following.

68. Morgan, Dan, *Merchants of Grain*, New York: Viking Press, 1979, p. 229 and p. 123 and following; see also Andræ, Gunilla and Björn Beckman, *The Wheat Trap: Bread and Underdevelopment in Nigeria*, Third World Books, London; Totowa, NJ: Zed Books in association with Scandinavian Institute of African Studies, 1985.

69. Burns, William J., *Economic Aid and American Policy toward Egypt, 1955–1981*, Albany, NY: State University of New York Press, 1985, p. 114.

70. Ibid., pp. 119, 150.

71. US Senate Committee on Foreign Relations, memorandum to all members by Carl Marcy, 'PL 480 and other aid to NES 1960–73', 20 November 1973, McGovern Papers, Series 4c, Box 623: Middle East 1973, Near East Subcommittee (2) Folder (FRC).

72. Burns, *Economic Aid and American Policy toward Egypt*, p. 159 and following; after Nasser toned down his rhetoric there was a brief reinstatement of a shorter six months' P.L. 480 agreement, but it was not prolonged beyond the summer of 1966.

73. Burns, *Economic Aid and American Policy toward Egypt*, p. 193; Wallerstein, Mitchel B., *Food for War–Food for Peace: United States Food Aid in a Global Context*, p. 46.

74. Oesterdiekhoff, Peter and Karl Wohlmuth, 'The "Breadbasket" is empty: the options of Sudanese development policy', *Canadian Journal of African Studies/Revue Canadienne des Études Africaines*, vol. 1, no. 17 (1983), pp. 35–67; O'Brien, Jay, 'Sowing the seeds of famine: the political economy of food deficits in Sudan', *Review of African Political Economy*, vol. 33, no. 12 (1985), pp. 23–32.

75. Personal interview with John Block, Secretary of US Department of Agriculture under Reagan, Washington DC, 14 January 2010; Lippman, Thomas W., 'U.S. Gives Saudis No-Embargo Pledge', *Washington Post*, 10 May 1983.

76. Chaudhry, Kiren Aziz, *The Price of Wealth: Economies and Institutions in the Middle East*, Cornell Studies in Political Economy, Ithaca: Cornell University Press, 1997; Jones, *Desert Kingdom*; Elhadj, Elie, 'Experiments in achieving water and food self-sufficiency in the Middle East: the consequences of contrasting endowments, ideologies, and investment policies in Saudi Arabia and Syria', PhD dissertation, History Department, SOAS, London, 2006.

77. de Schutter, Olivier, 'Food commodities speculation and food price crises: regulation to reduce the risks of price volatility', Briefing Note 2, Geneva: United Nations Special Rapporteur on the Right to Food, 2010. Additional demand only occurred as far as financial investors started to take long-term positions in derivatives markets.

78. Fischer, Günther, Eva Hizsnyik, Sylvia Prieler, Mahendra Shah and Harrij van Velthuizen, 'Biofuels and food security', Vienna: International Institute for Applied Systems Analysis (IIASA), commissioned by OPEC Fund for International Development (OFID), 2009.

79. See chapter 8 in this volume: Seyfert, Karin, Jad Chaaban and Hala Ghattas, 'Food Security and the Supermarket Transition in the Middle East—Two Case Studies'.

80. See chapter 11 in this volume: ElObeid, Tahra and Abdelmonem Hassan, 'The Nutrition Transition and Obesity in Qatar'.

81. Winders, Bill, 'The food crisis and the deregulation of agriculture', *The Brown Journal of World Affairs*, vol. 1, no. XVIII (2011), pp. 83–95.

82. Sen, Amartya, *Poverty and Famines: An Essay on Entitlement and Deprivation*, Oxford; New York: Clarendon Press, Oxford University Press, 1981.

83. Glover, Dominic, 'The corporate shaping of GM crops as a technology for the poor', *Journal of Peasant Studies*, vol. 1, no. 37 (2010), pp. 67–90; Weis, Anthony, *The Global Food Economy: The Battle for the Future of Farming*, New York: Zed Books, 2007.

84. Collier, Paul, 'The politics of hunger: how illusion and greed fan the food crisis', *Foreign Affairs*, vol. 6, no. 87 (2008), pp. 67–79.

85. Smil, Vaclav, *Enriching the Earth: Fritz Haber, Carl Bosch, and the Transformation of World Food Production*, Cambridge, MA: MIT Press, 2001.

86. See chapter 4 in this volume: Bush, Ray, 'Food Security in Egypt'.

87. Springborg, Robert, 'Egypt: attempting to improve "Quality of Administration" without

increasing "Public Accountability"', in *Governance in the Middle East and North Africa: A Handbook*, Kadhim, Abbas (ed.), New York: Routledge, 2012.

88. Breisinger, Clemens, Oliver Ecker and Perrihan Al-Riffai, 'Economics of the Arab awakening: from revolution to transformation and food security', *IFPRI Policy Brief*, Washington, DC: International Food Policy Research Institute (IFPRI), 2011.

89. Bush, Ray (ed.), 'Land reform and counter-revolution', in *Counter-Revolution in Egypt's Countryside: Land and Farmers in the Era of Economic Reform*, New York: Zed Books, 2002.

90. See chapter 7 in this volume: Tawk, Salwa Tohmé, Mounir Abi Said and Shadi Hamadeh, 'Urban Agriculture and Food Security in the Middle Eastern Context: a Case Study from Lebanon and Jordan'.

3. AN ECONOMIC ANALYSIS OF NATIONAL FOOD SOVEREIGNTY POLICIES IN THE MIDDLE EAST: THE CASE OF LEBANON AND JORDAN

1. Weinbaum, Marvin G., 'Food Security and Agricultural Development Policies in the Middle East', *Policy Studies Review*, vol. 4, no. 2 (1984), pp. 341–50.

2. Food and Agriculture Organization of the United Nations (FAO), *Near East Agriculture Towards 2050: Prospects and Challenges*, Rome: FAO, 2008; World Bank, *Improving Food Security in Arab Countries*, Washington, DC: World Bank, 2009.

3. International Food Policy Research Institute (IFPRI), *International Model for Policy Analysis of Agricultural Commodities and Trade (IMPACT)*, Washington, DC: IFPRI, 2008; FAO, 'Food Security', *Policy Brief No. 2* (June 2006); FAO, *Near East Agriculture Towards 2050*.

4. World Bank, *Improving Food Security in Arab Countries*; Fabiosa, Jacinto F., John C. Beghin, Fengxia Dong, Amani Elobeid, Simla Tokgoz, and Tun-Hsiang (Edward) Yu, 'Land Allocation Effects of the Global Ethanol Surge: Predictions from the International FAPRI Model', *Working Paper No. 08005*, Ames, IA: Iowa State University Department of Economics, 2008, available at: www.econ.iastate.edu/research/webpapers/paper_12877_08005.pdf (last accessed 18 Feb. 14); Gardener, Bruce L. and Daniel A. Sumner, 'US Agricultural Policy Reform in 2007 and Beyond', in *Agricultural Policy for the 2007 Farm Bill and Beyond*, Washington, DC: American Enterprise Institute, 2007; Cline, William R., *Global Warming and Agriculture: Impact Estimates by Country*, Washington, DC: Peterson Institute, 2007; FAO, *Near East Agriculture Towards 2050*; World Bank, *World Development Report 2008*, Washington, DC: World Bank, 2008; Oxfam, *Growing a Better Future*, 2011, www.oxfam.org/grow.

5. A fourth strategy which has recently gained importance is land acquisition in third party countries to secure food supplies directly without recourse to international food markets. See chapter 9 in this volume: Tétreault, Mary Ann, Deborah Wheeler, and Benjamin Shepherd, 'Win-Win Versus Lose-Lose: Investments in Foreign Agriculture as a Food Security Strategy of the Arab States of the Persian Gulf'; von Braun, Joachim and Ruth Meinzen-Dick, '"Land Grabbing" by Foreign Investors in Developing Countries: Risks and Opportunities', *IFPRI Policy Brief 13* (April 2009), available at: http://www.ifpri.org/sites/default/files/publications/bp013all.pdf (last accessed 18 Feb. 2014); Cotula, Lorenzo, Sonja Vermeulen, Rebeca Leonard, and James Keeley, *Land Grab or Development Opportunity? Agricultural Investment and International Land Deals in Africa*, London; Rome: IIED, FAO, IFAD, 2009, available at: http://www.ifad.org/pub/land/land_grab.pdf (last accessed 18 Feb. 14); World Bank, *Rising Global Interest in Farmland: Can it Yield Sustainable and Equitable Benefits?*, Washington, DC: World Bank, 2010a.

6. See Harrigan, Jane, 'Food Security Policies and Starter Pack: a Challenge for Donors?', *Starter Packs: A Strategy to Fight Hunger in Developing and Transition Countries: Lessons from the Malawi Experience, 1998–2003*, Levy, Sarah (ed.), Wallingford: CAB International, 2005, for an illustrated schema of both national and individual food security policy options.

7. Five exporters (Argentina, Australia, Canada, the EU, and the USA) supply 73 per cent of the world's traded cereal which makes access to imported cereal heavily dependent on events in these countries and Arab countries' relationships with them (FAO, *Near East Agriculture Towards 2050*).

8. FAO, *Near East Agriculture Towards 2050*; IFPRI, *Food Security and Economic Development in the Middle East and North Africa*, Washington, DC: IFPRI, 2010; World Bank, *Improving Food Security in Arab Countries*.

9. DeRosa, Dean A., *International Trade, Regional Integration and Food Security in the Middle East*, Washington, DC: IFPRI, 1995; Allan, J. A., 'Virtual Water: A Strategic Resource: Global Solutions to Regional Deficits', *Ground Water*, vol. 36, no. 4 (1998), pp. 545–6; Lofgren, Hans and Alan Richards, 'Food Security, Poverty, and Economic Policy in the Middle East and North Africa', *TMD Discussion Paper No. 111*, Washington, DC: IFPRI, 2003; World Bank, *World Development Report 2008*; World Bank, *Improving Food Security in Arab Countries*; IFPRI, *Food Security and Economic Development*; United Nations Economic and Social Commission for Western Asia (ESCWA), *Food Security and Conflict in the ESCWA Region*, New York: United Nations Economic and Social Commission for Western Asia, 2010.

10. World Bank, *Improving Food Security in Arab Countries*, p. 17.

11. The fieldwork and research for this chapter was made possible through a research grant provided by the Center for International and Regional Studies at Georgetown University School of Foreign Service in Qatar. Thanks are due for research assistance from Dr. Helen Tilley in London, Mr. Roland Riachi and Mr. Nicolas Haddad in Lebanon, and Professor Emad Al-Karablieh and Professor Samir Habbab in Jordan. The views expressed in this paper are those of the author alone.

12. In 2002, both countries figured in the world's top twenty per capita cereal importers.

13. Weinbaum, 'Food Security and Agricultural Development Policies'.

14. The extent of Jordan's renewable water resources in cubic meters per capita in 2005 was 163. For Lebanon, the comparable figure was 1,259 (FAO, *Near East Agriculture Towards 2050*).

15. Balassa, Bela, 'Intra-Industry Trade and the Integration of Developing Countries in the World Economy', in *On the Economics of Intra-Industry Trade*, Giersh, Herbert (ed.), Tübingen: J.C.B. Mohr, 1979; DeRosa, *International Trade*.

16. Monke, Eric A. and Scott R. Pearson, *The Policy Analysis Matrix for Agricultural Development*, Ithaca, NY: Cornell University Press, 1989; Ellis, Frank, *Agricultural Policies in Developing Countries*, Cambridge: Cambridge University Press, 1992; Harrigan, Jane, R. J. Loader, and Colin G. Thirtle, 'Agricultural Price Policy: Government and the Market', *Training Materials for Agricultural Planning No. 31*, Rome: FAO, 1992.

17. IFPRI, *Food Security and Economic Development*; Wilson, J. P. and H. J. Bruins, 'Food Security in the Middle East Since 1961', *Food Security Under Water Scarcity in the Middle East: Problems and Solutions*, Hamdy, Atef and Rossella Monti (eds), Bari: CIHEAM-IAMB, 2005; World Bank, *Improving Food Security in Arab Countries*.

18. The GHI is a multidimensional approach to measuring hunger combining three equally weighted indicators :1) the proportion of undernourished as a percentage of population, 2) the prevalence of underweight children younger than five, and 3) the mortality rate of

children younger than five. The index ranges from 0 to 100, with 100 being the worst score. See IFPRI, *Global Hunger Index, The Challenge of Hunger: Taming Price Spikes and Excessive Food Price Volatility*, Washington, DC: IFPRI, 2011.

19. World Bank, *Improving Food Security in Arab Countries*, uses import dependency and fiscal position. Wilson and Bruins, 'Food Security in the Middle East Since 1961', use food aid as a percentage of domestic consumption, imports as a percentage of domestic consumption and country income levels. IFPRI, *Food Security and Economic Development*, uses the ratio of total exports to food imports, food production per capita, Global Hunger Index, and GDP per capita. Breisinger, Clemens, Olivier Ecker, Perrihan Al-Riffai, and Bingxin Yu, *Beyond the Arab Awakening: Policies and Investments for Poverty Reduction and Food Security*, Washington, DC: IFPRI, 2012, uses the ratio of food imports to exports and net remittances and the percentage of stunted children.

20. World Bank, *Lebanon Agricultural Sector Note: Aligning Public Expenditures with Comparative Advantage*, Washington, DC: World Bank, 2010b, p. 1.

21. Central Intelligence Agency, 'World Factbook', available at: https://www.cia.gov/library/publications/the-world-factbook/ (last accessed 18 Feb. 2014).

22. UK Trade and Investment, 'Sector Report: Agriculture Lebanon', 2007, available at: www.tradeinvest.gov.uk; a large percentage of the country's arable land remains unutilised with the potential to be brought into production. Around 306,000 hectares of arable land are currently in use in Lebanon, but there are a further 269,000 hectares (an increase of 88 per cent) which could be cultivated—compared to Egypt with just 3 per cent more cultivatable land yet to be used. See Halabi, Sami, 'A Homegrown Shortfall: Lebanon's Over-Reliance on Food Imports Leaves it at the Mercy of Global Forces', 2011, available at: http://www.executive-magazine.com/economics-and-policy/3679/a-homegrown-shortfall (last accessed 18 Feb. 2014).

23. World Bank, *Lebanon Agricultural Sector Note*, p. 2.

24. The budget for the Ministry of Agriculture in 2008 was only 0.3 per cent of the Lebanese budget, but this represents only 14 per cent of the total expenditure allocated to the sector, with 49 per cent falling under the Ministry of Economy and Trade for the wheat subsidy, 27 per cent falling under the Ministry of Finance for tobacco subsidies, and 10 per cent falling under IDAL for the export subsidies. See Riachi, Roland and Jad Chaaban, 'The Agricultural Sector in Lebanon: Major Issues and Challenges', unpublished paper, American University of Beirut, 2011, p. 14.

25. Ibid.

26. Halabi, 'A Homegrown Shortfall', p. 2.

27. FAOSTAT, Trade STAT.

28. FAOSTAT, Food Balance Sheets.

29. These figures are from the Lebanese General Directorate of Cereals and Sugar Beet (GDCS) in the Ministry of Economy and Trade. The FAO Food Balance Sheet puts the figure at 400,000 MT plus or minus 15 per cent. Food consumption excludes wheat for seed, animal feed, exports, other utilisation, and losses in storage and transportation.

30. Note, these figures do not tally with FAO production data which put annual wheat production significantly above the GDCS purchases (see Figure 3.4).

31. Since 2007–8 there have been some years when the government support price was below or close to the international price and, as a result, farmers sold little of their crop to the government.

32. The issue of changing food consumption patterns in the MENA region, including the shift towards more refined cereals, has important nutritional implications. The links between nutrition and food security are discussed in chapter 11 in this volume: ElObeid,

Tahra and Abdelmonem Hassan, 'The Nutrition Transition and Food Security in Qatar', The food supply chains in Lebanon and Qatar are discussed in chapter 8 in this volume: Seyfert, Karin, Jad Chaaban and Hala Ghattas, 'Food Security and the Supermarket Transition in the Middle East: Two Case Studies'.

33. Government of Jordan and United Nations, *Food and Nutrition Security in Jordan Towards Poverty Alleviation 2010–2013*, Amman, 2010.
34. Al-Karablieh, Emad K., Amer S. Jabarin and M. Tabieh, 'Jordanian Horticultural Export Competitiveness from Water Perspective', *Journal of Agricultural Science and Technology* B1 (2011), pp. 964–74, Table 1.
35. See Appendix 1 Figure A.1.1, 1 dunum = approximately 0.1 hectare.
36. Government of Jordan and United Nations, *Food and Nutrition Security in Jordan*, p. 9.
37. Headley, Derek and Shenggen Fan, *Reflections on the Global Food Crisis*, Washington, DC: IFPRI, 2010.
38. IMF, *Food and Fuel Prices–Recent Developments, Macroeconomic Impact, and Policy Responses*, Washington, DC, 2008; Dessus, Sébastien, Santiago Herrera and Rafael De Hoyos, 'The Impact of Food Inflation on Urban Poverty and its Monetary Cost: Some Back-of-the-Envelope Calculations' *Agricultural Economics*, vol. 39 (2008), pp. 417–29.
39. Banque du Liban, www.bdl.gov.lb.
40. IMF, *Food and Fuel Prices–Recent Developments, Macroeconomic Impact, and Policy Responses*, Washington, DC, 2008.
41. Dessus, Herrera and de Hoyos, 'The Impact of Food Inflation on Urban Poverty and its Monetary Cost', pp. 419–20.
42. Riachi and Chaaban, 'The Agricultural Sector in Lebanon', p. 14.
43. Breisinger, Clemens, Olivier Ecker, and Perrihan Al-Riffai, 'Economics of Arab Awakening: From Revolutions to Transformation and Food Security', *IFPRI Policy Brief 18*, Washington, DC: IFPRI, May 2011, Table 1.
44. Ibid.
45. Personal interviews, July 2011.
46. Government of Lebanon, *Policy for Agriculture Sector Development*, Amman, 2009.
47. Personal interview, July 2011.
48. Personal interview, July 2011.
49. Personal interview, July 2011.
50. These differing statements from the Ministry of Agriculture and the Ministry of Trade and Industry regarding intended levels of wheat production are indicative of the institutional fragmentation within the Lebanese government. This is an issue which needs to be urgently addressed as a prerequisite for the country to be able to develop a comprehensive multi-agency food security strategy.
51. World Bank, *Lebanon Agricultural Sector Note*.
52. Ibid., pp. 3–4.
53. Ibid., p. 4.
54. United States Department of Agriculture, available at: http://www.ers.usda.gov/data-products/food expenditures.aspx#26654 (last accessed 18 Feb. 2014).
55. ESCWA, *Food Security and Conflict*.
56. Dessus, Herrera and de Hoyos, 'The Impact of Food Inflation on Urban Poverty and its Monetary Cost'.
57. Breisinger et al., 'Economics of Arab Awakening', Table 1.
58. Between 2008 and 2011, the size of the grain reserve was increased from 6 months of grain supplies to 9 months with the World Bank involved in a project under the Ministry

of Trade and Industry using the National Silos Company. However, the targeted expansion under the second and third phase has not yet been achieved due to lack of funding.

59. In 2008, the WFP also carried out the first ever food security survey at the household level by assessing food insecurity in poverty pockets (defined as areas where poverty rates exceed 25 per cent). They found that food insecurity in the pockets ranged from 8–35 per cent. See World Food Programme and the Jordanian Alliance Against Hunger, *Jordan Food Security Survey in the Poverty Pockets*, Amman, 2008; the WFP plans to continue monitoring food security in Jordan through bi-annual household income and expenditure surveys.

60. For example, the 2007 mid-term review of the National Strategy for Agricultural Development announced as a priority the reclamation of field crop lands in northern Jordan.

61. Government of Jordan and UN, *Food and Nutrition Security in Jordan*.

62. Personal interview, Amman, December 2011.

63. Government of Jordan and United Nations, *Food and Nutrition Security in Jordan*, Figure 1.

64. Personal interviews, Amman, December 2011.

65. For example, the UNICEF flour fortification and breast feeding programme and the WFP school feeding programme.

66. Frequent cabinet reshuffles meant that there were three different minsters for agriculture in 2011. This hampered the functioning of the Committee which only met twice in 2011.

67. Balassa, 'Intra-Industry Trade'; DeRosa, *International Trade*.

68. In 2008, the Ministry of Finance spent $51.1 million in supporting tobacco farmers. See World Bank, *Decoupling Income Support from Tobacco Production in Lebanon: Challenges and Opportunities*, Washington, DC: World Bank, 2009.

69. Ramirez-Vallejo, Jorge and Peter Rogers, 'Failure of the Virtual Water Argument', *Global Change: Impact on Water and Food Security*, Ringler, Claudia, Asit K. Biswas, and Sarah Cline (eds), Berlin: Springer, 2010.

70. Monke, *The Policy Analysis Matrix*; Ellis, *Agricultural Policies*; Harrigan et al., *Agricultural Price Policy*.

71. For example, if the export F.o.B. price is the highest price a producer can get for an extra marginal unit of output, then this price measures the opportunity cost of resources that could be used to produce another good. Likewise, if the import C.I.F. price is the lowest consumer price for another unit of a good, then this price will measure the scarcity value of the good.

72. ESCWA, *Assessment of Past Experiences in Using the Policy Analysis Matrix (PAM) Approach in Selected ESCWA Member Countries*, New York: United Nations, 2001.

73. Atif Abdallah Kubursi, 'Lebanon's Agricultural Potential: A Policy Analysis Matrix Approach', 2000, available at: http://socserv.mcmaster.ca/kubursi/ebooks/policy.htm (last accessed 18 Feb. 2014).

74. Ibid., p. 42.

75. FAO, 'Organic Agriculture', 2009, available at: http://www.foa.org/organicag/oa-faq/oa-faq5/en/ (last accessed 18 Feb. 2014); World Bank, *Lebanon Agricultural Sector Note*.

76. Potatoes, tomatoes, and wheat are also interesting crops to analyse in light of their dominance in terms of the share of arable land allocated to their production and their importance in terms of their output. In 2007, approximately 25 per cent of Lebanon's cultivated surface was devoted to cereals, 52,800 hectares of which was under wheat, whilst 17.5 per cent was under vegetables, of which 20,100 hectares were devoted to potatoes. See

Riachi and Chaaban, 'The Agricultural Sector in Lebanon'. In terms of value of production, tomatoes are the second most important crop and potatoes are the fourth most important crop whilst in quantity terms, potatoes are the number one crop, tomatoes the number two crop, with wheat number five. In terms of quantities exported, potatoes are the number two crop (FAOSTAT).

77. Lack of data makes this a difficult task. The data from the Agricultural Census carried out in 2010 is not yet available and the most recent data is ESCWA, *National Farm Data Handbook for Lebanon*, New York: United Nations, 1999.

78. Riachi and Chaaban, 'The Agricultural Sector in Lebanon', p. 7.

79. Group of 20, Ministerial Declaration, *Action Plan on Food Price Volatility and Agriculture*, Meeting of G20 Agricultural Ministers, Paris, 22 and 23 June 2011.

80. ESCWA, *Guide to the Application of the Sustainable Livelihoods Approach in the ESCWA Region*, United Nations, New York, 2011.

81. ESCWA, *Food Security and Conflict*; World Bank, *Improving Food Security*; African Development Bank 2012, 'The Political Economy of Food Sovereignty in North Africa', Economic Brief, Jane Harrigan, Tunis: African Development Bank, 2012.

82. Alami, Randa and Massoud Karshenas, 'Deficient Social Policies have helped Spark the Arab Spring', *Development Viewpoint No. 70*, London: Centre for Development Policy and Research, SOAS, 2012.

83. Harrigan, Jane, 'The Political Economy of Aid Flows to North Africa', *WIDER Working Paper*, no. 2011/72, Helsinki: UNU-WIDER, 2011.

4. FOOD SECURITY IN EGYPT

1. Thanks to Hannah Cross for research assistance, Habib Ayeb, Ali Kadri and contributors to this volume for comments on an early draft. I remain responsible for the contents of this chapter.

2. Food and Agriculture Organization of the United Nations (FAO), 'Country profile: food security indicators, country: Egypt', available at: http://www.fao.org/fileadmin/templates/ess/documents/food_security_statistics/country_profiles/eng/Egypt_E.pdf (last accessed 18 Feb. 2014).

3. World Food Programme (WFP), *Secondary Data Analysis of the Food Security Situation in Egypt*, Regional Bureau for the Middle East, Central Asia and Eastern Europe—ODC Egypt Country Office, May 2011, p. 5.

4. *Inter alia*, 'Symposium: The 2007–8 World Food Crisis', *Journal of Agrarian Change*, vol. 10, no. 1 (January 2010), pp. 69–129.

5. World Food Programme, *Secondary Data*, p. 5 and p. 15.

6. Breisinger, Clemens, Olivier Ecker, Perrihan Al-Riffai and Bingxin Yu, 'Beyond the Arab awakening: policies and investments for poverty reduction and food security', *Food Policy Report*, Washington, DC: International Food Policy Research Institute, February, 2012, p. 11.

7. Personal communication with Nader Fergany, previous lead convenor Arab Human Development Report, Cairo, March 2011.

8. World Bank, *Egypt's Food Subsidies: Benefit Incidence and Leakages*, Washington: Arab Republic of Egypt and the World Bank, 16 September 2010. *Baladi* bread or *Aish baladi* is the staple Egyptian local bread.

9. Ibid., p. i.

10. But the status of the budget was in debate following the dissolution of the Egyptian parliament by the SCAF and election of Mohamed Morsi that led in August 2012 to the

'retirement' of two leading members of the SCAF and the apparent attempt to reduce the influence of the military. An additional factor in the debate regarding the continued levels of subsidy was the projected negotiation for an IMF loan mid-2012. See *inter alia*, 'Egypt's 2012/13 budget a "Conspiracy" against next president: FJP official', *Ahram Online*, 21 June 2012, available at: http://english.ahram.org.eg/News/45797.aspx (last accessed 18 Feb. 2014); 'IMF's Lagarde to visit Egypt on 22 August, may raise loan to \$4.8 bn', *Ahram Online*, 15 Aug. 2012, available at: http://english.ahram.org.eg/NewsContent/3/12/50497/Business/Economy/IMFs-Lagarde-to-visit-Egypt-on--August,-May–raise-.aspx (last accessed 18 Feb. 2014).

11. 'Bread subsidies to hit record high in 2012/13: exclusive figures', *Al Ahram Online*, 6 June 2012.

12. World Bank, *Egypt's Food Subsidies*, p. i; see also Adams Jr., Richard H., 'Self-targeted subsidies: the distributional impact of the Egyptian food subsidy system', *Policy Research Working Paper No. 2322*, The World Bank, April 2000.

13. Ibid.

14. WFP, *Secondary Data*, p. 14.

15. Ibid.; Breisinger et al., 'Beyond the Arab awakening'.

16. WFP, *Secondary Data*, p. 24.

17. Ibid., p. 6.

18. Ibid., pp. 17–18.

19. WFP, *Secondary Data*, p. 5.

20. WFP, *Secondary Data*, p. 6.

21. *Inter alia*, see Raikes, Philip, *Modernising Hunger*, Portsmouth, UK: Heinemann, 1991 and Oya, Carlos, 'Agro-pessimism, capitalism, and agrarian change: trajectories and contradictions in sub-Saharan Africa', in *The Political Economy of Africa*, Padayachee, Vishnu (ed.), London: Routledge, 2010.

22. Bush, Ray, 'Poverty and neo-liberal bias in the Middle East and North Africa', *Development and Change*, vol. 35, no. 4 (2004), pp. 673–95.

23. This is an important issue reported by Saker el Nour in 'National geographical targeting of poverty in upper Egypt', in *Marginality and Exclusion in Egypt and the Middle East*, Bush, Ray and Habib Ayeb (eds.), London: Zed Books, 2012.

24. Breisinger et al., 'Beyond the Arab awakening', p. viii.

25. Ibid.

26. Ibid., p. 2.

27. Ibid., p. 3.

28. El-Ghonemy, M. Riad, 'Recent changes in agrarian reform and rural development strategies in the near East', *Land Reform*, vol. 1, no. 2 (1999), pp. 9–20.

29. Breisinger et al., 'Beyond the Arab awakening', p. 11.

30. Bresinger, Clemens, Olivier Ecker and Perrihan Al-Riffai, 'Economics of the Arab awakening: from revolution to transformation and food security', *IFPRI Policy Brief No. 18*, May 2011, p. 3.

31. *Inter alia* see 'Q&A: Economist Gouda Abdel Khaleq on crony capitalism in Egypt', *Masry al-Youm*, 22 October 2010.

32. Ministry of Agriculture and Land Reclamation, Government of Egypt and USAID, 'Agricultural policy reform programme', *RDI Policy Brief*, Cairo, 1999; USAID and Government of Egypt, 'The Egyptian agricultural policy reforms: an overview', paper presented at the Agricultural Policy Conference; 'Taking stock, eight years of Egyptian agricultural policy reforms', Cairo, 26–28 March, 1995; see also for a detailed critique that this section draws on Bush, Ray, *Economic Crisis and the Politics of Reform in Egypt*,

Boulder, CO: Westview, 1999; Bush, Ray, 'Mubarak's legacy for Egypt's rural poor: returning land to the landlords', in *Land, Poverty and Livelihoods in an Era of Globalization*, Haroon Akram-Lodhi, A., Saturnino M. Borras Jr. and Cristóbal Kay (eds), Oxford: Routledge, 2007.

33. Yapp, M. E., *The New East Since the First World War*, London: Longman, 1997.

34. El-Ghonemy, 'Recent changes in agrarian reform'.

35. See chapter 2 in this volume: Woertz, Eckart, 'Historic Food Regimes and the Middle East'.

36. See chapter 3 in this volume: Harrigan, Jane, 'An Economic Analysis of National Food Sovereignty Policies in the Middle East: The Case of Lebanon and Jordan'.

37. Faris, Mohamed A. and Mahmood Hasan Khan (eds), *Sustainable Agriculture in Egypt*, Boulder, CO: Lynne Reinner, 1993; Fletcher, Lehman B. (ed.), *Egypt's Agriculture in a Reform Era*, Ames, IA: Iowa State University Press, 1996.

38. See Ministry of Agriculture and Land Reclamation and USAID, 'Agriculture: Vision for 2003', *RDI Policy Brief*, Cairo: Agricultural Policy Reform Program, 1999.

39. Mitchell, Timothy, 'The market's place', in *Directions of Change in Rural Egypt*, Hopkins, Nicholas S. and Kirsten Westergaard (eds), Cairo: The American University Press, 1998.

40. Fergany, Nader, 'Poverty and unemployment in rural Egypt', in *Counter Revolution in Egypt's Countryside: Land and Farmers in the Era of Economic Reform*, Bush, Ray (ed.), London: Zed Books, 2002.

41. Field notes, April 2010 made during interviews with villagers in the Delta, Egypt; see also Bush, Ray, 'Coalitions for dispossession and networks of resistance? Land, politics and agrarian reform in Egypt', *British Journal of Middle Eastern Studies*, vol. 38, no. 3 (December 2011), pp. 391–405.

42. See chapter 9 in this volume: Tétreault, Mary Ann, Deborah Wheeler and Benjamin Shepherd, 'Win-Win versus Lose-Lose: Investments in Foreign Agriculture as a Food Security Strategy of the Arab States of the Persian Gulf', for a description of violence in relation to land rights.

43. Bush, 'Coalitions', p. 400.

44. Bush, Ray, 'Market violence in Egypt's countryside', *Peace Review: A Journal of Social Justice*, vol. 19, no. 1 (2007), pp. 15–21.

45. Ayeb, Habib, 'The marginalization of the small peasantry: Egypt and Tunisia', in *Marginality and Exclusion in Egypt*, Bush, Ray and Habib Ayeb (eds), London: Zed Books, 2012.

46. Ibid.

47. This term of social Darwinism is taken from Carlos Oya's suggestive analysis of 'Agro-pessimism, capitalism and agrarian change', p. 99. Several of his key arguments can be applied to Egypt.

48. *Inter alia*, Lewis, Martin W., 'The Toshka scheme: Egypt's salvation or Mubarak's folly?', 17 February 2011, available at: http://geocurrents.info/economic-geography/the-toshka-scheme-egypts-salvation-or-mubaraks-folly (last accessed 18 Feb. 2014).

49. Arab Republic of Egypt Ministry of Agriculture and Land Reclamation, *Sustainable Agricultural Development Strategy Towards 2030*, Cairo: Agricultural Research & Development Council October, 2009.

50. I say this despite the comment made by the head of economic affairs in the MALR who noted after the 25 January uprising: 'We should make it up to the peasants.' See El-Batran, Mohsen quoted in 'From liberalisation to self sufficiency: Egypt charts a new agricultural policy', *Ahram Online*, 28 April 2011.

51. Arab Republic of Egypt, *Sustainable Agricultural Development*, p. 20.

52. Ibid., pp. 24–5.
53. Ibid., p. 25.
54. Ibid.
55. Field notes, November 2010, interviews with farmers in Egypt's Delta.
56. Field notes, May 2010, interviews with farmers in middle Egypt.
57. Abdel Aal, Mohamed H., 'Agrarian reform and tenancy in Upper Egypt', in *Counter-Revolution in Egypt's Countryside: Land and Farmers in the Era of Economic Reform*, Bush, Ray (ed.), London: Zed Books, 2002.
58. For a provocative theoretical debate about what constitutes agrarian transition see Bernstein, Henry, *Class Dynamics of Agrarian Change*, London: Kumarian Press, 2010.
59. Author interview with founding member of the Peasant Solidarity Committee, Al Qalyubiya Governorate, 11 May 2010.
60. The systematic and systemic use of torture in Egypt is well-documented, see *inter alia*, Human Rights Watch, '"Work on him until he confesses" Egypt: impunity for torture fuels Days of Rage', 31 January 2011, available at: http://www.hrw.org/news/2011/01/31/egypt-impunity-torture-fuels-days-rage (last accessed 18 Feb. 2014).
61. *Inter alia*, Charbel, Jano, 'Egypt's farmers ready for independent organizing', *Al Masry Alyoum*, 23 June 2011, available at: http://www.egyptindependent.com/news/egypts-farmers-ready-independent-organizing (last accessed 18 Feb. 2014).

5. PROSPECTS FOR FOOD SELF-SUFFICIENCY IN IRAN IN 2025

1. In almost all annual public budgets and in all five economic development plans implemented after the Islamic revolution in 1979, 'self-sufficiency' is one of the main policy objectives that is directly or indirectly referred to.
2. See, for example, Timmer, Peter, 'Agriculture and economic development', in *Handbook of Agricultural Economics*, vol. 2A, Gardner, Bruce and Gordon Rausser (eds), Amsterdam: Elsevier, 2002, pp. 1487–546; Thirtle, Colin G., Lin Lin and Jennifer Piesse, 'The impact of research-led agriculture productivity growth on poverty reduction in Africa, Asia, and Latin America', *World Development*, vol. 31, no. 12 (2003), pp. 1959–75; and Christiaensen, Luc J. and Lionel Demery, *Down to earth: agriculture and poverty reduction in Africa, directions in development*, Washington, DC: The World Bank, 2007.
3. United Nations, *The Millennium Development Goals Report 2010*, New York: United Nations, 2010.
4. Food and Agriculture Organization of the United Nations (FAO), Office of Director-General, 'The Strategic Framework for FAO 2000–2015', FAO Document Repository, 1999, available at: http://www.fao.org/docrep/x3550e/x3550e00.htm (last accessed 18 Feb. 2014).
5. See for example, FAO, 'Statistical Year Book 2012', FAO Statistical Division.
6. 'Iran Country Report', Global Finance, available at: http://www.gfmag.com/gdp-data-country-reports/253-iran-gdp-country-report.html#axzz2uJf83t00 (last accessed 18 Feb. 2014).
7. Food and Agriculture Organization of the United Nations (FAO) Statistics Division (FAOSTAT): http://faostat3.fao.org/home/index.html
8. This is a target year in *Iran's 20-Year Economic Perspective*, documented in March 2005 by the Iranian government, in which the government outlined a road map for the country's economic, political, social and cultural developments for the next two decades.
9. See the equations in Appendix 2.

10. See more details in Appendix 2.
11. To see the complete Iranian Policy Simulation Model, please refer to: Mohtashami, T., 'Forecasting the Gap Between Demand and Supply in Major Agricultural Products: A Guideline for Investment in Agricultural Sector', PhD thesis, Department of Agricultural Economics, Faculty of Economic and Agricultural Development, University of Tehran, Iran.
12. See chapter 3 in this volume: Harrigan, Jane, 'An Economic Analysis of National Food Sovereignty Policies in the Middle East: The Case of Lebanon and Jordan', for a detailed discussion of trade-based food security strategies.
13. These projects include the construction of dams in different provinces of Iran which is predicted to increase irrigation water available to the agricultural sector from 83,787 to 95,290 million cubic metres by 2025.
14. Díaz-Bonilla, Eugenio, Marcelle Thomas and Sherman Robinson, 'Trade liberalization, WTO, and food security', *Trade and Macroeconomics Division Discussion Paper No. 82*, Washington, DC: International Food Policy Research Institute, 2002; Yu, Bingxin, Liangzhi You and Shenggen Fan, 'Toward a typology of food security in developing Countries', *IFPRI Discussion Paper* No. 945, Washington, DC: International Food Policy Research Institute, 2010.
15. See for example: FAO, 'Statistical Year Book 2012', FAO Statistical Division.

6. NEITHER SECURITY NOR SOVEREIGNTY: THE POLITICAL ECONOMY OF FOOD IN YEMEN

1. The 'Friends of Yemen' are a group of donors that includes the G-8, the Gulf Cooperation Council states, European Union members, multilateral donor organisations and other key partners.
2. Clements, Ashley Jonathan, 'Yemen: fragile lives in hungry times', *Oxfam Briefing Paper* No. 152, September 2011.
3. See Integrated Regional Information Networks (IRIN), 'Yemen malnutrition data should "shock"', 27 December 2011, available at: http://www.irinnews.org/Report/94533/YEMEN-Malnutrition-data-should-shock (last accessed 18 Feb. 2014), where a third of children are reported to suffer global acute malnutrition. In *The Comprehensive Food Security Survey (CFSS): Republic of Yemen*, March 2010, p. 80, the World Food Programme cites UNICEF data: 'Yemen's overall malnutrition status shows little improvement. On the contrary: more than half of the children in the country are chronically malnourished (55.7 per cent) or too short for their age, and 13.2 per cent are wasted and too thin for their height.'
4. Islamic Republic of Afghanistan, Ministry of Economy, 'Poverty and food security in Afghanistan', The World Bank, Economic Policy and Poverty Section: South Asia Region, February 2012, analysis based on national risk and vulnerability assessment of 2007–8.
5. World Food Programme (WFP), *The state of food security and nutrition in Yemen: Comprehensive Food Security Survey*, 2012, p. 18. See also Figures 1 and 2 of the International Food Policy Research Institute (IFPRI) and Ministry of Planning and International Cooperation, Yemen, *Yemen National Food Security Strategy: 1 Overview and Action Plan*, 2011, pp. 2–3. This is a policy paper for estimates of food insecurity in 2009, showing large areas of the country with 40 per cent severe food insecurity and 60 per cent or more stunting in children.
6. Yemen Ministry of Planning and International Cooperation (MOPIC), *Yemen's Third Socio-*

Economic Development Plan for Poverty Reduction (2006–2010), 2006, p. 42, states: 'Agriculture is the main direct or indirect source of income for 73.5% of the population in Yemen, making up 20.5% of the GDP, employing 31% of the labour force and accounting for 56.6% of non-oil exports during the period of the SFYP (2000–2005)'.

7. WFP, *The state of food security*, p. 57, states: 'Nationally, the average CSI (coping strategy index) in 2009 was 4.1. By 2011, it had risen to 8.4. That means that the frequency or severity of coping strategies adopted because of a lack of food had more than doubled'.

8. For a detailed discussion of food system transitions, see chapter 2 in this volume: Woertz, Eckart, 'Historic Food Regimes and the Middle East'.

9. See Ziegler, Jean, *Destruction Massive: Géopolitique de la Faim*, Paris: Editions du Seuil, 2011.

10. WFP, 'The state of food security', p. 30, states: 'Even farmers buy 73 per cent of their food—just over 10 per cent comes from their own production,' p. 52, and '46% of agricultural wage labourers have debt for food; 45% of non-agricultural wage labour do'.

11. Chaudhry, Kiren Aziz, *The Price of Wealth: Economies and Institutions in the Middle East*, Ithaca, NY: Cornell University Press, 1997, p. 127 and pp. 135–6; Al-Hamdi was assassinated in October 1977. His immediate successor al-Ghashmi, head of the army, was in turn assassinated eight months later, with Ali Abdullah Saleh, who was rumoured to have had a role in al-Hamdi's elimination, coming to power and continuing as president until 2011.

12. Ibid., pp. 193–9, p. 207, p. 215, pp. 220–5, and Mundy, Martha, *Domestic Government: Kinship, Community and Polity in North Yemen*, London: I.B. Tauris, 1995, pp. 8–10.

13. On NGOs see: Shalan, Thaira, 'Les organisations non gouvernementales et la société civile au Yémen' ('NGOs and civil society in Yemen'), in *Le Yémen contemporain* (*Contemporary Yemen*), Leveau, Remy, Franck Mermier and Udo Steinback (eds), Paris: Karthala, 1999, pp. 285–300; Carapico, Sheila, *Civil Society in Yemen: A Political Economy of Activism in Modern Arabia*, Cambridge: Cambridge University Press, 1998.

14. 'Doubly subsidised' means both the subsidies to agricultural production in a number of major producing countries (USA and the EU) and the subsidisation of prices of a number of basic foodstuffs from 1970–2000 in north Yemen (and then united Yemen). On the latter the World Bank, *Republic of Yemen: Country Social Analysis*, 2006, p. 10, states that: 'Growing imports of basic commodities such as wheat, sold to consumers at subsidized prices until 1999–2000, meant that local cereal farmers were no longer competitive'.

15. For a review of the work on the damage to terraces see Pelat, Frédéric, 'Economic & social impact of terraces & outcomes of terrace rehabilitation in Yemen: taking stock of existing literature on terraces & terraces' externalities in Yemen', study report (prepared for the World Bank), December 2009.

16. On Yemeni unity see al-Saqqaf, Abou Bakr, 'The Yemeni unity: crisis in integration', in *Le Yémen contemporain*, Leveau, Remy, Franck Mermier and Udo Steinback (eds), Paris: Karthala, 1999, pp. 141–60.

17. In *The Price of Wealth*, p. 302, Chaudhry writes: 'For the third time in Yemen's modern history, the transnational movement of an entire class rearranged the social and political structure of the country. The labor force returned, moreover, as primary property rights were being reallocated in the former socialist south in a context of renewed labor organization among public-sector workers in Aden. The entry of a million unemployed workers into the unified economy foreclosed the possibility of success for the southern workers'.

18. Dresch, Paul, *A History of Modern Yemen*, Cambridge: Cambridge University Press, 2000, p. 159 and p. 162.

19. Abd al-Wahid al-Maytami, Mohammed, 'La réforme économique au Yémen: résultats et implications' ('Economic reform in Yemen: results and implications'), in *Le Yémen Contemporain*, Leveau, Mermier and Steinback (eds), states that poverty had reached 33 per cent in 1996 and that the statistics in 1998 indicated the proportion had increased to 50–60 per cent of the population, 76.5 per cent of which was in the countryside.

20. 'Al-thawrah al-yamaniya wa-mustaqbal al-bilad' ('The Yemeni revolution and the future of the country'), *Al Akhbar*, 4 April 2011, available at: http://www.al-akhbar.com/node/8261 (last accessed 18 Feb. 2014).

21. Ibid., (print edition), p. 23.

22. Hill, Ginny, 'Riyadh will decide the fate of Ali Abdullah Saleh—and of Yemen', *The Guardian*, 23 March 2011, available at: http://www.guardian.co.uk/commentisfree/2011/mar/23/ali-abdullah-saleh-riyadh-house-of-saud (last accessed 18 Feb. 2104).

23. World Bank, *Republic of Yemen*, p. 36, and Phillips, Sarah, *Yemen's Democracy Experiment in Regional Perspective: Patronage and Pluralized Authoritarianism*, New York: Palgrave Macmillan, 2008, pp. 104–6.

24. Salisbury, Peter, *Yemen's economy: Oil, Imports and Elites*, Chatham House, Middle East and North Africa Programme Paper MENA PP 2011/02, October 2011, p. 17.

25. 'Yemen crude oil production by year', Index Mundi, available at: http://www.indexmundi.com/energy.aspx?country=ye&product=oil&graph=production (last accessed 18 Feb. 2014).

26. The beginnings of this process in the 1990s are described by Chaudhry, *The Price of Wealth*, p. 292.

27. This is presumably YECO, the present name for the former Military Economic Corporation (MECO), see Dresch, *A History*, p. 208. See also Phillips, Sarah, 'Yemen: developmental dysfunction and division in a crisis state', *Developmental Leadership Program Research Paper 14*, 2011, p. 27, where she writes: 'The climate for foreign investment is further undermined by President Saleh's insistence that the shadowy and unaudited Yemen Economic Corporation…be the local partner for prospective investors'. In fn. 71, Phillips writes that: 'YECO was established in the early 1970s and was initially owned by all military servicemen who contributed to its start-up capital, but was usurped and used as a commercial arm of the regime in the mid-1980s. It has business operations in a wide array of industries including basic commodities and foodstuffs, non-lethal military supplies, furniture, textiles, pharmaceuticals, agribusiness, (unlicensed) commercial fishing, and real estate. Many Yemeni observers view the corporation as a vast criminal enterprise.' She also notes that: 'President Saleh used to be the head of YECO', but that it is now run by Ali al-Kohlani who 'is the brother of Ahmed al-Kohali (former governor of Aden and now the Minister of Parliamentary Affairs), who is President Saleh's father-in-law'.

28. Longley Alley, April, 'Shifting light in the Qamariyya: the reinvention of patronage networks in contemporary Yemen', PhD. Dissertation, Department of Government, Georgetown University, 2008.

29. See Joubari, Bilqis Mohammed, 'Les politiques du planning familial au Yémen' ('Family planning policies in Yemen'), in *Le Yémen contemporain*, Leveau, Mermier and Steinback (eds), pp. 301–18.

30. 'Yemeni economist proposes strategy to tackle unemployment', *Yemen Observer*, 12 February 2012. While the economist cited, Dr Mohammed Ali Jubran of Sanaa University, calls for a series of massive projects to counter unemployment in rural, indus-

trial and infrastructural sectors, the first step proposed is persuading the GCC to import Yemeni labour about which Jubran is quoted as saying: 'Opening the hearts of the GCC population towards the Yemeni people before their pockets and convincing them that the Yemeni people are great and hardworking and can live with minimum requirements once they have to.'

31. Lackner, Helen, *P.D.R. Yemen: Outpost of Socialist Development in Arabia*, London: Ithaca Press, 1985, pp. 171–88.

32. Brehony, Noel, *Yemen Divided: The Story of a Failed State in South Arabia*, London: I.B. Tauris, 2011, p. 71; *Qat* (Catha edulis) is a shrub, the leaves of which when chewed have amphetamine with mild hallucinogenic qualities; it is not a narcotic.

33. For a detailed discussion of land dispossessions, see chapter 9 in this volume: Tétreault, Ann, Mary, Deborah Wheeler and Benjamin Shepherd, 'Win-Win versus Lose-Lose: Investments in Foreign Agriculture as a Food Security Strategy of the Arab States of the Persian Gulf'.

34. World Bank, *Republic of Yemen*, p. 15: 'There is a trend towards inequitable distribution of land in Yemen, with ownership increasingly concentrated in the hands of a few influential families. …. There is a trend towards increasing private appropriation of communal land.' And p. 16: 'In the southern governorates, in contrast, the holding of large agricultural land owners are expanding at the expense of small farmers. After unification…rampant land grabbing occurred, often by influential and powerful figures'. It should be noted that there was never a cadastre or comprehensive land registration in the north—calls to introduce such in the unified Republic of the early 1990s were silenced by the 1994 war.

35. Yemen Ministry of Planning and International Cooperation, *Yemen's Third Socio-Economic Development Plan*, p. 64, notes: 'Total annual renewable water resources are estimated at 2.5 billion cubic metres (1.500 billion m³ of groundwater and 1 billion m³ surface water). However, total annual water consumption stands at 3.4 billion m³, reflecting a groundwater depletion rate of 0.9 billion m³ (138 %) a year. On average, water tables in most aquifers drop by 6 metres a year, and are thus expected to run dry within 15–50 years'. Less pessimistic is the recent paper by van Steenbergen, Frank, Omar Bamaga and Adel al-Washali, 'Groundwater security in Yemen: who is accountable to whom?', *Law, Environment and Development Journal*, vol. 7, no. 2 (2011), p. 164, available at: http://www.lead-journal.org/content/11164.pdf (last accessed 18 Feb. 2014), which documents some successes at the local level in regulating extraction from the aquifer by pumps and restrictions on the sinking of pumps.

36. Yemen Ministry of Planning and International Cooperation, *Millennium Development Goals needs assessment: Yemen Country Report*, 2005.

37. Ibid.

38. UNDP Regional Bureau for Arab States, *Development challenges for the Arab region: food security and agriculture*, vol. 2 (2009), Cairo, Egypt.

39. This is the case for the UNDP Regional Bureau for Arab States, 'Development challenges'. But see World Food Programme, 'Market Study Yemen 2010', 2010, p. 16, where production statistics are given: 'Sorghum is the most important cereal in terms of production quantities, followed by wheat, millet, maize and finally barley'.

40. Livestock numbers do not appear to have dropped; hence there must be a greater reliance on imported feeds if the figures in Alabsi, Ali Abdulmalek, *Country pasture/forage resource profiles: Yemen*, FAO, 2006, are correct. The structure of livestock raising and the livestock market does not appear well documented. WFP, 'The state of food security',

p. 28, notes that 'Around 38 percent of households with livestock reduced the number of sheep and goats they kept over the previous year'. It explains, 'the main reasons for the fall in the number of livestock are lack of fodder and of grazing areas, along with animal pest. Only 21 percent of households have more than one animal, suggesting that livestock is not important in the livelihoods of most Yemenis—except for those dependent on agriculture and livestock'.

41. International Development Association and International Finance Corporation (IDA/IFC), 'Country assistance strategy for the Republic of Yemen for the period FY 2010–2013', *Report No. 47562-YE*, 2009; World Bank and Yemen Ministry of Planning and International Cooperation, 'Millennium Development Goals', p. 73, see Annex 2.

42. Varisco, Daniel Martin, 'Indigenous knowledge and traditional Yemeni irrigation', in *Savoirs locaux et agriculture durable au Yémen* (*Indigenous Knowledge and Sustainable Agriculture in Yemen*), Al-Hakimi, Amin and Frédéric Pelat (eds), *Les Cahiers du CEFAS #3*, Sanaa: Centre Français d'Archéologie et de Sciences Sociales, 2003, pp. 115–20.

43. The figure for 2009 appears egregious; it is not clear why it is so high.

44. These figures derive from several sources: Yemen's Ministry of Agriculture and Irrigation (MAI) agricultural statistics for the period 1997–2009 and World Bank, 'Republic of Yemen Agricultural Strategy Note', *Report No. 17973-YEM*, 1999.

45. Yemen Ministry of Planning and International Cooperation, *Yemen's third Socio-Economic Development Plan*, p. 47.

46. Grains include wheat, barley, sorghum, millet and maize.

47. Yemen Ministry of Agriculture and Irrigation, 'Agricultural Statistics Year Book 2007', Sanaa, Republic of Yemen: General Department of Statistics and Documentation, MAI, 2008.

48. Hazza, Abdel-Warith, 'Wheat production trade and nutritional level of Yemeni population', *Yemeni Journal of Agricultural Research & Studies*, no. 19 (2009), pp. 45–68.

49. International Development Association and International Finance Corporation (IDA/IFC), 'Country Assistance Strategy', p. 63.

50. van der Gun, Jac A. M., Abdul Aziz Ahmed and Abdallah Saleh Saif, 'The water resources of Yemen: a summary digest of the available information', *Report WRAY-35*, Sanaa, Yemen: Ministry of Oil and Mineral Resources; Delft, Netherlands: TNO Institute of Applied Geoscience, 1995. Note that in the eastern plain, the average temperature ranges between 19°–33°C, and the average rainfall ranges between 50–100ml.

51. van Steenbergen, Frank, Philip Lawrence, Abraham Mehari Haile, Maher Salman and Jean-Marc Faurès, 'Guidelines on spate irrigation', *FAO Irrigation and Drainage Paper No. 65*, Rome, FAO, 2010.

52. Compare Makin, M. J. (ed.), 'Yemen Arab Republic Montane Plains and Wadi Rima Project: a land and water resources survey. Irrigation and agricultural development in Wadi Rima'', 2 vols, Project Report No. 16, Surrey, UK: Ministry of Overseas Development, Land Resources Division Project Team, 1977; Pratt, D. J., 'Yemen Arab Republic Montane Plains and Wadi Rima Project: a land and water resources survey. An investment and development plan for Wadi Rima'', *Project Report No. 17*, YAR-01–30/Rep-17/77, Surrey, UK, Ministry of Overseas Development, 1977; and Williams, J. B., 'Yemen Arab Republic Montane Plains and Wadi Rima Project: a land and water resources survey. Physical aspects of water use under traditional and modern irrigation/farming systems in Wadi Rima Tihama', *Project Record No. 27*, YAR-01–40/REC-27/79, Land Resources Division, Surrey, UK: Ministry of Overseas Development, Yemen Arab Republic, 1977.

53. Mundy, Martha, *Tihama II Project: monitoring and evaluation report*, Ministry of Agriculture, Yemen Arab Republic, and World Bank/Kuwait Fund, 1980.

54. DHV Consulting Engineers, 'Wadi Rima Irrigation Development: Feasibility Study', vol. 1, Main Report, 1979.

55. Garcia, Conchitam, Nada Al-Syed Hassan and Carin Vijfhuizen, 'Women and water rights in Wadi Tuban, Yemen', n.d.

56. Clouet, Yves, 'Yémen, agriculture d'oasis' ('Yemen: oasis agriculture'), in *La Conquête de l'eau* (*The Conquest of Water*), Gandin, J. P., (ed.), *Fondation Pour le Progrès de l'homme* (*Dossier pour un débat, Synthèse réalisée par Jean-Paul Gandin*), 1995, pp. 26–8.

57. Vegetable group: gathers data for all vegetables, including potatoes and tomatoes.

58. Fruit group: gathers data for all fruit, including those detailed in this table.

59. Cash crop group: gathers data for all cash crops, including those detailed in this table.

60. Fodder group: gathers data for all fodders, including irrigated sorghum.

61. Yemen Ministry of Planning and International Cooperation, *Yemen's Third Socio-Economic Development Plan*, notes: 'Areas cultivated with *qat* (Catha edulis) have doubled 18 times during the last three decades, growing from 7 thousand hectares in 1970 to 127 thousand hectares by 2005, which represents 25% of irrigated agricultural land, and accounts for half a million jobs. Production has also increased from 108 thousand tons in 2000 to about 124 thousands in 2005, constituting about 30% of the annual agricultural water usage at around 850 million cubic metres per annum. The steady and strong rise of *qat* production has had impact on food security and resulted in an economic pattern that the rural areas have become dependent on in an unprecedented fashion'.

62. The levels of 2009 were as low as those of 1995.

63. Since the mid-2000s, the MAI has included dams and small tanks in the range of irrigation systems used in Yemen, besides spring (streams), spate flow (floods) and wells (aquifers). These may reflect a strategy developed by some farmers to adapt to underground water depletion.

64. Mundy, Martha, 'Irrigation and society in a Yemeni valley: on the life and death of a bountiful source', *Peuples Méditerranéens*, vol. 46, no. 1 (1989), pp. 97–128; Mundy, *Domestic Government*.

65. Riaz, Khalid, 'Tackling the issue of rural-urban water transfers in the Ta'iz region, Yemen', *Natural Resources Forum*, no. 26 (2002), pp. 89–100.

66. UNDP Regional Bureau for Arab States, 'Development challenges'.

67. As defined by Jean Lebel, an 'agroecosystem' is 'a coherent geographical and functional entity where agricultural production takes place. Agroecosystems consist of living and non-living components and their interactions. The agroecosystem concept allows one to understand the linkages between farming systems and their environment within the recent socioeconomic mutations and also to develop solutions at appropriate scales', *Health: An Ecosystem Approach*, Ottawa: International Development Research Centre, 2003.

68. Varisco, Daniel Martin, 'The future of terrace farming in Yemen: a development dilemma', *Agriculture and Human Values*, vol. 8, nos. 1–2 (1991), p. 169.

69. Lichtenthäler Gerhard, 'Adjusting to the extreme shortage of a common resource: runoff, resource capture and social adaptive capacity', *Les Cahiers du CEFAS*, vol. 3, in *Savoirs locaux et agriculture durable au Yémen* (*Indigenous Knowledge and Sustainable Agriculture in Yemen*), Al-Hakimi, Amin and Frédéric Pelat (eds), 2003, Les Cahiers du CEFAS #3, Sanaa: Centre Français d'Archéologie et de Sciences Sociales, p. 101.

70. Aw-Hassan, Aden, Mohammed Al-Sanabani and Abdul Rahman Bamatraf, 'Impact of land tenure and socioeconomic factors on mountain terrace maintenance in Yemen', *CAPRi Working Paper No. 3*, International Food Policy Research Institute, 2000.

71. al-Ghulaibi, Najib M., 'Traditional water harvesting on the mountain terraces of Yemen', study report submitted to the United Nations University, Tokyo, Japan, 2004.

72. At least 20 per cent of all the wells drilled nationwide are concentrated in the Sanaa basin.

73. Al-Ghulaibi, 'Traditional water harvesting'.

74. A 2002 landscape survey estimated that 9.63 per cent was land eroded by water without further details; see Yemen Ministry of Planning & International Cooperation, 'Yemen's Third Socio-Economic Development Plan', p. 47.

75. Yemen MAI, FAO, UNCCD, UNDP, *National Action Plan to combat desertification [NAPCD]*, 2000.

76. Rangelands represent the drier environments of the country. These marginal areas of low annual rainfall averages are home to a substantial proportion of the country's rural and poorest populations. Water is the over-riding constraint. The low and highly variable rainfall is often inadequate for economic crop production. So intervention in these extensive areas (rain-fed and rangelands) is needed if land degradation is to be halted or reversed and the productivity and livelihoods of rural communities are to be improved. Due to its limited resources and poor return on investments, development has been restricted. Moreover given the vulnerability and fragility of the natural resources, national policies have tended towards minimising interventions and disturbance to the system.

77. A chain of underlying causes and consequences affecting all zones along the water catchments from upstream to downstream was observed by Anthony Milroy in 1998 from the coastal *wadi* Zabid, in Tihama, as a conclusion to the 'Arid Lands Initiative Project': from 'denudation of shrubs, grasses and soil in upper escarpments and steep slopes' to 'abandonment, collapse and erosion of uneconomic upper terraces, (…) upper springs, cisterns and canals' in the upstream zone and leading to 'destruction of lower, wider and economically viable terraces, virtual destruction of upper *wadi* perennial and spate-irrigated lands by boulder/gravel deposits from eroded escarpments' and finally to 'the rapid depletion and salinisation of groundwater aquifers'. Milroy, Anthony, 'Yemen: development through cooperation', Arid Lands Initiative, available at: http://www.al-bab.com/yemen/env/arid.htm (last accessed 18 Feb. 2014).

78. Ibid.

79. Al-Jibly, Abdulmalek et al., *Climate change scenarios for Yemen*, Final Report submitted to the Environment Protection Authority, Sanaa Yemen (contribution of the Climate Change Scenario Group to the Yemen Climate Change Scenario Project), unpublished report, 1999, give prognostics for three scenarios: '1) Warm and wet; 2) Mid scenario; and 3) Dry and hot.' These are cross-tabulated with time horizons as far as 2020, 2050 and 2080.

80. Parry, Martin L. et al., *Report of the IPCC (Intergovernmental Panel on Climate Change) 2007: Climate Change: Technical Summary*, Cambridge: Cambridge University Press, 2007.

81. Bafadle, Omar and Amin Al-Hakimi et al., *A study on agriculture vulnerability and adaptation to climate change in the Republic of Yemen, final draft report*, Final Draft Report, Sanaa (contribution of the Agriculture Team of the National Committee for Climate Change to the National Communication on Climate Change [2 phases, 2000 and 2009]), 2009.

82. Yemeni Ministry of Water and Environment, *National Report on disaster risk reduction*, draft unpublished report, 2003.

83. The 'Yemen solution' of the GCC and international community entailed an election with one candidate and no option for voters but the one candidate; the Americans are in charge of the military restructuring; the French writing the constitution: and the Germans

'national dialogue'. Under international blessing, it accorded legal impunity to the former president who continues to be a force behind the scene.

7. URBAN AGRICULTURE AND FOOD SECURITY IN THE MIDDLE
   EASTERN CONTEXT: A CASE STUDY FROM LEBANON AND JORDAN

1. The fieldwork and research for this chapter was made possible through a research grant provided by the Center for International and Regional Studies at the Georgetown University School of Foreign Service in Qatar.

2. IFPRI, *International Model for Policy Analysis of Agricultural Commodities and Trade (IMPACT): model description*, Washington, DC: International Food Policy Research Institute, 2010; Wilson, J. P. and Hendrik J. Bruins, 'Food security in the Middle East since 1961', in *Food Security Under Water Scarcity in the Middle East: Problems and Solutions*, Hamdy, Atef and Rossella Monti (eds), Bari: CIHEAM-IAMB, 2005, pp. 49–56; The World Bank, *Improving food security in Arab countries*, Washington, DC, 2009, available at: http://siteresources.worldbank.org/INTMENA/Resources/FoodSecfinal.pdf (accessed 18 Feb. 2014).

3. Mougeot, Luc J. A., 'Urban agriculture: definition, presence, potentials and risks', in *Growing Cities, Growing Food, Urban Agriculture on the Policy Agenda*, Bakker, Nico, Marrielle Dubbeling, Sabine Guendel, Ulrich Sabel Koschella and Henk de Zeeuw (eds), Germany: Deutsche Stiftung für Internationale Entwicklung, Zentralstelle für Ernährung und Landwirtschaft, 2000, pp. 1–42.

4. World Bank, *Global Economic Prospects: Crisis, Finance, and Growth*, Washington, DC: World Bank, 2010.

5. Food and Agriculture Organization of the United Nations (FAO), 'Climate change: implications for agriculture in the Near East', 29th FAO Regional Conference for the Near East, Cairo, March 2008.

6. World Bank, *Global Economic Prospects*.

7. World Bank, *Improving food security*.

8. Ibid.

9. Harrigan, Jane, 'Did food prices plant the seeds of the Arab Spring?' SOAS Inaugural Lecture Series, 2011.

10. International Monetary Fund, 'World economic and financial survey', 2008, available at: www.imf.org/external/pubs/ft/weo/2008/02/weodata/index.aspx (last accessed 18 Feb. 2014).

11. World Bank, 'Improving food security'.

12. Mougeot, 'Urban agriculture'.

13. De Zeeuw, 'Urban food security'.

14. World Bank, *Improving food security*.

15. Homem de Carvalho, J. L., 'PROVE: small agricultural production virtualization programme', *Urban Agriculture Magazine*, no. 5, Appropriate Methods for Urban Agriculture, Leusden: RUAF, 2001.

16. Moustier, Paule and George Danso, 'Local economic development and marketing of urban produced food', in *Cities Farming for the Future, Urban Agriculture for Green and Productive Cities*, van Veenhuizen, René (ed.), Leusden, Netherlands: RUAF Foundation, International Institute of Rural Reconstruction, and International Development Research Centre, 2006.

17. Argenti, Olivio, *Food for the cities: food supply and distribution policies to reduce urban food*

insecurity, A briefing guide for mayors, city executives and urban planners in developing countries and countries in transition, Rome: FAO, 2000.

18. Joe, Nasr and Padilla Martine, 'Interfaces: agriculture et villes à l'est et au sud de la Méditerranée', Delta, Beyrouth, 2004.

19. Dixon, John, Aidan Gulliver and David Gibbon, *Global farming system study: challenges and priorities to 2030*, Rome: FAO, 2001.

20. Adam-Bradford, Andre, Femke Hoekstra and Rene van Veenhuizen, 'Linking relief, rehabilitation and development: a role for urban agriculture?', *Urban Agriculture Magazine*, no. 21 (2009), available at: http://ruaf.org/node/1995 (last accessed 18 Feb. 2014).

21. FAO, 'Making FIVIMS work for you, tools and tips (2002)', available at: http://www.gripweb.org/gripweb/sites/default/files/databases_info_systems/FIVIMS%20T%26T%20English_0.pdf (last accessed 18 Feb. 2014).

22. FAO, *Food Security Policy Brief* No. 2 (June 2006), available at: ftp://ftp.fao.org/es/esa/policybriefs/pb_02.pdf (last accessed 18 Feb. 2014).

23. Bickel, Gary, Mark Nord, Cristofer Price, William Hamilton and John Cook, *Guide to measuring household food security, food and nutrition service*. Alexanria, VA: United States Department of Agriculture, 2000.

24. Kabbani, Nader S. and Myra Yazbeck, 'The role of food assistance programs and employment circumstances in helping households with children avoid hunger', *Discussion Paper* No. 1280–04, Institute for Research on Poverty, University of Wisconsin–Madison, 2004.

25. Nord, Mark, Anoop Kumar Satpathy, Nikhil Raj, Patrick Web and Robert Houser, 'Comparing household survey-based measures of food insecurity across countries: case studies in India, Uganda, and Bangladesh', *Friedman School of Nutrition Science and Policy Discussion Paper* No. 7, Tufts University, 2002.

26. T. Ruel, Marie, 'Operationalizing dietary diversity: a review of measurement issues and research priorities', *The Journal of Nutrition*, vol. 133, no. 11 (2003); Kabbani, Nader S. and Yassin Wehelie, 'Measuring hunger and food insecurity in Yemen', prepared for the eleventh annual conference of the Economic Research Forum (ERF), 2004, available at: http://ideas.repec.org/p/erg/wpaper/0419.html (last accessed 18 Feb. 2014); Hoddinott, John and Yisehac Yohannes, 'Dietary diversity as a food security indicator', *Food Consumption and Nutrition Division Discussion Paper No. 136*, International Food Policy Research Institute, 2002.

27. Nord et al., 'Comparing household survey-based measures'.

28. Kabbani and Wehelie, 'Measuring hunger'.

29. Chaaban, Jad, Hala Ghattas, Rima Habib, Sari Hanafi, Nadine Sahyoun, Nisreen Salti, Karin Seyfert and Nadia Naamani, *Socio-economic survey of Palestinian refugees in Lebanon*, report published by the American University of Beirut (AUB) and the United Nations Relief and Works Agency for Palestine Refugees in the Near East (UNRWA), 2010.

30. Tohmé Tawk, Salwa, Ziad Moussa, Diana Marroush Abi Saiid, Mounir Abi Saiid and Shadi Hamadeh, 'Redefining a sustainable role for urban agriculture in the Middle East and North Africa', *Watch Letter No. 18*, International Centre for Advanced Mediterranean Agronomic Studies, 2011.

31. Ministry of Agriculture, Lebanon, *Stratégie de développement agricole du Liban*, Produced with FAO/Projet Assistance au Rencensement Agricole, 2004; Council for Development and Reconstruction, Republic of Lebanon, *Rural Development Strategy and Policy Statement*, 2002.

32. Council for Development and Reconstruction (CDR)—Economic and Social Fund for Development (ESFD): *Formulation of a strategy for social development in Lebanon: community development component*, 2005, available at: http://www.cdr.gov.lb/eng/progress_

reports/pr072005/Esocial.pdf (last accessed 18 Feb. 2014); Gambill, Gary C., 'Lebanese farmers and the Syrian occupation', *Middle East Intelligence Bulletin*, vol. 5, no. 10 (October 2003).

33. United Nations Development Program and International Poverty Centre, 'Poverty, growth and income distribution in Lebanon', *Country Study No. 13*, 2008.

34. Ibid.; United Nations Development Program, Lebanese Republic Ministry of Social Affairs, and Central Administration for Statistics: *Living conditions of the households in Lebanon: the National Survey of Household Living Conditions 2004*, 2006.

35. Greater Amman Municipality, *Towards the promotion of urban agriculture in Amman: an exploratory study*, Environment and Sustainable Development Unit of the American University of Beirut, Lebanon, 2007.

36. Directorate of Statistics, *Report on poverty in Jordan based on 2008 survey*, Jordan, 2010.

37. Dop, Marie Claude and Terri Ballard, *Measuring the impacts of food security-related programming*, Rome: Food and Agriculture Organization of the United Nations, December 2010.

38. Chaaban et al., *Socio-economic survey*.

39. Kabbani and Wehelie, 'Measuring hunger'; Chaaban et al., *Socio-economic survey*.

40. Swets, John A., 'Measuring the accuracy of diagnostic systems', *Science*, vol. 240, no. 4857 (1988), pp. 1285–93.

41. van Veenhuizen, Rene and George Danso, 'Profitability and sustainability of urban and peri-urban agriculture', *Agricultural Management, Marketing, and Finance Occasional Paper No. 19*, Rome: Food and Agriculture Organization of the United Nations, 2007.

42. World Bank, *Improving food security*.

43. Ibrahim, Saif, 'The food price crisis in the Arab countries: short-term responses to a lasting challenge', Web Commentary, Carnegie Endowment for International Peace, Middle East Program, June 2008.

44. Harrigan, 'Did food prices plant the seeds of the Arab Spring?'.

45. World Food Programme, *Fighting Hunger Worldwide: Annual Report 2010*, available at: http://documents.wfp.org/stellent/groups/public/documents/communications/wfp220666.pdf (last accessed 18 Feb. 2014).

46. Hunter, Elisabeth, 'Food security in rural Lebanon: links with diet and agriculture', MSc Thesis, Laval University Quebec Canada, 2008.

47. Kabbani and Wehelie, 'Measuring hunger'.

48. Prain, Gordon and Marielle Dubbeling, 'Urban agriculture: its contributions to poverty alleviation, food security and adaptation to climate change. Case studies of the cities of Accra, Nairobi, Lima, and Bangalore', RUAF Foundation and The World Bank, project No. 43, November 2011.

49. IFAD, *Rural Poverty Report*, 2011, available at: http://www.ifad.org/rpr2011/report/e/rpr2011.pdf (last accessed 18 Feb. 2014).

50. Chaaban et al., *Socio-economic survey*.

51. Kabbani and Wehelie, 'Measuring hunger'; Nord, Mark, Margaret Andrews and Steven Carlson, *Household food security in the United States, 2004*, USDA Economic Research Service, 2005, available at: http://www.ers.usda.gov/Publications/ERR11/ (last accessed 18 Feb. 2014); Bhattacharya, Jayanta, Janet Currie and Steven Haider, 'Food security or poverty? Measuring need-related dietary adequacy', *Working Paper No. 9003*, National Bureau of Economic Research, Cambridge, MA, 2002, available at: http://www.nber.org/papers/w9003.pdf (last accessed 18 Feb. 2014).

52. Kabbani and Wehelie, 'Measuring hunger'.

53. Nord et al., 'Comparing household survey-based measures'; Kabbani and Wehelie, 'Measuring hunger'.
54. Nord et al., *Household food security*.
55. Hunter, 'Food security in rural Lebanon'.
56. Kabbani and Yazbeck, 'The role of food assistance'.

8. FOOD SECURITY AND THE SUPERMARKET TRANSITION IN THE MIDDLE EAST: TWO CASE STUDIES

1. The fieldwork and research for this chapter was made possible through a research grant provided by the Center for International and Regional Studies at Georgetown University School of Foreign Service in Qatar.
2. Reardon, Thomas, C. Peter Timmer, Christopher B. Barrett and Julio A. Berdegue, 'The rise of supermarkets in Africa, Asia, and Latin America', *American Journal of Agricultural Economics*, vol. 85, no. 5 (1 December 2003), pp. 1140–6; Reardon, Thomas and C. Peter Timmer, 'Chapter 55: Transformation of Markets for Agricultural Output in Developing Countries Since 1950: How Has Thinking Changed?', in *Handbook of Agricultural Economic: Agricultural Development, Farmers, Farm Production and Farm Markets*, vol. 3, Evenson, Robert E. and Prabhu Pingali (eds), Netherlands: Elsevier, 2007, pp. 2807–55, available at: http://www.sciencedirect.com/science/article/pii/S1574007206030556 (last accessed 18 Feb. 2014).
3. Geopolitical and corporate processes of the third food regime and their impact on the region are discussed in chapter 2 in this volume: Woertz, Eckart, 'Historic Food Regimes and the Middle East'. See also Friedmann, Harriet and Philip McMichael, 'Agriculture and the state system: the rise and decline of national agricultures, 1870 to the present', *Sociologia Ruralis*, vol. 29, no. 2 (25 March 2008), pp. 93–117; Burch, David and Geoffrey Lawrence, 'Towards a third food regime: behind the transformation', *Agriculture and Human Values*, vol. 26, no. 4 (2009), pp. 267–79.
4. See chapter 11 in this volume: ElObeid, Tahra and Abdelmonem Hassan, 'The Nutrition Transition and Obesity in Qatar'; see also Shara, Nawar M., 'Cardiovascular disease in Middle Eastern women', *Nutrition, Metabolism and Cardiovascular Diseases*, vol. 20, no. 6 (July 2010), pp. 412–8; Gaziano, Thomas A., Asaf Bitton, Shuchi Anand, Shafika Abrahams-Gessel and Adrianna Murphy, 'Growing epidemic of coronary heart disease in low- and middle-income countries', *Current Problems in Cardiology*, vol. 35, no. 2 (February 2010), pp. 72–115; Alissa, Eman M., Suhad M. Bahjri, Nabeel Al-Ama, Waqar H. Ahmed and Gordon A. A. Ferns, 'High cardiovascular risk in young Saudi males: cardiovascular risk factors, diet and inflammatory markers', *Clinica Chimica Acta*, vol. 365, no. 1–2 (March 2006), pp. 288–96; de Onis, Mercedes and Monika Blössner, 'Prevalence and trends of overweight among preschool children in developing countries', *The American Journal of Clinical Nutrition*, vol. 72, no. 4 (1 October 2000), pp. 1032–9.
5. Mehio Sibai, Abla, Lara Nasreddine, Ali H. Mokdad, Nada Adra, Maya Tabet and Nahla Hwalla, 'Nutrition transition and cardiovascular disease risk factors in Middle East and North Africa countries: reviewing the evidence', *Annals of Nutrition & Metabolism*, vol. 57, no. 3–4 (2010), pp. 193–203.
6. El Taguri, Adel, Fawwaz Besmar, Ahmad Abdel Monem, Ibrahim Betilmal, Claude Ricour and Marie-Françoise Rolland-Cachera, 'Stunting is a major risk factor for overweight: results from national surveys in 5 Arab countries', *Eastern Mediterranean Health Journal*, vol. 15, no. 3 (June 2009), pp. 549–62.
7. Ghattas, Hala, *Food security, nutrition and health in the Arab world: the case of marginalized*

populations in Lebanon, paper presented at the Food Secure Arab World Conference, IFPRI-UN-ESCWA, Beirut, 6–7 February 2012, available at: http://www.slideshare.net/fsaw2012/session-3-b-hala-ghattas (last accessed 18 Feb. 2014).

8. Kingdom of Bahrain Ministry of Health, 'National nutrition survey for adult Bahrainis aged 19 years and above', 2002, available at: http://www.moh.gov.bh/pdf/survey/nut_survey1.pdf (last accessed 18 Feb. 2014); for data on Syria, see Bashour, Hyam N., 'Survey of dietary habits of in-school adolescents in Damascus, Syrian Arab Republic', *Eastern Mediterranean Health Journal,* vol. 10, no. 6 (2004), pp. 853–62.

9. Nasreddine, Lara, Nahla Hwalla, Abla Sibai, Mouin Hamze and Dominique Parent-Massin, 'Food consumption patterns in an adult urban population in Beirut, Lebanon', *Public Health Nutrition,* vol. 9, no. 2 (2006), pp. 194–203.

10. Mehio Sibai, Abla, Nahla Hwalla, Nada Adra and Boushra Rahal, 'Prevalence and covariates of obesity in Lebanon: findings from the first epidemiological study', *Obesity Research,* vol. 11, no. 11 (November 2003), pp. 1353–61.

11. Naja, Farah, Lara Nasreddine, Abla Sibai, Nada Adra, Marie Claire Chamieh, Leila Itani and Nahla Hwalla, 'Dietary patterns and their association with obesity and sociodemographic factors in a national sample of Lebanese adults', *Public Health Nutrition,* vol. 14, no. 9 (2011), pp. 1570–8.

12. Hassan, Abdelmonem S. and Sara N. Al-Dosari, 'Breakfast habits and snacks consumed at school among Qatari schoolchildren aged 9–10 years', *Nutrition & Food Science,* vol. 38, no. 3 (2008), p. 266.

13. Bener, Abdulbari and Abdulaziz A Kamal, 'Growth patterns of Qatari school children and adolescents aged 6–18 years', *Journal of Health, Population, and Nutrition,* vol. 23, no. 3 (September 2005), pp. 250–8.

14. Andrieu, Pedro Enrique, Nicole Darmon and Adam Drewnowski, 'Low-cost diets: more energy, Fewer nutrients', *European Journal of Clinical Nutrition,* vol. 60, no. 3 (23 November 2005), pp. 434–6; Drewnowski, Adam, Pablo Monsivais, Matthieu Maillot and Nicole Darmon, 'Low-energy-density diets are associated with higher diet quality and higher diet costs in French adults', *Journal of the American Dietetic Association,* vol. 107, no. 6 (June 2007), pp. 1028–32; Monsivais, Pablo and Adam Drewnowski, 'Lower-energy-density diets are associated with higher monetary costs per kilocalorie and are consumed by women of higher socioeconomic status', *Journal of the American Dietetic Association,* vol. 109, no. 5 (May 2009), pp. 814–22.

15. Mergenthaler, Marcus, Katinka Weinberger and Matin Qaim, 'The food system transformation in developing countries: a disaggregate demand analysis for fruits and vegetables in Vietnam', *Food Policy,* vol. 34, no. 5 (October 2009), pp. 426–36.

16. Beydoun, May A. and Youfa Wang, 'Do nutrition knowledge and beliefs modify the association of socio-economic factors and diet quality among US adults?', *Preventive Medicine,* vol. 46, no. 2 (February 2008), pp. 145–53.

17. Nabhani-Zeidan, Maya, Farah Naja and Lara Nasreddine, 'Dietary intake and nutrition-related knowledge in a sample of Lebanese adolescents of contrasting socioeconomic status', *Food and Nutrition Bulletin,* vol. 32, no. 2 (June 2011), pp. 75–83.

18. Naja et al., 'Dietary patterns'.

19. von Grebmer, Klaus, Maximo Torero, Tolulope Olofinbiyi, Heidi Fritschel, Doris Wiesmann, Yisehac Yohannes, Lilly Schofield and Constanze von Oppeln, *2011 Global Hunger Index: the challenge of hunger: taming price spikes and excessive food price volatility,* International Food Policy Research Institute, Concern Worldwide and Welthungerhilfe, 2011.

20. Chaaban, Jad, Hala Ghattas, Rima R. Habib, Sari Hanafi, Nadine Sahyoun, Nisreen

Salti, Karin Seyfert and Nadia Naamani, *Socio-economic survey on Palestinian refugees in Lebanon*, report published by the American University of Beirut (AUB) and the United Nations Relief and Works Agency for Palestine Refugees in the Near East (UNRWA), 2010.

21. Asfaw, Abay, 'Does supermarket purchase affect the dietary practices of households? Some empirical evidence from Guatemala', *Development Policy Review*, vol. 26, no. 2 (1 March 2008), pp. 227–43; Asfaw, Abay, 'Does consumption of processed foods explain disparities in the body weight of individuals? The case of Guatemala', *Health Economics*, vol. 20, no. 2 (February 2011), pp. 184–95.

22. Tessier, Sophie, Pierre Traissac, Nicolas Bricas, Bernard Maire, Sabrina Eymard-Duvernay, Jalila El Ati and Francis Delpeuch, 'Food shopping transition: socio-economic characteristics and motivations associated with use of supermarkets in a North African urban environment', *Public Health Nutrition*, vol. 13, no. 9 (2010), pp. 1410–8.

23. Reardon and Timmer, 'Chapter 55: Transformation of Markets'.

24. Tessier et al., 'Food shopping transition'.

25. Codron, Jean-Marie, Zouhair Bouhsina, Fatiha Fort, Emilie Coudel and Aurélie Puech, 'Supermarkets in low-income Mediterranean countries: impacts on horticulture systems', *Development Policy Review*, vol. 22, no. 5 (1 September 2004), pp. 587–602.

26. Minten, Bart, 'The food retail revolution in poor countries: is it coming or is it over?', *Economic Development and Cultural Change*, no. 56 (2008), pp. 767–89.

27. Mergenthaler, Weinberger, and Qaim, 'The food system transformation'.

28. Prabhu, Pingali, 'Westernization of Asian diets and the transformation of food systems: implications for research and policy', *Food Policy*, vol. 32, no. 3 (June 2007), pp. 281–98.

29. Devine, Carol M., Tracy J. Farrell, Christine E. Blake, Margaret Jastran, Elaine Wethington and Carole A. Bisogni, 'Work conditions and the food choice coping strategies of employed parents', *Journal of Nutrition Education and Behavior*, vol. 41, no. 5 (September 2009), pp. 365–70.

30. Gibson, Edward Leigh, 'Emotional influences on food choice: sensory, physiological and psychological pathways', *Physiology & Behavior*, vol. 89, no. 1 (30 August 2006), pp. 53–61.

31. Minten, Bart, Thomas Reardon and Rajib Sutradhar, 'Food prices and modern retail: the case of Delhi', *World Development*, vol. 38, no. 12 (December 2010), pp. 1775–87.

32. Reardon and Timmer, 'Chapter 55: Transformation of Markets'.

33. Ibid., p. 2841.

34. Tessier et al., 'Food shopping transition'.

35. Reardon and Timmer, 'Chapter 55: Transformation of Markets', p. 2841.

36. Haddock-Fraser, Janet, Nigel Poole and Mitsuhiro Doishita, 'The failure of multinational food retailers in Japan: a matter of convenience?', *British Food Journal*, vol. 111, no. 4 (18 April 2009), pp. 327–48.

37. Humphrey, John, 'The supermarket revolution in developing countries: tidal wave or tough competitive struggle?', *Journal of Economic Geography*, vol. 7, no. 4 (1 July 2007), pp. 433–50, citing Goldman, Arieh and Wilfred Vanhonacker, *The food retail system in China: strategic dilemmas and lessons for retail internationalization/modernization*, paper presented at the Globalizing Retail Conference, University of Surrey, Guildford, United Kingdom, 17 January 2006.

38. Codron et al., 'Supermarkets in low-income Mediterranean countries', p. 394.

39. Maruyama, Masayoshi and Le Viet Trung, 'Traditional bazaar or supermarkets: a probit analysis of affluent consumer perceptions in Hanoi', *The International Review of Retail, Distribution and Consumer Research*, vol. 17, no. 3 (2007), pp. 233–52; Goldman, Arieh,

Robert Krider and Seshan Ramaswami, 'The persistent competitive advantage of traditional food retailers in Asia: wet markets' continued dominance in Hong Kong', *Journal of Macromarketing*, vol. 19, no. 2 (1 December 1999), pp. 126–39.

40. Goldman, Arieh and Hayiel Hino, 'Supermarkets vs. traditional retail stores: diagnosing the barriers to supermarkets' market share growth in an ethnic minority community', *Journal of Retailing and Consumer Services*, vol. 12, no. 4 (July 2005), pp. 273–84.

41. However, home-cooking may not always be beneficial, especially for women. Interviews with south Asian women in Britain show that familial expectations towards women to prioritise cooking and family lead to overweight and non-communicable diseases, especially behavioural diabetes; Ludwig, Alison F., Peter Cox and Basma Ellahi, 'Social and cultural construction of obesity among Pakistani Muslim women in north west England', *Public Health Nutrition*, vol. 14, no. 10 (October 2011), pp. 1842–50.

42. Codron et al., 'Supermarkets in low-income Mediterranean countries'.

43. Maruyama and Trung, 'Traditional bazaar or supermarkets'.

44. Reardon and Timmer, 'Chapter 55: Transformation of Markets', p. 2833.

45. Codron et al., 'Supermarkets in low-income Mediterranean countries'.

46. Maruyama and Trung, 'Traditional bazaar or supermarkets'.

47. Abrahams, Caryn, 'Transforming the region: supermarkets and the local food economy', *African Affairs*, vol. 109, no. 434 (1 January 2010), pp. 115–34.

48. Minten, Reardon, and Sutradhar, 'Food prices and modern retail'.

49. Minten, 'The food retail revolution in poor countries'.

50. Schipmann, Christin and Matin Qaim, 'Modern food retailers and traditional markets in developing countries: comparing quality, prices, and competition strategies in Thailand', *Applied Economic Perspectives and Policy*, vol. 33, no. 3 (1 September 2011), pp. 345–62.

51. Popkin, Barry M., Linda S. Adair and Shu Wen Ng, 'Global nutrition transition and the pandemic of obesity in developing countries', *Nutrition Reviews*, vol. 70, no. 1 (1 January 2012), pp. 3–21; Goldman, Krider and Ramaswami, 'The persistent competitive advantage'.

52. Reardon and Timmer, 'Chapter 55: Transformation of Markets'.

53. Lawrence, Geoffrey and David Burch, 'Understanding supermarkets and agri-food supply chains', in *Supermarkets and Agri-food Supply Chains—Transformations in the Production and Consumption of Food*, Northampton: Edward Elgar Publishing, 2007.

54. van der Ploeg, Jan Douwe, *The food crisis, industrialized farming and the imperial regime*, *Journal of Agrarian Change*, vol. 10, no. 1 (24 December 2009), pp. 98–106.

55. Lawrence and Burch, 'Understanding supermarkets and agri-food supply chains'.

56. Ibid.

57. Reardon, Thomas and Julio Berdegué, *The retail-led transformation of agrifood systems and its implications for development policies*, background paper for the World Development Report 2008, Santiago, Chile: Rimisp-Latin American Center for Rural Development, 2006, p. 14.

58. Reardon et al., 'The rise of supermarkets in Africa, Asia, and Latin America'.

59. van der Ploeg, Jan Douwe, 'The food crisis, industrialized farming and the imperial regime'; Lawrence and Burch, 'Understanding supermarkets and agri-food supply chains'.

60. Codron et al., 'Supermarkets in low-income Mediterranean countries', p. 596.

61. Maruyama and Trung, 'Traditional bazaar or supermarkets'; Reardon and Berdegué, 'The retail-led transformation of agrifood systems', citing Boselie, David, 'Business case description: TOPS Supply Chain Project, Thailand', KLICT International Agri Supply Chain Development Program, Agrichain Competence Center, Den Bosch, 2002; and Berdegué, Julio A., Fernando Balsevich, Luis Flores and Thomas Reardon, 'Central American super-

markets' private standards of quality and safety in procurement of fresh fruits and vegetables', *Food Policy*, vol. 30, no. 3 (June 2005), pp. 254–69.

62. Humphrey, 'The supermarket revolution in developing countries'.

63. Echanove, Flavia and Thomas Reardon, 'Wholesale markets, horticulture products, and supermarkets in Mexico', *Staff Paper No. 11586*, Department of Agricultural, Food, and Resource Economics, Michigan State University, 2006, available at: http://ideas.repec.org/p/ags/midasp/11586.html (last accessed 18 Feb. 2014).

64. Codron et al., 'Supermarkets in low-income Mediterranean countries'.

65. Reardon and Berdegué, 'The retail-led transformation of agrifood systems', cite Wang, Honglin, Xiaoxia Dong, Scott Rozelle, Jikun Huang and Thomas Reardon, 'Producing and procuring horticultural crops with Chinese characteristics: a case study in the Greater Beijing Area', *Staff Paper 2005–06*, Department of Agricultural Economics, Michigan State University, 2006.

66. Reardon, Thomas, Christopher B. Barrett, Julio A. Berdegué and Johan F. M. Swinnen, 'Agrifood industry transformation and small farmers in developing countries', *World Development*, vol. 37, no. 11 (November 2009), pp. 1717–27.

67. Dinham, Barbara, 'Growing vegetables in developing countries for local urban populations and export markets: problems confronting small-scale producers', *Pest Management Science*, vol. 59, no. 5 (1 May 2003), pp. 575–82.

68. Reardon and Berdegué, 'The retail-led transformation of agrifood systems'; Reardon and Timmer, 'Chapter 55: Transformation of Markets.'

69. Echanove and Reardon, 'Wholesale markets, horticulture products, and supermarkets in Mexico'.

70. Reardon and Timmer, 'Chapter 55 Transformation of Markets.'

71. Ibid.

72. Cadilhon, Jean-Joseph, Paule Moustier, Nigel D. Poole, Phan Thi Giac Tam and Andrew p. Fearne, 'Traditional vs. modern food systems? Insights from vegetable supply chains to Ho Chi Minh City (Vietnam)', *Development Policy Review*, vol. 24, no. 1 (1 January 2006), pp. 31–49; Michelson, Hope, Thomas Reardon, and Francisco Perez, 'Small farmers and big retail: trade-offs of supplying supermarkets in Nicaragua', *World Development*, vol. 40, no. 2 (February 2012), pp. 342–54.

73. Berdegué et al., 'Central American supermarkets' private standards of quality'.

74. Hernández, Ricardo, Thomas Reardon and Julio Berdegué, 'Supermarkets, wholesalers, and tomato growers in Guatemala', *Agricultural Economics*, vol. 36, no. 3 (2007), pp. 281–90.

75. Reardon et al., 'Agrifood industry transformation and small farmers in developing countries'.

76. Stringer, Randy, Naiquan Sang and André Croppenstedt, 'Producers, processors, and procurement decisions: the case of vegetable supply chains in China', *World Development*, vol. 37, no. 11, (2009), pp. 1773–80.

77. Reardon and Timmer, 'Chapter 55: Transformation of Markets', p. 2844.

78. Amanor, Kojo Sebastian, 'Global food chains, African smallholders and World Bank governance', *Journal of Agrarian Change*, vol. 9, no. 2 (April 2009), pp. 247–62.

79. McMichael, Philip, 'Banking on agriculture: a review of the World Development Report 2008', *Journal of Agrarian Change*, vol. 9, no. 2 (April 2009), pp. 235–46.

80. Ploeg, 'The food crisis, industrialized farming and the imperial regime'.

81. See chapter 9 in this volume: Tétreault, Mary Ann, Deborah Wheeler, and Benjamin Shepherd, 'Win-Win versus Lose-Lose: Investments in Foreign Agriculture as a Food Security Strategy of the Arab States of the Persian Gulf'.

82. Ibid.
83. See chapter 6 in this volume: Mundy, Martha, Amin Al-Hakimi and Frédéric Pelat, 'Neither Security Nor Sovereignty: The Political Economy of Food in Yemen'.
84. Reardon et al., 'Agrifood industry transformation and small farmers in developing countries'.
85. Reardon and Timmer, 'Chapter 55: Transformation of Markets', p. 2846.
86. McLaughlin, Edward W., 'The dynamics of fresh fruit and vegetable pricing in the supermarket channel', *Preventive Medicine*, vol. 39, suppl. 2 (September 2004), pp. 81–7.
87. Cadilhon et al., 'Traditional vs. modern food systems?'
88. Michelson, Reardon, and Perez, 'Small farmers and big retail'.
89. McLaughlin, 'The dynamics of fresh fruit and vegetable pricing in the supermarket channel'.
90. Nasreddine et al., 'Food consumption patterns in an adult urban population'.
91. We are not quoting exact amounts consumed per day since the standard error and confidence interval of reported averages is quite large. We believe that the frequency ranking, in terms of which are the most frequently consumed fruit and vegetables is likely to be correct, however the absolute amounts reported in the study require validation.
92. Note that Nasreddine et al.'s 2006 study took place between April and September and may or may not have seasonal availability effects in it. Further, this study is based on a sample from Beirut and is likely to represent more affluent dietary habits than practiced by the average Lebanese. No similar data for Qatar is available.
93. Baruch, Yehuda and Brooks C. Holtom, 'Survey response rate levels and trends in organizational research', *Human Relations*, vol. 61, no. 8 (1 August 2008), pp. 1139–60.
94. Baruch and Holtom also find that while response rates increase as potential respondents receive reminders, response rates decrease with too many reminders. They hypothesise that respondents may react negatively to what they perceive as nagging.
95. Ibid.
96. Da, Hemin, 'Qatar as an oil emerging market', *International Journal of Marketing Studies*, vol. 3, no. 3 (2011), p. 141, doi:10.5539/ijms.v3n3p141.
97. James, Bonnie, 'Emadi farm to build more greenhouses', *Gulf Times*, 16 March 2012.
98. 'Statistics: Population Structure', Ministry of Development Planning and Statistics, 2014, available at: http://www.qsa.gov.qa/eng/PopulationStructure.htm (last accessed 18 Feb. 2014).
99. Qatar National Food Security Programme (QNFSP), 'Crop production', available at: http://www.qnfsp.gov.qa/programme/agriculture/crop-production/open-field-agriculture (last accessed 18 Feb. 2014).
100. James, 'Emadi farm to build more greenhouses'; James, Bonnie, 'Alfardan farm plan for home veg garden', *Gulf Times*, 15 March 2012; QNFSP, 'Crop production'.
101. AQUASTAT—FAO, 'Lebanon Country Overview', 2008.
102. Ministry of Agriculture, Lebanon, 'Recensement agricole 2010' ('Agricultural Census 2010'), Beirut, 2012.
103. This fraction has been calculated using ibid. as denominators and Ministry of Agriculture, Lebanon, *Strategy of the agricultural development in Lebanon*, Beirut, Lebanon, 2004, as numerator.
104. Hunter, 'Food security in rural Lebanon'; Riachi, Roland and Jad Chaaban, 'The agricultural sector in Lebanon: economical features and challenges', IBSAR American University of Beirut and University of Ottawa: IDRC funding; 'Food and Health in Rural Lebanon: Options to Improve Dietary Diversity, Food Security, Livelihoods and

105. Riachi and Chaaban, 'The agricultural sector in Lebanon'.

106. See chapter 3 in this volume: Harrigan, Jane, 'An Economic Analysis of National Food Sovereignty Policies in the Middle East: The Case of Lebanon and Jordan'.

107. Ministry of Agriculture, Lebanon, *Agricultural Census 2010*.

108. Franklin—AHT Consortium, 'Elements of agricultural policy and their Master Plan', Beirut, Lebanon, 2003.

109. Ibid.

110. Hunter, 'Food security in rural Lebanon'.

111. Referring to the Ministry of Agriculture press release: Le Commerce du Liban, 'Le Liban compte plus de 157.000 agriculteurs' ('Lebanon accounts for more than 157,000 farmers'), *Le Commerce Du Liban*, 5 September 2011, available at: http://www.lecommercedulevant.com/node/18788 (last accessed 18 Feb. 2014).

112. MoA, *Filiere de fruit et de legumes (The fruits and vegetables supply chain)*, Beirut, Lebanon, 2003.

113. Riachi and Chaaban, 'The agricultural sector in Lebanon.'

114. Consultation and Research Institute, *Competition in the Lebanese economy—a background report for a competition law for Lebanon*, commissioned by the Lebanese Ministry of Economy and Trade, Beirut, Lebanon, 2003, available at: http://www.economy.gov.lb/public/uploads/files/7982_8734_3466.pdf (last accessed 18 Feb. 2014).

115. Riachi and Chaaban, 'The agricultural sector in Lebanon'.

116. Ministry of Agriculture, Lebanon, *Recensement Aagricole* 2010, Beirut, 2012.

117. See chapter 4 in this volume: Bush, Ray, 'Food Security in Egypt'.

118. Figures vary across interview partners. Minimum and maximum numbers are given above.

119. 'Govt will not let vegetable prices go up', *The Peninsula*, 2 May 2011.

120. Franklin—AHT Consortium, 'Elements of agricultural policy'.

121. See chapter 7 in this volume: Tawk, Salwa Tohmé, Mounir Abi Said and Shadi Hamadeh, 'Urban Agriculture and Food Security in the Middle Eastern Context: a Case Study from Lebanon and Jordan'.

122. Codron et al., 'Supermarkets in low-income Mediterranean countries'.

123. Ibid., citing Gutman, Graciela E., 'Impact of the rapid rise of supermarkets on dairy products systems in Argentina', *Development Policy Review*, vol. 20, no. 4 (1 September 2002), pp. 409–27.

124. Hunter, 'Food security in rural Lebanon'.

125. Republic of Lebanon Ministry of Economy & Trade, *Info price 'Top Ten Supermarkets'*, March 2012, available at: http://www.economy.gov.lb/index.php/subCatInfo/2/86 (last accessed 18 Feb. 2014).

126. Qatarliving.com, 'Supermarkets', available at: http://www.qatarliving.com/doha-shopping/wiki/supermarkets (last accessed 18 Feb. 2014); Qatcom.com, 'Supermarkets', available at: http://www.qatcom.com/listings/qatar-search/supermarkets (last accessed 18 Feb. 2014); Qatar Online Directory, 'Companies: supermarkets & hypermarkets', available at: http://www.qataronlinedirectory.com/company_classif.asp?link=132200 (last accessed 18 Feb. 2014).

127. Hanna, Salma and Marah Aqeel, 'A market basket where Iraqi refugees reside in Lebanon', Undergraduate research project in Nutrition and Food Sciences, American University of Beirut, 2012.

128. Ministry of Agriculture, Republic of Lebanon, *A strategy for the renewal of the agricul-*

tural sector 2010–2014. 2009; and European Union—EEAS (European External Action Service), Agricultural and Rural Development Programme (ARDP), 2012, available at: http://eeas.europa.eu/delegations/lebanon/documents/news/20120113_1_en.pdf (last accessed 18 Feb 2014).

129. Qazi, Sarmad, 'Farms in Qatar "can meet 90% of vegetable needs"', *Gulf Times*, 25 May 2010. James, 'Emadi farm to build more greenhouses'.

130. James, 'Alfardan farm plan for home veg garden'.

131. Franklin—AHT Consortium, 'Elements of agricultural policy'.

132. Hunter, 'Food security in rural Lebanon'.

133. Chaaban, 'Socio-economic survey on Palestinian refugees in Lebanon'.

134. Ghattas Hala, and Nadine Sahyoun, 'Experiences of household food insecurity in Lebanon', unpublished research.

135. Popkin, Adair, and Ng, 'Global nutrition transition and the pandemic of obesity in developing countries'.

136. Wells, Jonathan C. K., 'Obesity as malnutrition: the role of capitalism in the obesity global epidemic', *American Journal of Human Biology*, vol. 24, no. 3 (2 March 2012), pp. 261–76, available at: http://www.ncbi.nlm.nih.gov/pubmed/22383142 (last accessed 18 Feb. 2014).

137. Williams, Peter G., 'Consumer understanding and use of health claims for foods', *Nutrition Reviews*, vol. 63, no. 7 (2005), pp. 256–64.

138. Roberto, Christina A., Marie A. Bragg, Kara A. Livingston, Jennifer L. Harris, Jackie M. Thompson, Marissa J. Seamans and Kelly D, Brownell, 'Choosing front-of-package food labelling nutritional criteria: how smart were "Smart Choices"?', *Public Health Nutrition*, vol. 15, no. 2 (February 2012), pp. 262–7.

139. Carter, Owen, Brennen Mills and Tina Phan, 'An independent assessment of the Australian food industry's Daily Intake Guide "Energy Alone" Label', *Health Promotion Journal of Australia*, vol. 22, no. 1 (April 2011), pp. 63–7.

140. Hassan and Al-Dosari, 'Breakfast habits and snacks consumed at school'.

141. Popkin, Adair, and Ng, 'Global nutrition transition and the pandemic of obesity in developing countries'.

142. Beydoun and Wang, 'Do nutrition knowledge and beliefs modify the association of socio-economic factors?'.

143. An exception being Wells' 'Obesity as malnutrition' paper.

144. See chapter 2 in this volume: Woertz, Eckart, 'Historic Food Regimes and the Middle East'.

9. WIN-WIN VERSUS LOSE-LOSE: INVESTMENTS IN FOREIGN AGRICULTURE AS A FOOD SECURITY STRATEGY OF THE ARAB STATES OF THE PERSIAN GULF

1. The fieldwork and research for this chapter was made possible through a research grant provided by the Center for International and Regional Studies at Georgetown University School of Foreign Service in Qatar; International Land Coalition, *Transnational land deals for agriculture in the global south: Analytical Report No. 1*, April 2012, pp. 21–2, available at: http://landportal.info/landmatrix/media/img/analytical-report.pdf (last accessed 18 Feb. 2014).

2. Shepherd, Benjamin, *Above carrying capacity: Saudi Arabia's external policies for securing food supplies*, paper presented at the World Congress of Middle East Studies, Barcelona,

July 2010; Al-Rasheed, Turki F., *Agricultural Development Strategies: the Saudi Experience*, Saarbrücken: LAP Lambert Adademic Publishing, 2012.

3. Interview with Khalid Al-Wrais, King Abdullah Chair for Food Security, King Saud University, Qatar, 14 November 2011; Al-Rasheed, Agricultural Development Strategies.

4. This social contract is widely believed to underpin regime-society relations in rentier states like the Gulf oil exporters. See Beblawi, Hazem, 'The rentier state in the Arab World', in *The Arab State*, Luciani, Giacomo (ed.), Berkeley, CA: University of California Press, 1990, pp. 85–98; and for a more recent view, Gray, Matthew, 'A theory of "Late Rentierism" in the Arab States of the Gulf', *CIRS Occasional Paper No. 7*, Center for International and Regional Studies, Georgetown University School of Foreign Service in Qatar, Doha, 2011.

5. Economist Intelligence Unit, 'The GCC in 2020: resources for the future', 2011, available at: http://graphics.eiu.com/upload/eb/GCC_in_2020_Resources_WEB.pdf (last accessed 18 Feb. 2014).

6. Tétreault, Mary Ann, 'Gulf Arab states' investment of oil revenues', in *Shifting Geo-Economic Power of the Gulf: Oil, Finance and Institutions*, Legrenzi, Matteo and Bessma Momani (eds), Surrey, UK: Ashgate, 2011, pp. 9–21.

7. Ibid.

8. Salomon, Margot, 'The ethics of foreign investment', *The Majalla*, updated 5 August 2010, available at: http://www.al-majalla.com/en/ideas/article94948.ece?service=print (last accessed 18 Feb. 2014); also Munif, Abd al-Rahman, *Cities of Salt*, trans. Peter Theroux, New York: Vintage International, 1989.

9. Tétreault, 'Gulf Arab states' investment'.

10. For example, Barger, Thomas C., *Out in the Blue: Letters from Arabia, 1937 to 1940*, Vista, CA: Selwa Press, 2000.

11. KCIC, 'Agri-business & real estate'; Qatar National Food Security Programme (QNSFP), 'Qatar urges creation of a global dry land alliance (GDLA) at the 66th Session of UN General Assembly', September 2011.

12. Tétreault, Mary Ann, *The Kuwait Petroleum Corporation and the Economics of the New World Order*, Westport, CT: Quorum Books, 1995, quote on p. 31.

13. See the keynote addresses in Bolton, Patrick, Frederic Samama and Joseph E. Stiglitz, (eds), *Sovereign Wealth Funds and Long-Term Investing*, New York: Columbia University Press, 2012, pp. 26–52.

14. See farmlandgrab.org, a continually updated collection of online materials on farmland acquisitions. The business press also has taken a critical perspective on the issue, for example, Janardhan, Meena, 'Gulf eyes oil-for-food pacts', *Asia Times*, 20 June 2008, available at: http://www.atimes.com/atimes/Middle_East/JF20Ak01.html (last accessed 18 Feb. 2014); International Land Coalition's 'Agriculture in the global south', along with academic studies reflect a range of judgements about these investments such as, for example, Rahmato, Dessalegn, 'Land to investors: large-scale land transfers in Ethiopia', *FSS Policy Debates Series No. 1*, Addis Ababa: Forum for Social Studies, 2011; and Salomon, 'The ethics of foreign investment'.

15. Kuwait China Investment Company (KCIC), 'Agri-business & real estate in Asia: a proposal', October 2009, available at: http://www.kcic-asia.com/UserFiles/file/Products/New%20Silk%20Road/Agri-business%20and%20Real%20Estate%20in%20Asia%20-%20A%20proposal%20-%20September%202009.pdf (last accessed 18 Feb. 2014); Cotula, Lorenzo, Sonja Vermuelen, Rebecca Leonard and James Keeley, *Land grab or development opportunity? Agricultural investment and international land deals in Africa*, London/Rome: IIED/FAO/IFAD, 2009.

16. For example, see Dessy, Sylvain, Gaston Gohou and Désiré Vencatachellum, 'Foreign Direct Investments in Africa's farmlands: threat or opportunity for local populations?', Centre Interuniversitaire sur le Risque, les Politiques Économiques et l'Emploi, *Working Paper No. 12–03*, Canada, January 2011.
17. In this context, 'The definition of long term is very simple. You are long term if you are never forced to sell and if you are never stopped-out': Skancke, Martin, 'Building long-term strategies for investment of sovereign wealth', in *Sovereign Wealth Funds and Long-Term Investing*, Bolton, Patrick, Frederic Samama and Joseph E. Stiglitz (eds), New York: Columbia University Press, 2012, p. 136.
18. Fahad Al-Attiya, Chair, of the Qatar National Food Security Programme (QNFSP), 'Qatar's Food Security Policy', presentation at the Center for International and Regional Studies, Georgetown University School of Foreign Service in Qatar, Doha, 14 November 2011; Al-Rasheed, Agricultural Development Strategies; interview with Al-Wrais; KCIC, 'Agri-business & real estate in Asia'.
19. This is especially so for Ethiopia, which is among the top ten investment targets for land investment worldwide according to the International Land Coalition. Cambodia is less popular but its status as a producer of rice for export, a commodity that figures heavily in the diets of Gulf citizens, makes it a desirable partner for GCC investors.
20. Akram-Lodhi, A. Haroun, 'Land, markets and neoliberal enclosure: an agrarian political economy perspective', *Third World Quarterly*, vol. 29, no. 8 (2007), pp. 1437–56; 'Seized: the 2008 land grab for food and financial security', Grain, 24 October 2008, available at: http://www.grain.org/article/entries/93-seized-the-2008-landgrab-for-food-and-financial-security (last accessed 18 Feb. 2014). Licadho, 'Harmful effects of economic land concessions on poor Cambodians', November 2005, available at: http://www.licadho-cambodia.org/reports.php?perm=74 (last accessed 18 Feb. 2014); Rahmato, 'Land to investors'.
21. For more information, see Shepherd, Benjamin, 'GCC states' land investments abroad: the case of Cambodia', *Summary Report No. 5*, Center for International and Regional Studies, Georgetown University School of Foreign Service in Qatar, 2012, available at: http://cirs.georgetown.edu/publications/summaryreports/104779.html (last accessed 18 Feb. 2014).
22. Shepherd interviews in Cambodia 2011; see also, Sothath, Ngo and Sophal Chan, 'Does large scale agricultural investment benefit the poor?', Cambodian Economic Association, 2010.
23. Ministry of Agriculture, Fisheries and Forestry (MAFF), Government of Cambodia, n.d.
24. Interview with a research analyst, NGO, Phnom Penh, 27 May 2011.
25. FAO STAT, using latest available data of 2009: http://faostat3.fao.org/home/index.html
26. Interview with an academic, Phnom Penh, 11 July 2011.
27. Royal Government of Cambodia, National Assembly, 'Land law' (English Translation), Phnom Penh, 2001.
28. Royal Government of Cambodia, Office of the Prime Minister, 'Sub-decree on economic land concession' (English Translation), Phnom Penh, 2005.
29. Rouen, Van, 'More Concessions Granted in Protected Areas', *Cambodia Daily*, 6 July 2011.
30. Interview with an academic, Phnom Penh, 11 July 2011.
31. Interview with a government official, Phnom Penh, 24 June 2011.
32. Interview with a lawyer, Phnom Penh, 21 June 2011.
33. Interview with an economist, Phnom Penh, 10 June 2011; also various NGOs interviewed.

34. Global Witness, 'Country for sale: how Cambodia's elite has captured the country's extractive industries', Washington, 2009, available at: http://www.globalwitness.org/sites/default/files/library/final_english.pdf (last accessed 18 Feb. 2014).

35. Interview with a representative of a Western advisory firm acting in Cambodia, Phnom Penh, 9 June 2011.

36. Interview with a lawyer, Phnom Penh, 2 June 2011.

37. Un, Kheang, 'The judicial system and democratization in post-conflict Cambodia', in *Beyond Democracy in Cambodia: Political Reconstruction in a Post-Conflict Society*, Oejendal, Joakim and Mona Lilja (eds), Copenhagen: NIAS, 2009.

38. Interview with the director of a civil society organisation, Phnom Penh, 30 May 2011.

39. In Addis Ababa, the kind of entrenched corruption that is common in other east African capitals is notably absent. Although Ethiopia's scores are roughly equivalent to those of its neighbours on many of Transparency International's rankings (for example, on press freedom, rule of law, judicial independence, and voice and accountability), it rates considerably better on the Corruption Perceptions index, ranking 120 out of 183. For comparison, Kenya is 154, Burundi 172, Sudan 177 and Cambodia 164. See Transparency International, available at: http://cpi.transparency.org/cpi2011/results/ (last accessed 18 Feb. 2014).

40. Interview with a representative of a foreign agri-business, Addis Ababa, 24 October 2011.

41. For information on the food situation in Ethiopia, see http://www.fao.org/fileadmin/templates/tc/tce/pdf/Executive_Briefs/02.02.12_Issue_10_HoA_FAOEB.pdf (last accessed 18 Feb. 2014) and http://www.fao.org/crisis/28468-0f4867a04e5f616834829d-544ce27de20.pdf (last accessed 18 Feb. 2014).

42. Ethiopian Investment Agency, 'Investment regime', Section 3, 2011.

43. Ethiopia, Population Census Commission, *Summary and Statistical Report of the 2007 Population and Housing Census*, Addis Ababa, 2007.

44. Alemu, Dawit, Bewket Woldemlak, Gete Zeleke, Yemisrach Assefa and Peter Trutmann, 'Extent and determinants of household poverty in rural Ethiopia in six villages', *Eastern Africa Social Science Research Review*, vol. 27, no. 2 (June 2011), pp. 21–49. This study which finds 'abject rural poverty in the study areas; annual average per capita income was estimated at Birr 1092.30' inexplicably uses an exchange rate of 9.6 Birr to the US dollar. The official, and on-the-street, rate is 17. At this rate of 17 Birr to the dollar, Birr 1092 is an annual income of just $64 or 17.5 cents per day.

45. Interview with a humanitarian aid agency, Addis Ababa, 30 September 2011.

46. Zewde, Babru, *A History of Modern Ethiopia 1855–1991*, Oxford: James Currey, 2001, pp. 14–5 and p. 87; and Nelson, Harold D. and Irving Kaplan, *Ethiopia, a Country Study*, Washington: U.S. Army, 1981, p. 151.

47. Al-Wrais, 2011.

48. International Crisis Group, 'Ethiopia: ethnic federalism and its discontents', *Africa Report 153*, September 2009, available at: http://www.crisisgroup.org/~/media/Files/africa/horn-of-africa/ethiopia-eritrea/Ethiopia%20Ethnic%20Federalism%20and%20Its%20Discontents.pdf (last accessed 18 Feb. 2014).

49. Interview with a former agency official, Addis Ababa, 20 September 2011.

50. Interview with a former ministry official, Addis Ababa, 28 September 2011.

51. Interview with a public relations executive investor, Addis Ababa, 24 October 2011.

52. Interview with a representative of foreign agri-business, Addis Ababa, 24 October 2011.

53. The constitution became effective in 1999. The freedom accorded to foreign investors is outlined in Vuthy, Chea, '"Investment opportunity in Cambodia", presentation to for-

eign investors', Royal Government of Cambodia; Cambodia Special Economic Zone Board, Phnom Penh, 2011.

54. Special Economic Zone (SEZ) is an area within the territory of a state where normal regulatory practices, such as foreign exchange and remittance restrictions, and export levels, do not apply. By 2002, there were more than 5,000 SEZs in China. See also free trade zone in Mayhew, Susan (ed.), *A Dictionary of Geography*, Oxford: Oxford University Press, 2009.

55. Brinkley, Joel, *Cambodia's Curse: Modern History of a Troubled Land*, Melbourne: Black Ink, 2011, pp. 207–15 and pp. 249–54.

56. Brinkley estimates that the United Nations spent about $3 billion in state-building; see ibid., p. 74. The UN's official statement in this regard is available at: http://www.un.org/en/peacekeeping/missions/past/untacbackgr2.html#six (last accessed 18 Feb. 2014). A detailed analysis of this programme can be found in Findlay, Trevor, 'Cambodia: The Legacy and Lessons of UNTAC', *Stockholm International Peace Research Institute Research Report No. 9*, Oxford: Oxford University Press, 1995, available at: http://books.sipri.org/files/RR/SIPRIRR09.pdf (last accessed 18 Feb. 2014).

57. Official figures for 2009, available at: http://www.cdc-crdb.gov.kh/cdc/third_cdcf/aer_2010_en.pdf (last accessed 18 Feb. 2014), totalled $990 million. For 2010, the figure was reported in the press to be $1.1 billion. See, for example: http://www.voanews.com/content/cambodias-donors-pledge-11-billion-for-development-95519109/165789.html (last accessed 18 Feb. 2014).

58. Brinkley, *Cambodia's Curse*, pp. 289–96; and Boden, George, 'New Cambodian anti-corruption plan will not stop high-level offenders', Global Witness, 2010.

59. See ASEAN, 'Macroeconomic Indicators, 2010', available at: http://www.aseansec.org/18135.html (last accessed 18 Feb. 2014).

60. Interview, 13 June 2011.

61. See, for example, the story of Australian mining company BHP-Billiton paying bribes to the Cambodian government: Doherty, Ben, 'BHP's "tea money" missing in Cambodia', *The Sydney Morning Herald*, 15 May 2010, available at: http://www.smh.com.au/business/bhps-tea-money-missing-in-cambodia-20100514-v4fs.html (last accessed 18 Feb. 2014).

62. Interview with a government official, Phnom Penh, 24 June 2011.

63. Brady, Brendan, 'The Cambodian Army: open for corporate sponsors', *Time*, 10 June 2010, available at: http://editorials.cambodia.org/2010/06/cambodian-army-open-for-corporate.html (last accessed 18 Feb. 2014).

64. See, for example, AD HOC Cambodia: http://www.adhoc-cambodia.org/; Indigenous People NGO Network of Cambodia: http://www.elaw.org/node/5349; Licadho, 'Harmful effects'; Janardhan, Meena, 'Gulf eyes oil-for-food'.

65. Interview with a policy official, Addis Ababa, 14 October 2011.

66. Central Statistics Agency of Ethiopia, 'National statistics abstract—agriculture', Addis Ababa, 2010.

67. Interview with recently-retired Ministry of Agriculture official, Addis Ababa, 29 September 2011.

68. Ibid.

69. Interview with a Nuer tribesman, Gambela region, 20 October 2011.

70. Observations and conversations with villagers, near Debre Zeit, 9 October 2011.

71. Interview with a government official, Addis Ababa, 14 October 2011.

72. Interview with a foreign agribusiness representative, Addis Ababa, 25 October 2011.

73. Subsequent to the field research, one of Shepherd's Ethiopian contacts has reported addi-

tional instances where violence has erupted between evicted communities and authorities at some of these land deal locations. In one instance, he reported that up to twelve people were killed.

74. The official was interviewed by Deborah Wheeler, July 2012, in Chevy Chase, Maryland.

75. Ibid.

76. For example, Brazil, which exports a range of food products including sugar, meats and cereals, citrus, coffee, beans, wheat and poultry. See 'Brazilian food exports to Arab countries touch $10.6bn in 2011', AMEinfo.com, 19 June 2012, available at: http://www.ameinfo.com/blog/company-news/a/abcc/brazilian-food-exports-to-arab-countries-touch-bn-in/ (last accessed 18 Feb. 2014). Six of the top ten food exporters (expressed as a percentage of GNP) are located in Latin America.

77. Wheeler interview with US official.

78. al-Attiya, 'Qatar's food security policy'.

79. Hope, Bradley, 'Egypt freezes Kingdom farm land deal', The National, 12 April 2011, available at: http://www.thenational.ae/featured-content/channel-page/business/middle-teasers-list/egypt-freezes-kingdom-farm-land-deal (last accessed 18 Feb. 2014).

80. Ford, Peter, 'Iceland blocks Chinese businessman from buying land', Christian Science Monitor, 8 November 2011, available at: http://www.csmonitor.com/World/Asia-Pacific/2011/1128/Iceland-blocks-Chinese-businessman-from-buying-land (last accessed 18 Feb. 2014).

81. Beisecker, Randall, 'DP World and U.S. port security', Global Security Newswire, 1 March 2006, available at: http://www.nti.org/analysis/articles/dp-world-and-us-port-security/ (last accessed 18 Feb. 2014). Weisman, Jonathan and Bradley Graham, 'Dubai firm to sell U.S. port operations', Washington Post, 10 March 2006, available at: http://www.washingtonpost.com/wp-dyn/content/article/2006/03/09/AR2006030901124.html (last accessed 18 Feb. 2014).

82. Tétreault, The Kuwait Petroleum Corporation, no. 35, pp. 201–2; Wright, Vincent, 'Redrawing the public-private boundary: privatisation in the United Kingdom 1979–92', Estudio/Working Paper 1992/37, paper presented at a conference held at the Juan March Institute, 2 April 1992, available at: http://www.march.es/ceacs/publicaciones/working/archivos/1992_37_en.pdf (last accessed 18 Feb. 2014).

83. Ford, 'Iceland blocks'.

84. Stiglitz, Joseph E., 'Sovereign Wealth Funds—distinguishing aspects and opportunities', in Sovereign Wealth Funds and Long-Term Investing, Bolton, Patrick, Frederic Samama and Joseph E. Stiglitz (eds), New York: Columbia University Press, pp. 26–31; Lewis, Michael, 'The irresponsible investor', New York Times Magazine, 6 June 2004 available at: http://www.nytimes.com/2004/06/06/magazine/06ETHICS.html?action=click&module=Search&region=searchResults%230&version=&url=http%3A%2F%2Fquery.nytimes.com%2Fsearch%2Fsitesearch%2F%23%2Firresponsible%2Binvestor%2F (last accessed 18 Feb. 2014).

85. Drechsler, Denis and David Hallam, 'Buying land in developing nations: challenges and promises', Vox, 29 June 2009, available at: http://www.voxeu.org/index.php?q=node/3711 (last accessed 18 Feb. 2014); Biryabarema, Elias, 'Thousands evicted in Uganda "Land Grab"—Oxfam', Alertnet, 22 September 2011, available at: http://www.trust.org/alertnet/news/thousands-evicted-in-uganda-land-grab-oxfam/ (last accessed 18 Feb. 2014); Rahmato, 'Land to investors'; Salomon, 'The ethics of foreign investment'.

86. Farmer, Paul, Pathologies of Power: Health, Human Rights, and the New War on the Poor, Berkeley, CA: University of California Press, 2005, p. 139.

87. Union of Concerned Scientists, 'Impacts of industrial agriculture', n.d., available at:

http://www.ucsusa.org/food_and_agriculture/science_and_impacts/impacts_industrial_
agriculture/ (last accessed 18 Feb. 2014).

88. Gorton, Matthew and Sophia Davidova, 'Farm productivity and efficiency in the CEE
applicant countries: a synthesis of results', *Agricultural Economics*, no. 30 (2004), pp.
1–16; McKibben, Bill, *Deep Economy: The Wealth of Communities and the Durable Future*, New
York: Times Books, 2007.

89. Interviews by Tétreault and Wheeler in Kuwait, 2011–12; Al Rasheed, Turki F., *Agricultural
Development Strategies: The Saudi Experience*, Berlin: Lambert Academic Publishing, 2011.

90. Center for Human Rights and Global Justice, *Foreign land deals and human rights: case
studies on agricultural and bio-fuel investment*, Center for Human Rights and Global
Justice, New York University, 2010, p. 1.

91. Janardhan, N., *Boom amid Gloom: The Spirit of Possibility in the 21st Century Gulf*, Reading,
UK: Ithaca Press, 2011.

10. FOOD INSECURITY IN THE WEST BANK

1. The fieldwork and research for this chapter was made possible through a research grant
provided by the Center for International and Regional Studies at Georgetown University
School of Foreign Service in Qatar. We are especially thankful to Ron Smith for his invaluable advice on earlier versions. We are indebted to Haneen Ghazawneh (MAS) for her
continuous help and comments and the participants of the The Center for International
and Regional Studies (CIRS) research initiative on 'Food Security and Food Sovereignty
in the Middle East', Doha, Qatar, April 2012. We would to thank Mohammad Al Masri
(Nahja University), Kamal Issa (PWA), Issa Zboun (ARIJ), Mohammad Waheed (OCHA)
and PCBS for sharing their data with us. The responsibility for any errors or omission is
our own.

2. Sen, Amartya, *Poverty and Famines: An Essay on Entitlement and Deprivation*, Oxford:
Oxford University Press, 1981; Bouis, Howarth E., *The determinants of household-level
demand for micronutrients: an analysis for Philippine farm households*, Washington, DC:
International Food Policy Research Institute, 1991; Bouis, Howarth E. and Mary Jane
G. Novenario-Reese, *The determinants of demand for micronutrients: an analysis of rural
households in Bangladesh*, Washington, DC: International Food Policy Research Institute,
1997; Strauss, John and Duncan Thomas, 'Human resources: empirical modeling of household and family decisions', *Handbook of Development Economics*, vol. III, Amsterdam:
Elsevier Science, 1995.

3. Sanchez, Pedro A., 'Soil fertility and hunger in Africa', *Science*, no. 295 (2002), pp. 2019–
20; Sanchez, Pedro A., M.S. Swaminathan, Philip Dobie, et al., *Halving hunger: it can be
done*, Final Report of the UN Millennium Project Task Force on Hunger, London: UNDP,
2005; Godfray, H. Charles J., John R. Beddington, Ian R. Crute, et al., 'Food security:
the challenge of feeding 9 billion people', *Science*, vol. 327, no. 812 (2010), pp. 812–8.

4. Sen, Amartya, *Poverty and Famines*; Chambers, Robert, 'Editorial introduction: vulnerability, coping and policy', *IDS Bulletin*, vol. 20, no. 2 (1989), pp. 1–7; Drèze, Jean and
Amartya Sen, *Hunger and Public Action*, Oxford: Clarendon Press, 1989; Watts, Michael
J. and Hans G. Bohle, 'Hunger, famine and the space of vulnerability', *GeoJournal*, vol. 35,
no. 2 (1993), pp. 117–25; Watts, Michael J. and Hans G. Bohle, 'The space of vulnerability: the causal structure of hunger and famine', *Progress in Human Geography*, vol. 17,
no. 1 (1993), pp. 43–67.

5. Cutter, Susan L., Bryan J. Boruff and W. Lynn Shirley, 'Social vulnerability to environmental hazards', *Social Science Quarterly*, vol. 84, no. 2 (2003), pp. 242–61; Bohle, Hans

G., Thomas E. Downing and Michael J. Watts, 'Climate change and social vulnerability: toward a sociology and geography of food insecurity', *Global Environmental Change*, vol. 4, no. 1 (1994), pp. 37–48.

6. IMF, *Economic Monitoring Note. Report update*, Washington, DC: International Monetary Fund, 2010.

7. Ibid.

8. World Bank, *Coping with conflict: poverty and inclusion in the West Bank and Gaza*, Washington, DC: International Bank for Reconstruction and Development/The World Bank, 2011.

9. According to the Census 2007, the total number of communities in the West Bank is 510 (twenty-one communities are left out in our dataset due to lack of data other than population count). The 489 included communities cover 99.2 per cent of the total population.

10. Palestinian National Authority, Palestinian Central Bureau of Statistics, *Agricultural Census 2010 final results*. Report from the Palestinian Central Bureau of Statistics, 2010.

11. Hansen, Matthew, Ruth DeFries, John R.G. Townshend and Robert Sohlberg, *UMD global land cover classification, 1 kilometer, 1.0*, Department of Geography, University of Maryland, College Park, Maryland, 1981–94, 1998.

12. Prince, Stephen and Jennifer Small, *Global production efficiency model, mean_annual_NPP_Latlon*, Department of Geography, University of Maryland, College Park, Maryland 1997, 2003; Net Primary Productivity (NPP) is how much carbon dioxide vegetation takes in during photosynthesis minus how much carbon dioxide the plants release during respiration. As the amount of organic carbon that plants actually make available to other organisms in an ecosystem, NPP is an indicator of actual yield of vegetation. NPP can be measured in grams per square metre per day or grams per squared metre per year, as in our case. In both cases, higher values are areas of greater vegetation and hence, higher land fertility. Negative values indicate that respiration outweighs carbon absorption: more carbon was released to the atmosphere than the plants took in.

13. Trabucco, Antonio and Robert J. Zomer, *Global Potential Evapo-Transpiration (Global-PET) and Global Aridity Index (Global-Aridity) Geo-Database*, CGIAR Consortium for Spatial Information, 2009.

14. The Socio-Economic and Food Security Survey 2010 includes 500 households living in the East-Jerusalem area, currently under Israeli jurisdiction. Most of these people are allowed to enter the Israeli labour market and their level of income is substantially different from the Palestinians living inside the West Bank. In addition, given the current formal Israeli jurisdiction, these communities are excluded from the Census information. We therefore exclude these households and restrict our sample to the Palestinian population inside the West Bank. However, we maintain the information on a few communities in the Seam Zone which are currently separated from the West Bank by the Israeli barrier.

15. 'Rome Declaration on World Food Security', World Food Summit, 13–17 November 1996, Rome, Italy.

16. Webb, Patrick, Jennifer Coates, Edward A. Frongillo, Beatrice L. Rogers, Anne Swindale and Paula Bilinsky, 'Measuring household food insecurity: why it's so important and yet so difficult to do', supplement to *The Journal of Nutrition*, vol. 5, no. 136 (2006), pp. 1404–8.

17. Coates, Jennifer, Anne Swindale and Paula Bilinsky, *Household Food Insecurity Access Scale (HFIAS) for measuring of food access: indicator guide*, report version 3, Food and Nutrition Technical Assistance—USAID, 2007.

18. From a methodological point of view, it is important to note that a subset of Z(j) are not actual observations, but are derived from GIS layers. Thus, Z(j) may have its own error structure, potentially correlated with u(ij). This may arise for example if the two error terms have similar spatial patterns. In this case instrumental variables should be used to address the problem as explained in Anselin, Luc, 'Spatial effects in econometric practice in environmental and resource economics', *American Journal of Agricultural Economics*, vol. 83, no. 3 (2001), pp. 705–10. However, in our case, no instrumental variables were available to instrument the environmental factors we are interested in.

19. An alternative approach is to count households whose predicted probability is above a threshold, usually the national food insecurity rate. This approach is dependent on the choice of the threshold and it is not recommended by the literature. Haddad, Lawrence and Ravi Kanbur, 'How serious is the neglect of intra-household inequality?', *Economic Journal*, vol. 100, no. 402 (1990), pp. 866–81, elaborates on this point in the context of individual welfare. See Ravallion, Martin, 'Expected poverty under risk-induced welfare variability', *Economic Journal*, vol. 98, no. 393 (1988), pp. 1171–82 in the context of poverty.

20. Predicting (unobserved) local-area attributes, such as food insecurity incidence, observing households data, poses the challenge of how to aggregate household information. The question is at which stage to aggregate: the approach presented above estimates the model at the household-level and aggregates the household-level predictions. An alternative approach is to first aggregate the household information at community-level and estimate a community-level equation. In a linear model, the two procedures would be equivalent. However, non-linearity breaks down this property and coefficient estimates will differ. We also estimate the model at community-level, where the dependent variable is the proportion of food insecure households surveyed in community *j* and we weight the estimates by the number of households surveyed. Because of space, these are not presented here but available upon request. The distributions of food insecurity incidence by the latter method are very similar to those presented in this chapter and point to the same patterns.

21. World Bank, *Coping with conflict: poverty and inclusion in the West Bank and Gaza*, Washington, DC: International Bank for Reconstruction and Development/The World Bank, 2011.

11. THE NUTRITION TRANSITION AND OBESITY IN QATAR

1. Food and Agriculture Organization of the United Nations (FAO), 'Rome Declaration on World Food Security', World Food Summit, 13–17 November, 1996, Rome, Italy, available at: http://www.fao.org/docrep/003/w3613e/w3613e00.htm (last accessed 18 Feb. 2014).

2. Musaiger, Abdulrahman O., Hassan S. Abdelmonem and Omar Obeid, 'The paradox of nutrition-related diseases in the Arab countries: the need for action', *International Journal of Environmental Research and Public Health*, vol. 8, no. 9 (2011), pp. 3637–71; World Health Organization Eastern Mediterranean Regional Office, *Regional data on non-communicable diseases*', 2011, available at: http://www.emro.who.int/ncd/ (last accessed 18 Feb. 2014).

3. Musaiger et al., 'The paradox of nutrition-related diseases'; Musaiger, Abdulrahman O., 'Diet and prevention of coronary heart disease in the Arab Middle East countries', *Medical Principles and Practice*, vol. 11, no. 2 (2002), pp. 9–16; Musaiger, Abdulrahman O., Hamed R. Takruri, Abdelmonem S. Hassan and Hamza Abu-Tarboush, 'Food-based dietary guide-

lines for the Arab Gulf countries', *Journal of Nutrition and Metabolism*, (2012), pp. 1–10, doi:10.1155/2012/905303.

4. Bray, George A. and Barry M. Popkin, 'Dietary fat intake does affect obesity', *American Journal of Clinical Nutrition*, vol. 68, no. 6 (1998), pp. 1157–73.

5. Kerkadi, Abdelhamid, Abdelmonem S. Hassan and Adil Eltayeb M. Yousef, 'High prevalence of the risk of overweight and overweight among Qatari children ages 9 through 11', *Nutrition & Food Science*, vol. 39, no. 1 (2009), pp. 36–45.

6. Al-Mahroos, Faisal and Khaldoon Al-Roomi, 'Overweight and obesity in the Arabian Peninsula: an overview', *Journal of the Royal Society of Promotion of Health*, vol. 119, no. 4 (1999), pp. 251–3; Bener, Abdulbari and Abdulaziz A. Kamal, 'Growth of Qatari school children and adolescents aged 6–18 years', *Journal of Health Population and Nutrition*, vol. 23, no. 3 (2005), pp. 250–8; Kerkadi, Abdelhamid, Nassar Abo-Elnaga and Wissam Ibrahim, 'Study of obesity and related risk factors among primary school children in Al Ain', *Emirates Journal of Food and Agriculture Sciences*, vol. 17, no. 1 (2005), pp. 43–56.

7. See, for example, Bener and Kamal, 'Growth of Qatari school children'; Kerkadi et al., 'Study of obesity and related risk factors'.

8. Drewnowski, Adam and Barry M. Popkin, 'The nutrition transition: new trends in the global diet', *Nutrition Reviews*, vol. 55, no. 2 (1997), pp. 31–43.

9. Musaiger et al., 'Food-based dietary guidelines'.

10. WHO/EMRO, *Regional data on non-communicable diseases*.

11. Musaiger, Abdulrahman O., *Food composition tables for the Arab Gulf countries*, Arab Center for Nutrition, Bahrain, 2006.

12. Schmiduber, Josef and Prakash Shetty, 'Nutrition transition, obesity and non-communicable diseases: drivers, outlook and concerns', *SCN News*, no. 29 (2005), pp. 13–9.

13. Bray and Popkin, 'Dietary fat intake'.

14. Musaiger et al., 'Food-based dietary guidelines'.

15. Bener, Abdulbari and Ihab Tewfik, 'Prevalence of overweight, obesity, and associated psychological problems in Qatari's [sic] female population', *Obesity Reviews*, vol. 7, no. 2 (2006), pp. 139–45.

16. Bener and Kamal, 'Growth of Qatari school children'; Kerkadi et al., 'High prevalence of the risk of overweight'; Qotba, Hamda and Abdulwahab Naser Al-Isa, 'Anthropometric measurements and dietary habits of school children in Qatar', *International Journal of Food Sciences and Nutrition*, vol. 58, no. 1 (2007), pp. 1–5.

17. Bener and Kamal, 'Growth of Qatari school children'; Kerkadi et al., 'High prevalence of the risk of overweight'; Qotba and Al-Isa, 'Anthropometric measurements'.

18. Hassan, Abdelmonem S. and Sara N. Al-Dosari, 'Breakfast habits and snacks consumed at school among Qatari schoolchildren aged 9–10 years', *Nutrition and Food Science*, vol. 38, no. 3 (2008), pp. 264–70; Arab Center for Nutrition, *Nutritional and health status in the Arab Gulf countries*, 2009, available at: http://www.acnut.com/ (last accessed 18 Feb. 2014).

19. Musaiger, 'Diet and prevention of coronary heart disease'; State of Qatar, Supreme Council of Health, *Qatar National Health Accounts—1st Report Years 2009 & 2010: a baseline analysis of health expenditure and utilization*, June 2011.

20. Chanpong, Gail Fraser, 'Qatar 2006 WHO World Health Survey', proceedings of the 1st International Primary Health Care Conference, 1–4 November 2008, National Health Authority, Doha, Qatar.

21. Bener, Abdulbari, Mahmoud Zirie, Ibrahim M Janahi, Abdulla O. A. A. Al-Hamaq, Manal Musallam and Nick J. Wareham, 'Prevalence of diagnosed and undiagnosed dia-

betes mellitus and its risk factors in a population-based study of Qatar', *Diabetes Research and Clinical Practice*, vol. 84, no. 1 (2009), pp. 99–106.

22. WHO, *New study presents state of the world's health*, 2008, available at: http://www.who.int/mediacentre/news/notes/2008/np11/en/index.html (last accessed 18 Feb. 2014).

23. Bener, Abdulbari, Jasim Al-Suwaidi, Khalifa Al-Jaber, Saleh Al-Marri and Isam-Eldin A. Elbagi, 'Epidemiology of hypertension and its associated risk factors in the Qatari population', *Journal of Human Hypertension*, no. 18 (2004), pp. 529–30.

24. Popkin, Barry M., Linda S. Adair and Shu Wen Ng, 'Global nutrition transition and the pandemic of obesity in developing countries', *Nutrition Reviews*, vol. 70, no. 1 (2012), pp. 3–21; Popkin, Barry M. and Adam Drewnowski, 'Dietary fats and the nutrition transition: new trends in the global diet', *Nutrition Reviews*, no 55 (1997), pp. 31–44; Bray, George A., Samara Joy Nielsen and Barry M. Popkin, 'Consumption of high-fructose corn syrup in beverages may play a role in the epidemic of obesity', *The American Journal of Clinical Nutrition*, vol. 79, no. 4 (2004), pp. 537–43.

25. Popkin et al., 'Global nutrition transition'; Popkin and Drewnowski, 'Dietary fats and the nutrition transition'.

26. Gibson, Edward Leigh, 'Emotional influences on food choice: sensory, physiological and psychological pathways', *Physiology & Behavior*, vol. 89, no. 1 (2006), pp. 53–61.

27. Stender, Steen, Jørn Dyerberg and Arne Astrup, 'Fast food: unfriendly and unhealthy', *International Journal of Obesity*, vol. 31, no. 6 (2007), pp. 887–90.

28. Garber, Andrea K. and Robert Lustig, 'Is fast food addictive?', *Current Drug Abuse Reviews*, vol. 4, no. 3 (2011), pp. 146–62.

29. Ibid.; Bray et al., 'Consumption of high-fructose corn syrup'; Gibson, 'Emotional influences on food choice'.

30. Ibid.

31. Ibid.

32. Bener and Tewfik, 'Prevalence of overweight'.

33. Ibid.; Honkala, Sisko, Eino Honkala and Nameer Al-Sahli, 'Consumption of sugar products and associated life- and school-satisfaction and self-esteem factors among schoolchildren in Kuwait', *Acta Odontologica Scandinavica*, vol. 64, no. 2 (2006), pp. 79–88.

34. Chanpong, 'Qatar 2006 WHO World Health Survey'.

35. Bener, Abdulbari, Mariam Al-Ali and Georg F. Hoffmann, 'High prevalence of Vitamin D deficiency in young children in a highly sunny humid country: a global health problem', *Minerva Pediatrica*, vol. 61, no. 1 (2010), pp. 15–22.

INDEX

ing in, 208; trade on consignment in, 204

Domestic Resource Cost (DRC): 75–80, 84; calculation of, 74; coefficients, 80; of field crops, 83

Dubai Ports World: attempted acquisitions made by, 243

Dutch disease: 23

Effective Rate of Protection (ERP): 74, 78, 80, 83; calculation of, 77; coefficient of, 75

eggs: 28, 48, 70, 121, 147, 276; consumption rates of, 121; production of, 122; use of corn in production of, 123

Egypt: 14, 18–19, 23–4, 29, 31, 88–90, 113, 202; agricultural land of, 104, 106–8; agricultural policies of, 23, 111; agricultural production rate of, 11; agricultural sector of, 90, 92, 99, 108; Alexandria, 30; budget of, 92–3, 99; Cairo, 30, 92, 95, 103, 106–7, 114; capital accumulation of, 90; cotton cultivation in, 25; Dakahlia, 106, 111–12; Delta, 102–3, 106, 108, 111, 114; dependency on food imports in, 95, 109; Economic Reform and Structural Adjustment Programme (1991), 110; economy of, 14, 93, 96, 103; FDI in, 96; food exports of, 105–6; food price increase in (2006–11), 2; GDP per capita, 37, 92–3; government of, 23, 90, 92, 95–8, 104, 107–11, 113–14; grain exports of, 34; household income and expenditure and consumption survey (HIES), 96–7; *infitah*, 99, 103; land ownership in, 25, 27, 102–3, 113; Law 69 (1974), 103; Law 96 (1992), 103–4,

106–7, 114; Lower, 97; Luxor, 108; migrant workers from, 93; Ministry of Agriculture and Land Reclamation (MALR), 104–6, 108–11; Minya, 111–12; Napoleonic scientific mission to (1798), 24; New Valley Governorate, 108; poor population of, 95; Revolution (2011), 89, 96, 113–14; rural communities of, 111–12; Sarandu, 113; Shura Council, 106; Suez Canal, 25, 30–1, 93; Upper, 95, 97, 103, 112, 114; US food aid provided to, 34–5; wheat imports of, 92; wheat production in, 28, 92

emergency food aid: 135; flawed, 230

EMKE Group: 211

Environmental Impact Assessments (EIAs): 227–8

Ethiopia: 194, 224–5, 229, 231–2, 240–1, 245; Amhara, 231; Anuak population of, 239; Debre Zeit, 239; foreign investment in, 230, 237–41; Gambela, 238–40; government of, 229–30, 232, 240; import networks of, 230; Italian Occupation of (1936–41), 30; *killil* system of, 231–2; millet exports of, 31; Nuer population of, 239; Oromiya, 231; poverty level in, 229; Tigray, 231; rural poor population of, 244; wheat exports of, 31; *woreda* system of, 232

Ethiopia People's Revolutionary Democratic Front (EPRDF): 231–2, 237–8; members of, 231

European Economic Community (ECC): 35

European Union (EU): 36, 213; cereal exports of, 85; Common Agricultural Policy (2003), 36; food production subsidies in, 86

INDEX

INDEX

Qatar Media Corporation: 283
Qatar Museum Authority: 283
Qatar National Food Security Programme (QNFSP): 32, 212–14, 242, 283; nutrition assessment, 280
Qatar Olympic Committee: 283
Qatar Orthopaedic and Sports Medicine Hospital (ASPETAR): 283
Qatar Statistics Authority Report (2012): 271–2
Qatar University: 283; Sports Science programme, 284
Qatar Women's Sports Committee: 283

Reagan, Ronald: administration of, 35
receiver operation characteristics (ROC): 168, 180
retail/supermarkets: 197–8, 212; association with urbanisation, 188–91; expansion of, 191; price fluctuations in, 212, 214; procurement channels, 185, 191–3, 195, 199; taxation policies regarding, 215; transition process, 194–5, 218; wholesalers, 191–3, 195–6, 198–9, 202, 204–6, 208, 212, 215–16, 218
Revealed Comparative Advantage (RCA): 42, 58, 69–70, 72, 84, 86; calculation of, 67–9, 87; of vegetable and fruit, 69; values of, 68
rice: 34, 56, 92–3, 104–6, 116–18, 121–2, 127, 134, 140, 274, 278, consumption rates of, 120; elasticity of demand, 105; presence in diets, 24, 29, 129, 271; production of, 122–3; subsidies on, 63
River, Jordan: 263
River, Mekong: 226

Roman Empire: reliance on grain imports, 21
Romania: 24
Rome Declaration on World Food Security (1996): 255–6
Roosevelt, Franklin D.: 27
Rumelia: 24
rural agriculture: 161
Russian Federation: food export restrictions enacted by, 19; grain exports of, 20; wheat exports of, 92

Sadat, Anwar: assassination of (1981), 103; de-Nasserisation policies of, 102; economic policies of, 103
Saleh, Ali Abdullah: 139, 140
Ibn Saud: 31–2; agricultural policies of, 32
Saudi Arabia: 8, 32–3, 137–8, 142, 221, 273, 275; food imports of, 11; food price increase in (2006–11), 2; government of, 35; Jeddah, 30; landholdings in, 13; Riyadh, 241; subsidising of wheat production of, 23, 35
Second World War (1939–45): 20, 23, 27, 30, 33; changes in food regime following, 22; East African Campaign (1940–1), 30; impact on food supplies, 29–32
Sen, Amartya: 37
Sen, Hun: 234
share cropping: 171
smallholding agriculture: 136
Social Impact Assessments (SIAs): 227–8
Socio-Economic and Food Security Survey (2010): 255
soil fertility: 255, 260, 263; depletion, 250; use of crop rotation in preservation of, 85
Somaliland: Berbera, 230